The Bare Essentials
Form A

Eighth Edition

Sarah Norton Brian Green

NELSON EDUCATION

NELSON / EDUCATION

The Bare Essentials, Form A,
Eighth Edition

by Sarah Norton and Brian Green

Vice-President, Editorial
Higher Education:
Anne Williams

Executive Editor:
Laura Macleod

Marketing Managers:
Amanda Henry and Ann Byford

Developmental Editor:
Lisa Berland

Photo Researcher and Permissions
Coordinator:
Natalie Russell

Senior Content Production
Manager:
Natalia Denesiuk Harris

Copy Editor:
Cathy Witlox

Proofreader:
Kate Revington

Indexer:
Christopher Blackburn

Senior Production Coordinator:
Ferial Suleman

Design Director:
Ken Phipps

Managing Designer:
Franca Amore

Interior Design:
Greg Devitt

Cover Design and Illustration:
Jan-John Rivera

Cover Images:
khr128/iStockphoto (highrise
buildings); sx70/iStockphoto
(Fifth Ave. Towers); Elenamiv/
Shutterstock (sky)

Compositor:
Nelson Gonzalez

Library and Archives Canada
Cataloguing in Publication Data

Norton, Sarah

   The bare essentials : form A /
Sarah Norton, Brian Green. —
8th ed.

Includes index.
ISBN 978-0-17-666205-9

   1. English language—
Grammar—Textbooks. 2. English
language—Rhetoric—Textbooks.
I. Green, Brian II. Title.

PE1408.N674 2013   808'.042
C2012-908090-X

PKG ISBN-13: 978-0-17-666205-9
PKG ISBN-10: 0-17-666205-7

CONTENTS

UNIT 2 SENTENCES

UNIT 3 GRAMMAR

UNIT 4   PUNCTUATION

UNIT 5   PARAGRAPHS AND ESSAYS

UNIT 6   READINGS

APPENDIXES

PREFACE

TO THE INSTRUCTOR

Welcome to the eighth edition of *The Bare Essentials, Form A*, a Canadian text designed for college and university students who need to learn to write correctly for academic and professional purposes. We've written this book to answer not only students' needs but also the needs of teachers who want a text that provides simple explanations, Canadian examples, and plenty of practice exercises.

NEW TO THIS EDITION

Grammar à la Carte comes packaged with every new copy of *The Bare Essentials, Form A*. This homework and practice platform, built specifically for English composition, is integrated with the book so students can practise both in their textbooks and online. For further details, see the section on Grammar à la Carte in the Instructor Resources section below.

HIGHLIGHTS OF THIS EDITION

Following is a summary of the highlights of this edition of the book:

- Units 1 through 4 begin with a "Quick Quiz" and conclude with a "Rapid Review." These tests preview and review the contents of each unit. They also provide practice in editing continuous prose passages.
- Chapter 1 focuses on audience-appropriate language. We begin with an overview of the levels and kinds of language that are and are not appropriate in written messages.
- Chapter 5 in the seventh edition, "Numbers," has been moved to the website.
- Chapter 26, "Revising Your Paper," includes exercises that give students practice in working through the three stages of a thorough revision.
- Chapter 27, "Using Research Resources Responsibly," provides examples illustrating the difference between paraphrase and plagiarism, together with exercises that give students practice in distinguishing between the two.

- Unit 6 consists of seven readings: four in the book and three on the website. Two of them are new to this edition. "Career Consciousness" appears first because it is the final product of the essay-writing process through which we guide students in Unit 5. We've moved three essays to the website in order to reduce the length of the book. Each reading is followed by discussion questions and writing suggestions. (Answers to the discussion questions are in the online *Instructor's Manual*.) Unit 6 includes one essay documented in APA style and one in MLA style.

- The "List of Useful Terms" (Appendix B) defines and illustrates terms that appear in bold print in the text, along with other grammatical terms with which you may wish your students to be familiar.

- On the inside front cover is a "Quick Revision Guide" that students can use as a checklist to guide them as they edit their work. Instructors can duplicate the guide, attach a copy to each student's paper, and mark ✓ or ✗ beside each point in the guide to identify the paper's strengths and weaknesses. This strategy provides students with clear and consistent feedback. Moreover, it saves hours of marking time.

- We have organized the book to build the mastery of writing skills progressively, from words (Unit 1) to syntax (Unit 2) to grammar (Unit 3) to punctuation (Unit 4) to paragraphs and essays (Unit 5). Many of the exercises are linked to the readings; thus, reading skills are reinforced along with writing skills. The units are independent of one another and may be introduced in any order. The chapters within each unit, however, should be introduced in the order in which they appear. The exercises within a unit are cumulative: those in later chapters often include questions that assume competence in skills covered in earlier chapters.

- Most of the exercises can be completed in the text, and the answers (in Appendix C) are easy to find. The first exercise in each chapter refers students to the page on which answers for that chapter begin. All exercises are numbered by chapter as well as by exercise: for example, Exercise 5.4 refers to Chapter 5, Exercise 4).

    Answers to the chapter Mastery Tests are not included in the book. They are available on the Instructors' page of the website and in the *Instructor's Manual*, where you will also find an alternative set of Mastery Tests equivalent to the ones in the book.

    We advise students to check their answers to each exercise (set of usually 10 questions) before moving on to the next. This process gives them immediate feedback, enables them to learn from their mistakes, and prevents them from reinforcing their errors. **We urge instructors to emphasize the importance of this procedure.**

- Students who need more practice than the exercises in the text provide will find supplementary, self-scoring exercises on the website (NELSONbrain.com).

Web icons in each chapter identify when and where to find these additional exercises.

- On the inside back cover, in the left-hand column, is a list of commonly used correction abbreviations and symbols. The middle column identifies the meaning of each and indicates where to find an explanation and examples. The right-hand column has been left blank so that students can write in the correction symbols that you use.

While *The Bare Essentials* can be used to support self-instruction and independent study, it works best for students lucky enough to have an instructor to guide them enthusiastically through its contents, adjust the level and pace of instruction to the needs of each class, and provide regular feedback and encouragement. We hope this new edition will satisfy your expectations and help you sustain your joy in teaching.

ACKNOWLEDGMENTS

We thank the following reviewers who helped us with the content of this edition.

Sandra Barber, University College of the North
Glen Boechler, Saskatchewan Institute of Applied Science and Technology
Karen Budra, Langara College
Simon Casey, Langara College
Richard Duffy, Seneca College
Tom Eades, Algonquin College
Heather Ferguson, Sault College
Jane Jacques, Keyano College
Shannon Kelly, British Columbia Institute of Technology
Tanya Lewis, Langara College
Tess MacMillan, Langara College
Dianna McAleer, Algonquin College
Jim McMullan, University of Toronto
Elaine Mullen, Mount Royal University
Catherine Patterson-Kidd, Algonquin College
Kathleen Stewart, Durham College
John Sturtridge, Cambrian College
Margaret Toye, Bow Valley College
Lorraine Wood-Gaines, University of Fraser Valley

Sarah Norton
Brian Green

RESOURCES AVAILABLE FOR *THE BARE ESSENTIALS, FORM A,* EIGHTH EDITION

INSTRUCTOR RESOURCES

The **Nelson Education Teaching Advantage (NETA)** program delivers research-based instructor resources that promote student engagement and higher-order thinking to enable the success of Canadian students and educators.

Instructors today face many challenges. Resources are limited, time is scarce, and a new kind of student has emerged: one who is juggling school with work, has gaps in his or her basic knowledge, and is immersed in technology in a way that has led to a completely new style of learning. Whether your course is offered in class, online, or both, Nelson is pleased to provide pedagogically driven, research-based resources to support you.

GRAMMAR À LA CARTE (NELSONbrain.com)

With **Grammar à la Carte**, students test their knowledge by completing a series of exercises and diagnostic tests. They can work through over 2000 exercise questions, covering all the major principles of written English.

For each chapter, students are encouraged to take the pre-test for each topic. The pre-tests assess the students' initial grasp of the subject content before they encounter the material in class and highlight areas students should review. Following the pre-test, students can focus on areas of weakness by completing an array of exercises, including fill-in-the-blank, short-answer, true/false, multiple-choice, and other types of questions.

Grammar à la Carte features a grade book so instructors can easily monitor and track students' progress.

INSTRUCTOR'S MANUAL

The online *Instructor's Manual* to accompany *The Bare Essentials, Form A*, Eighth Edition, includes teaching tips, classroom activities, and other features:

- the Creative Classroom
- Preventing Plagiarism: Why? What? How?
- answers to chapter Mastery Tests
- alternative chapter Mastery Tests and answers
- suggested answers to Discussion Questions (Unit 6)
- three essays to supplement those in Unit 6, with Questions for Discussion and Suggestions for Writing:
  - Brian Green, "The Case against Quickspeak"
  - Sun-Kyung Yi, "An Immigrant's Split Personality"
  - "The Myth of Canadian Diversity" (Editorial)

MICROSOFT® POWERPOINT®

Key concepts from *The Bare Essentials, Form A*, Eighth Edition, are presented in PowerPoint format, with generous use of examples to supplement those in the text.

ESSENTIALS ITESTS

Essentials iTests, a self-scoring CD-ROM version of the *Essentials Test Manual*, is now available to support instructors who use any textbook in the *Essentials* series. This comprehensive test bank includes diagnostic tests as well as pre- and post-tests for each unit and chapter. The tests address the six principal points of composition: organization, syntax, grammar, punctuation, diction, and spelling. Instructors can select pre-formatted tests, revise ready-made tests, or develop their own tests tailored to their curriculum.

With its easy-to-use assessment and tutorial system, *Essentials iTests* enables you to create and deliver customized tests in minutes. You can choose either Quick Test Wizard or an Online Test Wizard to guide you step by step through the process of creating individualized tests. Each test appears on-screen exactly as it will print or display online.

STUDENT RESOURCES

GRAMMAR À LA CARTE (NELSONbrain.com)

This icon in the book tells students that they can find the additional practice they need on Grammar à la Carte. Students can test their knowledge by completing a series of pre-tests and exercises. They can work through over 2000 exercise questions, covering all the major grammar rules.

Other online assets include

- Additional Readings
  - Brian Green, "The Case against Quickspeak"
  - Sun-Kyung Yi, "An Immigrant's Split Personality"
  - "The Myth of Canadian Diversity" (Editorial)
- Additional Examples
- How to Express Numbers
  - When to Use Words
  - When to Use Figures
  - When to Use Both Words and Figures
- Spelling Matters
- ESL Tips
- Format & Documentation
  - MLA Style
  - APA Style
- Student Survival Skills
- Reading, Writing, & Reference Links

INTRODUCTION

TO THE STUDENT:
WHY YOU NEED THIS BOOK

To get a job. To get promoted at your job. To find true love and eternal happiness. (Well, two out of three isn't bad.)

The fact is that **the ability to write well will be the most valuable skill you learn at college or university**. That's why English composition is part of your curriculum. College program advisory boards (made up of professionals in career fields) and university curriculum committees know that graduates who can communicate well will get hired more quickly, advance more quickly, and climb higher in their professions than graduates with poor communication skills. Companies from IBM to Imperial Oil, from the CBC to Ford, from the Royal Bank to Bell Canada, not to mention hospitals, police forces, the Canadian military, and all levels of government, have publicized their demand for superior communication skills as an essential hiring criterion.

Fairly or unfairly, no matter what field you're in, employers, peers, and subordinates will judge your ability—and even your intelligence—on the basis of your communication skills.

The good news is that writing skills can be learned, and that's where *The Bare Essentials* can help. There is no reason you can't write clear and correct reports, proposals, memoranda, and emails. This book will teach you how to write these and other professional documents, just as it has helped hundreds of thousands of Canadian students before you. All you need is the determination to improve. If you invest the time, effort, and care we ask of you, you will succeed.

WHAT'S IN THIS BOOK
(AND ON THE WEBSITE)

This book is divided into six units. Units 1 through 4 will help you identify and eliminate errors in your writing. Unit 5 explains and illustrates how to organize and develop your ideas in effective paragraphs, essays, and reports. Unit 6 contains essays on topics that we hope you will find interesting. These essays illustrate several practical organizational patterns as well as different levels of language, from informal to formal, that writers can use to suit their topic, audience, and purpose.

After Unit 6, you'll find three appendixes. Appendix A covers basic grammar, offering definitions and examples of the kinds and parts of sentences and the parts of speech. Appendix B defines and illustrates the grammatical terms used in the book, along with other grammatical terms you may wish to know. Whenever you find a **technical term** in bold type, you can turn to Appendix B to discover what it means and how to use it. Appendix C contains answers to the exercises in Units 1 to 5 (except the chapter Mastery Tests; your instructor will provide the answers to those).

Included with every new copy of this book is a registration code for Grammar à la Carte (go to NELSONbrain.com to sign in). Grammar à la Carte provides more examples and exercises, additional readings, and practice tests. Together, the book and the website give you all the resources you need to become a good writer. To sign on to Grammar à la Carte, go to NELSONbrain. com and enter your code.

If you are required to write a research paper as part of your composition course, go to the "Format & Documentation" section of the website, where you will find explanations and examples of both MLA and APA format and documentation styles.

HOW TO USE THIS BOOK

In each chapter, we do three things: explain a writing rule, illustrate it with examples, and give you exercises to help you master it. The exercises are usually arranged in sets of ten items that get harder as you progress. If you find you're struggling with a writing principle, look for the laptop symbol. This icon tells you where on the website you will find more exercises to help you master the point that's puzzling you. All exercises on the website are electronically scored, which means you will get instant feedback about your learning progress. By the time you finish a chapter, you should have a good grasp of the principle you've been practising. Then it's up to you to **apply what you've learned every**

time you write. Competence in writing is no different from competence in any other skill: it results from combining knowledge with practice.

THE STEPS TO SUCCESS

1. Read the explanation. Do this even if you think you understand the point.
2. Study the highlighted rules and the examples that follow them.
3. If you find an explanation easy and think you have no problem with the skill, try the last exercise in the section (the hardest). Then check your answers. If you've made no errors, go on to the next point.

   If you're less confident, don't skip anything. Start with the first exercise and work your way through all of them until you are sure you understand the point. (As a general rule, getting two exercises in a row entirely correct demonstrates mastery of the skill.)
4. **Always check your answers to one set of exercises before you go on to the next.** Only by checking your results after each set can you identify errors and correct them instead of repeating an error and possibly reinforcing it.
5. When you make a mistake, go back to the explanation and examples. Go over them again, and then look up the additional examples on the website. If you are truly stuck, check with your instructor. Continue with the exercises only when you are sure you understand where you went wrong and are confident that you won't repeat the error.

You can reinforce your understanding—and prepare for tests—by doing the practice tests posted on the website.

WHAT THE SYMBOLS MEAN

When the laptop symbol appears, it means that you will find on the website (NELSONbrain.com) more exercises that supplement the grammatical point you are working on. To get to additional exercises for the apostrophe in contractions, for example, log on to the website and click on Chapter 3 in the list, and then click on Contractions (the section heading). Web exercises are marked automatically, so you will know instantly whether or not you have understood the material.

When the symbol of partners reading appears beside an exercise, it means the exercise is designed to be done by two or more students working together. Often you are instructed to begin work in a pair or group, then to work individually on a writing task, and finally to regroup and review your writing with your partner(s). (Of course, your instructor may choose to modify these exercises for students working independently.)

The magnifying glass symbol means "Note this." We've used it to highlight writing tips, helpful hints, hard-to-remember points, and information that you should apply whenever you write, not just when you are dealing with the principle covered in the paragraph marked by the icon.

This image beside an exercise identifies the activity as a Mastery Test—an exercise designed to check your understanding of the principles covered in the chapter you have just completed. The answers to these exercises are not in the back of the book; your instructor will provide them.

TWO FINAL SUGGESTIONS

Inside the front cover, you'll find a "Quick Revision Guide." Use it to help you revise your papers before handing them in. This book is meant to be a practical tool, not a theoretical reference. Apply the lessons in all of the writing you do. We can identify writing problems and show you how to solve them, and exercises can give you practice in eliminating errors, but only your own writing and revising can bring real and lasting improvement.

Inside the back cover, you'll find "Correction Abbreviations and Symbols," a list of the most common editing and proofreading symbols—the shorthand forms your instructor may use to show you where you've made mistakes. For each error, we provide and explain the standard symbol and also leave space for you to write in your instructor's preferred symbol or abbreviation. See Chapter 26 for suggestions for using this list to maximize your improvement from one assignment to the next.

UNIT 1

Words

UNIT 1 QUICK QUIZ

This Quick Quiz is designed to test your competence in the writing skills covered in Unit 1. Revise the passage below so that it contains no inappropriate language (e.g., slang), no redundancies (i.e., wordiness), and no misused words, incorrect apostrophes, or unnecessary capital letters.

After you've made your corrections, turn to page 392 in Appendix C to see how successful you've been at finding and correcting the 15 errors. For each error you miss, the Answer Key directs you to the chapter(s) you need to work on to eliminate that error from your writing.

[1]Having decided to buy a new stereo system for my car, I went to Awesome Auto Audio, a store who's advertisements in the paper said they're quality and prices are unbeatable. [2]The salesperson could see that I was a more serious customer then the average car radio buyer and recommended that I consider V3A. [3]Of coarse, I didn't want to let him know that I didn't know what V3A was, so he lead me to a special showroom, where a spotted a sign that read "Voice-Activated Auto Audio (V3A)."

[4]The salesperson switched on the system and demonstrated by saying, "louder," which increased the radio's volume. [5]Then he said, "Techno," and the radio immediately switched to a techno station. [6]I thought this was way cool, so, irregardless of the price, I told him to install it in my car. [7]In actual fact, I had convinced myself that its safer to have a radio that doesn't need to be adjusted manually, by hand, while I was driving. [8]Once I had presented my

Credit Card and a peace of identification, I went to the parking lot to wait for the installation.

[9]Soon I was driving home and calling out, "Louder" and "Oldie's" and "Classic rock," and the radio was obeying every command. [10]Suddenly, as I was turning a corner, another driver cut right in front of me. [11]Annoyed, I yelled, "Stupid!" and the radio suddenly and abruptly switched to a call-in talk show.

1 Choosing the Right Words

The difference between the right word and the almost right word is the difference between lightning and the lightning bug.
—Mark Twain

Real estate salespeople say there are three things to consider when buying a property: location, location, location. Good writers know that there are three things to consider when sending a message: audience, audience, audience. Your readers and their expectations—what they need or want to know from you, the writer—should be your constant focus.

Whenever you write, you want your reader
- to understand your message and
- to think well of you as a writer

To achieve these goals, your writing must be correct and appropriate. If your readers are to understand you, your message must consist of accurate words organized into grammatical sentences and arranged in well-developed paragraphs.

The notion of "correctness" in writing has been developed over hundreds of years—and is still changing—to help writers create messages that say what their authors intend. Error-filled writing fails to meet the reader's expectation that a message will be clearly communicated. Mistakes in grammar, sentence structure, spelling, and punctuation mean that a message will not be easy to read.

Another reason to ensure that your writing is correct is that our culture associates correct language with education and intelligence. Careless, ungrammatical writing is often considered a sign of ignorance or laziness—or both.

But that's not all. Accuracy alone will not help you reach your goals. A message that is technically free of errors can still confuse or annoy a reader if it contains inappropriate language. Slang; racist, sexist, obscene, or blasphemous language; and even wordiness can interfere with your message. That's why we call them "errors." They divert the reader's attention from what you're saying to how you're saying it. They also lower the reader's opinion of you.

In this chapter, we provide a brief introduction to choosing language that is accurate and appropriate for your message and **audience**. We assume that you are writing for readers in an academic or professional environment. Our goals are to help you convey your message clearly and in a way that will leave your readers with a positive impression of you and your ideas.

Before you get started, you need to equip yourself with a few essential resources and an understanding of the levels of language that are available to you when you write.

> 1. Buy and use a good dictionary.

A dictionary is a writer's best friend. You will need to use it every time you write, so if you don't already own a good dictionary, you should buy one. For Canadian writers, a good dictionary is one that is Canadian, current, comprehensive (contains at least 75,000 entries), and reliable (published by an established, well-known firm).

A convenient reference is the *Collins Gage Canadian Paperback Dictionary*, available in an inexpensive paperback edition. Also recommended are the *Canadian Oxford Dictionary*, 2nd edition (Oxford University Press, 2004), which is also available online—**www.oupcanada.com/reference_trade/ canadian_oxford_dictionaries/dictionary_online.html**—and, for those whose first language is not English, the paperback *Oxford Advanced Learner's Dictionary*, 8th edition (Oxford, 2010).

Unless you have already done so (and most people haven't), begin by reading the introduction or the guide at the front of your dictionary. This information may not be very entertaining, but it is essential to understanding how to read your dictionary accurately. No two dictionaries are alike. Only if you are familiar with your dictionary's symbols, abbreviations, and item-entry format will you be able to use it effectively.

Knowing the information in your dictionary's guide will also save you time. For example, you do not need to memorize long lists of irregular plurals. Good dictionaries include irregular plurals in their entries. They also include irregular forms of verbs, adjectives, and adverbs. And if you've forgotten how to form regular plurals, verbs, adjectives, and adverbs, you'll find that information in your dictionary guide as well.

Read through the front matter in your dictionary. Then do the following sets of exercises. Be sure to check your answers to each set before going on to the next. Answers for exercises in this chapter begin on page 393.

EXERCISE **1.1**

1. What is another spelling of the word *humour*? Which spelling must you use when you add an ending such as *-ous* or *-ist* to the root word?
2. Is *harrassment* spelled correctly? Which syllable do you stress when you pronounce this word?
3. Is *tatoo* spelled correctly? Is the word a noun or a verb?
4. Are people who live in Saskatchewan more likely to experience a *tornado*, a *typhoon*, or a *tsunami*? Explain why.
5. Find alternative spellings for the words *programme, center, skillful, traveler,* and *judgement*. In each case, indicate the spelling most commonly used in Canada.

EXERCISE **1.2**

Write the plural form of each word.

1. basis
2. criterion
3. data
4. ratio
5. nucleus
6. appendix
7. formula
8. phenomenon
9. mother-in-law
10. syllabus

EXERCISE **1.3**

Combine each root word with the ending given.

1. delay + ed
2. journey + s
3. play + er
4. destroy + ing
5. repay + ment

6. lonely + ness
7. policy + s
8. easy + er
9. lazy + ness
10. necessary + ly

After you have checked your answers to this exercise, go back and look closely at the questions. What do the root words in questions 1 to 5 have in common? What do the root words in questions 6 to 10 have in common? How does this similarity affect the way these words are spelled when an ending is added? Can you write a rule to guide other writers who must deal with words like these?

EXERCISE **1.4**

Using hyphens, show where each word could be divided at the end of a line. (Some words can be divided in two or more places: *pol-it-ic-al*, for example.)

1. coffee
2. management
3. precise
4. through
5. distribute

6. monitor
7. gradually
8. technician
9. dictionary
10. business

EXERCISE **1.5**

The following words are not pronounced the way you might expect if you've had no previous experience with them. Look them up in your dictionary and, in the space beside each word, write its pronunciation (the information given immediately after it in parentheses). Using your dictionary's pronunciation key to help you, practise sounding out each word, one syllable at a time. No answers are given for this exercise.

1. quinoa
2. impotent
3. subtle

4. eulogy
5. indict
6. irreparable

7. corps

8. chassis

9. prenuptial

10. epitome

---

2. Use spelling and grammar checkers responsibly.

- Good spell-check programs can find typing errors and some common spelling mistakes. They have limitations, however. They can't tell if you meant to write "your" or "you're" and they won't flag either word, even if it's used incorrectly. (You'll learn more about such words in Chapter 2, "Hazardous Homonyms.") Also, since we use Canadian English, our spellings sometimes differ from the American spellings used in most word-processing programs. If your word processor can be set to Canadian spelling, make that adjustment. If it cannot, be aware that words such as *colour*, *honour*, *metre*, and *travelled*—all correct Canadian spellings—will be flagged as errors.
- Another useful tool is a hand-held spell checker. Pocket-sized and inexpensive, these devices contain a large bank of words and will provide the correct spelling if the "guess" you type in is not too far off. Some checkers even "talk," pronouncing the word for you. Ask your instructor if you can use this device (sound turned off, please) for in-class writing and exams.
- The best advice we can give you about grammar checkers (they announce their presence by producing a wavy green line under ungrammatical words or sentences in your word-processing program) is to use them with caution. No grammar checker has yet been able to account for the subtleties of English grammar. A grammar program is as likely to flag a perfectly good sentence, even to suggest an incorrect "fix," as it is to ignore a sentence full of errors. "I done real good on my grammar test," for example, escapes the dreaded wavy green line.

3. Buy and use a good thesaurus.

If you use the same words again and again, you will bore your reader. A thesaurus is a dictionary of synonyms—words with similar meanings. For any word you need to use repeatedly in a document, a good thesaurus will provide a list of alternatives. Note, however, that synonyms are not identical in meaning. Only you (or a knowledgeable friend) can decide which of the words listed in your thesaurus is appropriate for your message. Your dictionary will help you decide which terms are acceptable and which are not.

WHILE THE CITY SLEEPS, THE VIRUS INFECTS THE INNOCENT, TURNING THEM INTO... *THE UN-GRAMMATICAL!*

We recommend that you rely on a print thesaurus rather than on the thesaurus in your word-processing program, even though your computer's thesaurus will provide quick synonyms for words you don't want to repeat. A word-processor thesaurus provides a list of approximate synonyms, but no examples of usage. With unfamiliar or complex words, the information you need is whether the synonyms offered are nouns or verbs and whether they are in general use or are slang, technical, derogatory, or even obsolete. For this information, you need a book. Buy a good thesaurus and use it in conjunction with your dictionary.

Two good thesauruses are available in inexpensive paperback editions: *Oxford Paperback Thesaurus* (Oxford University Press, 2006), and *Roget's Thesaurus* (Penguin, 2004).

Inexperienced writers sometimes assume that long, obscure words will impress their readers. In fact, the opposite is true. Most readers are annoyed by unnecessarily "fancy" writing (see "Pretentious Language," pages 18 to 19).

NEVER use a word whose meaning you do not know. When you find a possible but unfamiliar synonym, look it up in your dictionary to make sure it means what you need it to say.

LEVELS OF LANGUAGE

Communication occurs on many levels, from grunts and mumbles to inspiring speeches; from unintelligible graffiti to moving poetry. Different levels of language are appropriate for different messages and different audiences. In academic and professional writing, you will be expected to use what is called standard written English.

Levels of language are defined by vocabulary, by length and complexity of sentences and paragraphs, and by tone (how the writing "sounds"). Most of the communication you encounter or are required to write in college will be at the **general level**, whether in postings to online course discussion groups or in voice-mail or email messages you leave for your instructor. Your relationship with your teacher is a professional one, and your language should reflect your understanding of that relationship.

Many colleges and universities expect students to write academic papers in **formal-level** English, which requires, among other things, third-person pronouns (*he, she, one, they*).[1] **Informal** writing, with its first- and second-person pronouns (*I, me, you*) may not be acceptable. For a talk you give to your class, however, an informal, conversational style may be appropriate.

The three levels of language we've identified are not fixed; they often overlap. In this book, for example, we use a variety of styles, ranging from informal through general (used for most of the text), with a few formal-level passages when they are appropriate. To help you choose the most appropriate level for your message and audience, the table on the next page outlines the basic features of informal, general, and formal written English.

No one level is "better" than another. Each has its place and function. Your message, your reader, and your purpose in writing should determine which level you choose. For college essays and term papers, unless your instructor specifically requires formal English or says you may use informal language in your written work, use general-level English.

In the past few years, text-messaging short forms have been creeping into written assignments, reports, and even research papers and résumés. In these contexts, "text messagese" is so inappropriate and reflects so poorly on the writer that we urge you never to use it except on your cellphone. Why? Because these short forms are a code that some people do not understand; they hinder rather than help communication. Read "The Case against Quickspeak" on our website (NELSONbrain.com) for a fuller explanation of how and why short forms such as text-message code are not effective in professional writing.

The three paragraphs that follow the table, all on the same topic, illustrate informal, general, and formal written English.

---

[1] See page 207 for an explanation of pronoun "person."

	Informal	General	Formal
Vocabulary and Style	Casual, everyday; usually concrete; some slang, colloquial expressions, contractions; written in first and second person.	The language of educated persons; non-specialized; balance of abstract and concrete; readily understood; can use first, second, and third person.	Often abstract, technical, or specialized; no contractions or **colloquialisms**; written in third person.
Sentence and Paragraph Structure	Sentences short, simple; some sentence fragments; paragraphs short.	Complete sentences of varying length; paragraphs vary in length but are often fairly short.	Complete sentences—often long, complex; paragraphs fully developed, usually at length.
Tone	Conversational, casual; sounds like ordinary speech.	Varies to suit message and purpose of writer.	Impersonal, serious, often instructional.
Typical Uses	Personal letters and blogs, some fiction, some newspapers, much advertising.	Most of what we read: websites, magazines, novels, business correspondence.	Academic writing, some textbooks, scientific reports, journal articles, legal documents.

INFORMAL LEVEL

So you're tired of paying through the nose at the pump! Well, the time has come to start paying attention to the alternatives out there. Everyone knows that our gas-guzzling cars and SUVs are responsible for a lot of the pollution that clogs the air, but not everyone knows that we can save money and feel good at the same time. The best bets to replace gas-powered cars are hybrid electric cars and fuel-cell electric cars. Hybrids use less gas than anything else on the road, and they are quickly becoming popular. But they are probably just a temporary fix until we move to fuel-cell cars that run on clean, plentiful hydrogen. The trouble is that we will have to change everything from refineries to fuel pumps before hydrogen-powered cars can become the standard. That's a big job!

GENERAL LEVEL

Gasoline prices are going up, but this news may not be all bad. The rise in gas prices has forced many of us to start looking at alternatives to our gas-guzzling vehicles. While our primary motivation is to save on fuel costs, we also know that reducing our use of fossil fuels will help clean up our environment. The two engines that are the current front-runner replacements for gasoline engines are the hybrid electric and the electric fuel cell. Hybrid cars use gas or diesel, but they are more efficient than anything now on the road, and they are already proving to be attractive to consumers. Hybrids, however, may be only a transition step to fuel-cell electric cars that run on clean, plentiful hydrogen. It's unlikely that this step will be taken soon, though, for we will have to transform our entire oil-based infrastructure—everything from refineries to fuel pumps—before we can all drive fuel-cell powered cars. That's an enormous undertaking!

FORMAL LEVEL

The higher gasoline prices rise, the more attention consumers and industry focus on alternatives to oil-based transportation. While the search for other options is driven primarily by the desire for cost savings, such alternatives have the additional appeal of being good for the environment. No one can be unaware of the atmospheric damage caused by carbon dioxide emissions, a large percentage of which are caused by burning fossil fuels in cars and trucks. Two alternative power sources compete for consumers' attention: hybrid electric vehicles and fuel-cell electric vehicles. The hybrid electrics, which do use gasoline or diesel but in significantly reduced amounts, are beginning to make an impact on consumers; however, many industrial observers see these cars as an interim step to fuel-cell electric vehicles that run on clean, plentiful hydrogen. Before the leap from gas-powered to hydrogen-powered cars can be made, however, the entire oil-based infrastructure must be redesigned, re-engineered, and replaced by a hydrogen-based infrastructure. A transformation of this magnitude is a daunting prospect.

Words

ONLY ONE MAN, WITH HIS DEDICATED ORGANIZATION, G.S.I. (GRAMMAR STANDARDS INVESTIGATIONS), STANDS BETWEEN COMMUNICATION AND CHAOS: *GUY GRAMMAR.*

EXERCISE **1.6**

Using the language-level chart on page 11, find some specific characteristics of vocabulary, sentence structure, and tone that identify the three paragraphs on pages 11 and 12 as informal, general, and formal. Then turn to pages 393 to 394 to compare your analysis with ours.

EXERCISE **1.7**

Working in pairs, study the following three sentences and identify the level of language of each.

1. The sport of professional cycling has been unfairly tarnished by revelations concerning the illicit use of performance-enhancing substances by some of its most celebrated practitioners, despite the preponderance of evidence suggesting that every sport is riddled with those who augment their capabilities artificially but who are seldom apprehended.
2. I don't think it's fair that bike racers get all the blame for using drugs just because their sport cracks down on doping, while other pro sports just ignore the problem or face up to it only when the media make a fuss.
3. While every professional sport has some participants who use performance-enhancing drugs, professional cycling seems to have been unfairly labelled as the worst offender, not because there are more cyclists who use drugs, but because the other sports organizations turn a blind eye to the problem.

Now, working alone, write three sentences of your own in different levels of language. (Choose topics with which you are familiar: e.g., music, sports, movies, fashion, fast food, work.)

Finally, exchange papers with your partner and see if he or she can identify the level of language you were aiming for in each sentence.

We've introduced you to the tools you'll need as a writer and to the levels of language you can choose from when writing a message for a specific audience. Let's turn now to the writing errors you must not commit in any message to any audience: wordiness, slang, pretentious language, clichés, offensive language, and "abusages."

WORDINESS

One of the barriers to clear communication is **wordiness**, the unnecessary repetition of information or the use of two or more words when one would do. As a courtesy to your reader, you should make your writing as concise as possible.

Sometimes wordiness results from careless revision. In the editing stage of writing a paper, you should tighten up your sentences and paragraphs. Wordy or awkward phrasing sometimes pops into your mind when you are struggling to express an idea, and it always appears in a first draft. However, there is no excuse for it to survive a careful edit and make its way into a final draft.

Here's an example of what can happen when a writer fails to prune his or her prose:

> In my personal opinion, the government of this country of ours needs an additional amount of meaningful input from the people of Canada.

The writer has chosen impressive-sounding phrases (*meaningful input, this country of ours*) and wordy but meaningless expressions (*personal opinion, an additional amount*) to produce a sentence so hard to read that it isn't worth a reader's effort to decipher. This wordy sentence could be nicely shortened to "In my opinion, our government needs to hear more from the people."

The following list contains some of the worst offenders we've collected from student writing, corporate memoranda, form letters, and advertisements.

Wordy	Concise
a large number of	many
absolutely nothing (or everything, complete, perfect, etc.)	nothing (or everything, complete, perfect)
actual (or true) fact	fact
almost always	usually
at that point in time	then
at the present time	now
consensus of opinion	consensus
continue on	continue
could possibly (or may possibly, might possibly)	could (or may, might)
crisis (or emergency) situation	crisis (or emergency)
due to the fact that	because
end result	result
equally as good	as good
few and far between	rare
final conclusion	conclusion
for the reason that	because
free gift	gift
I myself (or you yourself, etc.)	I (or you, etc.)
I personally think/feel	I think/feel
in actual fact	in fact
in every instance	always
in my opinion, I think ...	I think
in the near future	soon
in today's society/in this day and age	now (or today)
is able to	can
many different kinds	many kinds
mutual agreement (or cooperation)	agreement/cooperation
my personal opinion	my opinion
no other alternative	no alternative
personal friend	friend
real, genuine antique (or real leather, etc.)	antique (or leather, etc.)
red in colour (or small in size, etc.)	red (or small etc.)
repeat again	repeat
return back	return (or go back)
really, very	*These words add nothing to your meaning. Leave them out.*
8:00 a.m. in the morning	8:00 a.m.
such as, for example ...	such as

Wordy	Concise
take active steps	take steps
totally destroyed/surrounded, *etc.*	destroyed/surrounded, *etc.*
truly remarkable	remarkable
very (*or* most, quite, almost, rather) unique	unique

By studying these examples, you will see how such phrases add words but not meaning to your message. Teachers and editors call these phrases "fill" or "padding," and they urge students to eliminate them if they want to build a good relationship with their readers.

EXERCISE **1.8**

Working with a partner, revise these sentences to make them shorter and clearer. Then compare your answers with our suggestions on page 394.

1. Basically, I myself prefer modern contemporary furniture to old antiques.
2. I myself personally feel that there is absolutely no basis in fact for the idea that UFOs exist.
3. Getting up at 5 a.m. in the morning and repeating the exact same daily routine every day for three weeks wore me out and exhausted me.
4. In my opinion, I doubt that this particular new innovation will succeed in winning much in the way of market share.
5. Due to the fact that he is being transferred away from where he lives, Ravi plans to buy a brand-new car.
6. I personally think Holly is faking her illness and pretending to be sick so she can stay at home and not have to go to work.
7. Close personal friends almost always share tastes and opinions in common with each other.
8. In my opinion, I believe that my essay is equally as good as Kim's and deserves equally as good a mark, which it would have got if it weren't for the fact that our professor hates me.
9. There is absolutely nothing at the present time to suggest that this almost unique set of circumstances will ever again be repeated in the foreseeable future, so we can proceed ahead with real and genuine confidence.
10. It has come to my attention that our competitor's products, even though they are not equally as good as ours, are, at this point in time, selling better than those that we produce.

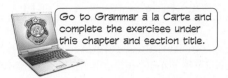

Go to Grammar à la Carte and complete the exercises under this chapter and section title.

SLANG

Amped, bugdust, and *spacker*: do you know what these words mean? Probably not. **Slang** is "street talk": nonstandard language used in conversation among people who belong to the same social group. It's a kind of private speech. Because slang expressions become outdated quickly and are understood by a limited group of people, they are not appropriate for a message intended for a general reader. There are thousands of slang expressions. If you're curious about them, browse through an online dictionary such as **www.slangsite. com**.

If you're in doubt about a word, check your print dictionary. The notation *sl.* or *slang* appears after words that are slang or have a slang meaning. (Some words—for example, *house, cool,* and *bombed*—have both a standard meaning and a slang meaning.) If the word you're looking for isn't listed, chances are it's a slang term, and you should not use it in writing. Taking the time to choose words that are appropriate to written English increases your chances of communicating clearly and earning your readers' respect.

EXERCISE **1.9**

- Working in groups of three or four, list five slang expressions that are outdated—they are no longer used by your peers.
- Now identify five current slang expressions that everyone in your group is familiar with.
- Define each current slang term in language appropriate to a general reader. (That is, write each definition in words your teachers would understand.)

PRETENTIOUS LANGUAGE

The opposite of slang is **pretentious language**: words that are too formal for general writing. Never use a long, difficult, or obscure word when a simpler word will do. Your writing will be easier to read and your message clearer and more convincing if you write to inform rather than to impress.

You can recognize pretentious language easily: the words and sentences are long, complicated, and unnatural-sounding. If the average reader needs a dictionary to "translate" your words into general English, then your writing is inflated and inappropriate. Consider these examples:

Before we embark on our journey, we must refuel our vehicle.

The refrigerator is bare of comestibles, so it is time to repair to the local emporium and purchase victuals.

After consulting your dictionary, you can translate these pompous sentences into plain English:

Before we leave, we need to put gas in the car.

The refrigerator is empty, so it's time to go to the store and buy some food.

But why would you? It's the writer's job to communicate, and a pretentious writer makes the reader do too much work. Here is a list of some common offenders, together with their general-level equivalents.

Pretentious	Clear
ascertain	find out
commence	begin
conceptualize	think
endeavour	try
facilitate	help
finalize	finish
manifest	show
reside	live
transmit	send
utilize	use
verbalize	say

The cure for pretentious language is simple: be considerate of your readers. If you want your readers to understand and respect you, write in a simple, straightforward style.

EXERCISE **1.10**

With a partner, read through the following paragraph and highlight the pretentious words and phrases.

On our recent excursion to Montreal, in close proximity to Dorval, we detected the presence of storm clouds in advance of our position, which led us to the realization that precipitation was probably imminent. Within a short period of time, heavy precipitation began, and our vehicle's windshield-clearing apparatus was inadequate to maintain visibility. When the rainfall began to descend in a congealed state due to falling temperatures, we repaired to the shelter of a hostelry in close proximity to the highway to bide our time until the storm should cease.

Now, working alone, revise this pretentious gobbledygook into a clear, concise statement. Then compare your revision with our suggestion on page 394.

CLICHÉS

Pretentious writing requires time and effort; clichéd writing requires neither. It is as easy and as thoughtless as casual talk. A **cliché** is a phrase that has been used so often it has lost its ability to communicate a meaningful idea.

> At this point in time, we have no choice but to focus our effort where it really counts: on the bottom line.

At this point in time, we have no choice, focus our effort, where it really counts, and *on the bottom line*—all these phrases are clichés. They do not create a picture in the reader's mind, and if your reader cannot "see" what you're saying, no communication takes place. After a few cliché-filled sentences, readers will conclude, "There's nothing new here. It's all been said before." And they will stop reading.

Spoken English is full of clichés—we use them as shortcuts to put our thoughts into words, and if our listener doesn't understand our meaning, we can always explain further. Writers, on the other hand, have time to plan what they want to say. They also have the opportunity to revise and edit. So writers are expected to communicate with more precision and more originality than speakers.

   If English is your first language, you will find clichés easy to recognize. When you can read the first few words of a phrase and fill in the rest automatically, you know the phrase is a cliché: *Better late than* _____; *easier said than* _____; *when push comes to* _____.

   The solution to a cliché problem involves time and thought, first to recognize the cliché and then to find a better way to express your idea. Think about what you want to say and then say it in your own words, not everyone else's.

EXERCISE **1.11**

Working with a partner, identify the cliché(s) in each sentence. Then rewrite the sentence, expressing the ideas in your own words. When you have finished, exchange your results with another group and check each other's work: have all clichés been eliminated? Have any new ones been introduced? Finally, compare your answers with our suggested answers on pages 394 to 395.

1. The financial adviser told us there was a window of opportunity open to investors who could think outside the box. Then she gave us an eye-popping ballpark figure of what our bottom line would look like in five years if we put our money in her capable hands.

2. While you may want cutting-edge stereo and television equipment and a state-of-the-art computer and car, you need to understand that your lifestyle choices must depend on your income, not your desires. At the end of the day, your take-home pay doesn't make the grade.

3. Kayla knew that she was in over her head when the meeting ground to a halt because she had not done her homework. When she became office manager, she thought it would be child's play to get everyone on the same page, but she soon learned that careful preparation is a must.

4. Experts agree that meaningful relationships are important to mental health, even as divorce rates have reached epidemic proportions and loneliness has become a fact of life.

5. Last but not least, I want to thank George and Navika, my tried-and-true friends who have stood by me through thick and thin, even when there

was no light at the end of the tunnel. The list of times when they have lent me a hand is endless.

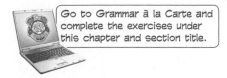

Go to Grammar à la Carte and complete the exercises under this chapter and section title.

OFFENSIVE LANGUAGE

The last thing you want to do when you write is offend your reader, even if you are writing a complaint. As we've seen, some words occasionally used in speech are *always* inappropriate in writing. Swear words, for example, are unacceptable in a written message. So are obscene words, even mild ones. Offensive language appears much stronger in print than in speech. It can shock or outrage a reader. Racist language and blasphemy (the use of names or objects that are sacred to any religion) are always unacceptable and deeply offensive.

Many writers have suffered the embarrassment of having a message read by someone for whom the message was not intended. What may seem when you write it to be an innocent joke or an emphatic expression could, if it is read by someone other than the person you sent it to, prove shocking to readers and mortifying to you. Before you send an angry email, save it as a draft and reread it later. You may decide to tone it down. And make sure you don't accidentally hit Reply All when you intend to reply only to a message's sender. Always THINK before you click Send.

Language has power. Our language shapes as well as reflects our attitudes and values. People who use racist, blasphemous, sexist, or profane terms reinforce the attitudes represented by those terms and also project a negative image to their readers.

LANGUAGE ABUSAGES

Some words and phrases, even ones we hear in everyday speech, are *always* incorrect in written English. Technically, they are also incorrect in speech, but most people tolerate them as part of the casual standard that is common in informal conversation. If these expressions appear in your writing, your reader will assume you are uneducated, careless, or both. In some conversations, particularly in academic and professional environments, these expressions make a poor impression on your listeners.

Carefully read through the following list and highlight any words or phrases that sound correct to you. These are the ones you need to find and fix when you revise.

alot	There is no such word. Use *much* or *many*. (*A lot* is acceptable in informal usage.)
anyways (anywheres)	The *s* on these words betrays the writer as uneducated.
between you and I	A very common error. Use *between you and me*.
can't hardly (couldn't hardly)	The correct expression is *can* (or *could*) *hardly*.
could of (would of, should of)	Using the preposition *of* instead of the auxiliary verb *have* in these verb phrases is a common error. Write *could have, would have,* and *should have*.
didn't do nothing	All double negatives are errors. Some familiar examples are *couldn't see nothing, won't go nowhere,* and *can't find nobody*. Write *didn't do anything, couldn't see anything, won't go anywhere,* and *can't find anybody*.
***good* used as an adverb**	"How are you?" "I'm good." This all-too-common expression is incorrect (unless you mean to say that you are moral or ethical or saintly). If you want to say that you are healthy, then say, "I'm *well*."
irregardless	There is no such word. *Regardless* is the word you may want, but check your thesaurus for other, possibly more appropriate, choices.
***media* used as singular**	The word *media* is plural. It is incorrect to say, "Television is a mass media." It is a mass *medium*. Newspapers, magazines, and the Internet are mass media. Radio is an electronic medium.

off of	Use *off* by itself: "I fell *off* the wagon." Or use *from*: "I fell *from* the balcony."
***prejudice* used as an adjective**	It is incorrect to write "He is *prejudice* against blondes." Use *prejudiced*.
prejudism	There is no such word. Use *prejudice* (a noun): "He showed *prejudice* in awarding the prize to his daughter."
***real* used as an adverb**	*Real good*, *real bad*, and *real nice* are not acceptable. You could use *really* or *very* and be correct, but such filler words add nothing to your meaning.
the reason is because	Write *the reason is that*: "The reason is that my dog ate my essay."
sort of speak	If you must use this expression, get the words right: "so to speak."
suppose to	Like *use to*, this phrase is incorrect. Write *supposed to* and *used to*.
themselfs	Also *ourselfs, yourselfs*. The plural of *self* is *selves*: *ourselves, yourselves,* and *themselves. Theirselves* is non-standard English and is not used by educated speakers and writers.
youse	There is no such word. *You* is both the singular and the plural form of the second-person pronoun. While occasionally heard in restaurants or retail stores, "Can I help youse?" labels the speaker as a high-school dropout.

EXERCISE **1.12**

Working with a partner, revise the following sentences to eliminate any abusages. Then compare your revisions with our suggestions on page 395.

1. I would be happy to meet youse any time, anywheres.

2. Don't be discouraged that Jessa's father can't hardly stand you; he's prejudice against alot of her friends.

3. Television is probably the best example of a media that remains popular irregardless of the quality of the programming.

4. This course was suppose to be real easy, but I could not of passed it without alot of help.

5. Between you and I, the reason our group got a C+ on our project is because Jamie didn't do nothing to contribute to it.

EXERCISE **1.13**

Eliminate the 15 abusages from the following paragraph.

My friend Tim did real good in his last year of high school, so his parents gave him some money for a trip to Europe as a reward. He and two friends got a cheap flight to Amsterdam and then rented a car off of an agent who gave them a real good discount. They drove south to the French Riviera, where there were suppose to be alot of other young travellers, but it rained most of the time they were there. Irregardless of the rain and cold temperatures, they would of gone swimming, but when they discovered the beach was not sand but rocks, they became real discouraged and decided to go north to Paris.

In Paris, they should of been more careful because at the Arc de Triomphe, they got into a minor accident even though they didn't do nothing to cause it. Another problem was that they were unprepared for the real high prices in restaurants and cafés. Tim thought charging six euros for an espresso and nine euros for a beer was proof of the Parisians' dislike of tourists, but he and his friends couldn't do nothing about it. The reason was because they couldn't speak French well enough.

The three boys were delighted to get off the plane in Calgary. While they agreed that their trip could of been worse, they concluded that Europe was nothing like what they had expected. Like so many other things in life, it just wasn't the way it use to be.

GRAMMAR À LA CARTE

- Looking for more opportunities to practise? Want to see what you need to review before the big test? Visit NELSONbrain.com and log in to **Grammar à la Carte** for *The Bare Essentials, Form A*, to access additional exercises! These Web exercises are graded automatically, so you will know instantly whether or not you have mastered the material.

THE VIRUS EFFECTS GRAFFITI ARTISTS BY MAKING THEM CHOSE THE WRONG WORD.

GUY CRAMER, EXCEPT ARE ADVISE AND QUITE, YOU LOOSER!

2 Hazardous Homonyms

This chapter focuses on **homonyms**—words that sound alike or look alike and are easily confused: *accept* and *except*; *weather* and *whether*; *whose* and *who's*; *affect* and *effect*. Your word processor will not help you find spelling mistakes in these words because the correct spelling depends on the sentence in which you use the word. For example, if you write, "Meat me hear inn halve an our," no spell checker will find fault with your sentence, and no reader will understand what you're talking about.

Below you will find a list of the most common homonym hazards. Only some of the words in this list will cause you trouble. Careful pronunciation can sometimes help you tell the difference between words that are often confused. For example, if you pronounce the words *accept* and *except* differently, you'll be less likely to use the wrong one when you write. It's also useful to make up memory aids to help you remember the difference in meaning between words that sound or look alike. The list that follows includes several examples that you may find helpful.

Make your own list of problem pairs and keep it where you can easily refer to it. Tape it inside the cover of your dictionary, or post it over your computer. Get into the habit of checking your document against your list every time you write.

accept **except**	*Accept* means "ta**k**e" or "receive." It is always a verb. *Except* means "**ex**cluding."

> I **ac**cepted the spelling award, and no one **ex**cept my mother knew I cheated.

advice **advise**	The difference in pronunciation makes the difference in meaning clear. *Advise* (rhymes with *wise*) is a verb. *Advice* (rhymes with *nice*) is a noun.

> I *advise* you not to listen to free *advice.*

affect **effect**	*Affect* as a verb means "to ch**a**nge." Try substituting *change* for the word you've chosen in your sentence. If it makes sense, then *af-FECT* is the word you want. As a noun, *AF-fect* means "a strong feeling." *Effect* is a noun meaning "r**e**sult." If you can substitute *result,* then *effect* is the word you need. Occasionally, *effect* is used as a verb meaning "to bring about."

> Learning about the *effects* (results) of caffeine *affected* (changed) my coffee-drinking habits.
> Depressed people often display an inappropriate *affect* (feeling).
> Antidepressant medications can *effect* (bring about) profound changes in mood.

a lot **allot**	*A lot* (often misspelled *alot*) should be avoided in formal writing. Use *many* or *much* instead. *al-LOT* means "distribute" or "assign."

>   many   much
> He still has ~~a lot of~~ problems, but he is coping ~~a lot~~ better.
> The teacher will *allot* the marks according to the difficulty of the questions.

allusion **illusion**	An *allusion* is an implied or indirect reference. An *illusion* is something that appears to be real or true but is not what it seems; it can be a false impression, idea, or belief.

> Many literary *allusions* can be traced to Shakespeare's works.
> A good movie creates an *illusion* of reality.

are **our**	*Are* is a verb. *Our* shows ownership. Confusion of these two words often results from careless pronunciation.

> Where *are our* leaders?

beside **besides**	*Beside* is a preposition meaning "by the side of" or "next to." *Besides* means "also" or "in addition to."

> One evening with Dwayne was more than enough. *Besides* expecting me to buy the tickets, the popcorn, and the drinks, he insisted on sitting *beside* Lisa rather than me.

choose **chose**	Pronunciation gives the clue here. *Choose* rhymes with *booze*, is a present tense verb, and means "select." *Chose* rhymes with *rose*, is a past tense verb, and means "selected."

> Please *choose* a topic.
> I *chose* to write about fuel-cell technology.

cite **sight** **site**	To *cite* means "to quote from" or "to refer to."

> A lawyer *cites* precedents; writers *cite* their sources in articles or research papers; and my friends *cite* my tweets as examples of comic writing.

Sight means "vision," the ability to see. It can also mean something that is visible or worth seeing.

> She lost her *sight* as the result of an accident.
> With his tattoos and piercings, Izzy was a *sight* to behold.

A *site* is the location of something: a building, a town, or a historic event.

> The *site* of the battle was the Plains of Abraham, which lies west of Quebec City.

coarse **course**	*Coarse* means "rough, unrefined." (The slang word **arse** is co**arse**.) For all other meanings, use *course*.

> That sandpaper is too *coarse* to use on a lacquer finish.
> *Coarse* language only weakens your argument.
> Of *course* you'll do well in a *course* on the history of pop music.

complement
compliment

A *complement* completes something. *A compliment* is a gift of praise.

> A glass of wine would be the perfect *complement* to the meal.
> Some people are embarrassed by *compliments*.

conscience
conscious

Your *conscience* is your sense of right and wrong. *Conscious* means "aware" or "awake"—able to feel and think.

> After Ann cheated on the test, her *conscience* bothered her.
> Ann was *conscious* of having done wrong.
> The injured man was *unconscious*.

consul
council
counsel

A *consul* is a government official stationed in another country. A *council* is an assembly or official group. Members of a *council* are *councillors*. Counsel can be used to mean both "advice" and "to advise."

> The Canadian *consul* in Mexico was helpful.
> The Women's Advisory *Council* meets next month.
> Maria gave me good *counsel*.
> She *counselled* me to hire a lawyer.

desert
dessert

A *DE-sert* is a dry, barren place. As a verb, *de-SERT* means "to abandon" or "to leave behind." *Des-SERT* is the part of a meal you'd probably like an extra helping of, so give it an extra *s*.

> The tundra is Canada's only *desert* region.
> If you *desert* me, I'll be all alone.
> I can't resist any *dessert* made with chocolate.

dining
dinning

You'll spell *dining* correctly if you remember the phrase "wining and dining." You'll probably never use *dinning*, which means "making a loud noise."

> The dog is not supposed to be in the *dining* room.
> We are *dining* out tonight.
> The noise from the karaoke bar was *dinning* in our ears.

does
dose

Pronunciation provides the clue. *Does* rhymes with *buzz* and is a verb. *Dose* rhymes with *gross* and refers to a quantity of medicine.

> Josef *does* drive fast, *does*n't he?
> My grandmother used to give me a *dose* of cod liver oil every spring.

forth
fourth

Forth means "**for**ward." *Fourth* contains the number **four**, which gives it its meaning.

> Please stop pacing back and *forth*.
> The Raptors lost their *fourth* game in a row.

hear
here

Hear is what you do with your **ear**s. *Here* is used for all other meanings.

> Now *hear* this!
> Ranjan isn't *here*.
> *Here* is your assignment.

it's
its

It's is a shortened form of *it is*. The apostrophe takes the place of the *i* in *is*. If you can substitute *it is*, then *it's* is the form you need. If you can't substitute *it is*, then *its* is the correct word.

> *It's* really not difficult. (*It is* really not difficult.)
> The book has lost *its* cover. ("The book has lost it is cover" makes no sense, so you need *its*.)
> *It's* is also commonly used as the shortened form of *it has*. In this case, the apostrophe takes the place of the *h* and the *a*.
> *It's* been a good month for new car sales.

knew
new

Knew is the past tense of *know*. *New* is an adjective meaning "having recently come into being," "fresh," or "original."

> We *knew* our *new* pool would attract friends just as surely as fruit attracts flies.
> Who would have thought that cropped pants, a style from the 1950s, would be considered a *new* fashion 60 years later?

know
no

Know is a verb meaning "to understand" or "to recognize." *No* can be used as an adverb to express refusal or denial, or as an adjective to express a negative state or condition.

> We do not *know* the results of the test yet.
> Why are there *no* cookies left in the jar?

later
latter

Later rhymes with *gator*, and has the word *late* in it. *Latter* rhymes with *fatter*, means "the second of two," and has two *t*s. It is the opposite of *former*.

> It's *later*, alligator.
> You take the former, and I'll take the *latter*.

lead
led

Lead is pronounced to rhyme with *speed* and is the present tense of the verb *to lead*. (*Led* is the past tense of the same verb.) The only times you pronounce *lead* as "led" is when you are referring to the writing substance in a pencil or to the metal used to make bullets and leaded windows.

> You *lead*, and I'll decide whether to follow.
> Your suitcase is so heavy it must be filled with either gold or *lead*.
> When our sergeant *led* the charge, I decided to retreat.

loose
lose

Pronunciation is the key to these words. *Loose* rhymes with *goose* and means "not tight" or "unrestricted." *Lose* rhymes with *booze* and means "misplace" or "be defeated."

> There's a screw *loose* somewhere.
> When Moosehead beer is served, people say, "The moose is *loose*!"
> Some are born to win, some to *lose*.
> You can't *lose* on this deal.

miner
minor

A ***miner*** works in a **mine**. *Minor* means "lesser" or "not important" or "a person who is not legally an adult."

> Liquor can be served to *miners*, but not if they are *minors*.
> For some people, spelling is a *minor* problem.

moral
morale

Again, pronunciation provides the clue you need. *MO-ral* refers to the understanding of what is right and wrong; *mo-RALE* refers to the spirit or mental condition of a person or group.

> Most religions are based on a *moral* code of behaviour.
> Despite his shortcomings, he is basically a *moral* man.
> Low *morale* is the reason for our employees' absenteeism.

passed
past

Passed is the past tense of the verb *pass*, which has several meanings, most of which have to do with movement on land or water, but some of which have to do with sports or games. *Past* describes something that happened or existed in an earlier time. *Passed* is always a verb; *past* can be a noun, adjective, adverb, or preposition, but it is never a verb.

> George *passed* the puck to Henry, who slammed it *past* the goalie to win the game.

peace **piece**	*Peace* is what we want on **Ea**rth. *Piece* means a part or portion of something, as in "a **pie**ce of **pie**."

Everyone hopes for *peace* in the Middle East.
A *piece* of the puzzle is missing.

personal **personnel**	*PER-sonal* means "priv**a**te." *Person-NEL* refers to the group of people working for an employer or to the office responsible for maintaining employees' records.

The letter was marked "*Personal* and Confidential."
We are fortunate to have highly qualified *personnel*.

principal **principle**	*Principal* means "m**a**in." A *principl**e*** is a ru**le**.

A *principal* is the main administrator of a school.
The federal government is the *principal* employer in Summerside, P.E.I.
The *principal* and the interest totalled more than I could pay. (In this case, the principal is the main amount of money.)
One of our instructor's *principles* is to refuse to accept late assignments.

quiet **quite**	If you pronounce these words carefully, you won't confuse them: *quiet* has two syllables (kwy-et); *quite* has only one.

The chairperson asked us to be *quiet*.
We had not *quite* finished our assignment.

stationary **stationery**	*Stationary* means "fixed in place." *Stationery* is writing pap**er**.

A *stationary* bicycle will give you a good cardio workout without stressing your knees.
Please order a new supply of *stationery*.

than **then**	*Than* is used in comp**a**risons: bigger than, better than, slower than, etc. Pronounce it to rhyme with *can*. *Then* refers to time and rhymes with *when*.

Kim is a better speller *than* I.
I'd rather be here *than* there.
Pay me first; *then* you can have my notes.

their
there
they're

Their indicates ownership. *There* points out something or indicates place. It includes the word ***here***, which also indicates place. *They're* is a shortened form of *they are*. (The apostrophe replaces the *a* in *are*.)

> It was *their* fault.
> *There* are two weeks left in the term.
> Let's walk over *there*.
> *They're* late, as usual.

threw
through

Threw is the past tense of the verb *throw*. *Through* can be used as a preposition, adjective, or adverb, but never as a verb.

> James *threw* the ball *through* the kitchen window. When he climbed *through* to fetch it, his mother angrily told him that his days of playing catch in the yard were *through*.

too
two
to

The *too* with an extra *o* in it means "more than enough" or "also." *Two* is the number after one. For all other meanings, use *to*.

> It's *too* hot, and I'm *too* tired *to* go for another hike.
> There are *two* sides *to* every argument.
> The *two* women knew *too* much about each other *to* be friends.

wear
were
where
we're

If you pronounce these words carefully, you won't confuse them. *Wear* rhymes with *bear* and can be a noun or a verb. *Were* rhymes with *purr* and is a verb. ***Where*** is pronounced "hwear," includes the word ***here***, and indicates place. *We're* is a shortened form of *we are* and is pronounced "weer."

> After 360,000 km, you shouldn't be surprised that your car is showing signs of *wear* and tear.
> What should I *wear* to the wedding?
> You *were* joking, *weren't* you?
> *Where* did you want to meet?
> *We're* on our way.

weather
whether

Weather refers to climatic conditions: temperature and humidity, for example. *Whether* means "if" and is used in indirect questions or to introduce two alternatives.

> We're determined to go camping this weekend, no matter what the *weather* is like. We'll pack enough gear to be prepared *whether* it rains or shines.

| who's whose | *Who's* is a shortened form of *who is* or *who has*. If you can substitute *who is* or *who has* for the *who's* in your sentence, then you have the right spelling. Otherwise, use *whose*. |

> *Who's* coming to dinner? (*Who is* coming to dinner?)
> *Who's* been sleeping in my bed? (*Who has* been sleeping in my bed?)
> *Whose* paper is this? ("*Who is* paper" makes no sense, so you need *whose*.)

| woman women | Confusing these two is guaranteed to irritate your women readers. *Woman* is the singular form; compare **man**. *Women* is the plural form; compare **men**. |

> Only one *woman* responded to our ad.
> Our company sponsors both a *women*'s team and a men's team.

| you're your | *You're* is a shortened form of *you are*. If you can substitute *you are* for the *you're* in your sentence, then you're using the correct form. If you can't substitute *you are*, use *your*. |

> *You're* welcome. (*You are* welcome.)
> Unfortunately, *your* hamburger got burned. ("You are hamburger got burned" makes no sense, so *your* is the word you want.)

In the exercises that follow, choose the correct word. If you don't know an answer, go back and reread the explanation. Check your answers after each set. Answers for exercises in this chapter begin on page 395.

EXERCISE **2.1**

1. A (conscious/conscience) is what hurts when all of (your/you're) other parts feel good.
2. On my (fourth/forth) try, I (passed/past) the fitness test without cheating.
3. The "forgive and forget" (principal/principle) doesn't always apply to school (principals/principles).
4. (Weather/Whether) we win or (loose/lose) this game, (we're/wear) planning a great end-of-season party.
5. Gloria Steinem is often incorrectly credited with the phrase "A (woman/women) needs a man like a fish needs a bicycle." In fact, (its/it's) author is Irina Dunn.

EXERCISE **2.2**

1. I'll serve you when you show me identification to prove (your/you're) not a (miner/minor).
2. Edie knew the (coarse/course) was too difficult for her when in the first class she was asked to (cite/site) her favourite play by Aristophanes.
3. I was surprised when my date suggested a vintage Pepsi would be the perfect (complement/compliment) to our formal (dining/dinning) experience.
4. On (who's/whose) (advice/advise) did you decide to wear your plaid jacket with those striped pants?
5. You know (your/you're) (passed/past) your prime when your arms are (to/too) short for you to read the newspaper.

EXERCISE **2.3**

1. First, (loose/lose) 15 kg, and (then/than) worry about (your/you're) bald spot.
2. I was (conscience/conscious) that I'd be sorry tomorrow, but I ordered (desert/dessert) anyway.
3. "Football combines (to/two/too) of the worst aspects of American life: (its/it's) nothing but violence punctuated by committee meetings." (George Will)
4. When my fiancée broke (are/our) engagement, she destroyed the (allusions/illusions) I cherished about love.
5. "Although golf was originally restricted to wealthy, overweight Protestants, today (its/it's) open to anyone (whose/who's) clothing is sufficiently hideous." (Dave Barry)

EXERCISE **2.4**

1. (Dose/Does) anyone (hear/here) remember the nineties?
2. The (coarse/course) wool of my (knew/new) scarf makes my neck itch.
3. "If you owe the bank $100, that's (you're/your) problem. If you owe the bank $100 million, (than/then) that's the bank's problem." (J. P. Getty)
4. Overeating at (diner/dinner) (lead/led) to a sleepless night.
5. "If a (women/woman) has to (chose/choose) between catching a fly ball and saving an infant's life, she will (chose/choose) to save the infant's life without even considering if there are men on base." (Dave Barry)

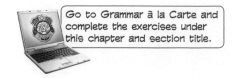

Go to Grammar à la Carte and complete the exercises under this chapter and section title.

EXERCISE **2.5**

1. An experienced manager (accepts/excepts) the fact that (a lot of/allot of/ many) employees hate Mondays.
2. "I am returning this otherwise good (stationery/stationary) to you because someone has written gibberish all over it and put (you're/your) name at the top." (Comment by a professor at Ohio State University on a student's essay)
3. (Wear/Where) were you when our tour group assembled for the camel ride into the (desert/dessert)?
4. In old gangster films, people who (where/were/we're) shot were said to have got "a (does/dose) of (led/lead) poisoning."
5. When I asked to be referred to a lawyer who was competent, (affective/ effective), and inexpensive, I was told to (chose/choose) one of the above.

EXERCISE **2.6**

Find and correct the 15 errors in the following sentences.

1. The hiring committee will not here from any candidate who's application is late.

2. Other then hope that the voters will chose our candidate, there isn't much more we can do.

3. I bruise easily, and beside, I faint at the site of blood.

4. Whose the idiot who said that our principle purpose in life was to serve as a warning to others?

5. Driving threw the deserted streets, we past only a police officer and a stray dog.

6. You would do well to chose a morale rather than an unprincipaled coarse of action.

EXERCISE **2.7**

Find and correct the 15 errors in the following paragraph. Watch carefully for the one error we've included that is not on our list of hazardous homonyms.

Nothing causes more arguments between men and woman then money. Recently, my husband and I were driving threw the countryside and became involved in a miner disagreement about weather to treat ourselves to a vacation or buy a new refrigerator. I argued that if we bought the appliance, this would be the forth year in which we had not had a holiday. He countered that our fridge had past it's useful life, and a functioning refrigerator took precedents over having fun. What began as a spat quickly lead to a battle. Before we new it, our good sense desserted us, and we were having a serious fight. At this point, we past a farmyard containing several goats and pigs. Pointing to them, my husband asked if they were relatives of mine. "Of coarse," I replied. "There my in-laws."

EXERCISE **2.8**

Find and correct the 15 errors in this paragraph.

Many people today are chosing a quieter way of life, hoping to live longer and more happily by following the "slower is better" principal. Some, on the advise of they're doctors, have been forced to slow down. One heart surgeon, for example, tells his patients to drive only in the slow lane rather then use the passing lane. They may arrive a few minutes later, but their blood pressure will not be effected. Others don't need to be prompted by their doctors. They except that living at a slower pace doesn't mean loosing out in any way. In fact, the opposite is true: choosing a healthy lifestyle benefits everyone. The affect of increased piece and quite in your personnel life leads to increased productivity, higher moral, and greater job satisfaction. Sometimes the improvements are miner, but as anyone who has consciencely tried to slow the pace of life can tell you, the slow lane is the fast lane to longevity.

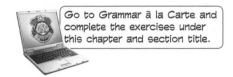

Go to *Grammar à la Carte* and complete the exercises under this chapter and section title.

EXERCISE **2.9**

Below is a list of word pairs that are often confused. Use each one in a sentence that clearly differentiates the word from the word or words that have the same sound. Use your dictionary to help you. When you are finished, exchange papers with another student and check each other's work.

1. altar, alter
2. breath, breathe
3. capital, capitol
4. stake, steak
5. waist, waste

6. cord, chord
7. cloths, clothes
8. emigrate, immigrate
9. hoard, horde
10. precede, proceed

EXERCISE **2.10**

The English language includes many words that can be used as nouns, verbs, even adjectives and adverbs, although they are often pronounced differently for different functions. Working with a partner or small group, make up 10 sentences using the word we've provided as two different parts of speech in each sentence.

Example: tear

I shed a tear when I saw the tear in my best blouse.

Hint: Use a dictionary if you are not familiar with both uses of the word.

1. wind
2. produce
3. dove
4. wound
5. present

6. refuse
7. object
8. lead
9. row
10. does

EXERCISE **2.11**

This exercise is more challenging. All the words in the following passage are correctly spelled. The problem is that 20 of them are the wrong words—they don't mean what the writer intended. Can you solve the puzzle by supplying the right words?

Between 1946 and 1964, about 90 million people were born in North America. Known as "baby boomers," this group, which now constitutes one-third of Canada's population, has had a greater affect on society then any previous generation. As anyone in marketing or retail knows, boomers have been big consumers, thanks to there parents, who tasted wealth for the first time after the Depression and World War II. They're buying power made corporate giants of Coca-Cola, McDonald's, Levi Strauss, and Bell; latter, IBM would join the club. Whatever products and services were knew, weather related to fitness, health, beauty, or home decorating, boomers bought them and made millionaires of inventors of everything from Clearasil to Frisbees. Of course, they were buying only the allusion of beauty or fitness, but theirs was a supremely image-conscience era.

The baby boomers profoundly effected popular music, to, embracing rock and roll in all it's forms and making stars of performers as diverse as Elvis Presley, Tiny Tim, Diana Ross, Stevie Wonder, and the Beatles. Their sometimes fickle enthusiasms lead to short-lived celebrity status for other musicians who's music made a brief impact and than disappeared.

The boomers themselves where shaped by the assassination of President Kennedy, the Vietnam War, the moon landing, Woodstock, and Canada's Centennial. However, the most profound influence on the men and woman of the generation was not an event but the gradual introduction of television into every home. This was the first generation to experience television as the dominant mass medium, and it's influence on everything from fashion to career goals, from family dinning to family dynamics, cannot be overestimated. Like it or not (and many resent the huge influence of the baby boomer generation), we still are living in a world largely shaped by their interests, values, morales, and whims.

GRAMMAR À LA CARTE

- Looking for more opportunities to practise? Want to see what you need to review before the big test? Visit NELSONbrain.com and log in to **Grammar à la Carte** for *The Bare Essentials, Form A,* to access additional exercises! These Web exercises are graded automatically, so you will know instantly whether or not you have mastered the material.

The Apostrophe **3**

What, you may ask, is a chapter on apostrophes doing in a unit on words? Why isn't it in Unit 4 with the other punctuation marks? Here's the reason: while all other punctuation marks show the intended relationship among parts of a sentence, apostrophes show the relationship between two words (in a possessive construction) or two parts of one word (in a contraction). Misused apostrophes change the meaning of words, and that is why we are discussing them here.

Can you spot how this sentence from a letter of application revealed the applicant's poor writing skills?

> I would like to contribute to you're companies success as it enters it's second decade of outstanding service to customer's.

Misused apostrophes can confuse, amuse, and sometimes annoy readers. Using them correctly is an indication that the writer is competent and careful. The example above contains four apostrophe errors, which irritated the reader so much that the applicant didn't even make it to the interview stage.

- Sometimes you need an apostrophe so that your reader can understand what you mean. For example, there's a world of difference between these two sentences:

  The instructor began class by calling the students' names.
  The instructor began class by calling the students names.

- In most cases, however, misused apostrophes just amuse or annoy an alert reader:

  The movie had it's moments.
  He does a days' work every week.
  The Conservative's thank you for your contribution.

It isn't difficult to avoid such mistakes. Correctly used, the apostrophe indicates either contraction or possession. It never makes a singular word plural. The following three sentences show where to use—and not use—apostrophes.

1. The dog's chasing cars again. (Contraction: *dog's = dog is*)
2. The dog's bark is more reliable than the doorbell. (Possessive: the bark belongs to the dog)
3. The dogs bark all night long. (Plural, so no apostrophe)

CONTRACTION

Contraction is the combining of two words into one, as in *they're* or *can't*. Contractions are common in conversation and in informal written English. Unless you are quoting someone else's words, however, you should avoid them in the writing you do for school or work.

> When two words are combined into one, and one or more letters are left out, the apostrophe goes in the place of the missing letter(s).

Here are some examples.

I am	→ I'm	they are	→ they're
we will	→ we'll	it is	→ it's
she is	→ she's	it has	→ it's
do not	→ don't	who has	→ who's

EXERCISE **3.1**

Place apostrophes correctly in these words, which are intended to be contractions. Notice that when the apostrophe is missing, the word often has a different meaning. Answers for exercises in this chapter begin on page 397.

1. cant   6. hasnt

2. shed   7. youre

3. hell   8. wont

4. wed   9. shell

5. lets   10. well

EXERCISE **3.2**

Make these sets of words into contractions.

1. they are   6. could not

2. I will   7. who has

3. it has   8. you are

4. would not   9. we would

5. everyone is   10. will not

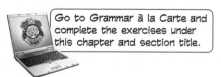

Go to Grammar à la Carte and complete the exercises under this chapter and section title.

EXERCISE **3.3**

Correct these sentences by placing apostrophes where they are needed.

1. Theres no way wed go without you.

2. There wont be any problem if youve got an invitation.

3. Im sure that contractions shouldnt be used in formal writing.

4. They're acceptable only in conversation and in informal writing.

5. Lets see if shell do what she said shed do.

6. Dont worry about your heart; its going to last as long as you do.

7. When everythings coming your way, youre probably in the wrong lane.

8. Wouldnt it be great if everyone whos celebrating a birthday today could get together for a big party?

9. Id support the idea only if the party wasnt held anywhere near my apartment.

10. "A mans got to do what a mans got to do. A womans got to do what he cant." (Rhonda Hansome)

EXERCISE **3.4**

In some formal kinds of writing—academic, legal, and technical, for example—contractions are not acceptable. A good writer is able not only to contract two words into one but also to expand any contraction into its original two-word phrase. In the following paragraph, find and expand the contractions into their original form.

I'm writing to apply for the position of webmaster for BrilloVision.com that you've advertised in the *Daily News*. I have the talent and background you're looking for. Currently, I work as a web designer for an online publication, Vexed.com, where they're very pleased with my work. If you click on their website, I think you'll like what you see. There's little in the way of web design and application that I haven't been involved in during the past two years. But it's time for me to move on to a new challenge, and BrilloVision.com promises the kind of opportunity I'm looking for. I guarantee you won't be disappointed if I join your team!

POSSESSION

The apostrophe is also used to show ownership or **possession**. Here's the rule that applies in most cases:

> If the owner word is singular, add 's to indicate possession.
> If the owner word is plural and ends in s, add only an apostrophe.

Here are some examples that illustrate the rule.

singer + 's = singer's voice	women + 's = women's voices
band + 's = band's instruments	student + 's = student's report card
players + 's = players'$\cancel{s}$ uniforms	students + 's = students'$\cancel{s}$ report cards
ships + 's = ships'$\cancel{s}$ sails	colleges + 's = colleges'$\cancel{s}$ teams

To form a possessive, first find the word in the sentence that identifies the owner. Then decide if the owner is singular or plural. For example, "the managers duties" can have two meanings, depending on where you put the apostrophe:

the manager's duties (the duties belong to one *manager*)
the managers' duties (the duties belong to two or more *managers*)

> To solve an apostrophe problem, follow this two-step process:
> 1. Find the owner word.
> 2. Apply the possession rule.

Problem: Laras hair is a mess.
Solution: 1. The owner word is *Lara* (singular).
　　　　　　2. Add 's to *Lara*.

Lara's hair is a mess.

Problem: The technicians strike stopped production.
Solution: 1. The owner word is *technicians* (plural).
                  2. Add an apostrophe: *technicians'*.

The *technicians'* strike stopped production.

Sometimes, the meaning of your sentence is determined by where you put the apostrophe.

Problem: The writer was delighted by the critics response to her book.

You have two possibilities to choose from, depending on your meaning.

Solution A: 1. The owner word is *critic* (singular).
                     2. Add *'s* to *critic*.

The writer was delighted by the *critic's* response to her book.

Solution B: 1. The owner word is *critics* (plural).
                     2. Add an apostrophe to *critics*.

The writer was delighted by the *critics'* response to her book.

Both solutions are correct, depending on whether the book was reviewed by one critic (Solution A) or by more than one critic (Solution B).

Possession does not have to be literal. It can be used to express the notion of "belonging to" or "associated with." That is, the owner word need not refer to a person or group of people. Ideas or concepts (abstract nouns) can be "owners" too.

today's news = the news of today
a month's vacation = a vacation of one month
a year's salary = the salary of one year

Words

EXERCISE **3.5**

In each of the following phrases, make the owner word possessive.

1. Cass voice
2. heaven gate
3. families budgets
4. crew mutiny
5. soldiers uniforms

6. everyone choice
7. the all-candidates debate
8. witness testimony
9. teacher attitude
10. Lady Gaga style

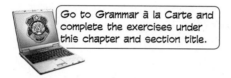

Go to Grammar à la Carte and complete the exercises under this chapter and section title.

A few words, called **possessive pronouns**, are already possessive in form, so they don't have apostrophes.

yours	ours
hers, his, its	theirs
whose	whose

The decision is *hers*, not *yours*.
Whose story do you believe, *theirs* or *ours*?
The dog has lost *its* bone.

Four possessive words (*its, theirs, whose,* and *your*) are often confused with the contractions that sound like them. When deciding which spelling to use, expand the contraction into its original two words and try those words in your sentence. If the sentence still makes sense, use the contraction. If it doesn't, use the possessive.

Possessive		**Contraction**	
its	= *it* owns something	it's	= it is/it has
their	= *they* own something	they're	= they are
whose	= *who* owns something	who's	= who is/who has
your	= *you* own something	you're	= you are

Error: They're (they are) going to sing they're (~~they are~~) latest song.
Revision: They're going to sing *their* latest song.

Error: It's (it is) you're (~~you are~~) favourite song.
Revision: It's *your* favourite song.

Error: Who's (~~Who is~~) CD are you listening to?
Revision: *Whose* CD are you listening to?

Error: That car has a hole in it's (~~it is~~) muffler.
Revision: That car has a hole in *its* muffler.

EXERCISE **3.6**

Make the words in parentheses possessive. This exercise will help you discover how well you understand the difference between possessive pronouns and their sound-alike contractions.

1. This (book) cover is more interesting than (it) contents.

2. (Bikers) equipment is on sale this week at (Larry) Leather Boutique.

3. My parents would like to know (who) yogurt has been in (they) fridge for months.

4. (Dennis) phone is ringing, but he's in the (men) room.

5. After only a (month) wear, my (son) jacket fell apart.

6. (Texas) execution record is one of the (United States) most notorious statistics.

7. This (month) *Fashion* magazine devotes two pages to (men) spring styles and twenty pages to (women).

8. WD-40 is a product (who) name comes from the fact that it was the fortieth formula created by San Diego Rocket Chemical for the (company) new "water displacement" compound in 1953.

9. According to (consumers) testimonials, one of (WD-40) unexpected uses is to remove ketchup stains from clothing.

10. If you spray WD-40 on your balcony railing, (it) smell is supposed to keep away pigeons, while if you spray it on (you) fishing lures, you'll attract more fish.

In the two exercises that follow, correct the sentences by placing apostrophes where they are needed in contractions and possessive constructions. Delete any misused apostrophes. There are 10 errors in each exercise.

EXERCISE **3.7**

1. A countrys health care system is one of it's greatest assets.

2. Who says nobodys perfect? In my mothers opinion, I am.

3. Most mothers beliefs about their childrens characters are unrealistically positive.

4. Most fathers opinions are negative when they first meet their daughters boyfriends.

5. Did you ever notice that when you blow in a dogs face, he gets mad at you, but when you take him on a car ride, he stick's his head out the window?

EXERCISE **3.8**

1. This years hockey schedule puts the Stanley Cup final's halfway through baseball season.

2. The candidates debate was deadly boring until the heckler's in the audience started a fistfight.

3. Todays styles and tomorrows trends are featured in every issue of our magazine.

4. My in-laws home is about a half-hours drive north of Green Lake.

5. Have you noticed that since everyones got a cellphone camera, theres been a dramatic drop in the number of UFO sightings?

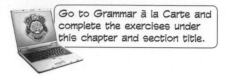

Go to Grammar à la Carte and complete the exercises under this chapter and section title.

PLURALS

The third apostrophe rule is very simple. Memorize it, apply it, and you will instantly correct many of your apostrophe errors.

> Never use an apostrophe to make a word plural.

The plural of most English words is formed by adding *s* to the root word, not *'s*. The *s* alone tells the reader that the word is plural: e.g., *memos, letters, files, broadcasts, newspapers, journalists*. If you add an apostrophe + *s*, you are telling your reader that the word is either a contraction or a possessive.

Incorrect: Never use apostrophe's to make word's plural.
Correct: Never use apostrophes to make words plural.

EXERCISE **3.9**

Correct the misused and missing apostrophes in the following sentences. There are 10 errors in this exercise. Check your answers against ours on page 399.

1. Jacques brilliance is outshone only by his wifes.

2. Forming plural nouns by using apostrophe's is one way to ensure that your writing attract's attention.

3. My iPods playlists need editing; they're full of song's I no longer want to listen to.

4. Good writing skill's may not guarantee success in you're career, but their lack will certainly contribute to failure.

5. Golf requires different club's for different shots: woods for long shots, irons for short one's, and a putter for character development.

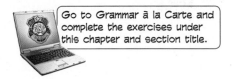

Go to Grammar à la Carte and complete the exercises under this chapter and section title.

Correct the misused and missing apostrophes in the two exercises that follow, and correct the spelling if necessary. There are 10 errors in each exercise.

EXERCISE **3.10**

1. "Candy is dandy, but liquors quicker." (Ogden Nash)*

2. Ive posted a sign on my front lawn: "Salespeoples visits are always welcome. Dog foods expensive."

3. I haven't started the essay thats due tomorrow. It was supposed to take three weeks work, so its going to be a long night.

4. In Canada, as soon as its warm enough to take off you're shirt, you know its mosquito season.

EXERCISE **3.11**

1. Brittany's Twitter report on her trip to Europe read like an Ogden Nash poem: "Britains a bore, Spains a pain, but Greece's grand."

2. Hedonist's are people who pursue pleasure for it's own sake.

3. We will need everybodies maximum effort if we are to meet tomorrows deadline.

* ©1931 by Ogden Nash, renewed. Reprinted by permission of Curtis Brown, Ltd.

4. Geoff devoted his two year's at Queens University to hard partying.

5. In todays competitive market, success depends on strategic thinker's who are familiar with a variety of cultures.

EXERCISE 3.12

Here's one more exercise to test your ability to recognize missing and misused apostrophes before you tackle the Mastery Test. There are 15 errors in these sentences.

1. Brain cell's come and brain cell's go, but fat cell's live forever.

2. One of our colleges objectives is to meet our students social needs as well as their academic goals.

3. The Three Tenors most spectacular concert was held in Romes ancient Colosseum.

4. The health of Canadas economy depends on two things: its abundant natural resource's and its pool of skilled labourer's and well-educated professional's.

5. Research tells us that people from different backgrounds encourage creativity in one another: one persons problem is anothers challenge.

6. "What do I think of computer dating? Its terrific if your a computer." (Rita Mae Brown)

Before you do the Mastery Test for this chapter, carefully review the information in the Summary box on the next page.

SUMMARY

APOSTROPHE RULES

- When contracting two words into one, put an apostrophe in the place of the missing letter(s).
- Watch for owner words: they need apostrophes.
- To indicate possession, add *'s* to the owner word. (If the owner word is plural and already ends in *s*, add just the apostrophe.)
- Possessive pronouns (e.g., *yours*, *its*, *ours*) do not take apostrophes.
- Never use an apostrophe to form the plural of a word.

EXERCISE **3.13**

This exercise will test your ability to use apostrophes correctly in contractions and possessive constructions—but *not* to form plurals. Find and correct the 15 errors in the following sentences.

1. If those bags are your's, then where are our's?

2. The federal governments announcement of huge infrastructure grant's prompted the 13 provincial and territorial governments accountant's to work overtime looking for ways to spend their share.

3. This college aims to meet our students social need's as well as their academic goal's.

4. I went to the librarys Help Desk and asked where I could find self-help book's, but the librarian said telling me would defeat the books purpose.

5. As knowledge worker's replace industrial worker's, the challenge of the 21st century will be to stimulate diversity in order to ensure our nations economic survival.

GRAMMAR À LA CARTE

- Looking for more opportunities to practise? Want to see what you need to review before the big test? Visit NELSONbrain.com and log in to **Grammar à la Carte** for *The Bare Essentials, Form A,* to access additional exercises! These Web exercises are graded automatically, so you will know instantly whether or not you have mastered the material.

THEY DESERVE CAPITALIZATION PUNISHMENT.

canadians demand more sundays, fewer mondays!

canadians demand more sundays, fewer mondays!

ungrammatical are people

Capital Letters 4

Capital letters belong in a few specific places and nowhere else. Some writers suffer from "capitalitis." They put capital letters on words without thinking about the words' position or function in a sentence.

Not many people have this problem. If you are in the majority, who generally use capitals correctly, skip this chapter and go on to something else. If you are puzzled about capital letters, though, or have readers who are puzzled by your use of them, read on.

Capitalize the first letter of any word that fits into one of the six categories highlighted below.

1. Capitalize the first word of a sentence, a direct quotation, or a sentence from a quoted source.

Are you illiterate? Write to us today for free help.

"It was a dark and stormy night," typed Snoopy.

Lister Sinclair once said, "The only thing Canadians have in common is that we all hate Toronto."

EXERCISE **4.1**

Revise the following sentences by adding the missing capital letters and deleting the incorrect ones. There are 10 errors in these sentences. Answers for exercises in this chapter begin on page 399.

1. The Pen is mightier than the Sword.

2. taped to the door was a sign that read, "do not use as entrance or exit."

3. Richard Harkness summed up my feeling about committees when he wrote, "a committee is a group of the unwilling, picked from the unfit, to do the unnecessary."

4. On the first day of class, our teacher told us, "for most of us, learning Standard Written English is like learning another Language."

5. Finally, I want you to remember the words of Wendell Johnson: "*always* and *never* are two words you should always remember never to use."

> 2. Capitalize the names of specific people, places, and things.

Names of people (and their titles):

> Norah Jones, Governor General David Johnston, the Reverend Henry Brock, Dr. Norman Bethune, Professor Ursula Franklin, Senator Hugh Segal

Names of places, regions, and astronomical bodies (but not general geographic directions):

> Stanley Park, Lake Superior, Cape Breton Island; Nunavut, the Badlands; Saturn, Earth, the Moon, the Asteroid Belt; south, north

Names of buildings, institutions, organizations, companies, departments, products, etc.:

> the National Art Gallery, the Museum of Civilization; McGill University, Red Deer College; the Liberal Party, the Kiwanis Club; Petro-Canada, Rogers; the Department of English, the Human Resources Department; Kleenex, Volvo, Labatt Blue

EXERCISE **4.2**

Add capital letters where necessary in the following sentences. There are 25 errors in this exercise.

1. At loblaws, we argued over the cornflakes. Should we buy kellogg's or president's choice?

2. After a brief stay in the maritimes, captain Tallman and his crew sailed west up the St. Lawrence river.

3. Do you find that visa is more popular than American express when you travel to faraway places like santiago, rome, or tofino?

4. Our stay at the seaview hotel, overlooking the pacific ocean, certainly beat our vacation at the bates motel, where we faced West, overlooking the city dump.

5. As a member of the Waterloo alumni association, I am working to raise funds from companies such as general motors, bell Canada, and the cbc, where our graduates have been hired.

> 3. Capitalize the names of major historical events, historical periods, religions, holy texts, and holy days.

> World War II, the Depression, the Renaissance; Islam, Judaism, Christianity, Buddhism, Hinduism; the Torah, the Koran, the Bible, the Upanishads; Easter, Ramadan, Yom Kippur

EXERCISE **4.3**

Add the 20 capital letters that are missing from the following sentences.

1. Many of the celebrations we think of as originating in the last 2,000 years have much older roots; halloween and easter are two such festivals.

2. The celebration of christmas has its origins in ancient babylon, where the birth of the son of isis was marked by feasting and gift-giving.

3. The romans, too, had a traditional celebration called saturnalia, held at the end of December. The tradition of seasonal songs, known to us as *carols*, began in roman times.

4. The Christmas tree and mistletoe date from pagan celebrations called yule, which were held in northern europe on the shortest day of the year.

5. The observance of ramadan is one of the five pillars of the islamic faith and is a month when muslims show obedience and submission by fasting.

6. At the end of ramadan, a huge feast called eid lasts the entire night.

7. In the jewish faith, the festival of hanukkah often occurs at the same time that christians are observing christmas.

8. The celebration of hanukkah involves the lighting of one candle each day on a nine-branched candelabrum.

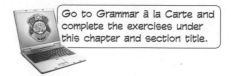

Go to Grammar à la Carte and complete the exercises under this chapter and section title.

4. Capitalize the days of the week, months of the year, and specific holidays—but not the seasons.

Wednesday; January; Remembrance Day, Canada Day; spring, autumn, winter

EXERCISE **4.4**

The following sentences contain both missing and unnecessary capitals. Find and correct the 15 errors.

1. My favourite months are january and february because I love all Winter sports.

2. This monday is valentine's day, when messages of love are traditionally exchanged.

3. In Summer, big meals seem to be too much trouble; however, after thanksgiving, we need lots of food to survive the winter cold.

4. In curaçao, people celebrate new year's day with elaborate fireworks displays.

5. By thursday, I'll have finished my St. patrick's day costume.

---

5. Capitalize major words in titles (books, magazines, films; essays, poems, songs; works of art; names of websites). Do not capitalize minor words (articles, prepositions, coordinating conjunctions) in titles unless the word is the first or last word in the title.

Eats, Shoots, and Leaves (book)   *David* (sculpture)
Of Mice and Men (book, film)   "An Immigrant's Split Personality" (essay)
Maclean's (magazine)   "In Flanders Fields" (poem)
A Room with a View (book, film)   *Facebook* (Internet site)

EXERCISE **4.5**

Add the 20 capital letters that are missing from the following sentences.

1. While I enjoyed the movie *The avengers*, I preferred the comic version and the old TV show of the same name.

2. Desperate for plot ideas, today's moviemakers turn to comic books or even fairy tales, as 2012's *Jack the giant killer*, *mirror mirror*, and *snow white and the huntsman* demonstrate.

3. Did you know that a small painting called *the scream* by Norwegian painter Edvard Munch recently sold for $120 million?

4. The album *blonde* by coeur de pirate is what I play most on my iPod; "ava" is my favourite single.

5. Most reviewers found Conrad Black's memoir, *A life in progress,* to be well written but wordy.

6. Although panned by reviewers and banned by libraries in several U.S. states, E. L. James's book *Fifty Shades of grey* is a bestseller on the *new york times* book list.

Pay special attention to this next category. It is one that causes every writer trouble.

6. Capitalize the names of specific school courses,

Marketing 101, Psychology 100, Mathematics 220, English 345,

but not the names of general school subjects

marketing, psychology, mathematics, literature

unless the subjects are languages or pertain to specific geographical areas.

English, Greek; the study of Chinese history, modern Caribbean literature, Latin American poetry

(Names of languages, countries, and geographical regions are always capitalized.)

In the space below, list the subjects you are taking this term, together with their specific course numbers and names. An example has been provided.

Subject	Course Number and Name
marketing	MA 101: Introduction to Marketing
English	_____
_____	_____
_____	_____
_____	_____
_____	_____

EXERCISE **4.6**

In this exercise, correct the spelling by adding or deleting capital letters as necessary. There are 25 errors.

1. Gore Vidal, author of *the best man*, once said, "it is not enough to succeed; others must fail."

2. You must take some Science courses, or you'll never get into the program you want at camosun college in the Fall.

3. Our youth group meets in the ottawa mosque every thursday evening.

4. We went to Ho lee chow for a bite to eat after the Game and then went home to watch *this hour has 22 minutes* on television.

5. In our english course at caribou college, we studied *the englishman's boy*, a novel about life among the settlers of the canadian west.

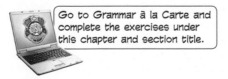

Go to Grammar à la Carte and complete the exercises under this chapter and section title.

The two exercises that follow contain capitalization errors from all six categories highlighted above. Correct the spelling by adding or deleting capital letters as necessary. Then check your answers on pages 401 and 402.

EXERCISE **4.7**

This exercise contains 25 errors.

1. My most difficult course is graphic design 201. We're required to submit both an essay and a Major Design project in which we demonstrate everything we have learned in all our Art courses.

2. I wonder how our College gets away with requiring students to take english and mathematics courses in addition to our Major subjects.

3. Leonard Cohen first became famous as a novelist when he published *beautiful losers*, but now he is better known as a singer-songwriter for albums such as *old ideas* and songs like "hallelujah."

4. The Aphorisms of Steven Wright, a scientist and Humorist, appeal to my sense of Irony. Here's an example: "I'd kill for a Nobel peace prize."

5. I was raised a baptist, but since taking professor Chan's course, introduction to world religions, I've been interested in hinduism and buddhism.

EXERCISE **4.8**

There are 15 errors in the following paragraph.

Sherlock Holmes and his friend dr. watson were on a camping trip in british columbia's rocky mountains. During the night, Holmes awakened his friend and said, "Watson, look up. what do you see?"

Watson replied, "I see millions and millions of stars."

"And what does that tell you?" enquired Holmes.

"If I recall correctly, my astronomy 200 course taught me that there are countless stars, Galaxies, and planets. From my knowledge of Astrology, I observe that taurus is in scorpio. From the position of the planets, I deduce it is about 3:30 in the morning, and according to my understanding of Meteorology, tomorrow will be a lovely Summer day."

Holmes was silent for a moment and then said, "you idiot, Watson! Someone has stolen our tent!"

EXERCISE **4.9**

The following exercise is the Mastery Test and contains 25 errors. Before you begin, it would be a good idea to review the six capitalization rules, which are highlighted on pages 55 to 60.

1. My wife's English is better than mine, even though her first language is french.

2. *The lion king*, which is based on disney's animated movie of the same name, is a spectacular musical with a gorgeous african setting.

3. My Mother and Father are still driving around town with an old bumper sticker that reads, "money isn't everything, but it sure keeps the kids in touch."

4. My Biology course is boring, Trigonometry is tedious, and Botany is bland. The only two courses I like this term are urban society, a Sociology course, and psychology of gambling, an upper-level Psychology course.

5. Luca plans to go to Paris next summer to study french and art history at the sorbonne, france's premier university.

6. When I moved North to thunder bay, I learned to appreciate the wonders of Winter and the ever-changing beauty of lake Superior.

UNIT 1 RAPID REVIEW

As a final test of your mastery of the skills you have worked on in Unit 1, correct the 15 errors in the following passage. Check the answers on page 402 to see whether you need to review any of the material in Unit 1.

[1]In 1908, travelers in the Nova Scotia wilderness reported being blown away by the cite of a beaver dam because beavers were almost extinct at that time. [2]What a change 100 years has brought! [3]Now, the beaver is so common and so prolific that its being hunted and trapped as a nuisance across Canada. [4]In fact, Canadian trappers are issued a quota for the number of beaver's they are aloud to trap in their territory, and they must reach that quota or loose their trapping licence.

[5]Were not alone in our struggle to control these humongous, pesky rodents. [6]A *Canadian Geographic* film called *the Super Beaver* documents the creatures introduction to Tierra del Fuego, at the tip of South America, which has led to the complete and total devastation of the ecosystem. [7]The film tells us that only coral and humans have had a greater impact on Earths environment than beavers! [8]They have migrated to the mainland of South America, where without rigorous and expensive government intervention, they threaten to destroy millions of hectares of Argentinas land as they expand their territory northward. [9]It's difficult to except the fact that only 100 years ago, travellers

in Canadas wilderness longed for a glimpse of what was then a rare and exotic

animal.

GRAMMAR À LA CARTE

- Looking for more opportunities to practise? Want to see what you need to review before the big test? Visit NELSONbrain.com and log in to **Grammar à la Carte** for *The Bare Essentials, Form A,* to access additional exercises! These Web exercises are graded automatically, so you will know instantly whether or not you have mastered the material.

UNIT 2

Sentences

Sentences

UNIT 2 QUICK QUIZ

This Quick Quiz will show you which chapters of Unit 2 you need to focus on. The passage below contains a total of 15 errors in sentence structure. You will find one or more examples of sentence fragments, run-ons, misplaced and dangling modifiers, and unparallel constructions. When you've made your corrections, turn to page 402 and compare your revisions with ours. For each error you miss, the Answer Key directs you to the chapter you need to work on.

[1]After enduring one of those awful days in which nothing seems to go right, we can be cheered up by a story about someone even less competent than ourselves sometimes. [2]I began the day by spilling my coffee, losing my car keys, and my debit card PIN slipped my mind. [3]Things got worse, I was late for an important meeting and then discovered I had left the documents I needed for the meeting in my car.

[4]Slinking back to my office after this disaster, a newspaper was open on my desk. [5]A Collingwood man had submitted a story about his neighbour, a woman who had recently moved from the city to enjoy the charms of country living. [6]The newcomer had written to the local town council. [7]To complain about a "deer crossing" sign on a post across the road from her house. [8]When the official in charge of road signs called her to ask why she objected to the sign. [9]She replied that too many deer were being hit on her road and the town should give them a safer place to cross. [10]Feeling better after reading this story, and the next story made me feel even better.

[11]A woman from Guelph had bought a new car, a loan with her bank was arranged, and arrived at the dealership to pick up her purchase. [12]There she was told that a worker had accidentally locked the keys in her car. [13]A mechanic working on the driver's door trying to unlock the vehicle. [14]While waiting for the mechanic to finish, the car looked so beautiful that she strolled around it, admiring her new purchase. [15]When she reached the passenger's side, she tried the door. [16]It opened! [17]When she told the mechanic that the car was open, he replied, "I know I've already done that side."

[18]I don't know who put the newspaper on my desk. [19]Must have been someone who knew the kind of day I was having. [20]After reading these examples about the stupidity of others, I realized my day hadn't been so bad. [21]In fact, by the time I got home from work, I felt quite cheerful. [22]At least in comparison to how I had felt eight hours before.

5 | Cracking the Sentence Code

A baby's first word is a big step, one that all parents mark as a significant stage of development. Not all parents recognize that an even more significant step in a baby's progress is the first time she puts together the two elements of a complete sentence: a subject and a verb. *Words* enable us to communicate images; *sentences* are the tools with which we communicate ideas.

There is nothing mysterious or difficult about sentences. You've been speaking them successfully since you were a toddler. The difficulty occurs when you try to write—not sentences, oddly enough, but paragraphs. Most postsecondary students, if asked to write 10 sentences on 10 different topics, could do so without error. But when those same students write paragraphs, errors such as fragments and run-ons appear. Sometimes these errors cause a failure of communication; at other times, they cause the reader to think poorly of the writer.

The solution to sentence-structure problems has two parts.

> Be sure every sentence you write
> - has both a subject and a verb and
> - expresses a complete thought

If English is your first language, test your sentences by reading them aloud. You should be able to tell from their sound whether they are complete and clear. Sometimes, however, your ear may mislead you, so this chapter will show you, step by step, how to decode your sentences to find their subjects and verbs. When you know how to decode sentences, you can make sure that every sentence you write is complete.

Read the following sentences aloud.

> Yak skiing is one of Asia's newest sports.
> Although yak skiing is still a young sport.

The second "sentence" doesn't sound right, does it? It does not make sense on its own and is in fact a sentence fragment.

Testing your sentences by reading them aloud won't work if you read your paragraphs straight through from beginning to end. The trick is to read from end to beginning. That is, read your last sentence aloud and *listen* to it. If it sounds all right, then read aloud the next-to-last sentence, and so on, until you have worked your way back to the first sentence you wrote.

Now, what do you do with the ones that don't sound right? Before you can fix them, you need to decode each sentence to find out if it has both a subject and a verb. The subject and the verb are the bare essentials of a sentence. Every sentence you write must contain both. There is one exception:

> In a **command**, the subject is suggested rather than stated.

Consider these examples.

> Sign here. = [You] sign here. (The subject you is implied or understood.)
> Charge it. = [You] charge it.
> Play ball! = [You] play ball!

FINDING SUBJECTS AND VERBS

A sentence is about *someone* or *something*. That someone or something is the **subject**.[1] The word (or words) that tells what the subject *is* or *does* is the **verb**. In the following sentences, the subject is underlined once and the verb twice.

Snow falls.
Akiko dislikes winter.
We love snowboarding.
Mt. Whistler offers excellent opportunities for winter sports.
In Canada, winter is six months long.
Some people feel the cold severely.

The subject of a sentence is always a **noun** (the name of a person, place, thing, or concept) or a **pronoun** (a word such as *I*, *you*, *he*, *she*, *it*, *we*, or *they* used in place of a noun). In the examples above, the subjects include persons (*Akiko*, *we*, *people*); a place (*Mt. Whistler*); a thing (*snow*); and a concept (*winter*). In one sentence, a pronoun (*we*) is the subject.

> Find the verb first.

One way to find the verb in a sentence is to ask what the sentence says about the subject. There are two kinds of verbs:

- **Action verbs** tell you what the subject is doing. In the examples above, *falls*, *dislikes*, *love*, and *offers* are action verbs.
- **Linking verbs** link or connect a subject to a noun or an adjective describing that subject. In the examples above, *is* and *feel* are linking verbs. Linking verbs tell you the subject's condition or state of being. (For example, "Tadpoles *become* frogs," "Frogs *feel* slimy.") The most common linking verbs are forms of *to be* (*am*, *is*, *are*, *was*, *were*, *have been*, etc.) and verbs such as *look*, *taste*, *feel*, *sound*, *appear*, *remain*, *seem*, and *become*.

Another way to find the verb in a sentence is to put a pronoun (*I*, *you*, *he*, *she*, *it*, or *they*) in front of the word you think is the verb. If the result makes sense, it is a verb. For example, you could put *she* in front of *falls* in the first sentence listed above: "she falls" makes sense, so you know *falls* is the verb in this sentence. Try this test with the other five example sentences.

---

[1] If you have forgotten (or have never learned) the parts of speech and the basic sentence patterns, you can find this information in Appendix A (beginning on page 364).

Keep this guideline in mind as you work through the exercises below:

> To find the subject, ask <u>who</u> or <u>what</u> the sentence is about.
> To find the verb, ask what the subject <u>is</u> or <u>is doing</u>.

EXERCISE **5.1**

In each of the following sentences, underline the <u>subject</u> with one line and the <u>verb</u> with two. At the end of each exercise, check your answers (beginning on page 403). If you make even one mistake, go to the website and do the exercises under the heading "Finding Subjects and Verbs." Be sure you understand this material before you go on.

1. I hate cellphones.

2. Today, however, cellphones are practically a necessity.

3. Public phone booths are very hard to find.

4. Turn your cellphone off, please.

5. Our rehearsal was a disaster.

6. Two of the players were half an hour late.

7. Take your time.

8. Few Canadians enjoy February.

9. Family Day makes no difference to the miserable weather.

10. The dance at Destiny's club was a rave riot.

EXERCISE **5.2**

Underline the subject with one line and the verb with two.

1. Canadians love doughnuts.

2. They eat more doughnuts than any other nation.

3. The Dutch invented doughnuts.

4. The Dutch word for doughnuts translates as "oily cakes."

5. An American sea captain created the doughnut hole.

6. Captain Hansen Gregory impaled his little cake on the ship's wheel.

7. Thus, Capt. Gregory created the hole—and the doughnut.

8. The most popular doughnuts in Canada are Tim Hortons'.

9. Tim Horton played hockey for the Toronto Maple Leafs from 1951 to 1970.

10. In 1964, Horton opened his first doughnut store in Hamilton, Ontario.

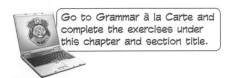

Go to Grammar à la Carte and complete the exercises under this chapter and section title.

Usually, but not always, the subject comes before the verb in a sentence.

Occasionally, we find the subject after the verb:

- In sentences beginning with *Here* + a form of *to be* or with *There* + a form of *to be* (*here* and *there* are never the subject of a sentence):

  Here <u>are</u> the test <u>results</u>. (Who or what <u>are</u> here? <u>Results</u>.)
  There <u>is</u> a <u>fly</u> in my soup. (Who or what <u>is</u> there? A <u>fly</u>.)

- In sentences that are inverted for emphasis or variety:

  Finally, at the end of the long, boring joke, <u>came</u> the pathetic <u>punch line</u>.
  Out of the stadium and into the rain <u>marched</u> the <u>demonstrators</u>.

- In questions:

  <u>Are</u> <u>we</u> there yet?
  <u>Is</u> <u>she</u> the one?

  But notice that in questions beginning with *who, whose, what,* or *which,* the subject and verb are in "normal" order: subject followed by verb.

  <u>Who</u> <u>ate</u> my sandwich?   <u>Whose</u> <u>horse</u> <u>came</u> first?
  <u>What</u> <u>caused</u> the accident?   <u>Which</u> <u>car</u> <u>uses</u> less gas?

EXERCISE **5.3**

Underline the subject with one line and the verb with two. Watch out for inverted-order sentences. Check your answers before going on. If you made even one mistake, go to the "Finding Subjects and Verbs" Web exercises for more practice.

1. Who wants the last piece?

2. Drive carefully.

3. Slowly down the spiral staircase came the bride.

4. Have you no heart?

5. Then give me a kilogram of liver and a couple of kidneys instead.

6. Into the pool leaped the terrified cat.

7. There are two electives to choose from.

8. Which one is more interesting?

9. Here is just the person to answer your question.

10. Were you happy with the answer?

MORE ABOUT VERBS

The verb in a sentence may be a single word, as in the exercises you've just completed, or it may be a group of words. When you are considering whether or not a word group is a verb, there are two points you should remember:

1. No verb form preceded by *to* is ever the verb of a sentence.[2]
2. **Helping verbs**[3] are often added to main verbs.

---

[2] The form *to* + verb—for example, *to speak, to write, to help*—is an infinitive. Infinitives can act as subjects, objects, or modifiers, but they are never verbs.

[3] If you are familiar with technical grammatical terms, you will know these verbs as **auxiliary verbs**.

The list below contains the most common helping verbs.

be (all forms, including *am, are, is, was, were, will be, have/had been*) can could/could have	do/did has/have; had may/may have might/might have must/must have	ought shall/shall have should/should have will/will have would/would have

> The complete verb in a sentence consists of any **helping verbs** + the **main verb**.

Below are a few of the forms of the verb *to take*. Study this list carefully, and note that when the sentence is in question form, the subject comes between the helping verb and the main verb.

We <u>are taking</u> a required
   English course.
You <u>can take</u> it with you.
<u>Could</u> Ray <u>have taken</u> it?
<u>Did</u> you <u>take</u> your turn?
The money <u>has been taken</u>.
We <u>have taken</u> too much time.
You <u>may take</u> a break now.

You <u>should have taken</u> our advice.
We <u>must take</u> the bus.
Lucy <u>ought to have taken</u> a course in
   stress management.
<u>Shall</u> we <u>take</u> his offer?
I <u>should take</u> more time.
We <u>will take</u> the championship.

One verb form always requires a helping verb. Here's the rule:

> A verb ending in *-ing* MUST have a helping verb (or verbs) before it.

Here are a few of the forms that a verb ending in *-ing* can take.

Farah <u>is taking</u> the test.
<u>Am</u> I <u>taking</u> your place?
You <u>are taking</u> an awfully long time.
These new computers <u>will be taking</u> over our jobs.
<u>Have</u> you <u>been taking</u> French lessons?

EXERCISE **5.4**

Underline the complete verb with a double line.

1. We are finding most of the verbs.

2. Someday my prince will come.

3. Have you planned a party to celebrate his arrival?

4. This book must have been written by a genius.

5. The verbs must be underlined twice.

6. Cam will have another coffee and a doughnut.

7. Do you know anything about grammar?

8. We have knocked on the door several times.

9. I will be looking for verbs in my sleep.

10. We must have practised enough by now.

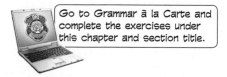

Go to *Grammar à la Carte* and complete the exercises under this chapter and section title.

Beware of certain words that are often confused with helping verbs.

> Words such as *always, ever, just, never, not, often, only,* and *sometimes* are not part of the verb.

These words usually appear in the middle of a complete verb, but they are modifiers, not verbs. Do not underline them.

Sophie is always chosen first.
They have just been married.
The question has not often
   been asked.

Do you ever have doubts about
   your ability?
Will you never learn?
I have sometimes wondered about that.

In the following two exercises, underline the subject with one line and the verb with two. Check your answers to the first set before going on to the next.

EXERCISE **5.5**

1. I am making a nutritious breakfast.

2. It does not include pop.

3. You can add fresh fruit to the cereal.

4. The toast should be ready now.

5. My doctor has often recommended yogurt for breakfast.

6. I could never eat yogurt without fruit.

7. With breakfast, I will drink at least two cups of coffee.

8. I don't like tea.

9. I simply cannot begin my day without coffee.

10. I should probably switch to decaf.

EXERCISE **5.6**

1. The security guard is sleeping again.

2. The security guard is often found asleep.

3. Have you ever been lonely?

4. There has never been a better time to invest.

5. Marie is carefully considering her options.

6. Where and when are we meeting?

7. Teenagers are sometimes embarrassed by their parents' behaviour.

8. Could you please explain one more time?

9. "Ladies are requested not to have children in the bar." (Sign in a Norwegian club)

10. "The manager has personally passed all our water." (Sign in an Acapulco hotel)

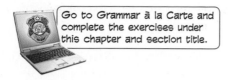

Go to Grammar à la Carte and complete the exercises under this chapter and section title.

MORE ABOUT SUBJECTS

Groups of words called **prepositional phrases** often come before the subject in a sentence or between the subject and the verb. When you're looking for the subject in a sentence, prepositional phrases can trip you up unless you know the following rule.

> The subject of a sentence is NEVER in a prepositional phrase.

You must be able to identify prepositional phrases so that you will know where *not* to look for the subject.

> A prepositional phrase is a group of words that begins with a preposition and ends with a noun or pronoun.

The noun or pronoun is called the object of the preposition. It is this word that, if you're not careful, you might think is the subject of the sentence.

Below is a list of prepositional phrases. The highlighted words are prepositions; the words that follow them are their objects.

about your message	between them	near the wall
above the door	by the way	of the memo
according to the book	concerning your request	on the following day
after the meeting	despite the shortfall	onto the floor
against the wall	down the corridor	over the page
along the hall	except the contract workers	through the window
among the staff		to the staff
around the office	for the manager	under the table
before lunch	from the office	until the meeting
behind my back	in the afternoon	up the corridor
below the window	inside the office	with permission
beside my computer	into the elevator	without the software

Before you look for the subject in a sentence, lightly cross out all prepositional phrases and identify the verb.

A bird ~~in the hand~~ is messy.   (What is messy? The bird, not the hand.)

This deck ~~of cards~~ is unlucky.   (What is unlucky? The deck, not the cards.)

Several houses ~~in our neighbourhood~~ need painting.   (What need painting? The houses, not the neighbourhood.)

In the following exercises, first cross out the prepositional phrase(s) in each sentence. Then underline the subject with one line and the verb with two.

EXERCISE **5.7**

1. Any of your friends is welcome at any time.

2. Henry asked for an extension on the grounds of mental incompetence.

3. This is the last of my money for the month.

4. Exaggeration in your writing is a million times worse than understatement.

5. Your flu, despite your precautions, has infected everyone in the office.

6. In their secret dreams, many grown men would still like to own a train set.

7. Nothing in the known universe travels faster than a bad cheque.

8. During the trial, before the decision, you must have been nervous.

9. Ninety-eight percent of all statistics are made up.

10. A day without sunshine is, in most respects, just like night.

Check your answers to Exercise 5.7 on page 405, and if you make even one error, practise with the "More about Subjects" Web exercises before going on to Exercise 5.8.

EXERCISE **5.8**

1. According to my financial adviser, my earliest possible retirement date is 2052.

2. By waiting on tables, baby-sitting, and borrowing from friends, I manage to make ends meet.

3. Except for me, everyone understands prepositions.

4. With the permission of the professor, I will demonstrate my mastery of verb identification.

5. No book of Canadian humour would be complete without some shots at American tourists.

6. Despite its strong taste, espresso contains no more caffeine than regular coffee.

7. A daily intake of more than 600 mg of caffeine can result in headaches, insomnia, and heart palpitations.

8. Six to ten cups of coffee will usually contain about 600 mg of caffeine.

9. One of the network's foreign correspondents will speak at noon in the auditorium about her experiences in Afghanistan.

10. Our teacher's uncertainty about the date of the War of 1812 made us curious about his knowledge of Canadian history.

EXERCISE **5.9**

1. In my opinion, fear of flying is entirely justifiable.

2. In our basement are stacks of magazines dating from the 1950s.

3. The rats in our building have written letters of complaint to the Board of Health.

4. Some of us are staying for a planning session after the meeting.

5. For reasons of privacy, I am listed in the telephone book under my dog's name.

6. After eight hours of classes, the thought of collapsing in front of the TV is very appealing.

7. In future, be sure to read through your notes before the exam.

8. Deciding between right and wrong, for most people, is not difficult.

9. Acting on that decision, however, for many people, often is.

10. Of all the great Italian innovations, from Fellini films to opera, from spaghetti to Chianti, the best, in my opinion, is cappuccino.

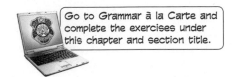

Go to Grammar à la Carte and complete the exercises under this chapter and section title.

MULTIPLE SUBJECTS AND VERBS

So far, you have been decoding sentences containing a single subject and a single verb, even though the verb may have consisted of more than one word. Sentences can, however, have more than one subject and one verb. Multiple subjects are called **compound subjects**; multiple verbs, **compound verbs**.

Here is a sentence with multiple subjects:

<u>French fries</u> and <u>onion rings</u> <u>are</u> Sanjay's idea of a balanced diet.

This sentence has multiple verbs:

Maya <u>dresses</u> and <u>walks</u> like a supermodel.

And this sentence contains both multiple subjects and multiple verbs:

<u>Alan</u> and <u>Dave</u> <u>drove</u> to the mall and <u>shopped</u> for hours.

The parts of a multiple subject are usually joined by *and* or *or*, sometimes by *but* or *nor*. Compound subjects and verbs may contain more than two elements. Look at the following examples.

<u>Clarity</u>, <u>brevity</u>, and <u>simplicity</u> <u>are</u> the basic qualities of good writing.

<u>Raj</u> <u>deleted</u> his work, <u>shut down</u> the computer, <u>unplugged</u> it, and <u>dropped</u> it out of the window.

Identify the subjects and verbs in the three exercises that follow. First, cross out any prepositional phrases. Then underline the subjects with one line and the verbs with two. Be sure to underline all elements of a multiple subject or verb (there may be more than two). Check your answers to each set (see pages 406 and 407), and if you've made any errors, go to the "Multiple Subjects and Verbs" Web exercises for more practice before you go on to the next exercise.

EXERCISE **5.10**

1. Maple sugar and wild rice are native Canadian products.

2. Professor Dasgupta handed out the tests and wished us luck.

3. The screen blinked twice and then went blank.

4. Elgar and Grieg are the names of my two unfortunate nephews.

5. My weird brother and his equally weird wife chose the names in honour of their favourite composers.

6. They could have done worse and chosen Humperdinck and Shostakovich.

7. "A good sermon writer creates a brilliant opening, develops a stirring conclusion, and puts the two as close together as possible." (George Burns)

8. Today my neighbour and I raked the leaves, dug up our gardens, and put away the lawn furniture.

9. Students with good time-management skills can research, organize, draft, and revise a first-class paper by the deadline.

10. Those with excellent time-management skills can keep on top of their schoolwork, hold a part-time job, volunteer at a local charity, and still find time for a social life.

EXERCISE **5.11**

1. Video games and Facebook take up about three-quarters of my waking hours.

2. With the rest of my time, I watch, read, and talk about sports.

3. The West Indies, British Isles, Australia, and India claim to have the greatest cricket teams.

4. In Canada, cricket, rugby, and jai alai are not played or followed as much as elsewhere.

5. For Canadians, the Habs, Sens, Leafs, Jets, Flames, Oilers, and Canucks are household words.

6. Referees control the game, call penalties, enforce the rules, and stay out of the way.

7. Soccer or football, despite its many faults, delights and infuriates the greatest number of fans around the world.

8. A good golfer drives, chips, putts, and lies with skill and confidence.

9. Winston Churchill, Gerald Ford, and Bill Clinton have all made witty remarks about the game of golf.

10. A hot bath, a good meal, and a *Seinfeld* rerun will help me recover from my stressful day.

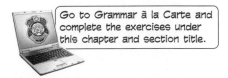

Go to Grammar à la Carte and complete the exercises under this chapter and section title.

EXERCISE **5.12**

During the holiday season, shopping for gifts and entertaining relatives are, for me, trials equivalent to medieval tortures. Stretching limited funds to buy presents for an ever-growing number of relatives and fighting through throngs of maddened consumers at the mall make me think fondly of the thumbscrew and the rack. I stagger from store to store, overwhelmed by the variety of goods for sale and pray for inspiration. How could I possibly know what to buy for Aunt Mildred, Uncle Morty, and cousin Millie and the rest?

After my shopping ordeal, I desperately need a nap. But it's entertainment time! Relatives, friends, neighbours, more relatives, and total strangers arrive in hordes. We eat. We drink. We pretend to enjoy the traditional holiday meal. We eat some more. We exchange gifts and pretend to like our presents. We eat again. We reminisce and pretend to enjoy one another's company. And then, once more, we eat.

That's Christmas. Give me the rack any time. I'd be a lot richer—and a lot thinner.

Below is a summary of what you've learned in this chapter. Keep it in mind as you complete Exercise 5.13, the Mastery Test.

SUMMARY

1. The subject is *who* or *what* the sentence is about.
2. The verb tells what the subject *is* or *does*.
3. The subject normally comes before the verb (exceptions are questions, sentences that begin with *here* or *there*, and some sentences that begin with prepositional phrases).
4. An infinitive (a phrase consisting of *to* + verb) is never the verb of a sentence.
5. The complete verb consists of any helping verbs + a main verb.
6. A word ending in *-ing* is not, by itself, a verb.
7. The subject of a sentence is never in a prepositional phrase.
8. A sentence can have more than one subject and verb.

EXERCISE **5.13**

Before you do this exercise, review the information in the Summary box above. This exercise will test your ability to identify subjects and verbs in different kinds of sentences. First, lightly cross out any prepositional phrases. Next, underline the subject(s) with one line and the verb(s) with two. Be sure to underline all elements in a compound subject or verb.

1. Turn the corner, put the past behind you, and get on with life.

2. Of all the emotions, sincerity is the most difficult to fake.

3. "The difference between the right word and almost the right word is the difference between lightning and the lightning bug." (Mark Twain)

4. Old age may be difficult, but it is better than the alternative.

5. After a huge argument with Brad, Marita threw his clothes out of the window, changed the locks on the doors to the house and the garage, and checked in at her favourite spa for a week.

6. According to Mame's obituary, clubs, all-night parties, and martinis for breakfast were her favourite pleasures during her short life.

7. Her lawyer, my lawyer, the accountant, and the mediator picked up the pen in turn, signed the document, and shook my hand.

8. The floors are cold, the windows are drafty, and the roof leaks in my newly purchased dream home.

9. Out of the pages of an illustrated history book stepped a coureur de bois and an Iroquois warrior.

10. Among the students in Irena's singing class are a grandmother of 12, a student chef with a nose ring, and an aspiring actor with a huge ego.

GRAMMAR À LA CARTE

- Looking for more opportunities to practise? Want to see what you need to review before the big test? Visit NELSONbrain.com and log in to **Grammar à la Carte** for *The Bare Essentials, Form A,* to access additional exercises! These Web exercises are graded automatically, so you will know instantly whether or not you have mastered the material.

Sentences

6 Solving Sentence-Fragment Problems

Every complete sentence has two characteristics: it contains a subject and a verb, and it expresses a complete thought. Any group of words that is punctuated as a sentence but lacks one of these characteristics is a **sentence fragment**. Fragments are appropriate in conversation and in some kinds of writing, but normally they are not acceptable in college, technical, or business writing.

> There are two kinds of fragments you should watch out for:
> - the "missing piece" fragment and
> - the dependent clause fragment

"MISSING PIECE" FRAGMENTS

Sometimes a group of words is punctuated as a sentence but is missing one or both of the essential parts of a sentence: the subject and the verb. Consider these examples:

> Won an award for creativity.
> (<u>Who</u> or <u>what</u> won an award? The sentence doesn't tell you. The subject is missing.)

> The hamster under the bed.
> (The sentence doesn't tell you what the hamster <u>was</u> or <u>did</u>. The verb is missing.)

> During their lunch break.
> (<u>Who</u> or <u>what</u> <u>was</u> or <u>did</u> something? Both subject and verb are missing.)

> The team missing two of its best players.
> (Part of the verb is missing. Remember that a verb ending in -*ing* needs a helping verb to be complete.)

Finding fragments like these in your work is the hard part. Fixing them is easy. There are two ways to correct sentence fragments. Here's the first one:

> To change a "missing piece" fragment into a complete sentence, add whatever is missing: a subject, a verb, or both.

You may need to add a subject:

> Her <u>essay</u> won an award for creativity.

You may need to add a verb:

> The hamster <u>was</u> under the bed. (linking verb)
> The hamster under the bed <u>chewed</u> my socks. (action verb)

You may need to add both a subject and a verb:

> Many desk-bound <u>workers</u> <u>enjoy</u> running in the park during their lunch break.

Sentences

Or you may need to add a helping verb:

The team <u>was missing</u> two of its best players.

Don't let the length of a fragment fool you. Students sometimes think that if a string of words is long, it must be a sentence. Not so. No matter how long the string of words, if it doesn't contain both a subject and a verb, it is not a sentence. For example, here's a description of a woman paddling a canoe on a lake in summertime:

The paddle dipping into the lake, sliding beneath the surface, and emerging at the end of the stroke, the face of the paddle glistening in the sun and droplets from its edge making a trail in the water as she reaches forward to dip again just as before, repeating the movement hundreds of times, thousands of times, in a hypnotic rhythm that becomes as natural as breathing, as calming as meditation.

At 71 words, this "sentence" is long, but it is a fragment. It lacks both a subject and a verb. If you add "<u>She</u> <u>watches</u>" at the beginning of the fragment, it becomes a complete sentence.

EXERCISE **6.1**

In the following exercise, decide whether each group of words is a complete sentence or a "missing piece" fragment. Write "S" in the space before each complete sentence and "F" before each fragment. Make each fragment into a complete sentence by adding whatever is missing: the subject, the verb, or both. Then compare your answers with our suggestions. Answers for exercises in this chapter begin on page 407.

1. _____ According to the government.

2. _____ Exhausted, I slept.

3. _____ Happy to help.

4. _____ Hoping to hear from you soon.

5. _____ Take another.

6. _____ In case you were wondering.

7. _____ Close the door quietly on your way out.

8. _____ Pausing to think of an appropriate reply.

9. _____ Working as a server in a cheap restaurant is not rewarding.

10. _____ Sentence fragments such as these.

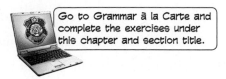

Go to Grammar à la Carte and complete the exercises under this chapter and section title.

Most of us can identify a fragment when it stands alone. But when we write, of course, we write in paragraphs, not in single sentences. Fragments are harder to identify when they occur in a context, as you'll see in the next exercise.

EXERCISE **6.2**

Read the following selections carefully and decide whether each question contains only complete sentences or whether it contains one or more sentence fragments. Put "S" beside the questions that contain only sentences. Put "F" beside those that contain fragments. Then check your answers.

1. _____ I wanted to stay home, but my girlfriend wanted to go to the movies. To see the Coèn brothers' new film.

2. _____ In volleyball, our college is well respected. Our team won the provincial championship last year. Placing three players on the all-star team.

3. _____ Whenever I go fishing, the fish aren't biting, but the mosquitoes are. Maybe I should give up fishing. And start collecting insects instead.

4. _____ My son is a genius. On his last birthday, he was given a toy that was guaranteed to be unbreakable. Guess what? Used it to break all his other toys.

5. _____ We weren't lost, but we certainly were confused. I realized this when we drove past City Hall. For the third time.

6. _____ Place the paper in the feed tray. Select the quality of copy that you want. Print.

7. _____ My friends and I often go to the hockey arena during the winter. Not to watch sports, but to hear concerts by some of the best local bands. These concerts give new meaning to the word *cool*.

8. _____ According to the weather reporter at our local radio station, a storm with high winds and heavy rain is approaching our region. Yesterday, when the temperature hit 0°C, she predicted light snow.

9. _____ I enjoy reading travel blogs. About faraway places that I have never visited and will probably never get to see. The fun is in the dreaming, not the doing.

10. _____ Spending my days skiing and my nights dining and dancing. That's how I picture my retirement.

Once you have learned to identify fragments that occur within a paragraph, it's time to consider the best way to correct them. You could fix all of them the way you did in Exercise 6.1, by adding the missing piece or pieces to each one, and in some cases, that is your only choice. However, there is another, shorter, way that can often be used to correct fragments in a paragraph.

> You can sometimes correct a "missing piece" fragment by attaching it to a complete sentence that comes before or after it—whichever makes better sense.

Sometimes you need to put a comma between a "missing piece" fragment and the complete sentence to which you attach it. (See Chapter 17, "The Comma," Rule 3, page 224, and Rule 4, page 225.)

EXERCISE **6.3**

Now go back to the sentences in Exercise 6.2 and correct the fragments. As you go through the exercise, try to use both techniques we've identified for fixing fragments:

- Add the missing piece(s).
- Join the fragment to a complete sentence before or after it.

When you've finished, compare your answers with ours on page 407.

EXERCISE **6.4**

Read through the following paragraph, and put "S" before each complete sentence and "F" before each fragment. Then check your answers.

(1) _____ Ed forgot his wife's birthday. (2) _____ Knowing he was in trouble from the moment he got home from work and saw her angry face. (3) _____ Apologizing and asking how he could make it up to her. (4) _____ She replied that she wanted to find something in the driveway that would go from zero to 100 in less than five seconds. (5) _____ No later than tomorrow morning. (6) _____ The next day, Ed left for work early. (7) _____ Leaving a colourful package tied with a large bow in the middle of the driveway. (8) _____ Ed's wife eagerly tore the paper and ribbon off the package. (9) _____ Discovering a new bathroom scale. (10) _____ Ed is still missing.

EXERCISE **6.5**

Now correct the fragments you identified in the paragraph above. Use both fragment-fixing techniques we've highlighted for you on pages 89 and 92. Then compare your answers with ours on page 408.

Sentences

DEPENDENT CLAUSE FRAGMENTS

Any group of words containing a subject and a verb is a **clause**. There are two kinds of clauses. An **independent clause** is one that makes complete sense. It can stand alone as a sentence. A **dependent clause**, as its name suggests, cannot stand alone as a sentence. It depends on (and must be attached to) another clause to make sense. Dependent clauses (also known as **subordinate clauses**) begin with words or phrases such as these:

Dependent Clause Cues

after	that
although	though
as, as if	unless
as long as	until
as soon as	what, whatever
because	when, whenever
before	where, wherever
even if, even though	whether
if	which, whichever
since	while
so that	who, whose

Whenever a clause begins with one of these words or phrases, it is dependent.

A dependent clause must be attached to an independent clause.
If it stands alone, it is a sentence fragment.

Here is an independent clause:

She writes a daily blog.

If we put one of the **dependent clause cues** (also known as **subordinating conjunctions**) in front of it, it can no longer stand alone:

Although she writes a daily blog.

We can correct this kind of fragment by attaching it to an independent clause:

Although she writes a daily blog, she has almost nothing to say.

EXERCISE **6.6**

Let's start with an easy exercise. Put an "S" before each clause that is independent and therefore a sentence. Put an "F" before each clause that is dependent and therefore a sentence fragment. Highlight the dependent clause cue in each fragment. Then check the answers on page 408.

1. _____ After my first attempt failed.

2. _____ If there is life on other planets

3. _____ Although many people think sentence fragments are fine.

4. _____ Unless there is a change in the weather, I will go.

5. _____ Soon, when our oil reserves are depleted.

6. _____ Even though the chef insists she does not overuse salt.

7. _____ If he were any dumber, he'd have to be watered twice a week.

8. _____ All of the salespeople who have not reached their quotas.

9. _____ Although there is plenty of evidence that fish stocks are declining and water quality is deteriorating in the headwaters of our biggest rivers.

10. _____ When you choose a hybrid car, whether it is gas-electric or diesel-electric, as your next vehicle.

Most sentence fragments are dependent clauses punctuated as sentences. Fortunately, these are the easiest fragments to fix.

> To correct a dependent clause fragment, join it either to the sentence that comes before it or to the one that comes after it—whichever linkage makes the most sense.

Problem: We want to move into our new apartment. As soon as the current tenants leave. It's perfect for our family.

The second "sentence" is incomplete; the dependent clause cue *as soon as* is the clue you need to identify it as a sentence fragment. You could join the fragment to the sentence that follows it, but then you would get "As soon as the current tenants leave, it's perfect for our family," which doesn't make sense. This fragment should be linked to the sentence before it.

Revision: We want to move into our new apartment as soon as the current tenants leave. It's perfect for our family.

If, as in the example above, your revised sentence *ends* with a dependent clause, you do not need to use a comma before it. If, however, your revised sentence *begins* with a dependent clause, put a comma between it and the independent clause that follows.

As soon as the current tenants leave, we want to move into our new apartment. It's perfect for our family.

(See Chapter 17, "The Comma," Rule 3, on page 224.)

EXERCISE **6.7**

Correct the fragments in Exercise 6.6 by attaching each one to an independent clause that you have made up. Then compare your answers with our suggestions on page 408. Be sure to put a comma after a dependent clause that comes at the beginning of a sentence.

Check your fragment-finding skills by trying the following exercises.

EXERCISE **6.8**

The items in this exercise each contain three clauses, one of which is dependent and therefore a fragment. Highlight the dependent clause fragment in each item.

1. Walking is probably the best form of exercise there is. Unless you're in the water. Then, swimming is preferable.

2. The modern world is confusing for all of us. If you can keep your head when all about you are losing theirs. Perhaps you just don't understand the situation.

3. "The world is divided into good and bad people. The good ones sleep better. While the bad ones enjoy their waking hours much more." (Woody Allen)

4. Doing the job right the first time gets the job done. While doing the job wrong again and again gives you job security. This principle explains how my brother stays employed.

5. You know you have been teaching too long. When capital punishment seems a reasonable response to sentence fragments. Now is the time to think about early retirement.

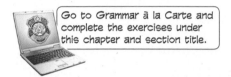

Go to Grammar à la Carte and complete the exercises under this chapter and section title.

EXERCISE **6.9**

The following exercise is more challenging. Each item contains one or more dependent clauses punctuated as sentences. Highlight the fragments in each item.

1. Internship programs provide experience and skill development for senior students. For small and mid-size companies, they are an important recruitment tool. Companies get to audition prospective hires at little cost. While training the students in their systems and practices. Since both the students and the businesses gain. Internships are a win-win.

2. Superglue is a remarkable product. That can bond anything to almost anything else. Nevertheless, all parents of toddlers know there is another substance. That is much harder and stronger than Superglue. The glue that outperforms all others is mashed banana. Especially after it has dried in an infant's hair.

3. The names of many Canadian landmarks have been changed over the years. One example is Kitchener. Which was called Berlin until the First World War. A second example is the Oldman River. Until the residents of

Lethbridge petitioned for a change to a more dignified name. It was called the Belly River.

4. Most historians agree that Canada was named by Jacques Cartier. Who thought natives were referring to the entire land mass when they told him their word for *village*. Another legend says that Cartier overheard a Portuguese crewman who muttered, "Aca nada." When he looked at the vast land. In fact, the sailor was saying, "Nothing here."

5. Where the word *golf* comes from is a mystery. Though we do know it does not stand for "Gentlemen only, ladies forbidden," as one legend suggests. Early references to the word are interesting. According to Katherine Barber, who is known as Canada's "Word Lady." One of the earliest comes from the 1400s. When the sport was banned because it was interfering with archery practice.

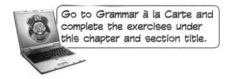

Go to Grammar à la Carte and complete the exercises under this chapter and section title.

EXERCISE **6.10**

Correct the sentence fragments you highlighted in Exercises 6.8 and 6.9 above. Make each fragment into a complete sentence by attaching it to the independent clause that precedes or follows it, whichever makes better sense. Remember to punctuate correctly: if a dependent clause comes at the beginning of your sentence, put a comma after it. Check your answers after each exercise.

EXERCISE **6.11**

In the following paragraph, you'll find a mixture of "missing piece" fragments and dependent clause fragments. Revise the six fragments any way you choose: either by adding the missing piece(s) or by joining fragments to appropriate independent clauses. Check your punctuation carefully.

Because the chances of winning are so small. Lotteries have been called a tax on people with poor math skills. Buying a lottery ticket will gain you about as much as betting that the next U.S. president will come from Moose Jaw. Or that the parrot in the pet store speaks Inuktitut. While winning a lottery is not impossible. It is so unlikely that you'd do better to use your money to light a nice warm fire. Although the winners are highly publicized. No one hears about the huge numbers of losers. Whose money has gone to pay the winners. In order for the lottery corporation to make its enormous profits. Millions of dollars must be lost whenever a lucky winner is declared.

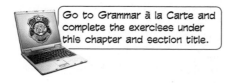

Go to Grammar à la Carte and complete the exercises under this chapter and section title.

EXERCISE **6.12**

Find and fix the 10 fragment errors in this selection.

A wealthy hunter took his pet dachshund with him on a hunting safari in Africa. Unfortunately, got lost while chasing butterflies around the camp. Before long, the dachshund realized he was being stalked by a leopard and

Sentences

knew he was about to become lunch. Thinking quickly, and noticing some bones on the ground. He crunched the bones between his teeth and said, "That leopard was delicious. I hope there's another around here!" The leopard stopped in mid-leap and slunk away into the bush. Thinking how lucky he was to escape.

A monkey, witnessing this incident and wanting to ingratiate himself with the dangerous leopard. Followed the leopard and told him how the dog had tricked him. The leopard was furious and immediately set out to tear the dachshund to bits. Taking the monkey with him on his back.

The dachshund saw the two coming and knew that his trick had been exposed. About to be torn limb from limb by the enraged leopard. Turning his back and pretending not to have seen the leopard and the monkey. Then said in a loud voice, "Now where has that darn monkey got to? Sent him off half an hour ago to bring me another leopard."

GRAMMAR À LA CARTE

- Looking for more opportunities to practise? Want to see what you need to review before the big test? Visit NELSONbrain.com and log in to **Grammar à la Carte** for *The Bare Essentials, Form A,* to access additional exercises! These Web exercises are graded automatically, so you will know instantly whether or not you have mastered the material.

SHE LOOKED HARMLESS, A COMMA SPLICE REVEALED THE TRUTH.

SHOULD HAVE USED A **SEMICOLON**, SWEETHEART!

Solving Run-On Sentence Problems

7

Some sentences lack essential elements and thus are fragments. Other sentences contain two or more independent clauses that are incorrectly linked together. A sentence with inadequate punctuation between clauses is a **run-on**. Run-ons tend to occur when you write in a hurry and don't take time to revise your work. If you remember the essential components of a sentence and punctuate carefully, you should have few problems with run-ons.

There are two kinds of run-on sentence to watch out for: comma splices and fused sentences.

COMMA SPLICES

As its name suggests, the **comma splice** occurs when two complete sentences (independent clauses) are joined (or spliced) by a comma. Consider these examples:

Broccoli is good for you, poutine is not.
This film is boring, it has no plot.

FUSED SENTENCES

A **fused sentence** occurs when two complete sentences are joined together with no punctuation between them. For example:

Broccoli is good for you poutine is not.
This film is boring it has no plot.

There are four ways to fix comma splices or fused sentences.

1. Make the independent clauses separate sentences.

Broccoli is good for you. Poutine is not.
This film is boring. It has no plot.

This solution works well if you do not use it too often. Writing that consists of nothing but single-clause sentences lacks smoothness and sounds immature. (See Chapter 10.)

2. Separate the independent clauses with a comma and one of these words: *and, but, or, nor, for, so, yet.*[1]

Broccoli is good for you, but poutine is not.
This film is boring, for it has no plot.

---

[1] These words are called **coordinating conjunctions** because they are used to join equal (or coordinating) clauses. See Appendix A, page 374, for an explanation and illustration of the different kinds of conjunctions and how to use them.

3. Make one clause dependent on the other by adding one of the dependent clause cues listed on page 94.

Broccoli is good for you although poutine is not.
This film is boring because it has no plot. (*Or:* Because it has no plot, this film is boring.)

4. Use a semicolon, either by itself or with a transitional expression, to separate the independent clauses.[2]

Broccoli is good for you; poutine is not.
This film is boring; for one thing, it has no plot.

Note: All four solutions to comma splices and fused sentences require you to use a word or punctuation mark strong enough to come between two independent clauses. A comma by itself is too weak, and so is a dash.

The sentences in the following exercises will give you practice in correcting comma splices and fused sentences. Correct the sentences with errors (note that there is one correct sentence in each set), and then check your answers, beginning on page 410. Since there are several ways to fix each sentence, your answers may differ from our suggestions. If you're confused about when to use a semicolon and when to use a period, read Chapter 18 before going on.

EXERCISE **7.1**

1. "Don't let your worries kill you, let the church help." (Sign outside a church)

2. I am busy right now you'll have to wait.

3. Remove your earbuds, you can't hear the speaker.

4. No one in the department supports her because she's arrogant and lazy.

5. Consider hiring an event planner you cannot arrange this function by yourself.

---

[2] If you are not sure when or why to use a semicolon, see Chapter 18, pages 233 to 242.

Sentences

6. "We do not tear your clothing with machinery, we do it carefully by hand." (Sign in a dry cleaner's)

7. Perfect your computer skills, then reapply for this position.

8. There are many factors to consider when hiring a new employee, attitude is key.

9. "I don't want to achieve immortality through my work, I want to achieve it through not dying." (Woody Allen)

10. Many good films are made in Canada, I just wish I could tell which ones they were before buying a ticket.

EXERCISE **7.2**

1. Computers do not prevent mistakes they just make them faster.

2. Our company wants to hire a telepath to predict market trends, the right person for the job will know where to apply.

3. All senior managers are required to attend the upcoming board meeting, it's in Bermuda.

4. Time is the best teacher, unfortunately, it kills all its students.

5. Allow enough time to complete the project, a rush job is not acceptable.

6. Place your hands on the table do not open your eyes.

7. I'm following the Toronto Maple Leafs this season, my doctor says I should avoid all excitement.

8. I enjoy driving to work in rush hour; it's a chance to see new faces and learn new hand signals.

9. "The English language makes no sense, people recite at a play and play at a recital." (Richard Lederer)

10. We have not inherited the earth from our ancestors, we are borrowing it from our children.

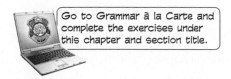

Go to Grammar à la Carte and complete the exercises under this chapter and section title.

EXERCISE **7.3**

Some of the items in the following exercise contain more than two independent clauses, so they are a bit more challenging to revise.

1. In Canada, winter is more than a season it's a bad joke.

2. Twice a week, my wife and I go to a nice restaurant for some good food, a little wine, and pleasant conversation, she goes Tuesdays, and I go Fridays.

3. Emma backed her car out of the driveway, she forgot to check her rear-view mirror as a result, she managed to produce a significant alteration to the front end of a passing Honda.

4. We understand his feelings of rejection, he discovered that his family had moved to another city while he was out getting a pizza.

5. Home-cooked meals are generally more nutritious than fast-food meals but this is not true of my mother's cooking, hers rates below cardboard in nutritional value as well as taste.

6. The biggest drawbacks to keeping tropical fish are that you get soaked whenever you pet them and they take a long time to grow big enough to eat.

7. There are two students in this class named Xan, one is from China, the other is from Russia, the latter's name is a nickname, a short form of Alexandra.

8. The first sign of adulthood is the discovery that the volume knob also turns to the left, this realization does not happen overnight for some people, the process takes years.

9. Football is always a great spectator sport, hockey is usually fun to watch in the last period, basketball is sometimes exciting for the last two minutes of a game but baseball is consistently boring.

10. Evaluating Frank's progress is difficult when you realize that he has submitted none of the assignments, written none of the tests, and attended less than a third of the classes, you can see why I despair.

EXERCISE **7.4**

In the paragraph that follows, correct the 10 run-on errors any way you choose. This would be a good time to review the four run-on solutions highlighted on pages 102 to 103. Your goal is to produce a paragraph in which the sentences are correct and effective. Then compare your revision to our suggestion on page 412.

"I'm about to graduate, I don't have any experience, all the jobs I'm interested in demand experience. What should I do?" This is a common question, many people are frustrated by the problem of how to get experience when no one will hire a person without it. According to employment experts and recruiters, there are several ways to overcome this problem. First, don't bother replying to job postings that clearly state experience is required, this wastes time and guarantees frustration. Second, look for part-time work in your field this is a productive route to full-time employment, it gives you a chance to prove your worth to the company. Third, consider an internship or a co-op placement, like part-time work, job placements allow you and the company to learn about each other and discover what both parties have to offer. Fourth, in your application, highlight how the skills and experience you gained in previous positions, even if they were unpaid, apply to the job you are seeking. Fifth, show initiative, research the company you want to work for and find out what skills they require. Join professional organizations and establish contacts through LinkedIn and other professional networks. Finally, be patient, it takes time to find the job of your dreams!

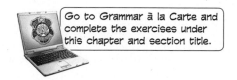

Go to Grammar à la Carte and complete the exercises under this chapter and section title.

EXERCISE **7.5**

The following exercise contains all four kinds of sentence structure error you have studied so far: "missing piece" fragments, dependent clause fragments, comma splices, and fused sentences. Work through the sentences slowly and carefully, and then compare your revisions with our suggestions on page 412.

1. "In answer to your letter, I have given birth to a boy weighing five kilos, I hope this is satisfactory." (From a letter applying for government assistance)

2. "That isn't food that's what food eats." (A meat eater's view of a vegetarian menu)

3. A cup of coffee in the middle of the afternoon. It helps to keep me alert, the caffeine chases away my after-lunch slump.

4. CRNC is the home of the million-dollar guarantee, you give us a million dollars, we guarantee to play any song you want.

5. It's far too hot, no one feels like working. Not even people who claim to like summer temperatures.

6. A fine wine during a special meal being my only vice, otherwise I'm perfect.

7. Eat sensibly, exercise regularly, die anyway.

8. People who do not turn off their cellphones in movie theatres are inconsiderate, they should be ejected without a refund.

9. When a football or hockey game is on TV. My husband becomes deaf, he doesn't hear a word I say.

10. Our dog loves children. Especially when they are eating French fries or hot dogs. In her excitement, she has sometimes frightened a child, she has never bitten anyone.

EXERCISE **7.6**

As a final test of your ability to identify and correct run-on sentence errors, supply appropriate sentence breaks to make this garble into a grammatically correct paragraph. You may need to add or delete a few words to make some of the sentences complete and clear. (There are 10 run-ons.)

Pet food is big business, just look at the products that line the supermarket shelves practically every label claims the box or tin contains "irresistible morsels of delectable goodness" with a "rich, meaty taste" it seems that people are easily persuaded that what a package says on the outside is a reliable indicator of what is to be found inside but this assumption is easily disproved if you open a can of cat food and examine the contents for any sign of the qualities advertised on the label I speak from experience, I recently bought a case of cat food, or "premium feline dinner," as the manufacturer calls it, because of the enticing description of the contents in particular, the words "scrumptious, succulent chunks of real chicken in an aromatic sauce" and "tender, savoury, prime cuts of real beef" caught my attention so the sticky, grey mess inside the can was a bit of a letdown, nevertheless, I emptied the muck onto a plate and probed it with my fork, looking for evidence of the "real chicken" or "real beef" I had been promised the more closely I examined my cat's supposedly gourmet dinner, the more certain I became that the label's insistent repetition of "real" with respect to every ingredient was a deliberate attempt to delude the consumer and anyone who believes that a label accurately describes the contents of a pet food product has more faith in the manufacturer's integrity than I do after my visual and olfactory examination of the evidence.

GRAMMAR À LA CARTE

- Looking for more opportunities to practise? Want to see what you need to review before the big test? Visit NELSONbrain.com and log in to **Grammar à la Carte** for *The Bare Essentials, Form A,* to access additional exercises! These Web exercises are graded automatically, so you will know instantly whether or not you have mastered the material.

GORGEOUS IN THE MOONLIGHT, HER DANGLING MODIFIERS BETRAYED HER.

8 Solving Modifier Problems

Having been underwater for 150 years, Dr. Philbrick found the ship in excellent condition.

Both students were expelled because of cheating by the college registrar.

For sale: A set of first-year medical textbooks by a needy student in almost perfect condition.

How could Dr. Philbrick stay underwater for 150 years? Was the college registrar cheating? Did the needy student write the medical textbooks, and is this student in almost perfect condition? As you can see, the meaning in these examples is not clear. The confusion comes from incorrect placement of modifiers.

A **modifier** is a word or phrase that adds information about another word in a sentence. In the examples above, the highlighted words are modifiers. Used correctly, modifiers describe, explain, or limit another word, making its meaning more precise. Used carelessly, modifiers cause confusion or, even worse, amusement.

You need to be able to recognize and solve two kinds of modifier problems: **misplaced modifiers** and **dangling modifiers**.

MISPLACED MODIFIERS

Modifiers must be as close as possible to the words they apply to. Readers usually assume that a modifier modifies whatever it's next to. It's important to remember this because, as the following examples show, changing the position of a modifier can change the meaning of your sentence.

(Only) I love you. (No one else loves you.)

I (only) love you. (I have no other feelings for you.)

I love (only) you. (You are the only one I love.)

> To make sure a modifier is in the right place, ask yourself, "What does it apply to?" and put it beside that word.

When a modifier is not close enough to the word it refers to, it is said to be misplaced.

> • A misplaced modifier can be a single word in the wrong place:

My boss told me that the payroll department needs someone who can use accounting software (badly).

Is some company really hiring people to do poor work? Or does the company urgently need someone familiar with accounting software? The modifier *badly* belongs next to the word it applies to, *needs*:

My boss told me that the payroll department (badly) needs someone who can use accounting software.

Be especially careful with these words: *almost, nearly, just, only, even, hardly, merely, scarcely.* Put them right before the words they modify.

Misplaced: I (nearly) passed every course I took in college.

Correct: I passed (nearly) every course I took in college.

Misplaced: The NDP leader was (almost) elected by 50 percent of his riding's voters.

Correct: The NDP leader was elected by (almost) 50 percent of his riding's voters.

Misplaced: I (only) have eyes for you.

Correct: I have eyes (only) for you.

• A misplaced modifier can also be a group of words in the wrong place:

(Playing happily), the new mother watched her baby.

The modifier, *playing happily,* is too far away from the word it applies to: *baby.* It seems to modify *mother,* making the sentence ridiculous. We need to revise the sentence.

The new mother watched her baby (playing happily.)

Look at this example:

I work for my aunt, who owns a variety store (during the summer.)

During the summer applies to *work* and should be closer to it:

(During the summer,) I work for my aunt, who owns a variety store.

Notice that a modifier need not always go right next to what it modifies. It should, however, be as close as possible to it.

Occasionally, as in the examples above, the modifier is obviously out of place. The writer's intention is often clear, and the sentence is easy to correct. Sometimes, however, modifiers are misplaced in such a way that the meaning is not clear, as in this example:

My supervisor told me (on Friday) I was being let go.

Did the supervisor speak to the employee on Friday? Or did she tell the employee that Friday would be his last day? To avoid confusion, we must move the modifier. Depending on the meaning we want, we might write

(On Friday,) my supervisor told me I was being let go.

or

My supervisor told me I was being let go (on Friday.)

Rewrite the following sentences, placing the modifiers correctly. Check your answers to each set before going on. Answers to exercises in this chapter begin on page 412.

EXERCISE **8.1**

1. I applied for every job that was posted almost.

2. We were run over by practically every car that passed.

3. This recipe can be made by anyone who has mastered basic cooking skills in about an hour.

4. Alice discovered a magic mushroom walking through Wonderland.

5. She just ate one bite and found herself growing larger.

6. The rabid dog was captured before anyone was bitten by the canine control officer.

7. The online classified page lists the names of people who want to buy used cars for less than a dollar.

8. We were only told at the end of the test that it was worth 10 percent of our grade.

9. We could not remember which building Luca lived in when we drove down his street.

10. Proud of his new tattoo—a python around his neck—Wayne's father told him to grow a long beard before he even thought of applying for a job.

EXERCISE **8.2**

1. Up to 1970, Canadians almost won every hockey tournament in the world.

2. Following my performance review, the company nearly gave me a raise of 10 percent.

3. Employees who are late frequently are dismissed without notice.

4. I will just ask you once more if you were present when your picture was taken.

5. Each year, 500,000 Canadian men nearly have vasectomies.

6. Our instructor reminded us on Monday we would have a test.

7. My bank is stingy; it only gives two percent interest on long-term savings accounts.

8. I want to play badly, but the coach thinks I should save my strength for the playoffs.

9. Professor Davies told us at the end of the term we would get our marks by mail.

10. Increasing numbers of Canadians are finding that they cannot feed, clothe, and shelter their children in today's economy properly.

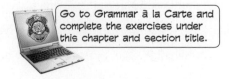

Go to Grammar à la Carte and complete the exercises under this chapter and section title.

DANGLING MODIFIERS

A *dangling modifier* occurs when there is no specific word or phrase in the sentence to which the modifier can sensibly refer. With no appropriate word to refer to, the modifier seems to apply to whatever it's next to, often with ridiculous results:

(After a good night's sleep,) [my teachers] were impressed by my alertness.

(This sentence seems to say that the teachers had a good night's sleep.)

(While paying for our purchases,) [a security guard] watched closely.

(The security guard paid for our purchases?)

(Torn from the old maple by the storm,) [our front window] was shattered by a huge branch.

(The front window was torn from the old maple?)

Dangling modifiers are harder to fix than misplaced ones. You can't simply move danglers to another spot in the sentence. There are two ways to correct them. One way requires that you remember the following guideline.

> When a modifier comes at the beginning of the sentence, it modifies the subject of the sentence.

There are two ways to avoid dangling modifiers.

> 1. Make sure that the subject is an appropriate one for the modifier to apply to.

To determine whether a subject is appropriate, ask yourself *who* or *what* the modifying phrase refers to. For example:

Who had a good night's sleep? *I* did. (not my teachers)

Who paid for our purchases? *We* did. (not the security guard)

What was torn from the maple tree? *A huge branch.* (not our front window)

Using this method, we can correct our three examples by changing the subjects.

(After a good night's sleep,) I impressed my teachers with my alertness.

(While paying for our purchases,) we were closely watched by a security guard.

(Torn from the old maple by the storm,) a huge branch shattered our front window.

> 2. Change the dangling modifier into a dependent clause.

After I had a good night's sleep, my teachers were impressed by my alertness.

While we paid for our purchases, a security guard watched us closely.

When the storm tore a huge branch from the old maple tree, our front window was shattered.

Sometimes a dangling modifier comes at the end of a sentence.

A Smart is the car for me, (looking for efficiency and affordability.)

Can you correct this sentence? Try it; then look at the suggestions we've given at the bottom of the page.

Here are two possible corrections for the Smart car sentence:

1. **Add an appropriate subject:** (Looking for efficiency and affordability,) I decided a Smart was the car for me.
2. **Change the dangler to a dependent clause:** A Smart is the car for me since I am looking for efficiency and affordability.

SUMMARY

1. Ask "What does the modifier refer to?"
2. Be sure there is a word or word group in the sentence for the modifier to apply to.
3. Put the modifier as close as possible to the word or word group it refers to.

The sentences in Exercises 8.3 and 8.4 contain dangling modifiers. Correct them by changing the subject of each sentence to one the modifier can appropriately apply to or by changing the dangler into a dependent clause. Then compare your answers with our suggestions on pages 414 to 415.

EXERCISE **8.3**

1. When applying for a job, experience is often the most important factor.
2. As a college English teacher, dangling modifiers are annoying.
3. When writing, a dictionary is your best friend.
4. Opening the hood carefully, the engine was still smoking.
5. The surface must be sanded smooth before applying the varnish.
6. Attempting to hot-wire a '99 Jeep Cherokee, the police had no trouble arresting the suspect.
7. As an advocate of healthy eating, fast-food restaurants are purveyors of poison, in my opinion.
8. Driving recklessly, the police stopped Kara at a roadblock.
9. Arriving at the meeting room 20 minutes late, everyone had left.
10. Travelling abroad, much can be learned from the sights you see and the people you meet.

EXERCISE **8.4**

1. After changing the tire, the jack should be released.
2. The next question is whether to order beer or soft drinks, having decided on pizza.

3. After waiting for you for an hour, the evening was ruined.

4. Jogging through Stanley Park, a cluster of totem poles came into view.

5. After four days on the trail, a hot shower and a cold drink were necessities rather than luxuries.

6. Having set the microwave on "Automatic," the turkey was cooked to perfection.   .

7. Having completed the beginning, the ending is the second most important part of an essay.

8. Convicted of aggravated assault, the judge sentenced her to two years in the penitentiary.

9. After scoring the goal in overtime, a huge victory parade wound through the city.

10. After living with the same roommate for two years, my parents suggested trying living alone.

Correct the misplaced and dangling modifiers in Exercise 8.5 in any way you choose. The answers on page 415 are only suggestions.

EXERCISE **8.5**

1. In our program, the women almost outnumber the men by a two-to-one ratio.

2. Slow-cooked in red wine for two hours, my guests were amazed by the tenderness of my *boeuf bourguignon*.

3. Police officers are only allowed to cross the line into the hotel where the heads of state are meeting.

4. Gnawing his stolen steak and growling, Henry could not coax his dog to come out from under the table.

5. Swimming in the bay is forbidden if polluted.

6. Because they do not shed hair, our neighbours bought a Cornish Rex cat.

7. Please summarize what you have read with your textbook closed.

8. Having been to Monte Carlo and visited its magnificent casino, Las Vegas seems trashy and cheap by comparison.

9. A Guatemalan bishop was murdered on page 23 of *The New York Times*.

10. A 53-year-old truck driver who has lived in Canada since he was a baby has been deported to England, where he was born after being convicted on drug charges.

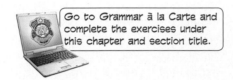

Go to Grammar à la Carte and complete the exercises under this chapter and section title.

EXERCISE **8.6**

Now it's time to test your mastery of modifiers. Carefully read each item in the following exercise before you revise it. Some sentences may contain more than one error.

1. After finishing high school, college seemed like a good idea.

2. As a computer programmer, the days are long and exhausting.

3. Having spilled coffee while working on my novel, the keyboard was sticky and the *g* wouldn't work.

4. The video that accompanies this sound system explains how to configure it clearly.

5. After reading her favourite book from cover to cover twice, the baby was finally ready to go to sleep.

6. My jeans almost fit as well now as they did 15 years ago, when I nearly wore them to class every day.

7. Camping in Cape Breton, magnificent sunsets ended our days.

8. Pierced with a freshly cut branch and roasted over a slow fire, you won't taste anything better than a vegetarian hot dog.

9. While attempting a back flip from the high board, my bathing suit somehow ripped at the seam.

10. Feeling totally prepared for the afternoon's employment interview, a few drinks at lunch with friends could not do any harm.

GRAMMAR À LA CARTE

- Looking for more opportunities to practise? Want to see what you need to review before the big test? Visit NELSONbrain.com and log in to **Grammar à la Carte** for *The Bare Essentials, Form A*, to access additional exercises! These Web exercises are graded automatically, so you will know instantly whether or not you have mastered the material.

The Parallelism Principle   9

Brevity, clarity, and force: these are three characteristics of good writing style. **Parallelism** will reinforce these characteristics in everything you write.

When your sentence contains a series of two or more items, they must be grammatically parallel. That is, they must be written in the same grammatical form. Consider this example:

> College requires us to manage our time, to work independently, and critical thinking.

The three items in this series are not parallel. Two are infinitive phrases (*to manage, to work*), but the third ends in *ing* and is a noun phrase. To correct the sentence, you must put all items in the same grammatical form. You have two choices. The first appears at the top of the next page.

College requires us *to manage* our time, [*to*] *work* independently, and [*to*] *think* critically. (all infinitive phrases)

Or you can write

College requires time management, independent work, and

critical thinking. (all noun phrases)

Now look at an example with two non-parallel elements:

Most people seek happiness in long-term relationships and work that provides them with satisfaction.

Again, you could correct this sentence in two ways. You could write "Most people seek happiness *in relationships that are long-term* and *in work that provides them with satisfaction*," but that solution produces a long and clumsy sentence. The shorter version works better: "Most people seek happiness in *long-term relationships* and *satisfying work*." This version is concise, clear, and forceful.

> Correct faulty parallelism by writing all items in a series in the same grammatical form: all words, all phrases, or all clauses.

One way to tell whether the items in a series are parallel is to write them out in list form, one below the other. That way, you can see at a glance if all of the elements "match"—that is, are in the same grammatical form.

Not Parallel

My supervisor is *demanding, short-tempered*, and *an obnoxious person*.

(This list has two adjectives and a noun phrase.)

I support myself by *delivering pizza, poker*, and *shooting pool*.

(This list has two phrases and one single word as objects of the preposition *by*.)

Parallel

My supervisor is *demanding, short-tempered*, and *obnoxious*.

(This list has three adjectives.)

I support myself by *delivering pizza, playing poker*, and *shooting pool*.

(This list has three phrases as objects of the preposition *by*.)

Not Parallel

Jules wants a job that *will interest him,*
                        will challenge him,
            and   *pays well.*

(This series of clauses contains two future tense verbs and one present tense verb.)

Parallel

Jules wants a job that *will interest him,*
                        challenge him,
            and   *pay him well.*

(All three subordinate clauses contain future tense verbs.)

As you can see, achieving parallelism is partly a matter of developing an ear for the sound of a correct list. A parallel sentence has a smooth, unbroken rhythm. Practice and the exercises in this chapter will help you recognize non-parallel structures. Once you have mastered parallelism in your sentences, you will be ready to develop ideas in parallel sequence—in thesis statements, for example—and thus to write clear, well-organized prose. Far from being a frill, parallelism is a fundamental characteristic of good writing.

Working with a partner, make any necessary corrections in the following exercises. Read each sentence aloud and try to spot parallelism errors from the change in rhythm that the faulty element produces. Then revise each sentence to bring the faulty element into line with the other element(s) in the series. Check your answers to each set of 10 before going on. Answers for this chapter begin on page 415.

EXERCISE **9.1**

1. I am overworked and not paid enough.

2. Our new office is ergonomic, functional, and it looks attractive.

3. The three main kinds of speech are demonstrative, information, and the kind intended to persuade the audience about something.

4. Wielding his knife swiftly and with skill, the chef turned a tomato into a centrepiece that looked just like a rose.

5. My doctor advised me to take two aspirins and I should call her in the morning.

6. Most people would prefer to work rather than living on welfare.

7. You need to develop skill and strategy and be agile to be a competitive skateboarder.

8. Will and Kate are a perfect couple: attractive, with good minds, and lots of energy.

9. My name is hard to pronounce, and you can't spell it easily, either.

10. I had a hard time deciding whether to continue my education or trying to find a job.

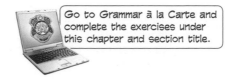

Go to Grammar à la Carte and complete the exercises under this chapter and section title.

EXERCISE **9.2**

1. To me, Kahlil Gibran's poetry is sentimental and not very interesting.

2. Garlic and when it gets light are the two things Dracula detests.

3. We're seeking a roommate who is responsible, self-supporting, reliable, and doesn't make a lot of noise.

4. I'm looking for a car that is cheap to run, easy to park, and driving one is fun.

5. The apostrophe is used for two purposes: contraction and in possessive constructions.

6. The Internet provides us with limitless possibilities for research, access to convenient shopping, and endless ways to waste time.

7. Olympic athletes in the modern era can be categorized as able bodied, physically challenged, and the ones who are enhanced chemically.

8. Travel provides an education in independence, ability to be patient, resourceful, and humility.

9. Our cafeteria now offers a number of healthy choices: there are plenty of items without glucose, lactose-free items, and no trans-fat items on the menu.

10. We are offering this once-in-a-lifetime opportunity for the discriminating buyer to purchase a unique home that is superbly constructed, thoughtfully designed, with beautiful landscaping, and a competitive price.

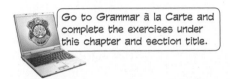

Go to Grammar à la Carte and complete the exercises under this chapter and section title.

EXERCISE **9.3**

Make the following lists parallel. In each case, there's more than one way to do it because you can make your items parallel with any item in the list. Therefore, your answers may differ from ours. Here's an example:

Incorrect:	prepare reports ... analysis
Correct:	prepare reports ... analyze
Also correct:	report preparation ... analysis

1. Incorrect: mechanically   manually   by using electronics

    Correct:

2. Incorrect: security   valuable   safety

    Correct:

3. Incorrect: achieve her goals   finding true happiness   enjoy her family

    Correct:

4. Incorrect: sense of humour   wealthy   intelligent

    Correct:

5. Incorrect: daily exercise   wholesome food   getting a checkup regularly

    Correct:

6. Incorrect: creative   skilful   good thinking
                                                     ability

   Correct:

7. Incorrect: generous   kind spirit   consideration for
                                                     others

   Correct:

8. Incorrect: look for bargains quality should be value comes first
                                  chosen

   Correct:

9. Incorrect: lavish   cost a great deal   attended by many
                                                     guests

   Correct:

10. Incorrect: waiting with   reading quietly   softly humming
               patience

    Correct:

EXERCISE **9.4**

Create a sentence for each of the parallel lists you developed in Exercise 9.3. There are no answers for this exercise. Example:

Madison's data analysis was superb, but her report preparation was pitiful.

EXERCISE **9.5**

Many errors in parallelism occur in the bulleted points that are commonly featured in reports and presentations. Working with a partner, create a parallel list out of each of the following sets of bulleted points. Your answers may vary from our suggestions, depending on which item in each list that you choose as the model for the other items to parallel.

1. In order to improve office morale, our committee recommends that we
   take the following steps:

   • Install nameplates on all office doors

   • Computers in all offices should be upgraded

- New furniture to replace damaged items
- Institute weekly office meetings
- Flexible hours where practical

2. The consultants' report identifies five changes that must be made to return our team to profitability:

- Improved food at stadium concession stands
- Lower prices for general admission
- Advertising budget should be increased by 20 percent
- High-profile players should be acquired
- Update team logo and uniforms

3. After a careful study of your son's time management practices, we conclude that the following recommendations, if adopted at once, could salvage his college career:

- Be in bed by 10:00 p.m. on weekdays
- All classes and labs must be attended
- 50 percent less spending on entertainment
- Assignments submitted on time
- Restricted hours for Internet surfing and computer gaming
- His current crowd of friends should be replaced

4. Before we choose your hotel for our convention, we would like to confirm that the following facilities will be available for our delegates' use:

- A conference room for 150 people
- We would like to book a nearby 18-hole golf course
- Full exercise facilities, including pool
- Our dining room must be separate from restaurants used by other guests
- Wireless Internet access in each room

5. The successful applicant for this position will have these qualifications:

- Able to work independently

- College diploma in business administration, hotel and restaurant management, or related program
- Experience in the travel/tourism industry
- High-level computer skills are required
- Must be fluent in at least one of French, German, Spanish, or Italian

EXERCISE 9.6

Correct the faulty parallelism in the following paragraphs. This exercise contains 10 errors.

There can no longer be any question about the fact that our planet is getting warmer. The melting glaciers, the winters that are getting shorter, record-breaking temperatures, and expanding deserts all point to a rapid warming trend. Many of us shrug our shoulders and leave solutions to this complex problem in the hands of governments, business leaders, those who work in the field of science, and activists. We think, "How can one person do anything to make a difference?" We forget that if we all acted together, we could bring about a significant change for the better.

Buying more fuel-efficient cars, using our automobiles less, and even do without them altogether would be a start, and imagine the impact if a million city dwellers decided to switch to public transit! We can turn our thermostats down in the winter and up in the summer—even a couple of degrees means a huge energy saving—and changing to energy-efficient light bulbs. Would it be such a hardship to wear an extra sweater in the winter, air conditioning off in the summer when we're out, or switching off the lights when we leave a room? Individual actions like these, if undertaken by enough of us, will not only save energy and reduce pollution but also demonstrate to business and government that we're serious, and motivating them to do more.

On a larger scale, we need to put more resources into research that will enable us to exploit wind power, capture solar energy, and tidal forces must be harnessed. We must insist on intelligently designed, energy-efficient buildings. Every project, whether large or small, will require the support and encouragement of individuals who buy thoughtfully, consume wisely, and strategic voting. All of us—individuals, corporations, and governments—need to dedicate ourselves to reducing, reusing, and recycling. Our comfort, our children's health, and the lives of our grandchildren depend on it.

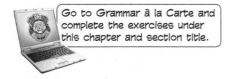

Go to Grammar à la Carte and complete the exercises under this chapter and section title.

EXERCISE **9.7**

As a test of your ability to correct faulty parallelism, revise the following sentences.

1. My doctor, who is asthmatic, diabetic, and weighs too much, tells me that he doesn't believe in exercise because he says making your heart beat faster to make it stronger is like driving your car faster to make it last longer.

2. The first hint I had that the company I had applied to was in trouble was that the offices were ill-equipped, poorly lighted, and there wasn't any heat.

3. Books provide us with information, education, and an enjoyable experience.

4. Tonight's program has all the ingredients of a successful reality show: ambition, greedy characters, jealous people, and sex.

5. I made two resolutions this New Year: to improve my work habits and getting my spending under control.

6. Lots of swimming, fishing, and seeing all the sights I can are what I plan to do this summer on Vancouver Island.

7. Sleeping all day and awake all night: I've been doing this for two weeks now.

8. When they buy a car, most people consider such factors as safety, the styling, how fast it goes, whether or not it is reliable, and how much it costs.

9. An article I read in a magazine said that the symptoms of stress are impulse buying, eating more than you should, and driving recklessly. That's what I call a perfect day!

10. According to famed chef Julia Child, any cooking disaster can be rescued. If it's a main course, cover it with parsley; if it's a dessert, whipped cream will disguise it.

GRAMMAR À LA CARTE

- Looking for more opportunities to practise? Want to see what you need to review before the big test? Visit NELSONbrain.com and log in to **Grammar à la Carte** for *The Bare Essentials, Form A*, to access additional exercises! These Web exercises are graded automatically, so you will know instantly whether or not you have mastered the material.

Refining by Combining | 10

SENTENCE COMBINING

If you have worked carefully through Unit 2 to this chapter, you should now be writing in complete sentences—a solid achievement, but one that does not yet meet the requirements of academic and professional writing. Your paragraphs may consist of sentences that are short, choppy, and monotonous; that is, your writing may be lacking in style. Now is the time to try your hand at **sentence combining**, a technique that enables you to produce correct and pleasing sentences. Sentence combining accomplishes three things: it reinforces your meaning; it refines and polishes your writing; and it results in a style that will keep your reader alert and interested in what you have to say.

Let's look at two short, technically correct sentences that could be combined:

My boss is demanding.
She expects quick results.

There are several ways of combining statements like these into a single sentence. Note that the meanings of the resulting sentences are slightly different. These differences are important when you're deciding which method to use in a particular situation.

1. You can connect sentences with an appropriate linking word, such as *and*, *but*, *or*, *nor*, *for*, *so*, and *yet*.

My boss is demanding, and she expects quick results.
My boss is demanding, for she expects quick results.

2. You can change one of the sentences into a subordinate clause.

My boss, who is demanding, expects quick results. (*Or:* Because my boss is demanding, she expects quick results.)

3. You can change one of the sentences into a modifying phrase.

Being demanding, my boss expects quick results. (*Or:* My boss, a demanding supervisor, expects quick results.)

4. Sometimes you can reduce one of your sentences to a single-word modifier.

My demanding boss expects quick results.

In sentence combining, you are free to move parts of the sentence around, change words, add or delete words, or make whatever other changes you want. Anything goes, as long as you don't drastically alter the meaning of the base sentences. Remember that your aim in combining sentences is to create effective sentences—not long ones.

COORDINATION OR SUBORDINATION?

When you join two or more short independent clauses, you need to think about their logical relationship. Are the ideas equally significant? If so, link them with an appropriate coordinating conjunction: a linking word such as *and, but, so, for, or, nor,* or *yet.* Is one idea more significant than the other? Put it in the main clause and put the less important idea in a subordinate construction: a clause, phrase, or word.

The most common way of linking ideas is with **conjunctions**. Every conjunction has its own meaning and purpose. If you choose your conjunctions carefully, you will reinforce the meaning you wish to convey. If you choose them carelessly, you will not say what you mean and may confuse your reader.

COORDINATION

To join two ideas that are equal in content or importance, use either
- a **coordinating conjunction** (*and, but, so, for, or, nor, yet*) or
- **correlative conjunctions** (*either ... or, neither ... nor, not only ... but also, both ... and*) or
- a semicolon

Consider these examples:

1. Illogical relation:

    Water is vital to life, for it must be protected.

    Logical relation:

    Water is vital to life, so it must be protected. (coordinating conjunction)

    Logical relation:

    Water must be protected, for it is vital to life. (coordinating conjunction)

2. Illogical relation:

I reread the text and reviewed my notes, so I failed the test anyway.

Logical relation:

I reread the text and reviewed my notes, but I failed the test anyway.
(coordinating conjunction)

3. Poor logical relation:

Mr. Benson teaches school, and he is a writer also.

Logical relation:

Mr. Benson is both a teacher and a writer. (correlative conjunction)

4. Poor logical relation:

I am not young, and I am not experienced either.

Logical relation:

I am neither young nor experienced. (correlative conjunctions)

EXERCISE **10.1**

Combine the following sentences by using a coordinating conjunction or a pair of correlative conjunctions, as appropriate. Make your combined sentences as concise as possible by eliminating unnecessary words. Answers for exercises in this chapter begin on page 417.

1. Our town may be small. Our town is not backward.

2. The final exam will be held on Friday afternoon. Or it will be held on Monday morning.

3. This book promises to help me manage my money. I will buy it.

4. I have completed all the exercises. My sentence skills are gradually improving.

5. This man is not my father. He is not my husband either.

SUBORDINATION

To connect ideas of unequal importance, put the dominant idea in a main clause and the less significant idea in a subordinate clause beginning with either

- a **relative pronoun** (*who, whom, whose, which,* or *that*) or
- a **subordinating conjunction** such as *although, because, if, when, where,* or *after* (see list on page 94)

Consider these examples:

1. Illogical relation:

    Ryan did well on his tests, and he began working with a tutor.

    Logical relation:

    After he began working with a tutor, Ryan did well on his tests. (subordinating conjunction)

    Logical relation:

    Ryan did well on his tests after he began working with a tutor. (subordinating conjunction)

2. Illogical relation:

    No day is depressing to my English teacher, and he is an incurable optimist.

    Logical relation:

    No day is depressing to my English teacher, who is an incurable optimist. (relative pronoun)

    Logical relation:

    Because he is an incurable optimist, no day is depressing to my English teacher. (subordinating conjunction)

EXERCISE **10.2**

For each item below, consider the two sentences together with the two possible conjunctions that we've provided in parentheses. Only one conjunction expresses a logical relationship between the sentences. Decide which conjunction is appropriate and write the combined sentence in the space provided. Check your answers against ours on page 417.

Sentences

1. The office will close early today. This storm keeps up. (and/if)

2. My favourite team is the Vancouver Canucks. My father prefers the Montreal Canadiens. (for/but)

3. Politicans often complain. Newspapers distort the facts. (yet/that)

4. The protestors left the scene. The police arrived. (but/when)

5. Art is long. Life is short. (where/but)

In the following exercises, combine the pairs of sentences. We have provided two possible conjunctions to join each pair. First decide if the ideas in the sentences are equal or unequal in significance. If the ideas are of equal logical weight, use the coordinating conjunction to join them. If one idea is less important, express it in a dependent clause beginning with a subordinating conjunction. *Remember that dependent clauses can come before or after the main clause*, so some of your answers may differ from ours. After you finish each exercise, check your answers against ours on pages 418 to 419.

EXERCISE **10.3**

1. I sometimes have nightmares. They don't usually bother me unless I eat pepperoni pizza as a bedtime snack. (but/even if)

2. The tortoise is slow but steady. It will win the race. (for/because)

3. Declan procrastinates by playing video games. His homework lies unfinished. (for/while)

4. I don't mind doing this exercise. I'll be glad when it's finished. (although/ and)

5. Olivia blogs incessantly. She thinks all her thoughts are interesting. (who/ so)

EXERCISE **10.4**

In the following sentences, which are adaptations of one-liners by humorist Steven Wright, try each conjunction before the first statement and then the second before you decide which construction is the best choice.

Example:

Everything seems to be going well. You have overlooked something (because/when)

a. *Because* everything seems to be going well, you have overlooked something. (doesn't make sense)

b. Everything seems to be going well *because* you have overlooked something. (doesn't make sense)

c. *When* everything seems to be going well, you have overlooked something. (Bingo!)

d. Everything seems to be going well *when* you have overlooked something. (makes no clear sense)

1. You want the rainbow. You've got to put up with the rain. (and/if)

2. Borrow money from pessimists. They won't expect it back. (so/because)

3. The early bird may get the worm. The second mouse gets the cheese.

   (while/but)

4. Everything is coming your way. You're in the wrong lane. (for/when)

5. Hard work pays off in the future. Laziness pays off now. (but/though)

In the following exercises, try your solutions aloud before you write them. Combine the two sentences in each item, using the cues in parentheses as your guide to linking the ideas together. Answers begin on page 418.

EXERCISE **10.5**

1. Don't worry about your heart.
   Your heart will last as long as you do. (for)

   _____

   _____

2. The bank has added new service charges.
   I think the service charges are unjustified. (that)

   _____

   _____

3. Office morale improved.
   She changed jobs. (when)

   _____

   _____

4. "Reality" television shows are, in fact, scripted.
   Many people are not aware of this fact. (that)

   _____

   _____

5. Ancient scientists looked to the stars for guidance.
   Modern scientists look forward to travelling to the stars.
   Amanda looks for stars in dance clubs. (while, and)

   _____

   _____

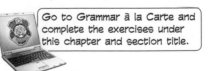

Go to Grammar à la Carte and complete the exercises under this chapter and section title.

EXERCISE **10.6**

Use a variety of sentence-combining techniques to join each set of statements into longer, more interesting units.

Hint: Read through each set of statements before you begin to combine them. Try several variations aloud or in your head before writing down your preferred solution. There are many ways to combine these short statements to make smooth, effective sentences. Our answers are only suggestions.

1. I have a new computer.
   It is a tablet.
   It came with e-reader and GPS apps.

   _____

   _____

   _____

2. Some people enjoy hockey.
   Other people prefer soccer.
   Soccer is the world's most popular spectator sport.

   _____

   _____

   _____

3. I want to leave class now.
   I want to go home.
   I want to lie down.
   My brain is full.

   _____

   _____

   _____

4. Nova Scotia is where I was born.
   I was born in Sidney Mines.
   I have not lived there since I was 10.

   _____

   _____

   _____

5. The Slow Food Movement began in 1986.
   It began in Italy.
   It was a reaction against fast food.
   It has now spread to 150 countries.

   _____

   _____

   _____

EXERCISE **10.7**

This set of exercises is more challenging. In some questions, you may need to combine the statements into two or even three sentences. Again, be sure to read through all of the statements in each question to identify related ideas before you begin revising. Turn to page 418 to compare your sentences with our suggested revisions.

1. Most of my friends hate to cook.
   I create special dishes whenever I can.
   I am going to college.
   I am taking a chef program.
   The program will enable me to do what I love as a career.

2. I have no ambition.
   I never move quickly except to avoid work.
   I believe that all deadlines are unreasonable.
   I believe that it is always possible that no one will notice that I am late.
   I believe that it is always possible that no one will notice that my work is unfinished.
   I begin a task when I get around to it.
   I never put off until tomorrow what I can avoid altogether.

3. China is a country with a huge population.
   There are more than a billion people in China.
   It is not easy to be an individual in China.
   You may think of yourself as "one in a million."
   There are a thousand other people just like you!

4. Lawyers are professionals.
   Doctors are professionals.
   Businesspeople are professionals.
   These professionals make up less than 10 percent of Canada's workforce.
   These professionals occupy almost three-quarters of the seats in the House of Commons.

5. Blue-collar workers make up nearly 50 percent of the population.
   They hold less than 10 percent of the positions in Parliament.
   Women are also underrepresented in Canada's government.
   First Nations people are also underrepresented in Canada's government.
   Minorities are also underrepresented in Canada's government.
   This underrepresentation calls into question Canada's commitment to democracy.

Now that you have completed Unit 2, you are ready to begin revising whatever you write. Read your work aloud. How your sentences sound is important. Test your writing against the seven characteristics of successful sentences, outlined in the Summary box below.

SUMMARY

1. **Meaning:** Have you said what you meant?
2. **Correctness:** Have you avoided fragments, run-ons, misplaced and dangling modifiers, and unparallel constructions?
3. **Clarity:** Is your sentence clear? Can it be understood on the first reading?
4. **Coherence:** Do the parts of your sentence fit together logically and smoothly?
5. **Emphasis:** Are the most important ideas either at the end or at the beginning of the sentence?
6. **Conciseness:** Is the sentence direct and to the point? Have you cut out all redundant or repetitious words?
7. **Rhythm:** Does the sentence flow smoothly? Are there any interruptions in the development of the key idea(s)? Do the interruptions help to emphasize important points, or do they distract the reader?

If your sentences pass the seven tests of good sentence style, you may be confident that they are both technically correct and easy to read. No reader could ask for more.

EXERCISE **10.8**

To practise what you have learned in this unit, write a short paper on a topic of your choice or on one your instructor assigns. When you have completed a first or, preferably, a second draft, read it over carefully. While your spell checker may have corrected some of your errors, remember that no program can flag your use of a correctly spelled wrong word: for example, *accept* instead of *except*, *their* when you mean *they're*, or *than* when the meaning requires *then*. Check your sentence structure by reading your work aloud from the last sentence back to the first. Look for fragments, run-ons, and errors in modifiers and parallelism. Here are some topics you may wish to consider for your paper.

1. Write a memorandum to the appropriate administrator of your school requesting exemption from a course you are currently taking. (Determining who this administrator is and his/her job title will require some research on your part.) Provide substantial reasons for your request.

2. Write a letter to a company whose product you use and tell the company why you like it. Even if you are satisfied with the product, you may have a suggestion for improvement. If so, let the company know. Most successful companies welcome positive suggestions.

3. Write to a club or association requesting information about membership and an application form. Briefly outline why you wish to join this organization.

4. Write a letter of support for a colleague whose probationary period is coming to an end, outlining your reasons for thinking this person is a good employee who should be retained.

5. Write to one of your former instructors or employers, requesting permission to use that person's name as a reference in your current job search. Explain the nature of the position you are applying for and outline what you have been doing since this instructor/employer last supervised you.

UNIT 2 RAPID REVIEW

As a final test of your ability to use correct sentence structure, read the following passage carefully. It contains a total of 15 errors, including one or more sentence fragments, run-ons, misplaced and dangling modifiers, and unparallel constructions. *Tip:* Read each paragraph through before you begin revising. For errors you miss, the Answer Key on page 420 will direct you to the chapter you should review.

[1]What simple activity can improve a child's grades, lessen the likelihood of drug use, and reduce the incidence of teen obesity and depression? [2]Research shows that eating together as a family produces these amazing results, here's the proof.

[3]A recent study from the University of Minnesota concluded that shared mealtimes were the primary cause of significant improvements in children's health and well-being. [4]Especially among girls. [5]Not surprisingly, the research shows that adolescents who eat meals with their family consume more fruit and vegetables, more calcium is consumed, and fewer soft drinks. [6]However, the benefits of sitting down to a family meal extend beyond better nutrition. [7]Studies show a correlation between family meals and improved academic performance, better mental health, and the incidence of substance abuse is reduced. [8]These benefits increasing with each additional family meal per week.

[9]Television is the biggest obstacle to family mealtimes, according to the Canadian Paediatric Society, by the age of 15, children have spent more

time in front of television than in front of teachers. [10]Rather than fight with their children to turn off the television and come to the table, meals are served to suit the children's TV schedule instead of the family's convenience. [11]Television-friendly frozen pizzas, TV dinners, and other fast foods are high in fat, carbohydrates, and sodium. [12]While their nutritional value is generally low.

[13]Accepting the benefits of eating together as a family is one thing doing something about it is another. [14]Most teenagers are not convinced that family activities are beneficial (let alone "cool"), and there are many more interesting pursuits for adolescents. [15]From part-time jobs to sports to video games to computers to cellphones to television, and even homework.

[16]Experts in child and adolescent psychology offer some helpful guidelines. [17]First, turn off the television and agree to turn off cellphones and let the household phone take messages as a family during mealtimes. [18]Second, keep the conversation light, upbeat, supportive, and comfortable. [19]Family meals are not the time for serious, sensitive, or subjects that involve controversy. [20]Third, set a goal. [21]You might begin with a commitment to sit down together twice a week and gradually increase the frequency. [22]As everyone gets used to the idea.

[23]The experts' suggestions may not work for everyone, each family will have to work out its own set of principles if family mealtimes are to succeed.

[24]Negotiating your own "family rules" takes time but the rewards are worth it!

GRAMMAR À LA CARTE

- Looking for more opportunities to practise? Want to see what you need to review before the big test? Visit NELSONbrain.com and log in to **Grammar à la Carte** for *The Bare Essentials, Form A,* to access additional exercises! These Web exercises are graded automatically, so you will know instantly whether or not you have mastered the material.

UNIT 3

Grammar

Grammar

UNIT 3 QUICK QUIZ

The following quiz will show you which chapters of Unit 3 you need to pay special attention to. The paragraph below contains 15 errors in grammar: verb forms, subject–verb agreement, verb tense consistency, pronoun form, pronoun–antecedent agreement, and pronoun consistency.

When you have made your corrections, turn to page 420 and compare your revisions with ours. For each error you miss, the Answer Key directs you to the chapter you need to work on.

[1]A Scottish newspaper reported recently that Scottish scientists had digged an excavation to a depth of 10 metres and discovered traces of copper wire that dated back more than 100 years. [2]Each of the artifacts were examined in a lab, and scientists conclude that Scotland had had a primitive telephone network more than 100 years ago.

[3]In the following weeks, English archeologists begun their own excavations in the hope of finding something that would outdo the Scots. [4](Anyone that is familiar with relations between Scotland and England know about the rivalry between the two long-time enemies.) [5]At the 20-metre mark in their excavation, the English made a discovery that them and their experts believed to be significant. [6]Laboratory analysis revealed what they had suspected: remnants of copper wire in the hole was evidence that the English had had an advanced communications network long before the Scots. [7]Everyone

who were following the controversial discoveries now waited for the next revelation, the one which would settle the dispute once and for all.

[8]They did not have to wait long. [9]Within a week of the English announcement, a startling discovery was reported by amateur archeologist Wilf Johnson of Fenwick, Ontario. [10]His two cousins had been hired by Wilf to help him dig down nearly 30 metres in an old apple orchard near his home, and, incredibly, them and Wilf found absolutely nothing. [11]The crack team of analysts from the Fenwick Lions Club were unanimous about the significance of this result: while the Scots and the English had been using copper wire for communication longer than anyone had thought possible, us in Canada had already been wireless for years.

11 Choosing the Correct Verb Form

Errors in grammar are like flies in soup. Most of the time, they don't affect meaning any more than flies affect flavour, but they are distracting and offputting. You must eliminate grammar errors from your writing if you want your readers to pay attention to what you say rather than to how you say it.

The **verb** is the most complex and essential part of a sentence. In fact, a verb is to a sentence what an engine is to a car: the source of power and a frequent cause of trouble.

This chapter looks at two verb problems that occur in many people's writing: incorrect use of irregular verbs and difficulties with the passive voice.

THE PRINCIPAL PARTS OF VERBS

All verb formations are based on a verb's **principal parts**. Technically, the principal parts are the elements that are used to construct the various **tenses** (time indicators) of verbs.

> Every verb has four forms, called its *principal parts*.
> 1. The base or **infinitive** form: the form used with *to*
> 2. The **simple past** (also called the **past tense**)
> 3. The **present participle**: the *-ing* form
> 4. The **past participle**: the form used with *has* or *have*

Here are some examples:

Infinitive	Simple Past	Present Participle	Past Participle
A. (to) call	called	calling	(has) called
(to) dance	danced	dancing	(has) danced
(to) work	worked	working	(has) worked
B. (to) do	did	doing	(has) done
(to) eat	ate	eating	(has) eaten
(to) say	said	saying	(has) said

If you study the list above, you will notice an important feature of principal parts. In the first group of three verbs (A), the simple past and the past participle are identical: they are both formed by adding *-ed* (or simply *-d* if the verb ends in *-e*, as *dance* does). When both the simple past and the past participle of a verb are formed with *-ed*, the verb is called a **regular verb**. Fortunately, most of the many thousands of English verbs are regular.

In the second group (B), the verbs are called **irregular verbs** because the simple past and past participle are not formed by adding *-ed*. With *do* and *eat*, the simple past and the past participle are different words: *did/done, ate/eaten*. The simple past and past participle of *say* are the same, *said*, but they are not formed with the regular *-ed* ending.

Unfortunately, although there are only a few hundred irregular verbs in English, these verbs are among the most common in the language; for example, *begin, come, do, go, see,* and *write* are all irregular. Their simple past tenses and past participles are formed in unpredictable ways.

If you are not sure of the principal parts of a verb, check your dictionary. If the verb is irregular, you will find the principal parts listed after the entry for the base form. For instance, if you look up *sing* in your dictionary, you will

Grammar

find *sang* (simple past), *sung* (past participle), and *singing* (present participle). If no principal parts are listed after the verb you are checking, it is regular; you form its simple past and past participle by adding *-ed*.

The verbs listed on pages 152 to 155 are used so frequently you should take the time to learn their principal parts. We have not included the present participle (the *-ing* form) because it rarely causes difficulty. The good news is that only some of the verbs on this list will cause you trouble.

To identify the verbs that cause you problems, cover the middle and right-hand columns of the list with a blank piece of paper. Begin with the infinitive form of the first verb, *be*. Say the past tense and past participle of *be*. Move the paper down one line to check your responses. If your answers are correct, go to the next verb in the left-hand column, *bear*. Again, say the past tense and the past participle, check your responses, and move on to the next verb, *beat*. Continue this exercise until you reach the end of the list.

Whenever you come to a verb whose past tense or past participle you aren't sure of or misidentify, highlight that verb across all three columns (infinitive, simple past, past participle). After you've gone through the list once, you'll have a quick and easy reference to the correct forms of verbs you need to watch out for.

THE PRINCIPAL PARTS OF IRREGULAR VERBS

Infinitive (Use with *to* and with helping/auxiliary verbs)	**Simple Past**	**Past Participle** (Use with *has, have, had*)
be (am, is)	was/were	been
bear	bore	borne
beat	beat	beaten
become	became	become
begin	began	begun
bend	bent	bent
bind	bound	bound
bite	bit	bitten
bleed	bled	bled
blow	blew	blown
break	broke	broken
bring	brought (*not* brang)	brought (*not* brung)
broadcast	broadcast	broadcast

Infinitive	Simple Past	Past Participle
(Use with *to* and with helping/auxiliary verbs)		(Use with *has, have, had*)
build	built	built
burst	burst	burst
buy	bought	bought
catch	caught	caught
choose	chose	chosen
cling	clung	clung
come	came	come
cost	cost	cost
cut	cut	cut
deal	dealt	dealt
dig	dug	dug
dive	dived/dove	dived
do	did (*not* done)	done
draw	drew	drawn
dream	dreamed/dreamt	dreamed/dreamt
drink	drank (*not* drunk)	drunk
drive	drove	driven
eat	ate	eaten
fall	fell	fallen
feed	fed	fed
feel	felt	felt
fight	fought	fought
find	found	found
flee	fled	fled
fling	flung	flung
fly	flew	flown
forbid	forbade	forbidden
forget	forgot	forgotten/forgot
forgive	forgave	forgiven
freeze	froze	frozen
get	got	got/gotten
give	gave	given
go	went	gone (*not* went)
grow	grew	grown
have	had	had
hear	heard	heard
hide	hid	hidden
hit	hit	hit
hold	held	held
hurt	hurt	hurt
keep	kept	kept
know	knew	known

Grammar

Infinitive	Simple Past	Past Participle
(Use with *to* and with helping/auxiliary verbs)		(Use with *has, have, had*)
lay (to put or place)	laid	laid
lead	led	led
leave	left	left
lie (to recline)	lay	lain (*not* layed *or* laid)
light	lit/lighted	lit/lighted
lose	lost	lost
make	made	made
mean	meant	meant
meet	met	met
mistake	mistook	mistaken
pay	paid	paid
raise	raised	raised
ride	rode	ridden
ring	rang	rung
rise	rose	risen
run	ran	run
say	said	said
see	saw (*not* seen)	seen
seek	sought	sought
sell	sold	sold
set	set	set
shake	shook	shaken (*not* shook)
shine	shone	shone
shoot	shot	shot
show	showed	shown
shrink	shrank	shrunk
sing	sang	sung
sink	sank	sunk
sit	sat	sat
sleep	slept	slept
slide	slid	slid
speak	spoke	spoken
speed	sped	sped
spend	spent	spent
spin	spun	spun
stand	stood	stood
steal	stole	stolen
stick	stuck	stuck
sting	stung	stung
strike (affect)	struck	stricken
strike (hit)	struck	struck
strive	strove	striven

Infinitive	Simple Past	Past Participle
(Use with *to* and with helping/auxiliary verbs)		(Use with *has, have, had*)
swear	swore	sworn
swim	swam	swum
swing	swung (*not* swang)	swung
take	took	taken
teach	taught	taught
tear	tore	torn
tell	told	told
think	thought	thought
throw	threw	thrown
understand	understood	understood
wear	wore	worn
weave	wove	woven
win	won	won
wind	wound	wound
withdraw	withdrew	withdrawn
write	wrote	written

The sentences in the exercises below require both the simple past and the past participle of the verb shown at the left. Write the required form in each blank. Do not add or remove helping verbs. Check your answers after each exercise. Answers for exercises in this chapter begin on page 421.

EXERCISE **11.1**

1. ride   Having _____ a cow once, I wouldn't mind if I never _____ one

   again.

2. tear   Albert _____ his sheet into strips, tied the strips he had _____ into

   a long cord, and escaped through the window.

3. lie   The cat _____ defiantly right where the dog had _____ all morning.

4. shake   After I had _____ the money out of the envelope, I _____ the

   envelope again to be sure I had it all.

5. grow   Britney _____ the plant in a pot on her balcony, where she had

   _____ similar plants successfully in the past.

Grammar

6. know   We _____ at the time that we should have _____ better than to believe it was a geranium.

7. lay   Dev confidently _____ his passport on the officer's desk where the other tourists had _____ theirs.

8. lend   I _____ Jessa the $50 she asked for, even though she hasn't paid back the money I'd previously _____ her.

9. take   We _____ sweaters with us to the concert, but when it snowed, we wished we had _____ parkas.

10. go   They _____ where no human being had ever _____ before.

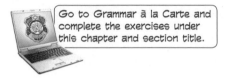

Go to Grammar à la Carte and complete the exercises under this chapter and section title.

EXERCISE **11.2**

Correct the 25 verb errors in the following sentences.

1. I would have call more often if I had knowed you cared.

2. The phone rung and rung, but no one answered because they had all went out for pizza.

3. After laying around all day watching TV, Emma sweared she would do her chores before bedtime.

4. "Strike three!" called the umpire as I swang the bat, but I run around the bases anyway.

5. While some have swam in the fountain of knowledge and others have drank from it, Gary just gargles.

6. Claudio should have knowed better than to challenge me at chess because I have seldom been beat.

7. Yasmin has stole his car and broke his heart, or maybe it was the other way around.

8. Too late, we figured out that if we had went to class and had did the homework, we would have past the course.

9. We should have went out and did something interesting this evening instead of setting around watching TV.

10. The lake had froze solid, so after we had ate supper, we brung our skates out and spended a couple of hours on the ice.

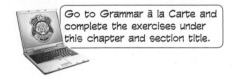

Go to Grammar à la Carte and complete the exercises under this chapter and section title.

CHOOSING BETWEEN ACTIVE AND PASSIVE VOICE

Verbs have another quality besides tense (or time). Verbs also have **voice**, which is the quality of being either active or passive. In sentences with **active-voice** verbs, the "doer" of the action is the grammatical subject of the sentence.

Active voice: <u>Helmets</u> <u>protect</u> cyclists.
My <u>dog</u> <u>ate</u> my homework.
<u>Someone</u> <u>will show</u> a movie in class.

In sentences with **passive-voice** verbs, the grammatical subject of the sentence is the "receiver" of the action (that is, the subject is "passively" acted upon), and the "doer" becomes an object of the preposition *by* or is absent from the sentence entirely, as in the third example below.

Passive voice: <u>Cyclists</u> <u>are protected</u> by helmets.
My <u>homework</u> <u>was eaten</u> by my dog.
A <u>movie</u> <u>will be shown</u> in class.

Notice that active and passive verbs can be in any tense. Present, past, and future tense verbs are used in both sets of examples above.

Passive-voice verbs are formed by using a form of *be* + a past participle. To use the passive voice correctly, you must know the past participle form of irregular verbs. For instance, in the third example above, the correct passive construction is *will be shown*, not *will be showed*. In the examples below, note the different tenses and pay special attention to the passive-voice verb forms.

	Active	**Passive**
present	The clerk *signs* the invoice.	The invoice *is signed* by the clerk.
past	The clerk *signed* the invoice.	The invoice *was signed* by the clerk.
future	The clerk *will sign* the invoice.	The invoice *will be signed* by the clerk.
present progressive	The clerk *is signing* the invoice.	The invoice *is being signed* by the clerk.
past progressive	The clerk *was signing* the invoice.	The invoice *was being signed* by the clerk.

EXERCISE 11.3

Use two lines to underline the verbs in the sentences below. Then identify the verbs as either active (A) or passive (P). The first one is done for you. The answers to the exercises in this part of the chapter begin on page 422.

1. __A__ Do not <u>number</u> your pages.

2. _____ Our cable line was gnawed through by a squirrel.

3. _____ Each year, Mount Washington is visited by thousands of tourists.

4. _____ "Some weasel took the cork out of my lunch!" (W. C. Fields)

5. _____ Your essay was not formatted properly.

6. _____ The test questions were read to us by our instructor in a mumbling monotone.

7. _____ *Whale Music* was written by Canadian author Paul Quarrington.

8. _____ A small Canadian company made Quarrington's novel into a successful movie.

9. _____ Mandarin is spoken by most of China's 1.3 billion people.

10. _____ "Children should neither be seen nor heard—ever again." (W. C. Fields)

EXERCISE **11.4**

Now rewrite the sentences in Exercise 11.3, changing active-voice verbs to passive and passive-voice verbs to active. We've done the first sentence for you as an example.

1. Your pages should not be numbered by you.

2.

3.

4.

5.

6.

7.

8.

9.

10.

Exchange papers with a partner, check each other's sentences, and decide whether active or passive voice is preferable in each case. Finally, compare your answers with ours on page 422.

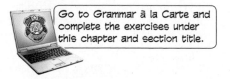

Go to Grammar à la Carte and complete the exercises under this chapter and section title.

Active-voice verbs are more direct and emphatic than passive verbs. Good writers use the active voice unless there is a specific reason to use the passive. There are three situations in which the passive voice is preferable.

1. The person or agent that performed the action is not known.

This workstation <u>is</u> not ergonomically <u>designed</u>.
The telephone <u>was left</u> off the hook.
The name of our street <u>has been changed</u> from Primate Road to Primrose Lane.

2. You want to place the emphasis on the person, place, or object that was affected by an action rather than on the subject performing the action.

The computer lab <u>was broken</u> into by a group of angry students.

This sentence focuses the reader's attention on the computer lab rather than on the students. If we reconstruct the sentence in the active voice, we produce a quite different effect:

A group of angry students <u>broke</u> into the computer lab.

3. You are writing a technical or scientific report or a legal document.

Passive verbs are the appropriate choice when the focus is on the facts, methods, or procedures involved in an experiment, situation, or event rather than on the person(s) who discovered or performed it. Passive verbs establish an impersonal tone that is appropriate to these kinds of writing. Contrast the emphasis and tone of these sentence pairs:

Passive: The heat <u>was increased</u> to 150°C and <u>was maintained</u> at that temperature.
Active: My lab partner and I <u>increased</u> the heat to 150°C and <u>main-tained</u> it at that temperature.

Passive: Our annual report <u>was approved</u> by the board on February 15.
Active: The board <u>approved</u> our annual report on February 15.

In general, because active verbs are more concise and forceful than passive verbs, they add focus and strength to your writing. When you find a passive verb in your writing, think about *who* is doing *what* to *whom*. Ask yourself why the *who* is not the subject of your sentence. If there is a good reason, then use the passive voice. Otherwise, change the verb.

EXERCISE **11.5**

Rewrite the sentences below, changing the verbs from passive to active voice. You may need to add a word or phrase to identify the doer of the action expressed by the verb.

1. Two days after the test, the students' results were posted by the department.

2. The car was packed the night before we left on our vacation.

3. Her new boyfriend is being tutored by my sister.

4. After a slow start, three runs were scored in the fourth inning.

5. My screen saver, a picture of a clear-cut forest was downloaded by my activist brother.

6. In English, the sound "ough" can be pronounced eight different ways.

7. Something must be done about persistent telephone solicitors.

8. "Shoes are required to eat in the dining room." (Sign in a hotel restaurant)

9. This piece of music is thought to have been written by Mozart.

10. After disappointing results were achieved by the class in the first semester, a different approach was tried by our professor.

EXERCISE **11.6**

Rewrite the sentences below, changing the verbs from passive to active voice. Then compare your revision to the original and, keeping in mind the three reasons for choosing the passive voice (page 160), decide which version is more effective.

1. The white part at the base of the fingernail is called the "lunula."

2. Payment was made as soon as the invoice was received.

3. A memo will be sent to your bank by the human resources department to confirm that you are a full-time employee.

4. More food than I needed was eaten by me when I came off my diet.

5. The remote was broken by Miranda in a fit of rage when she couldn't watch her favourite show.

Grammar

6. The letter carrier was barked at by the neighbour's dog until she was too terrified to deliver our mail.

7. The cause of the accident has not yet been determined by the investigators.

8. Next term, the honours seminar will be taught by a senior professor.

9. The little indentation that connects your upper lip to the bottom of your nose is called the "philtrum."

10. The word *assassination* was created by Shakespeare.

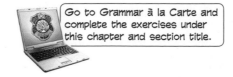

Go to Grammar à la Carte and complete the exercises under this chapter and section title.

EXERCISE 11.7

Rewrite the following passage, changing passive-voice verbs to active where appropriate. Ten changes are required.

Shortly after his graduation, a job was found by Gordon as a props buyer—someone who purchases special items needed for stage productions—at the Shaw Festival Theatre in Niagara-on-the-Lake, Ontario. In Gordon's first month on the job, a difficult challenge was presented to him by the set designer for *Arms and the Man*. In one of the scenes, two special ashtrays were required. During the Boer War, these ashtrays had been presented to the troops by the British government, and now they were very difficult to find. It was impossible that the ashtrays would be noticed by anyone in the audience, but Gordon did not think it would be useful to point this out to the designer, who was very particular. He found one ashtray at an antique store in Quebec after a two-week search. Eventually, Gordon turned his attention to other projects, but the ashtray was left on his desk to remind him that another was needed.

One day, Gordon's office in the props shop was visited by the director. She saw the ashtray on Gordon's desk and said, "Cool ashtray! My great-uncle has one just like it." To her surprise, she was given a big hug by Gordon. Another seemingly impossible assignment had successfully been completed by Gordon, Shaw Festival props buyer extraordinaire!

GRAMMAR À LA CARTE

- Looking for more opportunities to practise? Want to see what you need to review before the big test? Visit NELSONbrain.com and log in to **Grammar à la Carte** for *The Bare Essentials, Form A,* to access additional exercises! These Web exercises are graded automatically, so you will know instantly whether or not you have mastered the material.

Grammar

IN THIS VICTIM'S SENTENCES, THE SUBJECTS AND VERBS DOESN'T AGREE.

YOU HAVE THE RIGHT TO REMAIN SILENT...

12 Mastering Subject–Verb Agreement

SINGULAR AND PLURAL

One of the most common writing errors is lack of agreement between the subject and verb. Both must be singular, or both must be plural. If one is singular and the other plural, you have an agreement problem. You have another kind of agreement problem if your subject and verb are not both in the same "person" (see Chapter 16).

Let's clarify some terms. First, it's important to distinguish between **singular** and **plural**.

- *Singular* means one person or thing.
- *Plural* means more than one person or thing.

Second, it's important to know what we mean by the concept of **person**:

- *First person* is the person(s) speaking or writing: *I, me; we, us*
- *Second person* is the person(s) being addressed: *you*
- *Third person* is the person(s) being spoken or written about: *he, she, it; they, them*

Here's an example of the singular and plural forms of a regular verb in the present tense.

	Singular	**Plural**
First person	I win	we win
Second person	you win	you win
Third person	she wins (*or* he, it, the horse wins)	they win (*or* the horses win)

The third-person singular form often causes trouble because the endings of the verb and its subject do not match. Third-person singular present tense verbs end in *-s*, but their singular subjects do not. Third-person plural verbs never end in *-s*, while their subjects normally do. Look at these examples.

A <u>fire</u> <u>burns</u>.
The <u>car</u> <u>skids</u>.
A <u>neighbour</u> <u>cares</u> for our children.

The three singular verbs, all of which end in *-s* (*burns, skids, cares*), agree with their singular subjects (*fire, car, neighbour*), none of which ends in *-s*. When the subjects become plural, the verbs change form, too.

Four <u>fires</u> <u>burn</u>.
The <u>cars</u> <u>skid</u>.
The <u>neighbours</u> <u>care</u> for our children.

Now all of the subjects end in *-s*, and none of the verbs do.
To ensure **subject–verb agreement**, follow this basic rule:

> A verb and its subject must both be either singular or plural.

This rule causes difficulty only when the writer doesn't know which word in the sentence is the subject and so makes the verb agree with the wrong word. As long as you decode the sentence correctly (see Chapter 5), you'll have no problem making every subject agree with its verb.

If you have not already done so, now is the time to memorize this next rule:

> The subject of a sentence is NEVER in a prepositional phrase.

Here's an example of how errors occur:

Only one of the 20,000 ticket buyers are going to win.

What is the subject of this sentence? It's not *buyers*, but *one*. The verb must agree with *one*, which is clearly singular. The verb *are* does not agree with *one*, so the sentence is incorrect. It should read

Only <u>one</u> of the 20,000 ticket buyers <u>is going</u> to win.

If you are careful identifying the subject of your sentence, especially when it is separated from the verb by other words or phrases, you'll have no difficulty with subject–verb agreement. Before you try the exercises in this chapter, reinforce what you've learned by studying the following examples.

Incorrect: One of my sisters speak five languages.
Correct: <u>One</u> ~~of my sisters~~ <u>speaks</u> five languages.

Incorrect: Alix, one of the few girls on the team, keep trying for a perfect score.
Correct: Alix, <u>one</u> ~~of the few girls on the team~~, <u>keeps</u> trying for a perfect score.

Incorrect: One of the students continually write graffiti on the walls of the staff room.
Correct: <u>One</u> ~~of the students~~ continually <u>writes</u> graffiti ~~on the walls of the staff room~~.

EXERCISE **12.1**

Underline the subject in each sentence. Answers for exercises in this chapter begin on page 423.

1. The key to power is knowledge.

2. Here are the invoices for this shipment of software.

3. In the future, instead of live animals, people may choose intelligent machines as pets.

4. At the front of the line stood Professor Temkin, waiting to see Santa.

5. Jupiter and Saturn, the solar system's largest planets, appear close together in the western sky.

Pay special attention to words that end in *-one*, *-thing*, or *-body*. They cause problems for nearly every writer.

> Words ending in *-one*, *-thing*, or *-body* are always singular.

When used as subjects, these pronouns require singular verbs.

anyone	anything	anybody
everyone	everything	everybody
no one	nothing	nobody
someone	something	somebody

The last part of the pronoun subject is the tip-off here: every*one*, any*thing*, no*body*. If you focus on this last part, you'll remember to use a singular verb with these subjects.

These words tend to cause trouble when modifiers come between them and their verbs. For example, you would never write "Everyone are here." But when you insert a word or phrase between the subject and the verb, you might, if you weren't careful, write this: "<u>Everyone</u> involved in implementing the company's new policies and procedures <u>are</u> here." The meaning is plural: several people are present. But the subject (*everyone*) is singular, so the verb must be *is*.

Most subject–verb agreement errors are caused by violations of this rule. Be sure you understand it. Memorize it, and then test your understanding by doing the following exercise before you go any further.

EXERCISE **12.2**

Circle the correct verb for each of the following sentences, then check your answers against ours.

1. Somebody with a taste for Reese's Pieces (has/have) found my hidden stash of candy.
2. Nothing (succeed/succeeds) like success.
3. Nobody on the team (show/shows) much respect for the coach.

4. Why is it that everyone we meet (talk/talks) to you instead of me?

5. No one carrying a cellphone or any type of recording device (is/are) permitted into this meeting.

The next two exercises will give you practice in pairing singular subjects with singular verbs and plural subjects with plural verbs.

EXERCISE **12.3**

Change the subject and verb in each sentence from plural to singular. Underline the subject once and the verb twice. Then check your answers.

1. These policy changes affect all divisions of our company.

2. Articles on the Internet do not always contain reliable information.

3. Have the lucky winners collected the lottery money?

4. Above all, good teachers demonstrate respect for students.

5. The pressures of homework, part-time work, and nagging parents have caused many students to drop out of college.

EXERCISE **12.4**

Rewrite each sentence, changing the subject as indicated and revising the verb accordingly. Then check your answers. For example:

Computer <u>games</u> <u>are</u> my favourite pastime.
My favourite <u>pastime</u> <u>is</u> computer games.

1. Trees are a primary source of Earth's oxygen.

   A primary source _____

2. They insist on doing whatever they please.

   She _____

3. Good managers consult with their subordinates before making decisions.

   A good manager _____

4. He does his best work when he is unsupervised.

   We _____

5. A civil servant with an indexed pension stands to gain from future inflation.

   Civil servants _____

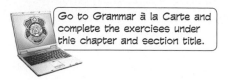

Go to *Grammar à la Carte* and complete the exercises under this chapter and section title.

So far, so good. You can find the subject, even when it's hiding on the far side of the verb or separated from the verb by one or more prepositional phrases. You can match up singular subjects with singular verbs and plural subjects with plural verbs. Now let's take a look at a few of the complications that make subject–verb agreement such a disagreeable problem.

FIVE SPECIAL CASES

Some subjects are tricky. They look singular but are plural, or they look plural when they're really singular. There are five kinds of these slippery subjects, all of them common and all of them likely to trip up the unwary writer.

> 1. Multiple subjects joined by *or*; *either ... or*; *neither ... nor*; or *not ... but*

Most multiple subjects we've dealt with so far have been joined by *and* and have required plural verbs, so agreement hasn't been a problem. But watch out when the two or more elements of a compound subject are joined by *or*, *either ... or*, *neither ... nor*, or *not ... but*. In these cases, the verb agrees in number with the nearest subject. That is, if the subject closest to the verb is singular, the verb will be singular; if the subject closest to the verb is plural, the verb must be plural, too.

Neither the <u>federal government</u> nor the <u>provinces</u> effectively <u>control</u> environmental pollution.

Neither the <u>provinces</u> nor the <u>federal government</u> effectively <u>controls</u> environmental pollution.

EXERCISE **12.5**

Circle the correct verb.

1. Either "Dr." or "Ms." (is/are) fine with me.
2. Not the cats but the dog (sleep/sleeps) on our bed.
3. Either your friend or you (is/are) paying for the damage.
4. Not lower taxes but friendly people (is/are) what I miss most about Alberta.
5. According to a recent survey, not financial worries but disagreement over children (cause/causes) the most strain on a marriage.

2. Subjects that look multiple but really aren't

Don't be fooled by phrases beginning with words such as *with*, *like*, *as well as*, *together with*, *in addition to*, and *including*. These prepositional phrases are NOT part of the subject of the sentence. Since they do not affect the verb, you can mentally cross them out.

My math professor, as well as my counsellor, has advised me to change my major.

Two people were involved in the advising; nevertheless, the subject (math professor) is singular, so the verb must be singular (has advised).

All of my courses, including English, seem easier this term.

If you mentally cross out the phrase "including English," you can easily see that the verb (seem) must be plural to agree with the plural subject (courses).

EXERCISE **12.6**

Circle the correct verb for each of the following sentences. Then check your answers against ours on page 424.

1. One hot dog with condiments and a side of fries (contain/contains) more calories and sodium than you can imagine.
2. Full-time employment, along with lower taxes, (has/have) become an impossible dream.
3. Even on sale, this computer package, including monitor, disk drive, printer, and software, (is/are) too expensive for us.

4. My parents, as well as my brother and even the family dog, (want/wants) me to move out.
5. Anger, together with denial and despair, (is/are) almost inevitable during the grieving process.

3. *Each* (of), *either* (of), *neither* (of)

Used as subjects, these words take singular verbs. (Remember, the subject is never located in a prepositional phrase.)

Either is suitable for the job.
Each of us dreams of scoring the winning goal.
Neither of these stores is open after six o'clock.

EXERCISE **12.7**

Circle the correct verb.

1. Neither of the two available seats (is/are) close to the stage.
2. Each of the psychology professors (appear/appears) to be a bit eccentric.
3. If either of the teams (scores/score) more than four goals, I win the money in the pool.
4. We are pleased to announce that each of you (has/have) won a full tuition scholarship.
5. If neither of these software programs (works/work) with our system, we'll have to find another supplier.

4. Collective nouns

A collective noun is a word naming a group. Some examples are *audience, band, class, company, committee, crowd, family, gang, majority, orchestra, public,* and *team.* When you are referring to the group acting all together, as a unit, use a singular verb. When you are referring to the members of the group acting individually, use a plural verb.

The team is sure to win tomorrow's game. (Here *team* refers to the group acting as one unit.)

The <u>team</u> <u>are</u> getting into their uniforms now. (The members of the team are acting individually.)

EXERCISE **12.8**

Circle the correct verb.

1. The nuclear family (is/are) the fundamental unit of society.
2. The class (is/are) making Valentine cards for their parents.
3. (Has/Have) the jury reached a verdict?
4. Having waited for more than an hour, the crowd (was/were) growing restless.
5. The majority of immigrants (find/finds) Canada a tolerant country.

> **5. Units of money, time, mass, length, and distance**

These expressions require singular verbs.

<u>Three dollars</u> <u>is</u> too much to pay for a coffee.

<u>Two hours</u> <u>seems</u> like four in our sociology class.

<u>Eighty kilograms</u> <u>is</u> the mass of an average man.

<u>Ten kilometres</u> <u>is</u> too far to walk.

EXERCISE **12.9**

Circle the correct verb.

1. Six metres (is/are) the minimum length of cloth you need to make a sari.
2. Thirteen dollars an hour for flipping burgers (sounds/sound) good to me.
3. Seven hours of classes without a break (makes/make) for a very long day.
4. Unless you are cycling against a strong wind, 30 kilometres on good roads (do/does) not seem far.
5. Forty years in the desert (means/mean) a very long time between baths.

In Exercises 12.10 and 12.11, correct the errors in subject–verb agreement. Check your answers to each exercise before going on.

EXERCISE **12.10**

1. A group of unbiased students and faculty have been asked to study the problem.

2. Anybody who really want to succeed will do so.

3. Over the past 20 years, the number of couples living together has more than doubled.

4. The lack of these four nutrients are thought to contribute to depression.

5. You'll find that not only ragweed but also cat hairs makes you sneeze.

6. Each of the contestants think that she is Canada's next superstar.

7. Neither the children nor their mother were willing to taste the bacon and garlic ice cream.

8. The lack of things to write about cause the headaches.

9. Sophia, along with her agent, stylist, two bodyguards, and three Chihuahuas, were seen boarding a private jet.

10. The amount of money generated by rock bands on concert tours are astonishing.

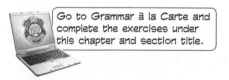

Go to Grammar à la Carte and complete the exercises under this chapter and section title.

EXERCISE **12.11**

There are 10 errors in this paragraph. Can you find and correct them?

There's many young people in Canada today carrying a large amount of debt. According to American Express, spending on fashion, travel, and fine dining have jumped dramatically in recent years. At the same time, wages among the group called Generation Y has stagnated, rising at a fraction of the increase in spending. Amex, for example, together with other financial institutions, report that spending on fine dining rose a staggering 102 percent over the past two years. At the same time, each of these institutions note that fewer than 40 percent of credit card holders between the ages of 18 and 34 makes the minimum payment on their card balance each month. This suggests that young people in the early stages of a career or even pre-career is sinking into debt while continuing to spend lavishly. It's the classic case of dousing a fire with gasoline! Parents, financial institutions, or the government are going to have to act to reverse this trend. But instead, bank representatives regularly visit campuses offering credit cards to undergraduates, and fewer than half of parents from the Baby Boomer generation believes it is important to save money for their children's inheritance. Generation Y, along with the Millennials and more recent generations, are going to have to get a grip on personal finances, or financial prosperity and even retirement will be an impossible dream.

EXERCISE 12.12

Find and correct the 10 subject–verb agreement errors in the following paragraphs.

In a recent interview, hockey coach Randy Carlisle noted that the Stanley Cup playoffs, in which his team was not involved, was hard fought, but didn't feature very much excitement. "It was a grinding type of puck movement," he noted, adding that this is the type of hockey he wants his team to play. "There wasn't a lot of goals scored off the rush," he said, since most of the scoring took place during penalties. "I think the games were played tight to the vest, but the pace of the games were up there," Coach Carlisle added.

So it is that fans of Randy Carlisle's team in the coming season is in for slow-moving, defensive hockey that will lull even the most enthusiastic fan to sleep. However, if the team along with Carlisle and his managers are successful, neither the fans nor the team owner are going to complain. Each fan, when assessing the success or failure of the players at the end of the season, have reason to applaud Carlisle's approach if the team wins. On the other hand, if the millionaire players and the organization itself is not successful, then this boring style of hockey will ensure that Carlisle's tenure behind the bench is short. Anyone in Carlisle's position, whether coach or players, feel the enormous pressure of fan expectations, and neither Coach Carlisle nor his general manager nor his highly paid players wants to fail to meet those expectations.

EXERCISE **12.13**

Complete the sentences below using present tense verbs. After you complete each set, check the answers on page 425 to see whether the verbs should be singular or plural.

1. Neither my supervisor nor her superiors

2. Everybody with two or more part-time jobs

3. Not the lead singer but the backup vocalists

4. A flock of geese

5. Every one of the company's employees

6. Fifty-five dollars

7. The actors, as well as the director,

8. Either French Fries or poutine

9. Not one of the witnesses

10. The department, including the clerical staff and the technicians,

EXERCISE **12.14**

Write 10 sentences, choosing the subjects we've suggested and using present tense verbs. Then exchange papers with your partner and check the subject–verb agreement in each sentence.

1. Use a unit of time as your subject (e.g., your age).

2. Use a compound subject.

3. Use *no one* as your subject.

4. Use *everything* as your subject.

5. Use *neither ... nor* as your subject.

6. Use *either ... or* as your subject.

7. Use a singular subject + *together with*.

8. Use a plural subject + *in addition to*.

9. Use your own height as your subject.

10. Use a compound subject joined by *or*.

The Summary box on the next page contains a summary of the rules governing subject–verb agreement. Review these rules carefully before you do the Mastery Test for this chapter.

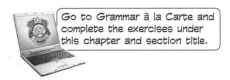

Go to Grammar à la Carte and complete the exercises under this chapter and section title.

SUMMARY

- Subjects and verbs must agree: both must be singular, or both must be plural.
- The subject of a sentence is never in a prepositional phrase.
- Pronouns ending in *-one*, *-thing*, or *-body* are singular and require singular verbs.
- Subjects joined by *and* are always plural.
- When subjects are joined by *or, either ... or, neither ... nor*, or *not ... but*, the verb agrees with the subject that is closest to it.
- When looking for the subject in a sentence, ignore phrases beginning with *as well as, including, in addition to, like, together with*, and so on. They are prepositional phrases.
- When *each, either*, and *neither* are used as subjects, they require singular verbs.
- Collective nouns are usually singular.
- Units of money, time, mass, length, and distance are always singular.

Grammar

EXERCISE **12.15**

As a final check of your mastery of subject–verb agreement, correct the following sentences. We suggest that you review the information in the Summary box before you tackle this exercise.

1. Not religious beliefs but ethnic hatred are to blame for much of the political unrest in the Middle East.

2. Everyone who knows egotists agree on their one good quality: they don't talk about other people.

3. There are three things I just don't understand: numbers and arithmetic.

4. Arguing against your position is the captain of the college debating team and a professor of English.

5. As a result of the loss in game seven, neither the coach nor the assistant coaches is going to be rehired.

6. The majority of students in our survey are against raising tuition or increasing class sizes.

7. Northern Dancer, along with Secretariat, Man O' War, and Nijinsky, are among the greatest thoroughbred horses of all time.

8. Every version of Murphy's Law apply to a common situation, but our favourite is the Law of the Bath: "When a body is fully immersed in water, the telephone will ring."

9. Either a hurricane or the tropical storms that swirl around the Caribbean in the fall are sure to disrupt our September vacation.

10. Whenever we push forward, the crowd around the musicians and their staff push back.

GRAMMAR À LA CARTE

- Looking for more opportunities to practise? Want to see what you need to review before the big test? Visit NELSONbrain.com and log in to **Grammar à la Carte** for *The Bare Essentials, Form A,* to access additional exercises! These Web exercises are graded automatically, so you will know instantly whether or not you have mastered the material.

Keeping Your Tenses Consistent 13

Verbs are time markers. Changes in tense express changes in time: past, present, or future.

I (was) hired yesterday; I (hope) this job (will last) longer than my last one.

past   present   future

Sometimes, as in the sentence above, it is necessary to use several different tenses in a single sentence to get the meaning across. But most of the time, whether you're writing a sentence or a paragraph, you use one tense throughout. Normally, you choose either the past or the present tense, depending on the nature of your topic. (Few paragraphs are written completely in the future tense.) The rule to follow appears at the top of the next page.

Don't change tense unless the meaning of the sentence requires it.

Readers like and expect consistency. If you begin a sentence with "I argued, protested, and even appealed to his masculine pride," the reader will tune in to the past tense verbs and expect any other verbs in the sentence to be in the past tense, too. So, if you finish the sentence with "... but he looks at me with those big brown eyes and gets me to pay for dinner," your readers will be yanked out of one time frame into another. Such abrupt jolts are uncomfortable, and readers don't like them.

Shifting tenses is like shifting gears: it should be done smoothly and when necessary—never abruptly, out of carelessness, or on a whim. Avoid causing verbal whiplash: keep your tenses consistent. Consider these two examples, both of which shift tenses inappropriately.

Problem:	I'm *standing* right behind Sula when she suddenly *screamed*.
Solution 1:	I *was standing* right behind Sula when she suddenly *screamed*.
Solution 2:	I'm *standing* right behind Sula when she suddenly *screams*.

Problem:	Kevin *procrastinated* until the last possible minute and then *begins* to write his paper. When he *gets* halfway through, he *decided* to change his topic.
Solution 1:	Kevin *procrastinated* until the last possible minute and then *began* to write his paper. When he *got* halfway through, he *decided* to change his topic.
Solution 2:	Kevin *procrastinates* until the last possible minute and then *begins* to write his paper. When he *gets* halfway through, he *decides* to change his topic.

Now look at this example, which expresses a more complex idea.

Problem:	I *handed* my paper in just before the deadline, but when I *see* the professor the next day, she *says* it was late, so I *will lose* marks.

This sentence is a hopeless muddle. It begins with the past tense, shifts to the present for no reason, and ends with the future.

Solution:	I *handed* my paper in just before the deadline, but when I *saw* the professor the next day, she *said* it was late, so I *will lose* marks.

Here the past tense is used consistently until the last clause, where the shift to future tense is appropriate to the meaning.

In the following exercises, most—but not all—of the sentences contain unnecessary tense shifts. Use the first verb in each sentence as your time marker and change the tense(s) of the other verb(s) to agree with it. Answers for exercises in this chapter begin on page 425.

EXERCISE **13.1**

1. I enjoy my work, but I was not going to let it take over my life.

2. The umpire stands there, unable to believe what he was seeing.

3. Even though he was tired from a long day at work, Jay makes it to the band rehearsal on time.

4. "The abdominal cavity contains the bowels, of which there were five: a, e, i, o, and u." (Student answer on a science test)

5. There will be a parade on Canada Day and the mayor is the grand marshal.

6. The goalie must not move from his stand until the penalty kicker makes contact with the ball.

7. When the server goes down, no one in the office was able to work.

8. We told Dana the exam was scheduled for 2:00 p.m., but she doesn't believe us and goes to the gym.

9. Mario goes to the fridge, gets a cold can of pop, and proceeded to drink it without offering me anything.

10. "I keep liquor on hand just in case I saw a snake, which I also kept on hand." (W. C. Fields)

EXERCISE **13.2**

1. The class had just ended when in walks Wesley.

2. The game was exciting to watch, but the wrong team wins on the last play.

3. First, he backcombed his hair into spikes, and then he coats it with glue.

4. The lights dimmed and the crowd held its breath; the Biebs keeps them waiting for another minute or so before he explodes onto the stage.

5. The Peter Principle states that every employee will rise to his or her level of incompetence.

6. Just as time ran out, Perry launches a three-point attempt from mid-court, but it misses the basket and the Chiefs lost their final home game.

7. The party was just getting started when she decides it's time to leave.

8. We'll do our best to be polite, but it was going to be difficult.

9. You will live a happy and healthy life until your forties, when you meet a beautiful, dark-haired woman who makes you miserable, breaks your heart, ruined your health, and left you for another man.

10. I used to smoke, drink, and eat poutine whenever I could until I had a bout of indigestion that I think is a heart attack and scares me into eating a healthier diet.

EXERCISE **13.3**

Correct the 25 faulty time shifts in the following paragraph. Use the italicized verb as your time marker. Then check your answers.

A woman *walked* into a veterinary office and places a very limp duck on the examination table. The vet checks the duck for vital signs and then shakes his head sadly and tells the woman that her pet is dead. Terribly upset, the woman insists the vet perform more tests to confirm that indeed her pet will be deceased. The vet leaves the room and comes back with a Labrador retriever, which proceeds to sniff the duck all over its body. After a moment, the dog sighs and shakes her head. Then a sleek Persian cat enters the room and examines the duck from head to toe or, rather, webbed foot. The cat, too, sadly shakes its head and sighs heavily. The vet tells the woman that the animals confirm his diagnosis: her pet is dead. Then he presents the woman with a bill for $350. She is outraged, given that the vet has spent less than 10 minutes examining her duck. The vet explains that his bill is $50. The Lab report and the cat scan are $150 each.

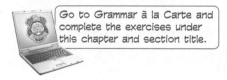

Go to Grammar à la Carte and complete the exercises under this chapter and section title.

EXERCISE **13.4**

Correct the 15 faulty time shifts in the following paragraph. Use the italicized verb as your time marker.

Movies *provide* us with guidelines that helped to shape our preferences in fashion, language, and even food. However, there were conventions common to almost all films that we accepted without critical thought, even though when we examined them, they will make no sense.

For example, in movies, people from other countries did not speak their own language but always spoke in heavily accented English. Kitchens did not have light switches, and characters entering the kitchen at night will always open the fridge to light the entire room. If a room other than the kitchen needed to be lit at night, a single match did the job nicely. Cars that crash almost always exploded and will burst into flames. All beds in movies had special L-shaped sheets that reached up to armpit level on a woman but only to waist level on the man lying next to her. There are hundreds of other examples of silly movie conventions, and spotting them can make even dull films more enjoyable!

GRAMMAR À LA CARTE

- Looking for more opportunities to practise? Want to see what you need to review before the big test? Visit NELSONbrain.com and log in to **Grammar à la Carte** for *The Bare Essentials, Form A,* to access additional exercises! These Web exercises are graded automatically, so you will know instantly whether or not you have mastered the material.

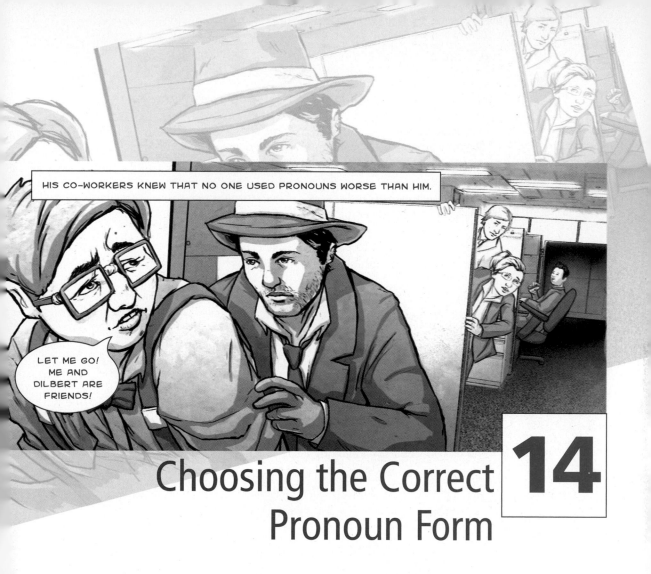

HIS CO-WORKERS KNEW THAT NO ONE USED PRONOUNS WORSE THAN HIM.

LET ME GO! ME AND DILBERT ARE FRIENDS!

Choosing the Correct Pronoun Form

14

"Pronoun? That's just a noun used by a professional!" When a character in a television sitcom spoke this line, the audience cracked up. His TV wife corrected him, pointing out that a pronoun is a word that stands in for a noun, replacing it in a sentence so the noun doesn't have to be repeated. His response: "Both answers are acceptable."

Of course, he's wrong, and his wife is right. (In sitcoms, the wife is always right.) Generally, pronouns are not well understood. In this chapter and the two following, we will look at the three aspects of pronoun usage that can trip you up if you're not careful: **pronoun form**, **agreement**, and **consistency**. We will also consider the special problem of using pronouns in a way that avoids sexist language.

Three kinds of pronouns can cause difficulty for writers:

Personal pronouns	Examples: *I, we, she, they*
Relative pronouns	Examples: *who, whom, which, that*
Indefinite pronouns	Examples: *any, somebody, none, each*

The first thing you need to do is be sure you are using correct pronoun form. Look at these examples of incorrect pronoun usage:

Her and me offered to pick up the car.
Between you and I, I think Ted's mother does his homework.

How do you know which form of a pronoun to use? The answer depends on the pronoun's place and function in your sentence.

SUBJECT AND OBJECT PRONOUNS

There are two forms of personal pronouns. One is used for subjects, and one is used for objects. Pronoun errors occur when you confuse the two. In Chapter 5, you learned to identify the subject of a sentence. Keep that information in mind as you learn the following basic rule.

> When the subject of a sentence is (or is referred to by) a pronoun, that pronoun must be in **subject** form; otherwise, use the **object** form.

Subject Pronouns

Singular	*Plural*
I	we
you	you
he, she, it, one	they

She and *I* offered to pick up the car.
(The pronouns are the subject of the sentence.)

The lucky <u>winners</u> of the free tickets to the World Wrestling Championships <u>are</u> *they*.
(The pronoun refers to the subject of the sentence, *winners*.)

The only <u>person</u> who got an A in the course <u>was</u> *she*.
(The pronoun refers to the subject of the sentence, *person*.)

We serious <u>bikers</u> <u>prefer</u> Harleys to Hondas.
(The pronoun refers to the subject of the sentence, *bikers*.)

Object Pronouns

Singular	*Plural*
me	us
you	you
him, her, it, one	them

Between you and *me*, <u>I</u> <u>think</u> Ted's mother does his homework.
(*Me* is not the subject of the sentence; it is one of the objects of the preposition *between*.)

Brooke <u>saw</u> *him* and *me* having coffee at Tim Hortons.
(*Him* and *me* are not the subject of the verb *saw*; Brooke is, so the pronouns must be in the object form.)

The <u>police</u> <u>are</u> always suspicious of *us* bikers.
(*Us* does not refer to the subject of the sentence, *police*; it refers to *bikers*, the object of the preposition *of*.)

Be especially careful with pronouns that occur in compound subjects or after prepositions. If you remember the following two rules, you'll be able to eliminate most potential errors in pronoun form.

1. All pronouns in a compound (multiple) subject are *always* in subject form.
2. Pronouns that follow a preposition are *always* in object form.

<u>*She*</u> and <u>*I*</u> <u>have</u> season's tickets.
(The pronouns are used as a compound subject.)

We are delighted for *you* and *her*.
(The pronouns follow the preposition *for*.)

When you're dealing with a pair of pronouns and can't decide which form to use, try this test. Mentally cross out one pronoun at a time, then read aloud the sentence you've created. Applying this technique to the first example above, you get "*She* has tickets" and "*I* have tickets." Both sound right and are correct. In the second sentence, if you try the pronouns separately, you get "We are delighted for *you*" and "We are delighted for *her*." Again, you know by the sound that these are the correct forms. (You would never say "*Her* had tickets" or "*Me* had tickets" or "We are delighted for *she*.") If you deal with paired pronouns one at a time, you are unlikely to choose the wrong form.

Note, too, that when a pair of pronouns includes *I* or *me*, that pronoun comes last. For example, we write "between *you* and *me*" (not "between *me* and *you*"); we write "*she* and *I*" (not "*I* and *she*"). There is no grammatical reason for this rule. It's based on courtesy. Good manners require that you speak of others first and yourself last.

EXERCISE **14.1**

Choose the correct pronouns from the words given in parentheses. Answers for exercises in this chapter begin on page 426.

1. Liam and (I/me) stayed up all night trying to complete our assignment.
2. There wasn't much (us/we) could do to rescue it, however.
3. Ava and Katy were supposed to be in our group, but neither of (they/them) showed up.
4. When (us/we) poor, sleep-deprived students submitted the assignment, our professor glared at (us/we).
5. Between (us/we), (us/we) had managed to produce barely four pages.
6. After all, what do Liam and (I/me) know about the topic assigned to (us/we)?
7. Both of (us/we) thought "relative deprivation" had something to do with families.
8. (He/Him) and (I/me) spent hours writing about being grounded by our fathers, forgetting our mothers' birthdays, and suffering our older siblings' bullying.
9. It never occurred to (he/him) or (I/me) that "relative deprivation" was a definition of poverty.
10. Liam and (I/me) have been frequently late and often absent from class this term, so when the prof adds our "class participation" mark to the grade we get on our major paper, whose topic we misinterpreted, it's unlikely that Liam and (I/me) can count on an A in sociology.

EXERCISE **14.2**

The following exercise contains 10 errors in pronoun form. Can you find and correct them?

1. Her and her family are strict vegans; they don't eat dairy products, honey, or eggs.

2. Him and his brothers started a yard maintenance company last summer.

3. The full moon affects humans and animals in strange ways, according to Lisbeth and she.

4. Mila returned the books to the library before me and my boyfriend had a chance to look at them.

5. It is not up to you or I to discipline your brother's children; that responsibility belongs to he and his partner.

6. Luigi seems to be quite comfortable living with his mother; do you think him and Sofia will ever get married?

7. The contract was not signed by the deadline, so me and my boss will be up all night renegotiating it.

8. Except for he and his brother, no one was affected by the poison ivy.

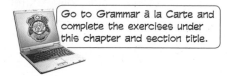

Go to Grammar à la Carte and complete the exercises under this chapter and section title.

USING PRONOUNS IN CONTRAST CONSTRUCTIONS

Choosing the correct pronoun form is more than a matter of wanting not to appear ignorant or careless. Sometimes the form determines the meaning of your sentence. Consider these two sentences:

Jill treats her dog better than *I*.
Jill treats her dog better than *me*.

There's a world of difference between the meaning of the subject form—"Jill treats her dog better than *I* [do]"—and the object form—"Jill treats her dog better than [she treats] *me*."

> When using a pronoun after *than*, *as well as*, or *as*, decide whether you mean to contrast the pronoun with the subject of the sentence. If you do, use the subject form of the pronoun. If not, use the object form.

Minnie would rather listen to Nelly Furtado than I.
(*I* is contrasted with *Minnie*.)

Minnie would rather listen to Nelly Furtado than me.
(*Me* is contrasted with *Nelly Furtado*.)

Here's a quick way to check that you've used the correct pronoun form. If you've used a subject form, mentally insert a verb after it. If you've used an object form, mentally insert a preposition before it. If your imagined sentences make sense, you have chosen correctly. For example,

Minnie would rather listen to Nelly Furtado than I [would].
Minnie would rather listen to Nelly Furtado than [to] me.

Some writers prefer to leave the additional verb or preposition in place, a practice that eliminates any possibility of confusion.

EXERCISE **14.3**

Correct the errors in the following sentences.

1. No one enjoys old movies more than me.

2. Only a few pasta fanatics can eat spaghetti as fast as him.

3. At last, I have met someone who enjoys grilled liver as much as me!

4. You seem to have even less money than me.

5. Few people in our company flatter the CEO as much as her.

6. Hans is more interested in history and archeology than him.

7. Although they have more talent than us, our team is in better condition.

8. No one in the world eats more doughnuts per capita than us Canadians.

9. Everyone wanted to watch the game except Max and I.

10. He doesn't write as well as me, but he does write faster.

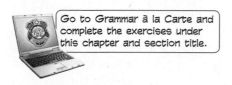

Go to *Grammar à la Carte* and complete the exercises under this chapter and section title.

EXERCISE **14.4**

Correct the faulty pronoun forms in the following sentences.

1. William and me took French lessons; him and his girlfriend are travelling to Normandy in the spring.

2. After my friend and me tried ice fishing, we decided the frostbite wasn't worth the few bony fish we caught.

3. The accounts manager will phone you and she regarding your credit card balances.

4. Kevin dislikes sociology class more than me, but him, more than any of us, needs to learn social skills.

5. Our enjoyment of travel and appreciation for other cultures have brought my partner and me closer together.

6. Him and his two sons have gone to the all-you-can-eat buffet with us several times, and they always eat twice as much food as us.

7. Once you and me get to know each other better, you'll understand why Dalia and I split up.

8. When she and me were chosen for the team, most of the players were veterans, and us goalies were the only rookies.

9. Our dance instructor pushes Megan and I really hard, but he still thinks she has more talent than me.

10. Montreal fans and Leafs fans don't agree on very much, but the time will come when us Leafs fans will have the last laugh. Unfortunately, I may be too old to enjoy it.

GRAMMAR À LA CARTE

- Looking for more opportunities to practise? Want to see what you need to review before the big test? Visit NELSONbrain.com and log in to **Grammar à la Carte** for *The Bare Essentials, Form A,* to access additional exercises! These Web exercises are graded automatically, so you will know instantly whether or not you have mastered the material.

Mastering Pronoun–Antecedent Agreement

15

I am writing in response to your ad for a server and bartender, male or female. Being both, I am applying for the position.

Pronoun confusion can take several forms, and some of the resulting sentences can be unintentionally hilarious. In this chapter, we'll look at how to use pronouns consistently throughout a sentence or paragraph to avoid confusing (and embarrassing) mistakes.

PRONOUN–ANTECEDENT AGREEMENT

The name of this pronoun problem may sound difficult, but the idea is simple. Pronouns are words that substitute for or refer to a person, place, or thing mentioned elsewhere in your sentence or paragraph. The word(s) that a pronoun substitutes for or refers to is called the **antecedent**.

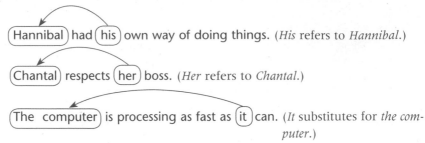

(Hannibal) had (his) own way of doing things. (*His* refers to *Hannibal*.)

(Chantal) respects (her) boss. (*Her* refers to *Chantal*.)

(The computer) is processing as fast as (it) can. (*It* substitutes for *the computer*.)

Usually, as in these three examples, the antecedent comes before the pronoun[1] that refers to it. Here is the rule to remember:

> A pronoun must agree with its antecedent in
> • number (singular or plural)
> • person (first, second, or third)
> • gender (masculine, feminine, or neuter)

Most of the time, you follow this rule without even realizing that you know it. For example, you would never write

Hannibal had *your* own way of doing things.

Chantal respects *its* boss.

The computer is processing as fast as *she* can.

You know these sentences are incorrect even if you may not know exactly why.

There are three kinds of pronoun–antecedent agreement that you need to learn. Unlike the examples above, they are not obvious, and you need to know them so you can watch out for them. The rules you need to learn involve indefinite pronouns ending in -*one*, -*body*, or -*thing*; vague references; and relative pronouns.

---

[1] Strictly speaking, possessive words such as *my*, *his*, *her*, *our*, and *their* are pronominal adjectives rather than pronouns. We are dealing with them in this chapter, however, because they follow the same agreement rule that governs pronouns.

PRONOUNS ENDING IN -*ONE*, -*BODY*, -*THING*

The most common pronoun–antecedent agreement problem involves **indefinite pronouns**:

anyone	anybody	anything
everyone	everybody	everything
no one	nobody	nothing
someone	somebody	something
each (one)		

In Chapter 12, you learned that when these words are used as subjects, they are singular and require singular verbs. So it makes sense that the pronouns that stand for or refer to them must also be singular.

> Antecedents ending in -*one*, -*body*, and -*thing* are singular.
> They must be referred to by singular pronouns: *he, she, it; his, her, its.*

Everyone deserves a break from *her* children now and then.

Everything has *its* place and should be in it.

Everybody is expected to do *his* share of the work.

No one had the courage to express *his* anger at the government's decision.

Now take another look at the last three sentences. Until about 50 years ago, the pronouns *he, him,* and *his* were used with singular antecedents to refer to both men and women. Modern readers are sensitive to gender bias in writing, and most think it inappropriate to use the masculine pronoun to refer to both sexes. As a writer, you should be aware of this sensitivity. If you want to appeal to the broadest possible audience, you should avoid what readers may consider sexist language.

In casual usage, it has become acceptable to use plural pronouns with -*one*, -*body*, and -*thing* antecedents. Although they are grammatically singular, they are often plural in meaning, and in conversation we tend to say

Everybody is expected to do *their* share of the work.

No one had the courage to express *their* anger at the government's decision.

This usage is acceptable in speech, but it is not acceptable in academic or professional writing.

Writers sometimes make errors in pronoun–antecedent agreement because they are trying to avoid identifying the gender of the person(s) referred to. "Everybody is expected to do *their* share of the work" is grammatically incorrect, as we have seen; however, it does avoid making "everybody" male or "everybody" female. The writer could replace the plural *their* with the singular and non-sexist *his or her*—"Everybody is expected to do *his or her* share of the work"—but *his or her* sounds clumsy if it is used frequently.

There are two better ways to solve the problem.

1. Revise the sentence to leave out the pronoun.

Everybody is expected to share the work.

No one had the courage to protest against the government's decision.

Such creative avoidance of gender-specific language or incorrect constructions can be an interesting intellectual challenge. The results sometimes sound a little artificial, however. The second solution is easier to accomplish.

2. Revise the sentence to make both the antecedent and the pronoun plural.

We are all expected to do *our* share of the work.

The staff did not have the courage to express *their* anger at the government's decision.

Here are a couple of examples for you to study:

Problem: *Everybody* has been given *his* assignment.
Revision 1: *Everybody* has been given *an* assignment.
Revision 2: *All* of the students have been given *their* assignments.

Problem: *No one* likes to have *his* writing corrected.
Revision 1: *No one* likes to have writing assignments corrected.
Revision 2: Most *people* dislike having *their* writing corrected.

If you are writing on a word processor, you may be able to use the grammar checker to ensure agreement between indefinite pronouns and their antecedents. Many grammar checkers will catch this error. The revisions offered by the checker may not be elegant, but they are usually technically correct. This revision step takes less time than you might think and is well worth it, especially if your instructor has asked for a formal paper or report.

EXERCISE **15.1**

Identify the most appropriate word(s) from the choices given in parentheses. The symbol *** means no pronoun is necessary. Read each sentence through to the end before deciding on your answers. Check your answers before continuing. Answers for this chapter begin on page 427.

1. Everyone is a product of (his or her/their/***) environment as well as heredity.
2. Nobody as smart as you are needs help with (her or his/their/your/***) homework.
3. The accident could not have been avoided, and fortunately no one was hurt, so no one should have to (say they are sorry/say he or she is sorry/apologize).
4. Everyone who pays (his or her/their/the/***) membership fee in advance will receive a free session with a personal trainer.
5. It seemed that everybody in the mall was talking on (his/her/their/a) cellphone.
6. We will do our best to return everything found in the locker room to (his/her/its/their) owner.
7. Everyone from the provincial premiers to front-line health care providers agrees that electronic health records could provide huge gains in (one's/their/***) efficiency.
8. Would someone kindly lend (a/her/his/their) copy of the text to Basil?
9. A bore is someone who sticks to (his/their) own opinion even after we have enlightened (him/them) with ours.
10. Anyone who wants an A for (his/their/this) essay should see me after class and give me (his/their/a) cheque.

EXERCISE **15.2**

1. If anyone wants to change (his or her/their) mind, now is the time.
2. Each of the candidates has (his/her/their) appeal, but I choose bachelorette number 3.
3. Anyone who faithfully watches *The Bachelorette* needs to get out of (his/her/the/their) house more often.
4. Every movie-, theatre-, and concert-goer knows how annoying it is to have (an/her/his/their) evening's enjoyment spoiled by a ringing cellphone.
5. Everyone from the Bank of Canada to academics, marketers, and urban planners uses Statistics Canada surveys as the basis for (her or his/their/***) research.
6. When you turn off the highway, (one/you) must be very careful because the roads leading to the lake are not well marked.

7. Ultimate Frisbee is a game that every player enjoys, whether (his/her/the/their) team finishes first or last.

8. Put the sign at the curb so anyone looking for our yard sale won't have to waste (his/ her/their/***) time driving around the neighbourhood.

9. A bandleader is someone who is not afraid to face (his/her/the/their) music.

10. Bridging the gap between the young upstarts who develop smartphone apps and the highly structured, rule-bound world of health care (she is/ he is/they are) creating them for is not easy.

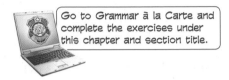

Go to Grammar à la Carte and complete the exercises under this chapter and section title.

VAGUE REFERENCES

Avoiding the second potential difficulty with pronoun–antecedent agreement requires common sense and the ability to put yourself in your reader's place. If you look at your writing from your reader's point of view, it is unlikely that you will break the following rule.

> Every pronoun must have a clearly identifiable antecedent.

The mistake that occurs when you fail to follow this rule is called **vague reference**.

> Luca pointed to his brother and said that he had saved his life.

Who saved whom? Here's another:

> Emma wrote a song about her sister when she was five years old.

Is the song about a five-year-old sister, or was Emma a musically talented child?

In sentences like these, you can only guess the meaning because you don't know who the pronouns refer to. The antecedents are not clear. You can make such sentences less confusing either by using proper names (Luca, Emma) more frequently or by changing the sentences around. These solutions aren't difficult; they just take a little time and some imagination. Try them on our examples.

Another type of vague reference occurs when there is no antecedent for the pronoun to refer to.

Yuri loves off-road rallies and would like to try *it* himself. (Try what?)

Snowboarding is Olivia's favourite sport, and she's hoping to get *one* for her birthday. (One what?)

My roommate chain-smokes constantly, *which* I hate. (There is no noun or pronoun for *which* to refer to.)

My sister's work schedule overlaps with her husband's. *This* creates child-care problems. (There is no noun or pronoun for *this* to refer to.)

How would you revise these sentences? Try it, and then see our suggestions below.

Suggestions: Yuri loves off-road rallies and would like to try *the sport* himself.

Snowboarding is Olivia's favourite sport, and she's hoping to get *a board* for her birthday.

My roommate is an incurable chain-smoker, *which* I hate.

My sister's work schedule overlaps with her husband's. *This* conflict creates child-care problems.

Make sure that every pronoun has a clear antecedent and that every pronoun agrees with its antecedent. Both must be singular, or both must be plural. Once you have mastered this principle, you'll have no trouble with pronoun–antecedent agreement.

EXERCISE **15.3**

Correct the following sentences where necessary. There are several ways to fix these sentences. In some cases, the antecedent is missing, and you need to supply one. In other cases, the antecedent is so vague that the meaning of the sentence can be interpreted in more than one way; you need to rewrite these sentences to make the meaning clear.

1. Whenever Connor and Carlos play poker, he stacks the deck.

2. Fishing is fun even when I don't catch one.

3. Every time Cameron looked at the dog, he barked.

4. If your pet mouse won't eat its food, feed it to the cat.

5. When the baby has finished drinking, it should be sterilized in boiling water.

6. The lifeguard didn't hear my cry for help, which was because he was wearing earplugs.

7. The payroll manager met with the chief steward to tell her it was not her responsibility to collect union dues.

8. My roommate and I, together with a couple of the girls from upstairs, play poker and blackjack once a week. They are a lot of fun.

9. Her son scored the winning goal three minutes into overtime, which Bella missed because she was arguing with another parent.

10. Our college strictly enforces the "no smoking" policy, so you can't have one even outside on campus.

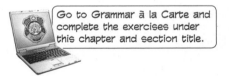

Go to Grammar à la Carte and complete the exercises under this chapter and section title.

RELATIVE PRONOUNS

The third potential difficulty with pronoun–antecedent agreement is how to use relative pronouns—*who, whom, which,* and *that*—correctly. Relative pronouns must refer to someone or something already mentioned in the sentence. Here is the guideline to follow:

Use *who* and *whom* to refer to people.
Use *that* and *which* to refer to everything else.

The chef *who* prepared this meal deserves a medal.

The servers *who* presented it deserve to be fired.

The appetizer *that* I ordered was buried under a gluey, tasteless sauce.

My soup, *which* was cold, arrived at the same time as my main course.

My father's meal, *which* was delicious, demonstrated the talent *that* the chef is famous for.

Whether you need *who* or *whom*[2] depends on the pronoun's place and function in your sentence. Apply the basic pronoun rule:

> If the pronoun is, or refers to, the subject of the sentence, use *who*. Otherwise, use *whom*. Or you can revise the sentence to eliminate the pronoun.

It was Madison *who* drew the winning ticket for a week's holiday in Moose Factory. (The pronoun refers to the subject of the sentence, *Madison*.)

The trip's promoters were willing to settle for *whomever* they could get. (The pronoun does not refer to the subject, *promoters*; it is the object of the preposition *for*.)

A better solution is to solve the problem by rewriting the sentence so that you don't need either *who* or *whom*.

Madison drew the winning ticket for a week's holiday in Moose Factory.

The trip's promoters were willing to settle for anyone they could get.

That is required more often than *which*. You should use *which* only in a clause that is separated from the rest of the sentence by commas. (See Chapter 17, "The Comma," Rule 4, page 225.)

The moose *that* I met looked hostile.
The moose, *which* was standing right in front of my car, looked hostile.

---

[2] The distinction between *who* and *whom* has all but disappeared in spoken English and is becoming increasingly rare in written English. Ask your instructor for guidance.

Grammar

EXERCISE **15.4**

Correct the pronoun errors in the following sentences. Remember: use *who* to refer to people; use *that* or *which* to refer to everything else.

1. We were pretty sure Miss Grundy knew who was responsible for the cartoon which she found on her board this morning.

2. A grouch is a person that knows himself and isn't happy about it.

3. The sales clerk that sold me my DVD player didn't know what he was talking about.

4. Everyone that was at the party had a good time, although a few had more punch than was good for them.

5. The open-office concept sounds good to anyone that has worked in a stuffy little cubicle all day.

6. I wonder why we are so often attracted to people that are totally unsuitable for us.

7. Is this the dog which attacked the mail carrier that carries a squirt gun?

8. I think the ideal domestic companions would be a cat who cuddles and a husband that purrs.

9. Thanks to the Internet, I regularly order supplies from companies which are located in cities around the world.

10. Sales staff that want to earn promotions must have good interpersonal skills as well as thorough knowledge of the products which they are selling.

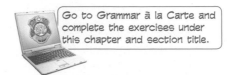

Go to Grammar à la Carte and complete the exercises under this chapter and section title.

EXERCISE **15.5**

Revise the following paragraphs to eliminate the 15 pronoun–antecedent agreement errors. If you change a subject from singular to plural, don't forget to change the verb to agree. Both must be correct for your answer to be right. Some of your answers may differ from our suggestions and still be correct. Ask your instructor to make the final call.

Computing is not something I take to naturally, and although I have quite a good one, I do not trust it. Anyone that is like me knows their communication with the outside world depends on their computer and the Internet, so when something goes wrong, we need help right away. Fortunately, I have a neighbour that is a computer genius. He is only 11 years old, but Raj is someone that seems to understand instinctively how they can solve computer issues.

Before calling Raj for help, I try everything I can think of to fix my frequent computer problems because Raj is a person with little patience for their less competent acquaintances. Raj is an intellectual that doesn't enjoy sports, but his parents make him go outside from time to time, and he and I kick one around in the yard. I waited until we had played for a few minutes before casually asking him if he would take a look at my current computing problem. He was delighted to quit kicking the soccer ball in favour of computing, and came right in.

Anyone that knows anything about computers knows when they are in the presence of genius. Raj's fingers flew over the keyboard, and the computer responded with screens of information I had never seen before, almost purring with satisfaction as someone who knew what they were doing took the machine through its paces. After a couple of minutes, Raj sat back and told me the problem was fixed.

No one wants to appear ignorant, especially in front of their 11-year-old neighbour, so, not really expecting to understand, I asked him if he could tell me what the problem was. Raj got up and headed for the door while telling me it was a common error with mine, an error called ID ten T. Seeing the puzzled look on my face, he told me to write it down and I would understand. As the door slammed behind him, I wrote out ID10T, and understood.

SUMMARY

- Every pronoun must agree with its antecedent (a word or phrase mentioned, usually earlier, in the sentence or paragraph). Both must be singular, or both must be plural.
- Antecedents ending in -one, -body, and -thing are singular and must be referred to by singular pronouns: *he, she, it; his, her, its.*
- A pronoun must clearly refer to a specific antecedent.
- Use *who/whom* to refer to people; use *that* and *which* to refer to animals, objects, and ideas.
- As a courtesy to your reader, try to make your writing gender neutral.

Correct the 15 errors in the following paragraph. Part of the challenge in this Mastery Test is to make the paragraph not only grammatically correct but also free of sexist language. Before you try the test, we suggest that you review the rules for pronoun–antecedent agreement in the Summary box on page 204.

Everyone that works in retail sales knows that their job has changed in the past 10 or 15 years. New emphasis on service and satisfaction has changed the way customers and salespeople interact. The sales clerk understands that satisfied customers that are likely to be repeat customers are the best job insurance they can have.

Recently, forward-thinking corporations and institutions have begun to apply "customer satisfaction" principles to another sector which has traditionally been ignored: its own employees. Each year, *Report on Business* magazine publishes a list of the top 50 best companies to work for. A few exceptional companies make the list every year, and all have several practices in common.

First, their employee feels recognized and valued for his contribution to corporate or institutional goals. Second, those goals are clear, meaningful, and realistic. Third, every manager maintains communication with their employees through regular meetings that allow them to get to know them.

Notice that compensation is not on this list of key attributes. Most corporations now recognize competitive pay rates and pay its employees appropriately. More

Grammar

important, the employee feels that they are fairly compensated for the work they do. And even more important than a paycheque is recognition, that may be something as simple as a manager personally congratulating an employee on their fifth-year anniversary with the company. It is no coincidence that, every year, the list of the top 50 best companies to work for includes some of the most successful companies in its field.

GRAMMAR À LA CARTE

- Looking for more opportunities to practise? Want to see what you need to review before the big test? Visit NELSONbrain.com and log in to **Grammar à la Carte** for *The Bare Essentials, Form A,* to access additional exercises! These Web exercises are graded automatically, so you will know instantly whether or not you have mastered the material.

ONE CAN BE AN UN-GRAMMATICAL EVEN IF YOU ARE RICH AND FAMOUS.

FAULTY PERSON AGREEMENT IS LOW CLASS ANYWHERE.

Maintaining Person Agreement 16

So far, we have focused on using pronouns correctly and clearly within a sentence. Now let's turn to the problem of **person agreement**, which means using pronouns consistently between sentences or throughout a paragraph or an essay. There are three categories of person that we use when we write or speak:

	Singular	Plural
First person	I; me	we; us
Second person	you	you
Third person	she, he, it, one; her, him and all pronouns ending in -one, -body, -thing	they; them

Here is the rule for person agreement:

> Do not mix "persons" unless the meaning requires it.

In other words, be consistent. If you begin a sentence using a second-person pronoun, you should use the second person all the way through. Look at this sentence:

If *you* want to succeed, *one* must work hard.

Mixing second-person *you* with third-person *one* is the most common error. Sometimes mixed pronouns can puzzle or mislead the reader, as in this sentence:

Everyone must shower before you go into the pool. (Why should everyone shower if you are the only person swimming?)

Most of the time, however, lack of agreement among pronouns is just poor style, as this example illustrates:

One can live happily in Vancouver if *you* have a sturdy umbrella.

We can correct this error by using the second person throughout:

(1) *You* can live happily in Vancouver if *you* have a sturdy umbrella.

We can also correct it by using the third person throughout:

(2) *One* can live happily in Vancouver if *one* has a sturdy umbrella.

or

(3) *One* can live happily in Vancouver if *he or she* has a sturdy umbrella.

These last three sentences raise two points of style that you should remember.

> 1. Don't overuse *one.*

All three revised sentences are grammatically correct, but they make different impressions on the reader, and impressions are an important part of communication.

- The first sentence, in the second person, sounds the most informal—like something you would say. It's a bit casual for general writing purposes.
- The second sentence, which uses *one* twice, sounds the most formal—even a little stuffy.
- The third sentence falls between the other two in formality. It is the one you'd be most likely to use in writing for school or business.

Although it is grammatically correct and non-sexist, this third sentence raises another problem. Frequent use of the *he or she* construction in a continuous prose passage, whether that passage is as short as a sentence or as long as a paper, is guaranteed to irritate your reader.

> 2. Don't overuse *he or she*.

He or she is inclusive, but it is a wordy construction. If used too frequently, the reader cannot help shifting focus from what you're saying to how you're saying it. The best writing is transparent—that is, it doesn't call attention to itself. If your reader becomes distracted by your style, your meaning is lost. Consider this sentence:

A student can easily pass this course if he or she applies himself or herself to his or her studies.

Readers deserve better. There are two better solutions to this problem, and they are already familiar to you because they are the same as those for making pronouns ending in *-one, -body,* or *-thing* agree with their antecedents.

- You can rewrite the sentence without using pronouns.

A student can easily pass this course by applying good study habits.

- You can change the whole sentence to the plural.

Students can easily pass this course if they apply themselves to their studies.

Grammar

EXERCISE **16.1**

Select the most appropriate word(s) from the choices given in parentheses. Answers for exercises in this chapter begin on page 430.

1. You might consider a career in broadcasting if (you have/one has) acting or public speaking experience.
2. If you are looking for sturdy, inexpensive shoes, (one/you) can get a pair at the bowling alley for only two dollars.
3. The penalties for plagiarism are severe, but most of us don't think about penalties until after (we've/you've) been caught.
4. When I was in grade school, (our/their/your) principal strictly enforced the rules.
5. Too late, we realized the test would have been easy if (one/you/we) had done (their/your/our) homework during the term.
6. When a man is hungry, (he is/you are) not likely to be satisfied with a slice of quiche and a cup of tea.
7. You can save a lot of time if (one fills/we fill/you fill) out the forms before going to the passport office.
8. Always read through the entire test before (one begins/you begin) to answer the questions.
9. Most people have encountered an inspiring teacher somewhere in (one's/ their/your) past.
10. Our happiness is determined by (one's/our/your/their) quality of life, not (one's/our/your/their) wealth.

EXERCISE **16.2**

Correct the errors in pronoun consistency in the following sentences.

1. A speed limit is the speed you go as soon as one sees a police car.

2. People who don't learn from history are doomed to find yourself back in Grade 9 for a second try.

3. If you want to succeed in business, one must be well groomed and conservatively dressed.

4. If you are convicted on that charge, a fine is the least of one's worries.

5. One cannot lead any farther than you have already gone.

6. "Middle age is that time of life when you've met so many people that everyone one meets reminds one of somebody else." (Ogden Nash)

7. "Never try to impress a woman, because if one does, she'll expect you to keep up that standard for the rest of their life." (W. C. Fields)

8. Many people are happy to ride with one in a limo, but what you want is someone who will take the bus with them when the limo breaks down.

9. Some women enjoy the pursuit of their ideal mate more than the capture and domestication of her prey.

10. When a company fails to maintain and upgrade their equipment, they often pay a high price for their neglect.

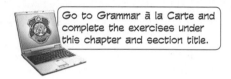

Go to Grammar à la Carte and complete the exercises under this chapter and section title.

EXERCISE **16.3**

Correct the following sentences where necessary. For those sentences containing language that might be considered sexist, try correcting them twice: first, to ensure person agreement; second, to avoid gender bias. Turn to page 430 to compare your answers with our suggestions.

1. It has taken Canadians far too long to acknowledge the seriousness of our environmental problems.

2. No one tests the depth of a river with both of their feet. (Ashanti proverb)

3. If you can't cope with the pressure, one must expect to be replaced by someone who can.

4. If any of you have signed up to attend the class party next Friday, their tickets are now available in the Student Association office.

5. Some people are like Slinkys: they have no useful purpose, but you can't help but smile when one sees them tumble down the stairs.

6. When they feel frustrated or angry, it can sometimes be difficult for a teenager to control his temper.

7. "Good health" is nothing more than the slowest rate at which he or she can die.

8. In the 1960s, some people took LSD to make the world seem weird; now the world *is* weird, and you take Prozac to make it seem normal.

9. When taking multiple-choice tests, don't stop and think about questions you aren't sure of. Finish the test and then go back to the questions that stumped one.

10. When you're gardening, the best way to make sure one is removing a weed and not a plant is to grasp it firmly at the base of the stem and pull. If they come out easily, they are a plant.

EXERCISE **16.4**

Find and correct the inconsistencies in pronoun person in the following paragraph. Revise the paragraph twice: (1) once in the second person and (2) once in the third person. Then compare your two revisions. Which version do you prefer? Why?

If one is a sports fan, you are already familiar with the astronomical salaries major players make. We fans sometimes lose sight of the fact that our favourite players live in the real world, and their salaries are sometimes out of touch with real life, at least as most people live it. You may be aware, for example, that all-time-favourite basketball player Michael Jordan made nearly $200,000 per day in the last year of his contract. If we compare Jordan's salary with the incomes of other famous people, however, one finds some interesting numbers. For instance, you learn that, in his last year in professional basketball, Jordan earned 200 percent more than the total income of all the presidents of the United States, from George Washington to Barack Obama, *combined*. If we do a little more research, we also discover that, if Jordan were to save and invest all of his income for 250 years, he would accumulate less money than Bill Gates has now.

EXERCISE **16.5**

Rewrite the following paragraphs, changing the 25 third-person pronouns to second-person pronouns and correcting any verb errors that result from your revisions.

If one is searching for a less stressful, more satisfying life, he or she could investigate the "Slow Movement." One could start with the original Slow Food Movement, begun in Italy in 1986 as a protest against fast-food restaurants, specifically McDonald's, which was planning to build a restaurant in Rome near the historic Spanish Steps. The movement's objectives include eating healthy, buying local products, and making meals convivial occasions instead of wolfing down one's food in a crowded, noisy, plastic environment.

One might also look into the Slow City Movement, an organization that certifies cities based on four criteria. To be declared a "Slow City," one's city must respect strict environmental rules, encourage consumption of local products, discourage dependence on cars, and emphasize a sense of community. If the population of one's city is more than 50,000, he or she need not apply, because cities over that size are automatically disqualified from Slow City status.

Third, why not check out the Slow Money Movement? This is an organization dedicated to changing the way one invests. Instead of putting one's money in huge corporations with destructive environmental practices or health issues, like the oil or tobacco industries, the Slow Money Movement encourages one to invest in small food producers, sustainable enterprises, and local farms. Slow Money investors are not aiming to make less money but hoping to use their investments to encourage more responsible, ethical practices.

Another possibility one might find consistent with his or her principles is called simply the "Slow Movement," which promotes the idea of "connectivity." One might find this an appealing concept, as it seeks to make connections among one's social network, environment, culture, food, and community. The Slow Movement promotes ideas such as Slow Travel, which encourages one to avoid packaged tours that zoom frenetically from place to place, in favour of slowing down, staying in one place for a few weeks, and getting to understand a little about the locale. The Slow Movement also promotes Slow Schooling, a type of education that seeks to replace one-size-fits-all learning and standardized testing with "connected learning": connecting students' learning to the community, culture, history, and geography of the place in which they live. The concept of the "edible schoolyard" might also appeal to one: students are responsible for producing, preparing, and serving the food they eat.

One can embrace several different aspects of the slower life, depending on his or her principles and preferences. One does not need to join a formal movement to change the way he or she lives. The concepts behind these movements may give one ideas for revising his or her lifestyle, but maybe one should just consider living life more slowly, whatever that phrase means to him or her.

EXERCISE **16.6**

Rewrite the paragraph in Exercise 16.5 by changing the pronouns from third-person singular to third-person plural throughout. Your first two sentences will read "**People who are searching** for a less stressful, more satisfying life ******* could investigate the "Slow Movement." **They** could start with the original Slow Food Movement ...

EXERCISE **16.7**

With a partner, compare the answers you composed for Exercises 16.5 and 16.6. Discuss the problems you encountered trying to ensure pronoun consistency while still making the paragraphs communicate clearly. Which conversion was more difficult: from third-person singular to second person? Or from third-person singular to third-person plural? Why?

Finally, which of the three versions do you think is easiest to read? Why?

EXERCISE **16.8**

Find and correct the inconsistencies in pronoun person in the following.

1. When one walks through a storm, hold your head up high.

2. "If one picks up a starving dog and makes him prosperous, he will not bite you; that is the principal difference between a dog and a man." (Mark Twain)

3. In this country, you receive more acclaim and a great deal more money as a hockey player than one would as a brain surgeon or even prime minister.

4. When one is revising a paper, you should check to be sure that your pronouns agree in person and number.

5. Why do we always wish for what you don't have, even when you have more than you'll ever need?

6. Denying one's guilt is always an option, but since you were found with syrup all over your face and pastry crumbs on your shirt, a "not guilty" plea may not be one's best option.

7. Ken collects art and wine because he knows that you can always get a return on your investment, and one can sometimes make a large profit; if all else fails, one can simply hang the art and drink the wine.

8. I enjoy living in the country because you don't have to deal with traffic or noise or pollution, and one can always get into the city if you want to.

9. "One can say any foolish thing to a dog, and the dog will give us that look that says, 'Wow, you're right! I never would've thought of that!'" (Dave Barry)

10. A variation of Murphy's Law states, "The probability of meeting someone we know increases exponentially when you are in the presence of someone with whom one does not want to be seen."

UNIT 3 RAPID REVIEW

The passage below contains a total of 15 errors in verb form, subject–verb agreement, pronoun form, pronoun–antecedent agreement, and tense and pronoun consistency. When you've made your corrections, turn to page 433 and compare your answers with ours. For each error you miss, the Answer Key directs you to the chapter you need to review.

[1]Having began a new venture in our lives, we sometimes find that the experience does not meet your expectations. [2]Consider, for example, students that leave home to go to college. [3]They move to a new city, begin a new course of study, start making new friends, and begin to realize how stressful change can be. [4]Add to these challenges the inevitable shift in status that accompany such a move, and we can see why the transition from school to college is found by many students to be far from smooth.

[5]A student accustomed to being an academic, athletic, or social star in high school may find that they have to prove themselves all over again. [6]This is too much for some to cope with, so some former high achievers who fail to measure up in their new environment drop out. [7]These students often tend to quit in their first year, when one should still be experimenting and exploring their options.

[8]Students who were academically successful in high school may have a hard time when them and their less gifted peers move on to college. [9]There is more to be lost by "brains" in an academic environment where marks are

awarded for performance, not effort, and deadlines are not negotiable. [10]These students were often shocked to receive a B or even a C on a mid-term paper. [11]On the other hand, students that made average grades in school are usually pleasantly surprised when they achieve a mark in the 60s or 70s in their first term at college.

[12]Those who were "late bloomers" in high school often treat the postsecondary environment as a fresh start and began to blossom as they find new friends with interests similar to theirs. [13]In contrast, students who were social stars in high school may be frustrated by a new environment that dislodges him or her from the pinnacle of the popularity pyramid.

[14]When they reach their 30s or 40s, people who claim that high school was the best time of their lives often do so because their years in college was disappointing—in part because of their earlier success.

GRAMMAR À LA CARTE

- Looking for more opportunities to practise? Want to see what you need to review before the big test? Visit NELSONbrain.com and log in to **Grammar à la Carte** for *The Bare Essentials, Form A,* to access additional exercises! These Web exercises are graded automatically, so you will know instantly whether or not you have mastered the material.

UNIT 4
Punctuation

Punctuation

UNIT 4 QUICK QUIZ

This Quick Quiz will let you see at a glance which chapters of Unit 4 you need to concentrate on. In the paragraph below, 15 punctuation marks are missing. Go through the paragraph carefully and supply the missing punctuation. (Note: Each pair of quotation marks counts as one punctuation mark.) When you've finished your corrections, turn to page 434 and compare your answers with ours. For each error you miss, the Answer Key that follows the corrected version directs you to the chapter you need to work on.

[1]A hunter who had just shot a duck sent his dog to retrieve it only to discover that the bird had fallen inside a fenced field. [2]The farmer who owned the field was standing nearby so the hunter said, Excuse me that's my duck. [3]The farmer replied, Why is it your duck It's on my property. [4]After some bickering the farmer suggested a groin-kicking contest to decide ownership of the duck. [5]The hunter agreed and braced himself for the first blow. [6]The farmer's reaction suggested he'd had experience with this kind of contest before he took a deep breath drew back his leg and kicked the hunter in the groin so hard that the hunter fell to the ground like a stone. [7]After five minutes, the hunter was able to haul himself to his feet. [8]After 10 minutes he felt well enough to say OK. Now it's my turn. [9]At that, the farmer said "Nah. You can keep the duck."

SHE HAD LEFT OUT THE COMMAS THAT ARE NEEDED TO SEPARATE WORDS PHRASES OR CLAUSES IN A LIST.

SMALL THINGS LIKE DIAMONDS, COMPUTER CHIPS, AND COMMAS CAN, IN SOME CASES, BE IMPORTANT.

The Comma 17

Many writers-in-training tend to sprinkle punctuation like pepper over their prose. Please do not use punctuation to spice up or decorate your writing. Punctuation marks are functional: they indicate to the reader how the various parts of a sentence relate to one another. By changing the punctuation, you can change the meaning of a sentence. Here are two examples to prove the point.

1. An instructor wrote the following sentence on the board and asked the class to punctuate it appropriately: "woman without her man is nothing."

   The men wrote, "Woman, without her man, is nothing."
   The women wrote, "Woman: without her, man is nothing."

2. Now it's your turn. Punctuate this sentence: "I think there is only one person to blame myself."

If you wrote, "I think there is only one person to blame, myself" the reader will understand that you believe only one person—who may or may not be known to you—is to blame.

If you wrote, "I think there is only one person to blame: myself" the reader will understand that you are personally accepting the blame.

The comma is the most frequently used—and misused—punctuation mark in English. Perhaps nothing is so sure a sign of a competent writer as the correct use of commas. This chapter presents four comma rules that cover most situations in which commas are required. If you apply these four rules faithfully, your reader will not be confused by missing or misplaced commas in your writing. And if, as occasionally happens, the sentence you are writing is not covered by one of our four rules, remember the first commandment of comma usage: WHEN IN DOUBT, LEAVE IT OUT.

FOUR COMMA RULES

RULE 1
Use commas to separate three or more items in a series. The items may be expressed in words, phrases, or clauses.

Words	The required subjects in this program are math, physics, and English.
Phrases	"Punctuation marks are the traffic signals of prose: they tell us to slow down, notice this, take a detour, and stop." (Lynne Truss)
Clauses	The wedding was delayed an hour because the groom was hung over, the best man had forgotten the ring, and the bride was in tears.

The comma before the *and* at the end of the list is optional, but we advise you to use it. Occasionally, misunderstandings occur if it is left out.

EXERCISE 17.1

Insert commas where necessary in the following sentences, and then check your answers. Answers for exercises in this chapter begin on page 435.

1. How many of you remember Sporty Baby Scary Posh and Ginger?
2. A panda is a bearlike marsupial that eats shoots and leaves.

3. In a typical Hollywood B Western, the villain rides into town and drinks shoots and leaves.

4. "Rachael Ray finds inspiration in cooking her family and her dogs." (Magazine cover teaser)

5. Early investment of time and money can lead to a luxurious lifestyle international fame and a comfortable retirement.

6. Lee is an all-round athlete; he enjoys skiing cycling swimming and showering.

7. Nicole has strong ambition a cool head good health and an inquiring mind; most people hate her.

8. A good education long-range planning and pure luck led him to wealth acclaim and happiness.

9. Much of the world sees Canada as a land where French is spoken ice and snow are year-round hazards and violent hockey is a favourite pastime.

10. In fluent English and Italian, our tour guide described the construction of Notre Dame Cathedral explained the causes of the French Revolution and listed the ingredients in bouillabaisse.

The second comma rule is already familiar to you. You encountered it in Chapter 7, "Solving Run-On Sentence Problems."

> **RULE 2**
>
> Put a comma between independent clauses when they are joined by
>
> | for | but | so |
> |-----|-----|----|
> | and | or | |
> | nor | yet | |
>
> (You can remember these words easily if you notice that their first letters spell "fanboys.")

I hope I do well in the interview, for I really want this job.

I like Feist, but I prefer Norah Jones.

"We shape our tools, and our tools shape us." (Marshall McLuhan)

I knew I was going to be late, so I went back to sleep.

Be sure that the sentence you are punctuating contains two independent clauses rather than one clause with a single subject and a multiple verb.

<u>We</u> <u>loved</u> the book but <u>hated</u> the movie.
(<u>*We*</u> is the subject, and there are two verbs, <u>*loved*</u> and <u>*hated*</u>. Do not put a comma between two or more verbs that share a single subject.)

<u>We</u> both <u>loved</u> the book, but <u>Kim</u> <u>hated</u> the movie.
(This sentence contains two independent clauses—<u>*We*</u> <u>*loved*</u> and <u>Kim</u> <u>*hated*</u>— joined by *but*. The comma is required here.)

EXERCISE **17.2**

Insert commas where they are needed in the following sentences. Check your answers when you're done.

1. Rudi and I are good friends yet we often disagree.
2. I wonder why the sun lightens our hair but darkens our skin.
3. Noah had the last two of every creature on his ark yet he didn't swat those mosquitoes.
4. Money can't buy happiness but it makes misery easier to live with.
5. *Con* is the opposite of *pro* so Congress must be the opposite of progress.
6. Canada and the United States have a complex relationship that is characterized by ignorance on one side and apprehension on the other.
7. Flying may be the safest form of transportation but why is the place where planes land called a "terminal"?
8. Pack an extra jacket or sweater for evenings in September can be cold.
9. The phone hasn't worked for days and the television has been broken for a month but I haven't missed either of them.
10. Please pay close attention for the instructions are a little complicated and failure to follow the process precisely can result in disaster.

> ### RULE 3
> Put a comma after an introductory word, phrase, or dependent clause that comes BEFORE an independent clause.

Word: Rob, you aren't paying attention.

Phrase: Exhausted and cranky from staying up all night, I staggered into class.

Phrase: No matter how hard I try, I will never forget you.

Clause: If that's their idea of a large pizza, we'd better order two.

Clause: Until she got her promotion, she was quite friendly.

But note that if a dependent (or subordinate) clause **FOLLOWS** an independent clause, no comma is needed: She was quite friendly until she got her promotion.

EXERCISE **17.3**

Insert commas where they are needed in the following sentences. Then check your answers against ours on page 436.

1. First you need to understand what an independent clause is.
2. In the end we will be judged by how much happiness we have given others.
3. "Unless I get my husband's money pretty soon I will be forced to live an immortal life." (From an application for government assistance)
4. According to company policy you may not personally collect Air Miles points accumulated on business-related travel.
5. If you live by the calendar your days are numbered.
6. According to my stomach lunchtime came and went about an hour ago.
7. In most newspaper and magazine advertisements the time shown on a watch is 10:10.
8. Even if a mixed metaphor sings it should be stifled.
9. As her 40th birthday approached Emily met the challenge by trading in her minivan for a sports car and one boyfriend for another who is 20 years her junior.
10. When the first robin heralds the return of spring I begin to dream of lazy summer days beside the pool, with a cool drink in my hand and a ball game on the radio.

> ### RULE 4
> Use commas to set off any word, phrase, or dependent clause that is **NOT ESSENTIAL** to the main idea of the sentence.

Following this rule can make the difference between your readers' understanding and misunderstanding of what you write. For example, the following two sentences are identical, except for a pair of commas. But notice what a difference those two tiny marks make to meaning:

The students who haven't done their homework will lose one full grade.
(Only the students who failed to do their homework will be penalized.)

The students, who haven't done their homework, will lose one full grade.
(All the students failed to do their homework, and all will be penalized.)

To test whether a word, phrase, or clause is essential to the meaning of your sentence, mentally put parentheses around it. If the sentence still makes complete sense (i.e., the main idea is unchanged; the sentence just delivers less information), the material in parentheses is *not essential* and should be set off from the rest of the sentence by a comma or commas.

Non-essential information can appear at the beginning of a sentence,[1] in the middle, or at the end of a sentence. Study the following examples.

Alice Munro (one of Canada's best-known novelists) spends the summer in Clinton and the winter in Comox.

Most readers would be puzzled the first time they read this sentence if it had no punctuation. They would assume all of the information is equally important. In fact, the material in broken parentheses is extra information, a supplementary detail. It can be deleted without changing the sentence's meaning, and so it should be separated from the rest of the sentence by commas:

Alice Munro, one of Canada's best-known novelists, spends the summer in Clinton and the winter in Comox.

Here's another example to consider:

The Queen (who has twice as many birthdays as anyone else) officially celebrates her birthday on May 24.

Again, the sentence is hard to read. You can't count on your readers to go back and reread every sentence they don't understand at first glance. As a writer, you are responsible for giving readers the clues they need as to what is crucial information and what isn't. In the example above, the information in broken parentheses is not essential to the meaning of the sentence, so it should be set off by commas:

The Queen, who has twice as many birthdays as anyone else, officially celebrates her birthday on May 24.

---

[1] Rule 3 covers non-essential information at the beginning of a sentence.

In this next sentence, the non-essential information comes at the end.

> Although she was born on April 21, the Queen officially celebrates her birthday on May 24 (the anniversary of Queen Victoria's birth).

The phrase "the anniversary of Queen Victoria's birth" is not essential to the main idea, so it should be separated from the rest of the sentence by a comma:

> Although she was born on April 21, the Queen officially celebrates her birthday on May 24, the anniversary of Queen Victoria's birth.

And finally, consider this sentence:

> Writing a letter of application (that is clear, complete, and concise) is a challenge.

If you take out "that is clear, complete, and concise," you change the meaning of the sentence. Not all letters of application are a challenge to write. Writing vague and wordy letters is easy; anyone can do it. The words "that is clear, complete, and concise" are essential to the meaning of the sentence, and so they are not set off by commas.

> Writing a letter of application that is clear, complete, and concise is a challenge.

EXERCISE **17.4**

Insert commas where they are missing in the following sentences. Check your answers on page 436.

1. Commas like road signs are signals that indicate how to proceed.
2. An optimist of course is someone who doesn't really understand the situation.
3. There is room in this world for all of God's creatures right beside the mashed potatoes.
4. Our office manager who recently received her MBA has transformed our dysfunctional environment into a productive workplace.
5. An opportunist is someone who goes ahead and does what the rest of us wish we had the courage to do.
6. A compliment like a good perfume should be pleasing but not overpowering.
7. The only person who is with you for your entire life is yourself.

Punctuation

8. One of our most experienced marketing people suggested to our surprise that we concentrate on making a better product instead of spending millions to persuade people to buy the inferior stuff in our current line.

9. Like some cheeses and fine wines some people improve with age.

10. The new office manager now in her second month in the job has made many changes to our procedures not all of them welcome.

The rest of the exercises in this chapter require you to apply all four comma rules. Before you begin, write the four rules on a sheet of paper and keep the sheet in front of you as you work through the exercises. Refer to the four rules frequently as you punctuate the sentences that follow. After you've finished each exercise, check your answers and make sure you understand any mistakes you make.

EXERCISE **17.5**

1. All power corrupts but we need electricity.
2. If Barbie is so popular why do you have to buy her friends?
3. No words in the English language rhyme with *month orange silver* or *purple*.
4. My Facebook page which now has more than 300 "likes" features pictures of me as an adorable baby.
5. "Our Superstore is unrivalled in size unmatched in variety and unparalleled inconvenience." (Sign as posted at a "big box" store opening)
6. Why is it that one match can start a forest fire but it takes a whole box of matches to start a campfire?
7. "The sooner you fall behind the more time you will have to catch up." (Steven Wright)
8. Yield to temptation for it may not pass your way again.
9. Sam packed a lunch took a shower changed into her hiking clothes and without a word to anyone began her trek.
10. Noticing that he was being followed by two men in raincoats and hats he slipped into a nearby café and exited by the back door.

EXERCISE **17.6**

In this exercise, after you have punctuated each sentence, identify the rule(s) you applied. For example:

On Tuesday I go to the dentist.

On Tuesday, I go to the dentist. **(Rule 3)**

1. There is something wrong with this proposal but I haven't yet figured out what it is.
2. George Washington the first president of the United States was an officer in the British army before the American Revolution.
3. While I respect your opinion and your right to express it I disagree with everything you say.
4. "Politics is the art of looking for trouble finding it misdiagnosing it and then misapplying the wrong remedies." (Groucho Marx)
5. Did you know that pound for pound the amoeba is the most vicious animal on Earth?
6. This department cannot support your proposal nor can we recommend that any other department provide funding.
7. The word *allegro* thought by some to be a type of leg fertilizer is actually a musical notation meaning "lively" or "quick."
8. Further to your letter of last week our personnel director will be pleased to meet with you on Thursday but she can spare only 10 minutes for the meeting.
9. The best feature of this book a compact concise and clever guide to grammar is its convenient spiral binding.
10. Charlottetown Quebec and Kingston were the sites of the conferences that eventually led to Confederation the birth of our nation in 1867.

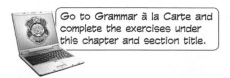

Go to Grammar à la Carte and complete the exercises under this chapter and section title.

EXERCISE **17.7**

Insert the 20 commas that are missing from the following paragraph.

While a winter storm raged outside their Winnipeg home a couple sat in their comfortable living room reading magazines watching television and snacking on popcorn. When a newscaster announced that all cars should be parked on the side of the street with even numbers to facilitate snow removal the husband sighed got up and put on his coat and boots to move the car. A week later another storm hit the city and this time the newscaster announced that cars must be parked on the side of the street with odd-numbered houses. Again the husband dutifully went out to move the car. Two weeks passed before another storm brought heavy snow to Winnipeg but this time just as the newscaster was about to announce snow-removal arrangements the power went out as it often did during storms. The husband distraught because he had not learned on which side of the street to park the car appealed to his wife for advice. The wife looked up from her magazine removed her glasses and said in a quiet voice "Dear why don't you just leave the car in the garage this time?"

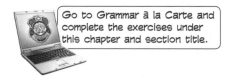

Go to *Grammar à la Carte* and complete the exercises under this chapter and section title.

EXERCISE **17.8**

Insert the 20 commas that are missing from the following paragraph.

As long as you are prepared and confident you'll find that an employment interview need not be a terrifying experience. Some people believe it or not actually enjoy employment interviews and attend them with enthusiasm. Most of us however are intimidated by the prospect of being interrogated by an interviewer or even worse a team of interviewers. To prepare for an interview you should first find out as much as you can about the company. Among the things you need to know are the title of the job you are applying for approximately how much it pays the name of the person or persons who will conduct the interview the address of the company and the location of the washrooms. Employment consultants usually recommend that you make an advance visit to the office of the firm to which you've applied in order to confirm how long it takes to get there and where the interview room is. While on your scouting mission you can learn valuable information about the company's working conditions employee attitudes and even dress code. On the day of the interview be sure to show up 10 or 15 minutes in advance of your scheduled appointment. When the interviewer greets you you should do three things: memorize his or her name identify yourself and extend your hand. Your handshake should be brief and firm not limply passive or bone-crushingly aggressive. Practise! Now all you have to do is relax and enjoy the interview.

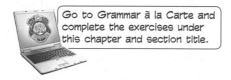

Go to Grammar à la Carte and complete the exercises under this chapter and section title.

SUMMARY

THE FOUR COMMA RULES

1. Use commas to separate three or more items in a series. The items may be expressed as words, phrases, or clauses.
2. Put a comma between independent clauses when they are joined by *for*, *and*, *nor*, *but*, *or*, *yet*, or *so*.
3. Put a comma after an introductory word, phrase, or dependent clause that comes before an independent clause.
4. Use commas to set off a word, phrase, or dependent clause that is NOT ESSENTIAL to the main idea of the sentence.

Punctuation

EXERCISE **17.9**

Insert commas where they are needed in the following sentences.

1. Once the wheel stops turning the pointer will indicate the prize you can claim.

2. I'm so broke, I can't even pay attention.

3. "In my business a flush beats a full house." (Sign on a plumber's truck)

4. Anything not nailed down is mine and anything I can pry loose is not nailed down.

5. Being a teacher requires the patience of a saint the stamina of a triathlete and the reflexes of a mongoose none of which I possess.

6. According to Dr. Steinberg who is quoting one of his patients "raising teenagers is like being pecked to death by a duck."

7. In sentence number seven you are required to insert commas not semicolons or periods in two places.

8. When I wind up a toy I start it but when I wind up this exercise I end it.

9. Propeller in Halifax McAuslan in Montreal Wellington in Guelph Alley Kat in Edmonton and Russell in Surrey are just five of the many microbreweries across Canada that are producing flavourful, interesting beers.

10. "Concentrating especially but not exclusively on its social political economic religious and philosophical impact on Europe Asia America and Africa describe the history of the papacy from its origins to the present day."* (This sentence from "The Final Exam" requires 10 commas.)

GRAMMAR À LA CARTE

- Looking for more opportunities to practise? Want to see what you need to review before the big test? Visit NELSONbrain.com and log in to **Grammar à la Carte** for *The Bare Essentials, Form A,* to access additional exercises! These Web exercises are graded automatically, so you will know instantly whether or not you have mastered the material.

---

* "The Final Exam." *Humor/Academic Jokes.* Wilson WindowWare. Web. 2001.

THE UN-GRAMMATICALS WERE BECOMING DESPERATE, THEY HAD NO IDEA WHERE OR WHEN TO USE A SEMICOLON.

The Semicolon | 18

The semicolon and the colon are often confused and used as if they were interchangeable. They have distinct purposes, however, and their correct use can dramatically improve a reader's understanding of your writing. The semicolon has three functions.

> 1. A semicolon can replace a period; that is, it can appear between two independent clauses.

You should use a semicolon when the two clauses (sentences) you are joining are closely connected in meaning, or when there is a cause-and-effect relationship between them.

Montreal is not the city's original name; it was once called Ville-Marie.

I can't stay awake any longer; I'm too tired.

A period could have been used instead of a semicolon in either of these sentences, but the close connection between the clauses makes a semicolon more effective in communicating the writer's meaning.

> 2. Certain transitional words or phrases can be put between independent clauses to show a causal relationship or the continuation of an idea.

Words or phrases used in this way are usually preceded by a semicolon and followed by a comma:

; also,	; furthermore,	; nevertheless,
; as a result,	; however,	; on the other hand,
; besides,	; in addition,	; otherwise,
; consequently,	; in fact,	; then,
; finally,	; instead,	; therefore,
; for example,	; moreover,	; thus,

My monitor went blank; nevertheless, I kept on typing.

"I'm not offended by dumb blonde jokes because I know I'm not dumb; besides, I also know I'm not blonde." (Dolly Parton)

In other words, A SEMICOLON + A TRANSITIONAL WORD/PHRASE + A COMMA = a link strong enough to come between two related independent clauses.

Note, however, that, when transitional words and phrases are used as nonessential expressions rather than as connecting words, they are separated from the rest of the sentence by commas (Chapter 17, Rule 4, page 225).

I just can't seem to master statistics, however hard I try.

Most of my courses this term are challenging but manageable. Statistics, however, remains a painful mystery to me.

> 3. To make a complex list easier to read and understand, use semicolons between the items instead of commas.

A complex list is one in which at least one component part already contains commas. Here are two examples:

I grew up in a series of small towns: Cumberland, British Columbia; Red Deer, Alberta; and Timmins, Ontario.

When we opened the refrigerator, we found a limp, brown head of lettuce; two small containers of yogurt, whose "best before" dates had long since passed; and a hard, dried-up piece of cheddar cheese.

EXERCISE **18.1**

Put a check mark (✔) before the sentences that are correctly punctuated. Answers for exercises in this chapter begin on page 438.

1. _____ Many are cold; but few are frozen.

2. _____ I'd really like to help you clean out the garage; however, my doctor has ordered me to rest as much as possible until my rash heals.

3. _____ This album is quiet and romantic; perfect for an intimate dinner.

4. _____ Knowledge is knowing that a tomato is a fruit; wisdom is not putting it in a fruit salad.

5. _____ I do not approve of political jokes; because I've seen too many of them get elected.

6. _____ Six of the First Nations bands joined together in a loose confederacy; they were called *Iroquois*.

7. _____ Max, our most creative classmate, wrote the script, Sam, an organizational genius, produced the film, Gina, our best camera operator, was the director of photography, and I was made director because I'm not particularly good at anything.

8. _____ The label on the bag of potato chips proclaimed, "You could be a winner! No purchase is necessary look for details inside."

9. _____ I think animal testing is wrong; the animals get terribly nervous and give the wrong answers.

10. _____ Here are the twins, looking adorable, their parents, who look in need of a good night's sleep, their babysitter, who appears to be on the verge of a nervous breakdown, and the family's four pet ferrets.

EXERCISE **18.2**

Correct the faulty punctuation in Exercise 18.1.

Punctuation

EXERCISE **18.3**

Put a check mark before the following sentences that are correctly punctuated.

1. _____ If life deals you a handful of lemons; make lemonade.
2. _____ Sadly, the swimming pool was closed, however, the hot tub was working just fine.
3. _____ The price of coffee is outrageous, yet that doesn't prevent me from having my morning cup or three.
4. _____ Our vacation in Europe was a huge success; except for Euro-Disney, which was a major disappointment.
5. _____ Erin is always late, nevertheless she is always worth waiting for.
6. _____ She made herself feel better by shopping for new shoes; a guaranteed strategy for chasing the blues.
7. _____ Cookie pieces have no calories; because all the calories leak out when the cookie is broken.
8. _____ Some people are skilled in many fields; Daisy, for example, is both a good plumber and a great cook.
9. _____ The weather is terrible, as it has been all month, I have a head cold that is making me miserable, the power has been out for several hours, so I can't cook; and, to top it all off, my in-laws are arriving for dinner in about an hour.
10. _____ Keep this book on your desk; that way, you can easily refer to it when you need to check on how or where to use semicolons.

EXERCISE **18.4**

Correct the faulty punctuation in Exercise 18.3.

EXERCISE **18.5**

Correct the following sentences by changing commas to semicolons where necessary.

1. I didn't say it was your fault, I said I was blaming you.

2. The airline pilots were on strike, and the train tracks were blocked by a washout in northern Ontario, our only choice was; to drive to Regina.

3. On my shopping list are carrots and onions for the stew, rhubarb and strawberries for the pie, Parmesan cheese, which Roshni likes to grate over the salad, and espresso coffee to have after the meal.

4. I'm reading a fascinating book on levitation, I just can't seem to put it down.

5. I already have a boyfriend, however, don't let that stop you from worshipping me from afar.

6. Dolphins are so smart that, within a few weeks of captivity, they can train people to stand at the edge of the pool and throw them fish.

7. Newfoundland and Labrador is Canada's newest province, actually, it was known as Newfoundland until 2004, when the full name was officially recognized.

8. Some people cause happiness wherever they go, some whenever they go.

9. Never argue with an idiot, he'll drag you down to his level and beat you with experience.

10. "For the physics section of your exam, explain the nature of matter, include in your answer an evaluation of the impact of the development of mathematics on the study of science."*

Punctuation

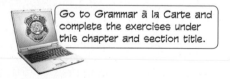

Go to Grammar à la Carte and complete the exercises under this chapter and section title.

EXERCISE **18.6**

Insert commas and semicolons where necessary in the following sentences. Then check your answers carefully.

1. Turn left when you come to the fork in the road otherwise you will end up at the nuclear waste-disposal site and come out all aglow.

---

* "The Final Exam." *Humor/Academic Jokes*. Wilson WindowWare. Web. 2001.

2. Watch your pennies the government will take care of your dollars.

3. As gasoline prices continue to rise hybrid cars make more and more sense the problem is their high purchase price.

4. If you can afford one however it will pay for itself in gas savings over the life of the vehicle in fact my calculations indicate that a hybrid will save me money after three years.

5. The Lord's Prayer is 66 words long the Gettysburg address is 286 words the Declaration of Independence is 1,322 words but U.S. government regulations on the sale of cabbage total 26,911 words.

6. When I am tired I listen to classic rock 'n' roll because it energizes me however when I am working at home nothing stimulates my creativity like Mozart.

7. I am nobody and nobody is perfect therefore I must be perfect.

8. "From the moment I picked up your book until I put it down I was convulsed with laughter someday I intend to read it." (Groucho Marx)

9. Buying a house involves enormous responsibilities not to mention enormous debt consequently I plan to live with my parents until I find a wealthy woman with her own home.

10. I'm sure you understand that I would like nothing better than for you to pass this course however there may be a small fee involved.

EXERCISE 18.7

Correct the faulty punctuation in these sentences.

1. I saw Michael Jackson, he sat right between the Sasquatch and me on the UFO.

2. Men never grow up; but some learn how to behave in public.

3. My new office chair was supposed to have been custom-fitted however when I sat down I discovered that it had been custom-fitted for someone else.

4. When we skied silently through the north woods we saw the tracks of a lynx that was stalking a snowshoe rabbit we heard the cracking, groaning, and sighing of the river as ice solidified on its surface and we felt the minus-40-degree temperatures nipping at our noses and fingers.

5. One movie reviewer loved this movie another hated it and a third thought it was so-so however audiences flocked to it and made the producers very rich. Apparently; critics do not have as much influence as they like to think.

6. In an advertisement for a product designed to help people quit smoking, Brooke Shields said, "Smoking kills, if you're killed, then you have lost an important part of your life."

7. Drive carefully and wear your seat belt, it's not only cars that can be recalled by their maker.

8. One of the products of the computer age was supposed to be increased leisure, however most of us are now working through evenings, weekends, and vacations, thanks to mobile computing.

9. Some biblical figures are familiar to many different cultures, for example the stories of Samson and Delilah and of David and Goliath are known throughout the world.

10. Every year at tax time, I am faced with the same problem: assembling my bills and receipts, figuring out my gas consumption, trying to recall which expenses were business-related and which were personal, finding my T-4s, T-5s, and other T-forms, and organizing this mess so my accountant can keep me out of jail for another year.

EXERCISE **18.8**

All of the punctuation marks that appear in the following paragraph are correct; however, 15 punctuation marks are missing. Correct the paragraph by inserting commas and semicolons where they are needed.

A friend of mine had not been feeling very well for some time so he finally went to the doctor for a complete physical examination. After many tests and two more visits he was told to come back once more he was also asked to bring his wife. When they arrived at the doctor's office the doctor asked the wife to wait outside while he examined her husband. After several minutes the husband emerged from the office and told his wife to go in the doctor wanted to see her alone. The doctor asked the wife to sit down, and then he told her that her husband was seriously ill. While she listened attentively, the doctor outlined what she must do to save her husband. The doctor revealed that stress was the cause of the husband's illness stress must be eliminated from his life. He must stop working immediately and stay at home. She would have to make sure he sat quietly in a comfortable chair while she brought him whatever he wanted. Even driving would be too stressful she would have to take him wherever he wanted to go. She would have to cook his favourite meals screen his telephone calls bring him snacks while he watched TV keep the children away from him, and cater to his every wish. The wife listened to these instructions with concern she left the office deep in thought. On the way home the husband finally asked her, "What did the doctor say, dear?"

She replied, "My dear, I'm so sorry unfortunately nothing can be done."

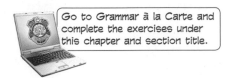

Go to Grammar à la Carte and complete the exercises under this chapter and section title.

EXERCISE **18.9**

Have you mastered the semicolon? Try this exercise and find out. Insert semicolons and change commas to semicolons and semicolons to commas where necessary in the following sentences.

1. Take my advice I'm not using it.

2. Tina says she has half a mind to marry Ben, perhaps she should check with the other half before she accepts his proposal.

3. The procrastinator's work is never done, our motto is "Never leave until tomorrow those chores you can get out of altogether."

4. Next time you wave at a driver who cuts you off, use all your fingers, there is a direct relationship between your gestures and your blood pressure.

5. "When I was in school; I cheated on the metaphysics exam, I looked into the soul of the boy sitting next to me." (Woody Allen)

6. The accused was travelling north on Main in a green Ford Flex when her vehicle apparently failed to stop at the intersection of High Street, resulting in her sideswiping a silver Honda Civic, however, it was the subsequent collision with a parked delivery truck that resulted in her arrest.

7. When the union was trying to recruit enough people to get certified at our plant, I was neutral, however, when they began harassing those who hadn't signed a card, I became resentful and joined those against certification.

8. Louis Riel led a Métis rebellion in Saskatchewan in 1885; but he was defeated, tried, and executed the same year, his death caused a deep rift between English and French Canada.

9. If you are intimidated by computers, you are a pre-boomer, if you use them but hate them, you are a boomer, if you think they are simply a part of life, you are Generation X, if they are your main link to the outside world, you are Generation Y.

10. When you come to write the final exam, please bring your text and any notes you may have taken in class, two pens, preferably with different colours of ink, a wi-fi-equipped laptop, scrap paper on which to work out problems, and, last but not least, your student card.

Punctuation

GRAMMAR À LA CARTE

- Looking for more opportunities to practise? Want to see what you need to review before the big test? Visit NELSONbrain.com and log in to **Grammar à la Carte** for *The Bare Essentials, Form A,* to access additional exercises! These Web exercises are graded automatically, so you will know instantly whether or not you have mastered the material.

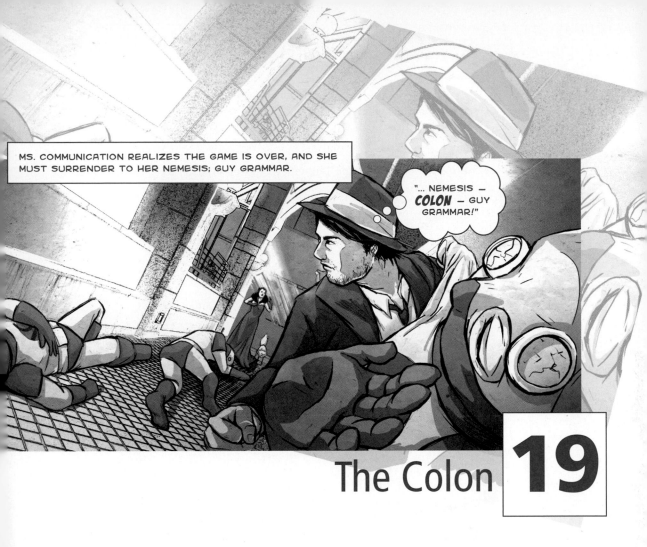

MS. COMMUNICATION REALIZES THE GAME IS OVER, AND SHE MUST SURRENDER TO HER NEMESIS; GUY GRAMMAR.

"... NEMESIS — *COLON* — GUY GRAMMAR!"

The Colon 19

The colon functions as an introducer. When a statement is followed by a list, one or more examples, or a quotation, the colon alerts the reader that some sort of explanatory detail is coming up.

When I travel, I am never without three things: sturdy shoes, a money belt, and my tablet.

There is only one enemy we cannot defeat: time.

We have two choices: to study or to fail.

Early in his career, Robert Fulford did not think very highly of intellectual life in Canada: "My generation of Canadians grew up believing that, if we were very good or very smart, or both, we would someday *graduate* from Canada."

> The statement that precedes the colon must be a complete sentence (independent clause).

A colon should never come immediately after *is, are, was,* or *were.* Here's an example of what *not* to write:

> The three things I am violently allergic to are: cats, ragweed, and country music.

This construction is incorrect because the statement before the colon is not a complete sentence.

There are three situations in which you need to use a colon.

> 1. Use a colon between an independent clause and a LIST or one or more EXAMPLES that define, explain, or illustrate the independent clause.

The information after the colon often answers the question "What?" or "Who?"

> I am violently allergic to three things: (what?) cats, ragweed, and country music.

> Business and industry face a new challenge: (what?) the rising value of the Canadian dollar.

> The president has found the ideal candidate for the position: (who?) her brother.

> 2. Use a colon after a complete sentence introducing a quotation.

> Maude Barlow of the Council of Canadians encourages young people to vote: "If you want to know who is going to change this country, go home and look in the mirror."

> 3. Use a colon to separate the title of a book, film, or television show from a subtitle.

Imagine: How Creativity Works (book)

Ai Weiwei: Never Sorry (film)

Seinfeld: "The Puffy Shirt" (TV show episode)

If you remember this summary, you'll have no more trouble with colons:

> The colon follows an independent clause and introduces one of three things: an example, a list, or a quotation.

EXERCISE **19.1**

Put a check mark (✔) next to those sentences that are correctly punctuated. Answers for the exercises in this chapter begin on page 441.

1. _____ Two of the most important traits for a good manager are good listening skills and superior problem-solving ability.

2. _____ We cannot write the report until we are given: accurate data.

3. _____ Our weekly shopping list always includes: pizza, pretzels, and pastries.

4. _____ My mechanic's solution could not be faulted: "I couldn't fix your brakes, so I made your horn louder."

5. _____ The essential characteristics of a good manager are: decisive leadership, clear communication, and meaningful consultation.

6. _____ There are three kinds of people: those who can count and those who can't.

7. _____ A shin is: a device for finding furniture in the dark.

8. _____ We are looking for a computer firm that can supply three critical components; reliable hardware, adaptable software, and timely support.

9. _____ Let me give you a perfect example of pride preceding a fall, Conrad Black.

10. _____ In an effort to encourage me, my parents gave me a book for my birthday, *The Dog Ate My Resumé, Survival Tips for Life after College.*

EXERCISE **19.2**

Correct the faulty sentences in Exercise 19.1.

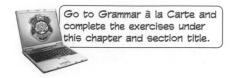

Go to Grammar à la Carte and complete the exercises under this chapter and section title.

EXERCISE 19.3

Correct the faulty punctuation in the following sentences, and then check your answers. If you've made any mistakes, review the explanation and examples, and be sure you understand why your answers were incorrect.

1. The only ways to get rich quickly are: to win the lottery or marry money.

2. According to Leah, men are like Kleenex, soft, strong, and disposable.

3. The pioneers made their own: candles, soap, butter, and beer.

4. The supplies cabinet is low on pencils, highlighters, scratch pads, and staples.

5. We expect to do well in two venues: the pool and the track.

6. My roommate, who loves horror movies, persuaded me to go with her to see *Nosferatu, the Vampyre* and *Evil Dead 2; Dead by Dawn.*

7. There are two sides to every divorce, yours and the idiot's.

8. My parents think I am: lazy, selfish, ignorant, and inconsiderate, but what do they know?

9. Your paper lacks three essential features, a title page, a Works Cited list, and some original content in between.

10. Every time I walk into a singles bar, I can hear my mother's warning "Don't pick that up! You don't know where it's been."

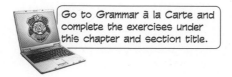

Go to Grammar à la Carte and complete the exercises under this chapter and section title.

EXERCISE **19.4**

The following paragraph will test all you have learned in the last three chapters. Insert commas, semicolons, and colons where appropriate in this passage. There are 15 errors.

After a long day at work Gina couldn't wait to get home, however she could not find: her car keys. She looked in her purse in her desk drawer even in the filing cabinet. Knowing that she had a bad habit of leaving the keys in the ignition she decided to check the car in the parking lot. When she saw that her car was missing she panicked and called the police to tell them that her car had been stolen because: she had stupidly left the keys in the ignition. Then she called the one person she didn't want to talk to at a time like this; her husband. When she explained what had happened there was a long pause, eventually he patiently reminded her that he had dropped her off at the office that morning. Embarrassed but relieved Gina sheepishly asked her husband to come and pick her up. There was an even longer pause. "I will: just as soon as I convince this police officer that I have not stolen your car."

Punctuation

EXERCISE **19.5**

Now test your ability to use colons correctly. Revise the punctuation in the following sentences where necessary.

1. Our dog knows only one trick: pretending to be deaf.

2. In studying this chapter, I learned that colons follow complete sentences and introduce: examples, lists, or quotations.

3. Four sure ways to cheer yourself up are: going shopping, watching a movie, exercising, and eating.

4. There is only one thing worse than getting old; the alternative.

5. Our canoe trip was a disaster it rained for three days, the tent leaked, and when it stopped raining, the mosquitoes were as thick as fog.

6. This program is one of the most difficult at college, but when we graduate, we can expect: interesting employment, good pay, and lots of opportunities to travel.

7. Here's my lawyer's definition of a will; a dead giveaway.

8. There is a secret to taking good notes, take them from someone who goes to class.

9. A palindrome is a word or sentence that reads the same backwards as it does forward, such as: *level, noon, Ogopogo, Laval,* and *madam.*

10. Probability analysts have devised the 50–50–90 law, "Any time there is a 50–50 chance you will get something right, there is a 90 percent chance you'll get it wrong."

GRAMMAR À LA CARTE

- Looking for more opportunities to practise? Want to see what you need to review before the big test? Visit NELSONbrain.com and log in to **Grammar à la Carte** for *The Bare Essentials, Form A,* to access additional exercises! These Web exercises are graded automatically, so you will know instantly whether or not you have mastered the material.

Quotation Marks 20

USING QUOTATION MARKS CORRECTLY

A quotation is one or more words originally spoken or written by another person that you want to include in your paper. Quotations can enhance meaning and add interest to your writing—as long as they are used sparingly, like spice. If you insert quotations into every other sentence, your own ideas will be buried under the weight of other people's words. Your reader wants to hear what you think about your topic. Use the words of others to support your ideas, not as substitutes for them.

When you quote, you need to provide a signal to your reader that these words are borrowed, not your own. Quotation marks (" ") are used to set off dialogue, short passages of quoted material, and some titles. Long passages of quoted material are treated differently, as you'll see later.

Quotation marks come in pairs. There must be a set to show where the quotation or title begins and a set to show where it ends. The words in between must be *exactly* what you heard or read. If you wish to omit or change a word or words and can do so without changing the meaning of the original, you may do so, but again you must alert your reader that you have altered the original. To find out how to add, delete, or alter an original source so that it fits smoothly into your paragraph, see the Student Resources page on this book's website at **www.NELSONbrain.com** and click on "Format and Documentation." The only other thing you need to know about quotations is how to introduce and punctuate them.

PUNCTUATING DIALOGUE

When you quote direct speech, start with a double quotation mark (") and use normal sentence punctuation. If you identify the speaker in your sentence, set the identification off with commas. Put a comma or an end punctuation mark—whichever is appropriate—inside the final set of quotation marks (").

> "Yes, officer , " said the young man, "that's her. That's the lady I stole the purse from."

Put quotation marks around a speaker's exact words. Do not use quotation marks with indirect speech (a paraphrase of someone's words).

> The young man confessed that the woman the officer pointed to was the woman from whom he had stolen the purse.

PUNCTUATING AND FORMATTING QUOTATIONS

Inserting quotations from print and electronic sources into your own writing smoothly and seamlessly is not easy. It takes practice. Quotations cannot simply be dropped (splash!) into your paragraphs. Every quotation must be introduced, usually in a phrase or clause that identifies the source.

> When you quote a *short passage* (three lines of print or less), you should work it into your own sentence using appropriate punctuation.

1. Normally, you use a short phrase and a comma to mark off a quotation of one or more sentences. Put your quotation marks at the beginning and end of the passage you are quoting, including the end punctuation mark.

   According to Margaret Atwood, "If you like men, you can like Americans. Cautiously. Selectively. Beginning with the feet. One at a time."

   "As you grow old," wrote Richard Needham, "you lose your interest in sex, your friends drift away, your children ignore you. There are other advantages, of course, but these would seem to me the outstanding ones."

   "My idea of long-range planning is lunch," confesses Frank Ogden, one of Canada's foremost futurists.

2. If your own introductory words form a complete sentence, use a colon to introduce the quotation.

   Frank Ogden, one of Canada's foremost futurists, confesses that he has little respect for traditional business-planning cycles: "My idea of long-range planning is lunch."

3. If the passage you are quoting is a couple of words, a phrase, or anything less than a complete sentence, do not use any punctuation to introduce it.

   Woody Allen's one regret in life is that he is "not someone else."

   Neil Bissoondath argues that racism is based on "willful ignorance and an acceptance of—and comfort with—stereotype."

4. A quotation *within* a quotation is punctuated by single quotation marks.

   According to John Robert Colombo, "the most widely quoted Canadian aphorism of all time is Marshall McLuhan's 'The medium is the message.' "

Punctuation

EXERCISE **20.1**

In the following sentences, place quotation marks where they are needed and insert any necessary punctuation before and after each quotation. Answers for exercises in this chapter begin on page 442.

1. There are not many quotations that everyone who speaks English knows, but Shakespeare's To be or not to be, that is the question must be one of the most familiar.

2. On the subject of exercise, Fred Allen remarked that he liked long walks, especially when they were taken by people who annoyed him.

3. It is good to obey the rules when you are young, wrote Mark Twain, so that you'll have the strength to break them when you're old.

4. A dedicated non-athlete, Twain also observed I take my exercise acting as pallbearer at the funerals of those who exercised regularly.

5. Will and Ian Ferguson describe Canadian cuisine in simple terms If you let a Canadian anywhere near a piece of food he (or she) is sure to fling it into a deep fryer. Or cover it with sugar. Or fling it into a deep fryer and *then* cover it with sugar.

EXERCISE **20.2**

For each of the topics below, read the quotation and write, in your own words, two or three sentences about the subject. Then revise your sentences to incorporate the quotation smoothly and effectively. You should end up with a short paragraph. Here's an example:

Topic:	College
Quotation:	"A place where pebbles are polished and diamonds are dimmed."
Source:	Robert G. Ingersoll

Original sentences:

My college experience has been positive, probably because I am taking courses that interest me and are directly related to the career I want. Some of my friends, however, are struggling, even though they did much better than I in high school. If I can keep up this success, then I will feel that I made a wise investment of money and time.

Revision:

> My college experience has been positive, probably because I am taking courses that interest me and are directly related to the career I want. Some of my friends, however, are struggling, even though they did much better than I in high school. I like to think that Robert G. Ingersoll got it right when he defined college as "a place where pebbles are polished and diamonds are dimmed." If I can graduate as a smoothly polished pebble, then I will feel that I made a wise investment of both money and time.

1. **Topic:**   Canadian culture
   Quotation: "Canada has never been a melting pot; [it's] more like a tossed salad."
   Source: Arnold Edinborough

2. **Topic:**   Winter
   Quotation: "In Canada, we have nine months of winter and three months of road repair."
   Source: Peter Hanson

3. **Topic:**   Lies
   Quotation: "A lie gets halfway around the world before the truth has a chance to get its pants on."
   Source: Sir Winston Churchill

4. **Topic:**   Equality of the sexes
   Quotation: "Whatever women do they must do twice as well as men to be thought half as good. Luckily, this is not difficult."
   Source: Charlotte Whitton (former mayor of Ottawa)

5. **Topic:**   Work/leisure
   Quotation: "No man on his deathbed ever said, 'I wish I'd spent more time at the office.' "
   Source: The originator of this modern proverb is unknown.

All of the lines of a *long quotation* (more than three lines of print) should be indented 10 spaces (2 cm) from the left margin. Do not use quotation marks around a long quotation that is set off from the text.

Punctuation

A block indentation indicates to the reader that the words set off in this way are not yours but some other writer's. Here is an example:

> In "An Immigrant's Split Personality," Sun-Kyung Yi describes the painful dilemma faced by the children of immigrants, who often feel torn between two worlds. She cites her own case as an example. Neither Korean nor Canadian, she
>
> > remain[s] slightly distant from both cultures, fully accepted by neither. The hyphenated Canadian personifies the ideal of multiculturalism, but unless the host culture and the immigrant cultures can find ways to merge their distinct identities, sharing the best of both, this cultural schizo-phrenia will continue. (A12)*

College writing normally requires that you indicate the source of any material you quote. In the example above, since the author's name and the article title are included in the introduction to the quotation, the full reference (which is given at the bottom of the page) would appear in a "Works Cited" or "References" list at the end of your paper or, if your instructor prefers, in a footnote or an endnote.

The following examples illustrate the two basic ways to incorporate a short quotation into your own writing and credit your source. The first example identifies the author in the sentence introducing the quotation; the second does not.

> Second marriages, according to Dr. Samuel Johnson, are "the triumph of hope over experience" (402).

> In the 18th century, a lifelong bachelor observed that second marriages were "the triumph of hope over experience" (Johnson 402).

These source identifications are called **parenthetical citations** and refer to entries in the "Works Cited" or "References" list. For further information on format and documentation, see our website at **www.NELSONbrain.com**.

Find out what format your instructor requires and follow it. Some institutions are very particular about documentation, so you would be wise to ask your instructor which style to use. As a general rule, if you are writing a paper for a humanities course and need more details than we provide on this text's website, we suggest you consult the *MLA Handbook for Writers of Research*

---

* Yi, Sun-Kyung. "An Immigrant's Split Personality." *Globe and Mail* 12 April 1992: A12. Print.

Papers, 7th ed. (New York: MLA, 2009), or access the Modern Language Association website at **www.mla.org**. These references provide information on citing all types of sources, including material obtained from Internet sites.

For papers in the social sciences, the standard reference is the *Publication Manual of the American Psychological Association*, 6th ed. (Washington, DC: APA, 2010). Check **www.apastyle.org** for specific details on using APA style, including instruction on citing online information.

The information and exercises that follow use the MLA format.

PUNCTUATING AND FORMATTING TITLES

- *Italicize* the titles of books, websites, and other works made up of parts.
- Use quotation marks around the titles of parts of books, the titles of website pages, and the titles of parts of other works.

The title of anything that is published or produced as a separate entity (e.g., books, magazines, newspapers, pamphlets, plays, movies, TV shows, CDs, blogs) should be italicized. The title of anything that has been published or produced as part of a separate entity (e.g., articles, essays, stories, poems, a single episode of a TV series, songs) should be placed in quotation marks. As you can see from the following examples, this rule is very simple, and it applies to all types of sources, both print and electronic.

Book:	*The Bare Essentials, Form A*
Chapter in a book:	"Quotation Marks"
Magazine:	*Maclean's*
Article in magazine:	"Yesterday's Canadian"
Newspaper:	*Calgary Herald*
Article in newspaper:	"The Ramallah Miracle"
TV program:	*The Nature of Things*
TV episode:	"The Hobbit Enigma"
Music CD:	*So Beautiful or So What*
Song on CD:	"The Afterlife"
Website sponsor:	*National Film Board of Canada*
Website page:	"The Facebook Challenge"

Punctuation

| **Blog:** | *SnailsSpace* |
| **Blog entry:** | "January: The French Resolution" |

Why the difference? The way you format and punctuate a title tells your reader what sort of document you are quoting from or referring to: it may be a complete work that the reader can find listed by title, author, or subject in a library, or it may be an excerpt that the reader can find only by looking up the name of the work in which it was published.

EXERCISE **20.3**

Insert the necessary punctuation (quotation marks or italics) in the following sentences. Check your answers before continuing.

1. Although Moneyball, The Iron Lady, and Lincoln are all biopics, none of them is a fully accurate portrayal of its subject.

2. The Huffington Post is the most popular of all blogs, but The Daily Beast has a large following, and its Children of War entry was one of the year's best articles.

3. Canada's national anthem, O Canada, was written by Calixa Lavallée in 1880, while the United States' Star-Spangled Banner was composed in 1814 by Francis Scott Key, using the melody of an old English drinking song, The Anacreontic Song.

4. In her bestselling book, Eats, Shoots and Leaves, Lynne Truss devotes a chapter entitled Airs and Graces to colons and semicolons.

5. The year 1997 saw the release of two of the bestselling albums in Canadian history: Shania Twain's Come on Over and Celine Dion's Let's Talk about Love.

6. British newspapers are famous for clever headlines; among my favourites are The Sun's How Do You Solve a Problem Like Korea? and, after Gordon Brown was elected prime minister, The Daily Mail's Gord Help Us Now!

7. Pierre Elliott Trudeau made many memorable statements during his years in Parliament, but he is probably best known for two: Just watch me! and Fuddle-duddle.

8. In her essay Motherload, Dana DiCarlo writes, My mother is the world's top travel agent for guilt trips.

9. The latest issue of Consumer Universe has an article about shopping aboard cruise ships entitled Veni. Vidi. Visa, which can be loosely translated as I came. I saw. I shopped.

10. The essay Early Television Westerns reveals that the musical theme for The Lone Ranger comes from The William Tell Overture by Gioachino Rossini, who also wrote the opera The Barber of Seville.

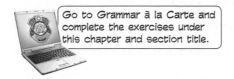

Go to *Grammar à la Carte* and complete the exercises under this chapter and section title.

EXERCISE **20.4**

Punctuation

This exercise is designed to test your understanding of how to punctuate short quotations and titles in your writing. When and where do you use quotation marks? Italics? Which punctuation marks precede and follow a quotation?

1. In their book How to Be a Canadian, Will and Ian Ferguson have a chapter entitled How the Canadian Government Works. The chapter consists of two words: It doesn't.

2. We are all immigrants to this place wrote Margaret Atwood even if we were born here.

3. My current favourite pop single is Natasha Gnostic's new hit, So Many Men, So Few Who Can Afford Me from her latest CD named Coffee, Chocolate, Men ... Some Things Are Just Better Rich.

4. In his book The Miracle of Language, Richard Lederer devotes a chapter entitled The Case for Short Words to the virtues of clarity and simplicity in writing.

5. The information in Chapter 2, The Perfect Poem, is based on William S. Baring-Gould's book The Lure of the Limerick.

6. Mark Twain, the author of the classic American novels Tom Sawyer and Huckleberry Finn, provides my favourite quote on anger: Anger is an acid that can do more harm to the vessel in which it is stored than to anything on which it is poured.

7. Time magazine has an annual award for the year's best blogs, and this year Talking Points Memo was number one, with The Huffington Post and Lifehacker following, while TechCrunch and Gawker were slammed as most overrated.

8. The great American poet Robert Frost, who wrote such memorable poems as Fire and Ice and The Road Not Taken, was not bad with a pithy observation, either: A jury, he said, consists of 12 persons chosen to decide who has the better lawyer.

9. In the chapter entitled Basics in the Inn on the Twenty Cookbook, Anna and Michael Olson write, Cooking requires the passion of an artist and the practical approach of a scientist.

10. The words Fools rush in where angels fear to tread were not penned by a pop singer but by the great English poet Alexander Pope, author of such classic works as Essay on Man and Essay on Criticism, as well as the observation A little learning is a dangerous thing.

GRAMMAR À LA CARTE

- Looking for more opportunities to practise? Want to see what you need to review before the big test? Visit NELSONbrain.com and log in to **Grammar à la Carte** for *The Bare Essentials, Form A,* to access additional exercises! These Web exercises are graded automatically, so you will know instantly whether or not you have mastered the material.

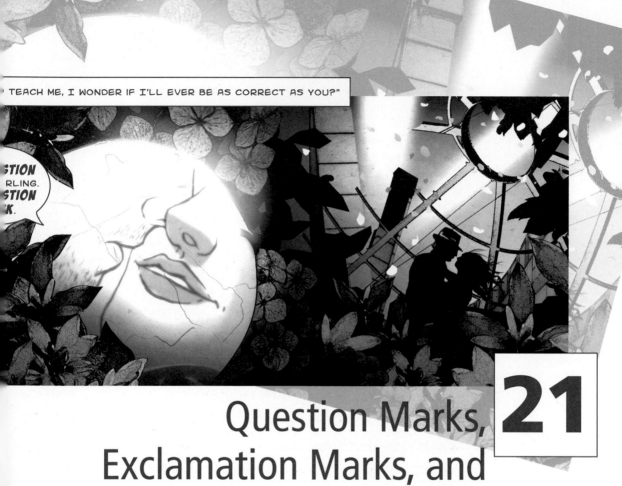

"TEACH ME, I WONDER IF I'LL EVER BE AS CORRECT AS YOU?"

Question Marks, Exclamation Marks, and Punctuation Review

THE QUESTION MARK

Everyone knows that a question mark follows an interrogative, or asking, sentence, but we all sometimes forget to include it. Let this chapter serve as a reminder not to forget!

> Put a question mark at the end of every interrogative sentence.

The question mark gives your readers an important clue to the meaning of your sentence. "There's more?" (interrogative) means something quite different from "There's more!" (exclamatory), and both are different from "There's more." (declarative). When you speak, your tone of voice conveys the meaning you intend; when you write, your punctuation tells your reader what you mean.

The only time you don't end a question with a question mark is when the question is part of a statement.

Question	Statement
Are you going?	I asked if you were going.
Do you know about them?	I wonder what you know about them.
Is there enough evidence to convict him?	The jury deliberated whether there was enough evidence to convict him.

EXERCISE 21.1

Write the correct end punctuation for the following sentences, and then check your answers. Answers for exercises in this chapter begin on page 443.

1. If we succeed, who will know

2. I wonder who won the game last night

3. Does the name Pavlov ring any bells

4. Wouldn't it be great if, whenever we messed up our lives, we could simply press "Ctrl Alt Delete" and start all over

5. The vice-president questioned our manager about the likelihood of completing this project on time and on budget

6. I am curious about what the new minister of finance plans to do about our chronic deficit

7. Please have a look at these tests and tell me if you agree that some of the students may have been cheating

8. How can anyone just stand by while a child is being bullied

9. If we continue to make a profit, I wonder if the new owners will close us down or move our operation offshore

10. Why can't the sports fans who yell so loudly at players' mistakes put themselves in the position of those they criticize and be a little more forgiving

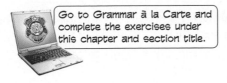

Go to Grammar à la Carte and complete the exercises under this chapter and section title.

THE EXCLAMATION MARK

Consider the difference in tone between these two sentences:

There's a man behind you.
There's a man behind you!

In the first sentence, information is being supplied, perhaps about the line of people waiting their turn at a grocery store checkout counter. The second sentence might be a shouted warning about a mugger.

> Use an exclamation mark as end punctuation only in sentences requiring extreme emphasis or dramatic effect.

Note that the exclamation mark will have "punch" or dramatic effect only if you use it sparingly. If you use an exclamation mark after every other sentence, how will your readers know when you really mean to indicate excitement? Overuse of exclamation marks is a technique used by comic book writers to heighten the impact of their characters' words. Ironically, the effect is to neutralize the impact: when all conversation is at top volume, top volume becomes the norm, and the writer is left with no way to indicate emphasis—other than by adding two, three, or more exclamation marks to punctuate each statement. This is why you seldom find exclamation marks in academic or business writing.

Almost any sentence could end with an exclamation, but remember that the punctuation changes the emotional force of the sentence. Read the following sentences with and without an exclamation mark, and picture the situation that would call for each reading.

Punctuation

They've moved   Don't touch that button
The file was empty   Listen to that noise
Alex is home   I quit

EXERCISE 21.2

Add the appropriate punctuation in the following sentences. Then compare your answers with our suggestions on page 443. (Answers may vary, depending on the tone and impact the writer wants to convey.)

1. Row faster It's gaining on us

2. Never introduce a quotation with a semicolon

3. Don't even think about it

4. Just imagine She actually got a job

5. Turn the heat up I'm freezing

6. She's here at last Let the celebrations begin

7. Try it You'll like it

8. The fans were on their feet, screaming "Skate "

9. "Lights, camera, action "

10. Go for it You'll never know unless you try

EXERCISE 21.3

Supply appropriate punctuation for the 15 sentences in the following paragraph.

[1]What a day [2]My daughter was going to make a presentation to her Grade 3 class, and the entire family was stressed [3]She and her mother had come up with a topic, but hadn't shared it with me [4]Why, I don't know [5]Aren't fathers supposed to be supportive and encouraging, even if they don't have a clue what the female side of the household is doing [6]Anyway, my wife took our daughter off to school to do the big demonstration, and when they left, I discovered some celery, raisins, and peanut butter on the kitchen counter [7]What was I supposed to do [8]I smeared the peanut butter on the celery and

put the raisins in the peanut butter [9]Was it ever a good breakfast [10]Just as I finished, the car zoomed up the driveway and screeched to a stop, and mother and daughter dashed into the house and ran into the kitchen [11]Where are the raisins and celery and peanut butter they screamed [12]I told them I had eaten them and asked what the fuss was about [13]There was more screaming [14]I had eaten my daughter's demonstration [15]The teacher told them later that was the first time she had heard the excuse My daddy ate my homework

PUNCTUATION REVIEW

The exercises that follow will test your knowledge of all the punctuation marks you have studied in Unit 4. All of the sentences below contain errors: punctuation or italics are either misused or missing. Work through the sentences slowly and carefully. Check your answers to each set before continuing. If you make a mistake, go back to the chapter that deals with the punctuation mark you missed, and review the explanation and examples.

EXERCISE **21.4**

1. Did you know that in English the word *karate* means empty hands

2. If your goal is to be a millionaire before you are 35 you will have to: make work the focus of your life and be uncommonly lucky

3. The question of whether evolution is fact or myth doesn't worry most of the people in my biology class, they're more concerned about whether there's a dance on Friday night

4. Do you think Deena has any idea how lucky she is that her supervisor didn't find out she took the day off to go to the casino

5. The cure is readily at hand drink plenty of liquids take an aspirin with each meal get lots of rest and take three grams of vitamin C daily

6. When her grandfather told her how large computers used to be the wide-eyed child exclaimed Gosh How big was the mouse

7. I think it was Mark Twain who once said Clothes make the man, naked people have little or no influence in society

8. This is the first entry in my new book, Words of Wisdom If at first you don't succeed skydiving is not the sport for you

9. Your resumé is the second piece of writing that an employer will see, the first is the cover letter, which is one of the most important documents you will write in your career

10. Today's passenger jets are so fast and the airlines so efficient that when you land in Amsterdam it takes them only a couple of days to locate your luggage and fly it in from Brazil

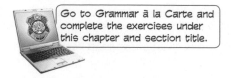

Go to Grammar à la Carte and complete the exercises under this chapter and section title.

EXERCISE **21.5**

Correct the 20 misused or missing punctuation marks in this passage.

No quality in business government or education is so widely discussed and studied as leadership, in fact leadership studies have become a significant industry. Many documents have been written on the subject, from General Rick Hillier's Leadership 50 Points of Wisdom for Today's Leaders to Patrick M. Lencioni's The Five Dysfunctions of a Team A Leadership Fable. The best known is undoubtedly Dale Carnegie's How to Win Friends and Influence People a bestseller since it was published in 1936. Organizations around the world offer courses seminars workshops, and conferences on leadership and most of them sell out quickly. While these various forms of leadership training are undoubtedly useful I cannot help thinking of great leaders like Winston

Churchill Mohandas Gandhi and Nelson Mandela. They did not read books or take courses on leadership, how did they master the art. Former American president and WWII general Dwight D. Eisenhower may have answered this question when he said The leadership instinct you are born with is the backbone. You develop the funny bone and the wishbone that go with it.

EXERCISE **21.6**

Insert the 25 punctuation marks that are missing or misused in the following paragraph.

Canada's climate is not always friendly to the farming of tender fruit crops like cherries peaches grapes pears, and apples. In fact only in very special regions of the country can such crops be grown, the Okanagan Valley the Niagara Peninsula the Annapolis Valley and a few other privileged spots in Quebec the Maritimes Ontario and B.C. Even with the effects of global warming growing tender fruit in Canada can be a risky business. Recently an unseasonably warm March seemed to be a good omen for the crop but when the fruit budded more than two weeks early an April frost which normally would not have affected the fruit destroyed almost the entire crop. Technology has come to the rescue, wind machines have begun making an appearance in Canada's orchards and vineyards. These machines look like miniature wind turbines but they are not driven by the wind, rather, they spin like a huge fan to drive warm air down onto the fruit trees and vines. At 20 metres the air can be as much as 10 degrees warmer than at the level of the fruit so pushing that warmer air down can prevent frost damage and save a valuable crop. There is a downside the machines cost up to $50,000 each cost about $40 an hour to run and sound like a helicopter hovering over the orchard. Neighbouring residential areas may not be too sympathetic.

Punctuation

EXERCISE **21.7**

Insert the punctuation marks that are missing in the following. You will need to use at least one colon, semicolon, and question mark, in addition to quotation marks, italics, and numerous commas. Be sure to read each sentence all the way through before you begin adding the missing punctuation.

1. The early bird gets the worm as the old saying goes, and I have always used this proverb to justify getting up as late as I possibly can.

2. When I told Brian on first meeting him that he sure was tall, he replied You certainly have a firm grasp of the obvious Sarah.

3. Woody Allen took a speed-reading course that enabled him to read Tolstoy's novel War and Peace in just over an hour then he provided a succinct summary of the book It's about Russia.

4. After reading the article Make Your Job Application Work for You! in the weekend paper, Shirlee began her cover letter as follows I am enclosing a summary of my qualifications for you to overlook.

5. Where are the great Canadian patriotic quotes that would compare to Nathan Hale's I regret that I have but one life to give for my country or Patrick Henry's Give me liberty or give me death

6. Agnes Macphail the first woman elected to Canada's Parliament had an answer to that question Patriotism is not dying for one's country it is living for one's country and for humanity.

7. A classically trained pianist jazz singer Nina Simone was famous for her ability to play one melody on the piano while singing another. Her song Little Girl Blue for example sounds hauntingly simple but is actually a complex merging of an old hymn and Simone's own melodic line.

8. George Bernard Shaw sent an invitation to his new play Major Barbara to Winston Churchill along with a note saying Here are two tickets to opening night. Bring a friend ... if you have one. Churchill replied I cannot attend the first night but will come on the second ... if there is one.

9. In an age when high-level computing skills are vital to employment advancement and even social interaction it may be time to rewrite the old Biblical message about the meek rising to prominence. It makes more sense to say The geek shall inherit the earth.

10. As the proud owner of a new Netbook computer you will be able to use wi-fi spots around the world check your email wherever you go write your novel while lying on a beach and access the Internet from airplanes hotel rooms and cafés in more than a hundred countries.

UNIT 4 RAPID REVIEW

Supply the 15 punctuation marks that are missing in the following paragraph. (Note: Each pair of quotation marks counts as one punctuation mark.)

[1]A man bought a parrot at the pet store only to find when he got it home that the bird's vocabulary was obscene. [2]He put up with the foul language for a while hoping that the parrot would tone it down once he got used to his new surroundings. [3]Unfortunately it just got worse and eventually the man had had enough. [4]"Quit it" he yelled. [5]That really irritated the parrot whose swearing became even more horrible. [6]Now really angry the man grabbed the bird threw him into the freezer and slammed the door. [7]At first there were sounds of a struggle then there was a terrible silence. [8]The man began to fear he had injured his pet. [9]He opened the freezer door. [10]The parrot climbed onto his outstretched hand and said these words "I'm awfully sorry about the trouble I gave you. I'll do my best to improve my vocabulary." [11]The man was astounded. [12]What could have brought about this miraculous change in the parrot's behaviour. [13]Then the parrot asked By the way, what did the chicken do?

GRAMMAR À LA CARTE

- Looking for more opportunities to practise? Want to see what you need to review before the big test? Visit NELSONbrain.com and log in to **Grammar à la Carte** for *The Bare Essentials, Form A,* to access additional exercises! These Web exercises are graded automatically, so you will know instantly whether or not you have mastered the material.

UNIT 5

Paragraphs and Essays

Paragraphs and Essays

Jim Lopes/Shutterstock

Finding Something 22
to Write About

Every writer knows that content is important. Not so many seem to know that form is just as important. In fact, you can't really separate the two: *what you say is how you say it*. Writing a paper (or an essay, a report, a letter, or anything else) is like doing a chemistry experiment or baking a cake: you need to put together the right amount of the right ingredients in the right proportions and in the right order. There are five steps to follow:

1. Choose a satisfactory subject.
2. Discover your thesis and main points.
3. Write a thesis statement and/or an outline.
4. Write the paragraphs.
5. Revise the paper.

If you follow these steps faithfully, in order, we guarantee that you will write clear, organized papers.

Note that, when you get to step 3, you have a choice. You can choose to plan your paper with a thesis statement or with an outline, or with both. The thesis statement approach works well for short papers—of about 500 words or less. An outline is necessary for longer papers. Ideally, you should learn to use both methods of organizing your writing. In fact, your teacher may require that you do so.

Steps 1, 2, and 3 make up the planning stage of the writing process. Be warned: done properly, these three steps will take you about as long as steps 4 and 5, which involve the actual writing. The longer you spend on planning, the less time you'll spend on drafting and revising, and the better your paper will be.

CHOOSING A SATISFACTORY SUBJECT

Unless you are assigned a specific subject (or topic) by a teacher or supervisor, choosing your subject can be the most difficult part of writing a paper. Apply the following guidelines carefully, because no amount of instruction can help you to write a good paper on something you know nothing about or on something that is inappropriate for your audience or purpose. Your subject should satisfy the **4-S test**.

> A satisfactory subject is SIGNIFICANT, SINGLE, SPECIFIC, and SUPPORTABLE.

1. Your subject should be SIGNIFICANT. Write about something that your reader needs or might want to know. Consider your audience and choose a subject that they will find significant. This doesn't mean that you can't ever be humorous, but, unless you're another Stephen Leacock, an essay on "How I deposit money in my bank" will not be of much interest to your readers. The subject you choose must be worthy of the time and attention you expect your readers to give to your paper.

2. Your subject should be SINGLE. Don't try to cover too much in your paper. A thorough discussion of one topic is more satisfying to a reader than a skimpy, superficial treatment of several topics. A subject such as "The challenge of government funding cutbacks to colleges and universities" is far too large to deal with in one paper. Limit yourself to a single topic, such as "How private sector donations are helping our college meet the challenge of funding cutbacks."

3. Your subject should be **SPECIFIC**. This requirement is closely tied to the "single" requirement. Given a choice between a general topic and a specific one, you should choose the latter. In a short paper, you can't hope to say anything new or significant about a large topic: "Employment opportunities in Canada," for example. But you could write an interesting, detailed discussion on a more specific topic, such as "Employment opportunities in Nova Scotia's hospitality industry."

You can narrow a broad subject by applying one or more limiting factors to it. Try thinking of your subject in terms of a specific *kind* or *time* or *place* or *number* or *person* associated with it. To come up with the hospitality topic, for example, we limited the subject of employment opportunities in Canada in terms of both place and kind.

4. Your subject must be **SUPPORTABLE**. You must know something about the subject (preferably, more than your reader does), or you must be able to find out about it. Your discussion of your subject will be clear and convincing only if you can include examples, facts, quotations, descriptions, anecdotes, and other details. Supporting evidence can be taken from your own experience or from the experience of other people. In other words, your topic may require you to do some research.[1]

EXERCISE **22.1**

Imagine that you have been asked to write a 500-word paper and given this list of subjects to choose from. Test each subject against the 4-S guidelines and identify what's wrong with it. Answers for exercises in this chapter begin on page 445.

1. Applying sunscreen
2. Samsung Galaxy, Apple iPad, and Rim Playbook
3. The Higgs boson particle
4. Combatting anorexia and obesity
5. Logging on to Facebook
6. Video games
7. The Chinese Secret Service

---

[1] Many colleges and most universities require students to write formal research papers in their first year. The five steps to essay writing that we outline in this unit apply to research papers as well as to informal and in-class essays. In addition to finding and incorporating information from sources in your essay, a research paper requires that you format and document your paper according to specific guidelines. On our website—NELSONbrain.com—you will find links to MLA and APA style guidelines, the two styles most frequently required in undergraduate courses.

8. Astrophysics
9. Parenting in the 22nd century
10. Velcro

EXERCISE **22.2**

Apply the 4-S guidelines to the following subjects. Some are possibilities for short papers but fail to satisfy one or more of the guidelines. Others are hopeless. Revise the "possible" subjects to make them significant, single, specific, and supportable.

1. Bottled water
2. Some people are very attractive
3. The proper way to load the dishwasher
4. The Russian economy
5. Plug-in electric cars
6. How to mix paint
7. Predicting the future
8. Canadian war heroes
9. Global positioning systems
10. Internet piracy

EXERCISE **22.3**

List three subjects that you might choose to write about. Make sure each subject is *significant*, *single*, *specific*, and *supportable*.

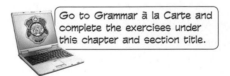

Go to Grammar à la Carte and complete the exercises under this chapter and section title.

DISCOVERING YOUR THESIS AND MAIN POINTS

Once you've chosen a suitable subject for your paper, you need to decide what you want to say about it. There are many possible ways of thinking and writing about any subject. In a short paper, you can deal effectively with only a few aspects of your topic. How do you decide what approach to take?

The approach to your subject that you choose is your **thesis**: a thesis is an idea about a limited subject. It is an opinion or point of view that needs to be explained or proved. A THESIS IS NOT A STATEMENT OF FACT. Compare the examples that follow.

Fact	Thesis
Most people experience some anxiety when they begin a first job.	The stress I experienced in my first job was caused by my employer, my co-workers, and—surprisingly—myself. (Needs to be explained.)
For several years, Canada ranked first on the UN's list of the world's best countries to live in.	Canadians don't know how lucky they are. (Needs to be explained.)
Some universities do not require students to demonstrate writing competence before graduation.	All universities should require students to demonstrate writing competence before graduation. (Needs to be proved.)

A thesis can be discovered in several ways. Brainstorming, freewriting, listing, and clustering are strategies that many college students are familiar with from high school. You should continue to use any technique you've learned that produces good results. However, if these approaches haven't worked well for you, you may need a more structured approach to discovering what it is you can and want to say about a subject.

Try questioning—asking lead-in questions about your subject. A lead-in question is one that guides you into your subject by pointing to an angle or viewpoint—a thesis—that you can explore in your paper. The answers to your lead-in question become the main points your paper will explain.

> **Six Questions to Ask about Your Subject**
>
> 1. How can my subject be defined or explained? What are its significant features or characteristics? Examples: "Generation Y," "HD TV," "The Canadian personality"
> 2. How is my subject made or done? How does it work? Examples: "How to choose the right college," "Hybrid electric cars," "How to set up a home network"
> 3. What are the main kinds, components, or functions of my subject? Examples: "Internet addicts," "The perfect workout," "What does a floor director do?"

Paragraphs and Essays

4. What are the main similarities and/or differences between my subject and something else like it? Examples: "Toyota and Honda hybrid systems," "A fan's view of professional vs. amateur hockey," "Differences between college and university"

5. What are the causes or effects of my subject? Examples: "Why parents and teenagers disagree," "The causes of ADD," "Some effects of high fuel prices"

6. What are the advantages or disadvantages of my subject? What are the reasons for or against it? Examples: "Our city's new recycling program," "Fast food," "Toll roads"

These questions suggest some common ways of looking at or thinking about a subject. Some questions will yield better results than others, and most subjects will produce answers to more than one of the questions. Choose as your subject the question that produces the answers you can or want to write about.

Here's an example of how the process works. Let's assume you've been asked to write a paper on the topic "A satisfying career."[2] Apply each question to your subject and make notes of the answers.

1. "What is a satisfying career?" What are its significant features or characteristics?

   This question produces useful answers. Answers might include a career that is interesting, highly paid, and respected and that provides opportunities for advancement.

2. "How is a satisfying career made or chosen?"

   This question would also work. Some answers might include self-analysis, career counselling, experience (perhaps through part-time or volunteer work), research, or aptitude tests.

3. "What are the main parts or components of a satisfying career?"

   We could use this question, too. The components of a satisfying career might include challenging work, good pay, compatible co-workers, and respect in the community.

---

[2] If your instructor has assigned the topic of your essay, don't grumble—be grateful. The way your instructor words the assignment may contain information that will help you decide what approach to take. Assignment instructions usually contain *direction words*, which are reliable clues to the kind of paper your instructor is looking for. For example, *Define* points you to question 1; *Describe* means you should apply questions 1 and 2; *Discuss* and *Explain* tell you to apply questions 3, 4, 5, and possibly 6; and *Evaluate* points you to question 6.

4. "How is a satisfying career different from something else?"

This question has limited possibilities. You could develop a contrast between a satisfying career and an unsatisfying one, but there isn't much new to say. The main points are obvious and could be explained more easily in response to question 1 than to question 4.

5. "Does a satisfying career have causes or effects?"

It has both.

"What causes a satisfying career?"

Self-analysis, planning, preparation.

"What are the effects of a satisfying career?"

Confidence, stability, recognition, happiness.

6. "What are the advantages or disadvantages of a satisfying career?"

Unless you can think of some unusual advantages (i.e., ones that are not covered by the answers to question 3), this question doesn't produce answers that are worth spending your or your readers' time on. You've already discovered the advantages in answering question 3, and there aren't many disadvantages to a satisfying career!

Asking these six questions about your subject will help you decide what approach would be best for your paper. The "best" approach is the one that is most original and most convincing: the main points your paper discusses not only should seem fresh to your readers but should also sound reasonable to an educated audience.

The questioning strategy we've outlined above will

- help you define your thesis by identifying the opinion you can best explain or defend and
- put you on the path to drafting your paper by providing some solid main points to work with

Don't rush this process. The more time you spend exploring your subject in the planning stage, the easier the actual drafting of the paper will be.

Below you will find eight sample subjects, together with main points that were discovered by applying the questions beginning on page 275. Study these examples carefully. Figure out the logic that leads from subject to question to main points in each case. When you're finished, you should have a good understanding of how the questioning process can work for you.

Subject	Selected Question	Main Points
A good teacher	1. What are the characteristics of a good teacher?	• knowledge of subject • ability to communicate • respect for students

Subject	Selected Question	Main Points
The hybrid automobile	1. What are the features of a hybrid car?	• gas engine for high speeds • electric engine for low speeds • momentum from gas engine and brakes to recharge batteries
A successful party	2. How do you give a successful party?	• invite the right mix of people • plan the entertainment • prepare the food in advance • provide a relaxed, friendly atmosphere
Internet users	3. What are the main categories of Internet users?	• dabblers • regulars • addicts
Quitting smoking	3. What are the main ways to quit smoking?	• cold turkey • taper off gradually • medical/chemical support (pills, gum, patch)
Refugees in Canada	5. What are the main causes of refugees coming to Canada?	• war in homeland • poverty in homeland • persecution in homeland
Nursing as a career	6. What are the main advantages of a career in nursing?	• opportunities to help people • opportunities for travel • career security
Smartphones	6. What are the main disadvantages of using a smartphone?	• keeps you tied to work 24/7 • compromises your privacy and "alone time" • replaces face-to-face social interaction • can be addictive • is an annoying disturbance in restaurants, classrooms, theatres, etc.

As a general rule, you should try to identify between *two* (the absolute minimum) and *five* main ideas to support your subject. If you have only one main idea, your subject is suitable for a paragraph or two, not for an essay. If you have discovered more than five main ideas that require discussion, you have too much material for a short paper. Either select the most important aspects of the subject or take another look at it to see how you can focus it more specifically.

EXERCISE **22.4**

In this exercise, select a question from the highlighted list beginning on page 275 and generate good main points for each subject.

Subject	Selected Question	Main Points
1. My chosen career	•	•
		•
		•
2. Owning a car versus using public transit	•	•
		•
		•
3. My family's (or my ancestor's) immigration to Canada	•	•
		•
		•
4. Leaving home	•	•
		•
		•
5. Reality television	•	•
		•
		•

Paragraphs and Essays

Subject	Selected Question	Main Points
6. Dressing for success	•	•
		•
		•
7. Time management	•	•
		•
		•
8. Blogs	•	•
		•
		•
9. Tattoos	•	•
		•
		•
10. Achieving a balanced life	•	•
		•
		•

EXERCISE 22.5

For each of the three subjects you chose in Exercise 22.3, list two to five main points. To discover suitable main points, apply to your subject the six questions highlighted on pages 275 and 276, one at a time, until you find the question that fits best. The answers to that question are your main points.

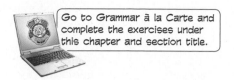

Go to *Grammar à la Carte* and complete the exercises under this chapter and section title.

TESTING YOUR MAIN POINTS

Now take a close look at the main points you've chosen for each subject in Exercise 22.5. It may be necessary to revise some of them before going any further. Are some points too trivial to bother with? Do any of the points overlap in meaning? Are there any points that are not directly related to the subject?

> Main points must be SIGNIFICANT, DISTINCT, and RELEVANT.

To be satisfactory, the main points you have chosen to write about must all be *significant*: they must require a paragraph or more of explanation. If you have any trivial ideas mixed in with the important ones, now is the time to discard them.

Each of the main points you've chosen must also be *distinct*. That is, each must be different from all the others. There must be no overlap in meaning. Check to be sure you haven't given two different labels to what is really one aspect of the subject.

Finally, each main point must be *relevant*; it must be clearly *related* to the subject. It must be an aspect of the subject you are writing about, not some other subject. For example, if you're writing about the advantages of a subject, cross out any disadvantages that may have appeared on your list.

EXERCISE **22.6**

Each of the following subjects is followed by some possible main points. Circle the unsatisfactory point(s) in each group.

1. Popular Canadian sports teams
   - Edmonton Oilers
   - Winnipeg Blue Bombers
   - Montreal Canadiens
   - Seattle Seahawks
   - Hamilton Tiger-Cats

Paragraphs and Essays

2. The advantages of getting into shape
- improved muscle tone
- weight loss
- improved appearance
- improved stamina
- better looks

3. Problems faced by new immigrants in Canada
- government bureaucracy and paperwork
- finding suitable work
- shovelling snow
- finding affordable and suitable housing
- learning a new language
- adjusting to the climate

4. Major causes of stress
- death of a loved one
- moving to a new location
- changing hairstyles
- beginning a new job
- making a major purchase

5. Characteristics of sharks
- tiny brain
- cartilaginous skeleton
- must move to breathe
- sharp, triangular teeth
- great white

6. Advantages of e-readers
- cause of eye strain
- portable, can carry many books in one tablet
- links to information and reference materials
- easy and quick access to books
- multi-function (video, email, word-processing, etc.)

7. Alternative energy sources
- sun
- wind
- tide
- geothermal
- solar

8. Lower taxes stimulate the economy
- businesses have more money to hire
- individuals have more money to spend on goods and services

- government can launch
  infrastructure projects to boost
  employment
- foreign investors are attracted to
  low-tax environment

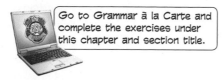

Go to Grammar à la Carte and
complete the exercises under
this chapter and section title.

EXERCISE **22.7**

Study the main points you chose in Exercise 22.5 on page 280. Cross out any
that are not *significant*, *distinct*, or *relevant* to the subject. If necessary, add
new main points so that you end up with at least three main points for each
subject.

ORGANIZING YOUR MAIN POINTS

Now that you've decided on three or four main points to discuss, you need to
decide on the order in which to present them in your paper. Choose the order
that is most appropriate for your subject and audience.

> There are four basic ways to arrange main points in an essay: CHRONOLOGICAL, CLIMACTIC,
> LOGICALLY LINKED, and RANDOM order.

1. **Chronological order** means in order of time sequence, from first to last.
   Here's an example:

   Subject

   The development of a
   relationship

   Main Points

   - attraction
   - meeting
   - discovery
   - intimacy

Paragraphs and
Essays

2. **Climactic order** means presenting your strongest or most important point last. Generally, you would discuss your second-strongest point first and the others in between, like this:

Subject	Main Points
Reasons for the federal government to legislate lower carbon emissions	• Airborne pollutants endanger the health of individual Canadians. • Damage to trees hurts the economy. • Our emissions affect the United States as well as Canada. • Global warming caused by carbon emissions threatens our very existence.

3. **Logically linked order** means that the main points are connected in such a way that one point must be explained before the next can be understood. Consider this example:

Subject	Main Points
Main causes of gang involvement	• lack of opportunity for work • lack of recreational facilities • boredom • need for an accepting peer group

The logical link here is this: because of unemployment, recreational facilities are needed, and because of both unemployment and inadequate recreational facilities, boredom becomes a problem. Bored by having nothing to do and nowhere to go, young people need an accepting peer group to bolster their self-esteem. The first three points must be explained before the reader can fully understand the fourth.

4. **Random order** means the points can be satisfactorily explained in any order. A random arrangement of points is acceptable only if the main points are *equally significant* and *not chronologically or causally linked*, as in this example:

Subject	Main Points
Reasons to cycle to school	• fitness • economy • enjoyment

These three points are equally important; they can be effectively explained in any order.

Below, we have identified eight subjects, together with several main points that could be used to develop them. For each subject, number the points so that they are arranged in the suggested order.

Subject	Order	Main Points
1. How to prepare for a job interview	chronological	_____ Visit the company's website.
		_____ Dress appropriately.
		_____ Prepare answers to standard interview questions.
		_____ Ask a friend to role-play the interview with you.
2. Differences between spoken and written language	climactic	_____ Speech is transitory; writing is permanent.
		_____ Speech is spontaneous; writing isn't.
		_____ Speech can't be revised; writing can.
3. How to write a research paper	chronological	_____ Read and take notes on selected research sources.
		_____ Draft the paper.
		_____ Compile a working bibliography of research sources.
		_____ Define the subject.
		_____ Type and proofread final draft.
		_____ Insert source citations and reference list.
		_____ Revise the paper.
4. How colleges benefit society	logical	_____ They provide students with a higher level of general education.
		_____ They contribute to increased national productivity.

Paragraphs and Essays

		_____ They provide students with job skills.
5. Effects of malnutrition	logical	_____ Malnutrition affects the productivity and prosperity of nations as a whole.
		_____ Malnutrition impedes the mental and physical development of children.
		_____ Undernourished children become sickly adults unable to participate fully in their society.
6. Why pornography should be banned	chronological	_____ It degrades those who make it.
		_____ It brutalizes society as a whole.
		_____ It desensitizes those who view it.
7. Reasons for student poverty	climactic	_____ lack of parental assistance
		_____ lack of government loan assistance
		_____ inability to manage money effectively
		_____ inability to find part-time work
8. Why Canadian professionals immigrate to the United States	climactic	_____ higher salaries
		_____ more jobs to choose from
		_____ warmer climate
		_____ better working conditions

EXERCISE 22.9

Using your list of subjects and main points from Exercise 22.7, arrange the main points for each subject in the most appropriate order. (*Note:* Keep your answer sheet. You will need it in some of the exercises that follow in the next chapter.)

In this chapter, you've learned how to choose a satisfactory subject; how to discover a thesis; and how to find, test, and arrange main points that support your thesis. Now it's time to think about how to plan your paper. Which will work best for you: the thesis statement method? Or the outline method? We think the former generally works best for short papers and the latter for long papers, but this distinction isn't hard and fast. Your wisest choice is to learn both. You will often get the best results if you use them together.

Paragraphs and Essays

23 The Thesis Statement

In Chapter 22, you chose a topic and selected some aspects of it to discuss. Your next task is to outline your paper. There are several different methods to choose from, ranging from a sentence or two (a thesis statement) to a formal outline. For short papers, we recommend that you use the method presented in this chapter. For longer papers, or for those for which your teacher requires a more detailed outline, you will find instructions in Chapter 24, "The Outline."

The key to a well-organized paper is a **thesis statement**—a statement near the beginning of your paper that announces its subject and scope. The thesis statement helps both you and your readers because it previews the plan of your paper. It tells your readers exactly what they are going to read about.

In fiction, telling readers in advance what they are going to find would never do. But for practical, everyday kinds of writing, advance notice works well. Term papers, technical reports, research papers, office memoranda, and business letters are no place for suspense or surprises. In these kinds of writing, you're more likely to get and keep your readers' attention if you indicate the subject and scope of your paper at the outset. A thesis statement acts like a table of contents. It's a kind of map of the territory covered in your paper: it keeps your reader (and you) on the right track.

> A thesis statement clearly and concisely indicates the SUBJECT of your paper, the MAIN POINTS you will discuss, and the ORDER in which you will discuss them.[1]

To write a thesis statement, you join your **subject** to your **main points**, which you arrange in an appropriate order. To join the two parts of a thesis statement, you use a **link**. Your link can be a word or a phrase such as *are, include, consist of, because,* or *since,* or it can be a colon.[2] Here is a simple formula for constructing a thesis statement. (*S* stands for your subject.)

> | *subject* | *link* | *main points* |
> |-----------|--------|----------------|
> | S | consists of | 1, 2, 3 … n. |

Here's an example:

subject   *link* *main points 1, 2, and 3*

Three characteristics of a good report (are) conciseness, clarity, and courtesy.

EXERCISE **23.1**

In each of the following thesis statements, underline the subject with a wavy line, circle the link, and underline the main points with a straight line. Answers for exercises in this chapter begin on page 448.

1. Three essential components of a strong and lasting relationship are good communication, sexual compatibility, and mutual respect.

---

[1] Not all thesis statements retain the preview portion (i.e., the main points in order of discussion) in the final draft. Nevertheless, we recommend that you begin the drafting process with a full thesis statement. You can always omit the preview of main points in your final copy if it seems redundant.

[2] Remember that a colon can be used only after an independent clause. See Chapter 19 if you need a review.

2. Don Cherry simultaneously amuses and provokes viewers with his opinions about hockey violence, his taste in clothing, and his perspective on international hockey.

3. If I were you, I would avoid eating in the cafeteria because the food is expensive, tasteless, and unhealthy.

4. The responsibilities of a modern union include protecting jobs, increasing wages, improving working conditions, and enhancing pensions and benefits.

5. If we are to compete internationally, our company needs a strong board of directors, creative executives, and dynamic middle managers.

6. The original Volkswagen Beetle, the Citroen CV, and the Morris Minor are three cars that will be remembered for their endearing oddness.

7. Fad diets are not the quick and easy fixes to weight problems that they may seem to be; in fact, they are often costly, ineffective, and even dangerous.

8. Taking the time and trouble to buy locally grown foods is better not only for you, but also for the local economy and the environment.

9. Do you lack basic skills, study skills, or motivation? If so, you are at high risk of failing your first year of college.

10. What makes a great movie? Not top stars or a huge budget. Great movies—those that are destined to be viewed generations from now—are based on a fortuitous combination of memorable stories, unforgettable characters, and brilliant direction.

When you combine your subject with your main points to form a thesis statement, there is an important rule to remember:

> Main points must be stated in *grammatically parallel form* (**parallelism**).

This rule means that, if main point 1 is a word, then main points 2 and 3 and so on must be words, too. If main point 1 is a phrase, then the rest must be phrases. If your first main point is a dependent clause, then the rest must be dependent clauses. Study the model thesis statements you analyzed in Exercise 23.1. In every example, the main points are in grammatically parallel form. For each of those thesis statements, decide whether words, phrases, or dependent clauses were used. If you think your understanding of parallelism is a bit wobbly, review Chapter 9.

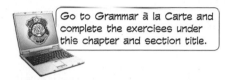

Go to Grammar à la Carte and complete the exercises under this chapter and section title.

EXERCISE **23.2**

Put a check mark (✔) before the sentences that are grammatically parallel. When you have completed the exercise, check your answers on page 448.

1. _____ An effective manager must have excellent knowledge of company products and procedures, superior leadership qualities, and a good work–life balance.

2. _____ The campus pub that we are designing should be open and inviting, efficiency for food preparation and serving, superior acoustics for concerts, and centrally located on campus.

3. _____ The company is seeking new employees who are well educated, honest, disciplined, and can be relied on.

4. _____ Some of the negative effects of caffeine include nervousness, unable to sleep, heart palpitations, and potential mild addiction.

5. _____ The new agreement includes a small pay increase, health benefits are improved, there is more sick time, and slightly higher pensions.

EXERCISE **23.3**

Now revise the incorrect sentences in Exercise 23.2.

EXERCISE **23.4**

Revise the following draft thesis statements. Be sure that the main points of each statement are significant, distinct, relevant, and grammatically parallel. Some sentences contain more than one kind of error. Make corrections as needed; then compare your revisions with our suggested answers.

1. Four types of essay writing are description, narrative, expository, and persuading somebody.

2. In a competitive environment, this corporation needs to improve its products, sales increases, a better logo, and workforce reduction.

3. Increasingly, scientists are finding links between the environment and health concerns such as diabetes, cancer, cold sores, and aging.

4. Cloud formations, the direction of wind, variation in temperature, and barometric pressure are all signs that even an amateur can use to predict the weather.

5. The Summer Olympic events that gain the largest television audience are track and field, volleyball, basketball, the 100-metre race, and gymnastics.

EXERCISE **23.5**

With a partner, for each of the following subjects, assess the main points we've provided to see if they are suitable for inclusion in a short essay. Then, using the points that pass the test, write a grammatically parallel thesis statement. Underline the subject with a wavy line, circle the link, and underline the main points with straight lines. We've done part of the first question for you as an example. (*Tip:* Read each question all the way through before you decide which main points can be kept and which should be discarded.)

When you have completed this exercise, go to Exercise 23.6 without checking your answers.

1. Subject: Watching television is a valuable way to spend time.

Choose main points that support the subject:

• learn things? Yes, you can learn many things watching TV.

• relax and laugh? Yes, TV provides good entertainment.

- wastes time? No, TV may do that, but this point doesn't support the thesis.

- provides topics for discussion? Yes, talking about shows we've watched brings us together with friends and family.

- violent video games? No (why?) _____

A. Thesis statement: <u>Watching television is a valuable way to spend time</u> (because) <u>it teaches us many things</u>, <u>it provides relaxation</u>, and <u>it supplies us with topics to discuss with others</u>.

Now rewrite the thesis statement using a colon as a link.

B. There are three reasons _____

_____

_____

_____

2. A 30-hour work week would increase our company's productivity.

- Employees will be less tired, more focused, and more productive.

- It would allow employees to get part-time jobs.

- Increased family time and leisure time make an employee more satisfied.

- Work hours will not be in sync with those of suppliers and clients.

- Reduction in work hours will be compensated for by reduction in absenteeism and sick leave.

A. Thesis statement: Three reasons why our company should reduce the work week to 30 hours are _____

_____

_____

_____

Rewrite the thesis statement using *because* as a link.

B. _____

_____

_____

_____

3. Immigration is a good policy for Canada.

- Immigrants offer new skills.

- Immigrants may find adjusting to life in Canada difficult.

- Immigrants may bring investment dollars.

- Immigrants must often learn a new language.

- Immigrants enrich Canadian culture.

A. **Thesis statement:** Immigration is a good policy for Canada because _____

_____

_____

_____

Rewrite the thesis statement using a colon as the link.

B. _____

_____

_____

_____

4. Most of us look forward to vacations, but the kind of vacation we enjoy depends on the kind of people we are.

- beach resorts

- gambling trips (e.g., Las Vegas, Orillia, Atlantic City)

- Cancun, Mexico

- adventure vacations

- Buckingham Palace

- too much sun

- mountain climbing

- touring cultural attractions

A. **Thesis statement:** Different people like different kinds of vacation; for

example, <u>some people like to relax at a beach resort</u>, _____

_____

_____

Rewrite the thesis statement using *are* as a link.

B. _____

_____

_____

_____

In the following question, you need first to create a subject statement. Next,
decide which points are usable (significant, distinct, and relevant). After deleting
any unsatisfactory points, write two different thesis statements, making sure
that both are grammatically parallel.

5. A satisfying career

- interesting

- well-paid

- respected

- provides opportunities for advancement

- makes employee feel needed and appreciated

A. Thesis statement: _____

_____

_____

_____

B. Thesis statement: _____

_____

_____

_____

EXERCISE **23.6**

Exchange with another student team the thesis statements you created for Exercise 23.5. Check each thesis statement for completeness and grammatical parallelism. Then decide which team's thesis statement for each subject you prefer and why. Be prepared to defend your choice by referring to the four highlighted guidelines found on pages 281, 283, 289, and 290. Finally, compare your answers with our suggestions on pages 449 and 450.

EXERCISE **23.7**

For each of the topics below, provide main points and write a thesis statement.

1. What I have learned from my family since I became an adult

   •

   •

   •

Thesis statement: _____

_____

_____

_____

2. Preparing for a career

   •

   •

   •

Thesis statement: _____

_____

_____

_____

3. What success means to me

-
-
-

Thesis statement: _____

_____

_____

_____

4. The characteristics of a great movie

-
-
-

Thesis statement: _____

_____

_____

_____

5. How not to impress a date

-
-
-

Thesis statement: _____

_____

_____

Paragraphs and Essays

EXERCISE **23.8**

Find the subjects and main points you produced for Exercise 22.9 in Chapter 22. Combine each subject with its main points to make a thesis statement. Be sure the main points are expressed in parallel form.

We said at the beginning of this chapter that a complete thesis statement provides a broad outline of your paper. Before we turn to the actual writing of the paper, you should have a general idea of what the finished product will look like.

In a short paper, each main point can be explained in a single paragraph. The main points of your subject become the *topics* of the paragraphs, as shown on the next page in the model format for a paper with three main points.[3] Once you've mastered this simple structure, you can modify, expand, and develop it to suit papers of any length or kind.

Please note that the model format on the next page is a basic guideline for anyone who is learning to write English prose. Not all essays are—or should be—five paragraphs long. As you will see in Unit 6, unified, coherent essays can be shorter or longer, depending on their subject and purpose. As you gain writing experience, you will learn how to adapt the basic format to suit your needs. A competent and confident writer always adapts form to content, never the other way around. But learners must start somewhere, and the five-paragraph format is an excellent structure to begin with.

Notice the proportions of the paragraphs in the model format. This format is for a paper whose main points are approximately equal in significance, so the body paragraphs are approximately equal in length. (In a paper in which your last main point is more important than the other points, however, the last paragraph will probably be longer than the other paragraphs.)

Notice, too, that the introductory and concluding paragraphs are shorter than the ones that explain the main points. Your introduction should not ramble on, and your conclusion should not trail off. Get to your main points as quickly as you can, and end with a bang, not a whimper. (Apologies to T. S. Eliot)

---

[3] Chapter 25 will show you how to develop your paragraphs fully and convincingly.

Title _____

Paragraph 1:
Contains your
introduction
and thesis
statement

_____
_____
_____
_____
S consists of 1, 2, and 3. _____

Paragraph 2:
Explains your
first main point

Topic sentence introducing main point 1. _____
_____
_____
_____
_____
_____
_____ .

Paragraph 3:
Explains your
second main
point

Topic sentence introducing main point 2. _____
_____
_____
_____
_____
_____
_____ .

Paragraph 4:
Explains your
third main point

Topic sentence introducing main point 3. _____
_____
_____
_____
_____
_____
_____ .

Paragraph 5:
States your
conclusion

_____
_____
_____
_____ .

EXERCISE **23.9**

An example of a paper based on the model format above is Brian Green's "Career Consciousness" on pages 344 to 345. Read it through; then go back and underline the thesis statement and the topic sentences.

Michel Stevelmans/Shutterstock

24 The Outline

For longer compositions—business and technical reports, research papers, and the like—an outline is often necessary. A good outline maps out your paper from beginning to end. It shows you what you have to say about each of your main points before you begin drafting. Outlining spares you the pain of discovering too late that you have too much information about one point and little or nothing to say about another.

Once you've chosen a satisfactory subject and main points, the next step is to expand this material into an organized plan for your paper. At this point, you may need to do some more thinking or reading to gather additional information. *Evidence*, the term used for supporting information, consists of data, facts, and statements that have been tested and validated by scholars through research or by writers through personal experience. (For the kinds of evidence you can choose from, see "Developing Your Paragraphs" in Chapter 25.) After you've assembled the information you need, prepare the outline.[1]

There are as many different approaches to outlining as there are writers. The outline you prepare will vary depending on your approach to the topic, the amount of time before the due date, and your instructor's preference (or requirement). Here are a few of the strategies you can choose from:

1. Some writers prefer to start with a "scratch" outline, which consists of one- or two-word points that act as a bare-bones guide.

2. Other writers prefer an informal outline that sketches out the parts of the paper in more detail, showing major headings and a few supporting points.

3. Some writers do best with a full, formal outline with main points, subheadings, and various levels of evidence (up to nine if you're using Word), which are identified by changes in indentation and font size.

4. Writers who like to begin with brainstorming, freewriting, or another inductive technique often choose to postpone outlining until after they see what their creative juices produce.

Whatever approach is appropriate for you, your topic, and your instructor, the time you spend on outlining is invested, not wasted. Your investment will pay off in time saved during drafting and revising.

SCRATCH OUTLINE

As we've seen in Chapters 22 and 23, writing an essay requires you to select a thesis and main points, which you arrange in an order that will make sense to your reader. A thesis and main points form the beginnings of a scratch outline. Key these into your word processor, together with a few of the ideas you will elaborate on as you develop the main points. Now you have a bare-bones outline to guide you as you draft the body of your paper. Here's an example:

Thesis: A satisfying career—interesting, rewarding, productive
- Interesting
  - enjoyable
  - like hobbies
  - Clive Beddoe

---

[1] The four ways to arrange main ideas in a paper, which we explained in Chapter 22, also apply to the arrangement of evidence within a paragraph. Choose whichever order best suits the nature of your topic and the needs of your audience.

- Rewarding
  - financial rewards
  - emotional rewards
- Productive
  - need to contribute
  - unproductive jobs

While this outline means nothing to anyone other than its author, this is the skeleton of a paper. Once the writer puts some meat on the bones, adds an introduction and a conclusion, he or she will have a good first draft.

INFORMAL OUTLINE

An informal outline carries the scratch outline a step further, adding notes and ideas that will form the content of each paragraph. If whole sentences occur to you, write them down, but generally the informal outline is in point form.

Introduction
Definition of "career"
Thesis: "A satisfying career should be interesting, rewarding, and productive"
- Interesting
  1. look forward to going to work
  2. leisure activities are stimulating, why not your career?
     Examples: artists, Clive Beddoe
  3. important not to waste your life doing something you hate
- Rewarding
  1. know yourself: What do you need to be happy?
     Are you ambitious? Do you need status? a high salary?
     Or do you want a relaxed, low-stress environment?
  2. success is what it means to you
     Examples: technician, news director—which one is "successful"?
- Productive
  1. human nature to want to contribute, to make a difference
  2. some jobs are easy but meaningless
     Examples: factory job, night shift
Conclusion
Understanding yourself is key.
Don't be swayed by opinions of others.
Strive to improve for your own sake, not your employer's.

FORMAL OUTLINE

A formal outline is more detailed than a scratch or informal outline. It may be drafted in point form, but even if it isn't, the finished outline usually consists of complete sentences. If you have access to a word-processing program with an outline feature, try it out. Most programs have a "document view" called "Outline," which can be invaluable: it will create a formal outline as fast as you can type. In Word, select the View tab and choose Outline. (In Apple's Pages, the "Template Chooser" has a variety of Outline options.)

Here's how to proceed:

1. Key in your main points, in the order you chose for your thesis statement, and hit Enter after each one.
2. Move the cursor to the end of your first main point, hit Enter, and select Level 2 from the window at the top of the screen. This will indent and reduce the font size of the next line you type, which should be a supporting point for the first main point.
3. Hit Enter again and select Level 3 to add examples or other evidence to develop this supporting point.

By repeating this process for each of your main points, you will end up with a clear visual plan of your essay. The outline will look something like this:

+ Introduction
  - Attention-getter
  - Thesis statement or statement of subject
+ First main point
  + Supporting point
    - Evidence
  + Supporting point
    - Evidence
+ Second main point
  + Supporting point
    - Evidence
  + Supporting point
    - Evidence
+ Third main point
  + Supporting point
    - Evidence
  + Supporting point
    - Evidence
  + Supporting point
    - Evidence

Paragraphs and Essays

+ Conclusion
  - Summary
  - Memorable statement

The outline stage is the time to decide how to present the supporting information under each main point and how much time to spend on a particular point. If, for example, you have six subheadings under your first main point and one under your second, you need to rebalance your paper. Main points should be supported by approximately equal amounts of information.

Creating a satisfactory outline takes time. Be prepared to spend time rearranging, adding, and deleting your ideas and supporting details until you're completely satisfied with their arrangement and proportions.

Now you are ready to draft your paper. Make the main points into paragraphs, develop the supporting points, and add an introduction and a conclusion. (Chapter 25 explains how.)

To show you the relationship between an outline and the final product, we've re-created the outline that was used to write "Career Consciousness," which you will find on pages 344 to 345.

Introduction

Attention-getter: Choosing your life's vocation is not a decision to be taken lightly.

Thesis statement: A satisfying career is one that is stimulating, rewarding, and productive.

I. A satisfying career is stimulating.
  A. When you get up in the morning, you look forward to your day.
      1. While not the image most people have of work, it is achievable.
      2. People can enjoy work just as they enjoy leisure activities.
  B. Many successful people have turned their interests into careers.
      1. Career professionals in the arts get paid for what they love to do.
          a. write, compose, paint, sculpt, etc.
          b. act, dance, sing, etc.
      2. Clive Beddoe: turned his love of flying into the development of WestJet.
  C. If you deny yourself the chance to do what you love, you will spend most of your life wishing you were doing something else.

II. A satisfying career is both financially and emotionally rewarding.

    A. To choose the right career, you must know yourself.

        1. Do you want power and status?

        2. Or do you want a less stressful position?

    B. Success is a state of mind.

        1. Contrast the careers of a small-town TV tech and a big-city news director.

            a. TV tech loves his job, family, community, and volunteer activities.

            b. News director thrives on deadlines, big-city life, money, and recognition.

        2. Both feel they are successful.

III. A satisfying career is productive.

    A. Everyone needs meaningful work.

        1. Everyone needs to feel they make a difference.

        2. Friendly co-workers, pleasant routine, and big salary do not make up for lack of appreciation.

    B. Many people go unnoticed in their working lives.

        1. Some read paperbacks on the job.

        2. Some sleep through the night shift and fish or golf during the day.

    C. Knowing that you are doing something worthwhile is essential to your sense of well-being.

Conclusion

    Summary: It's not easy to find a career that provides stimulating, enjoyable, and meaningful work.

    A. You need to understand yourself.

    B. Make career decisions consistent with your values and goals.

    C. Once you have found a satisfying career, keep working at it.

        1. Seek challenges and opportunities that stimulate you.

        2. Enjoy the rewards of doing your job well.

        3. Strive for improvement for your own sake (not your employer's).

    Memorable statement: Your career will occupy three-quarters of your life, so make the most of it!

Paragraphs and Essays

EXERCISE **24.1**

Turn to "Career Consciousness" on pages 344 to 345. Find the paragraphs and sentences that correspond to the headings and subheadings in the outline beginning on page 304. In the margins, label the paragraphs and sentences with the symbols that indicate their place in the outline: Attention-getter, Thesis statement, I, A, 1, 2, and so on. Appendix C does not provide answers for exercises in this chapter.

EXERCISE **24.2**

1. With a partner, choose an essay in Unit 6 that interests you. (Remember: three of the reading selections are on the website NELSONbrain.com.) Read the essay carefully, and create for it
   • a scratch outline
   • an informal outline
   • a formal outline
2. Exchange your work with another team that selected the same reading and compare outlines. Are there significant differences between the two teams' outlines? If so, which set of outlines best captures the essence of the essay?

EXERCISE **24.3**

Turn to the subjects and main points you developed for Exercise 22.9 in Chapter 22 and create scratch, informal, and formal outlines for a paper on one of those subjects.

©iStockphoto.com/sx70

Paragraphs 25

With your thesis statement and outline in front of you, you are ready to turn your main points into paragraphs. Does that sound like a magician's trick? It isn't. All you need to know is what a paragraph looks like and how to put one together.

A paragraph looks like this:

A sentence that introduces the **topic** (or main idea) of the paragraph goes here.

Three or more sentences that specifically support or explain the topic go in here.

A sentence that concludes your explanation of the topic goes here.

Sometimes you can explain a main point satisfactorily in a single paragraph. If the main point is complicated and requires lots of support, you will need two or more paragraphs. Nevertheless, whether it is explaining a main point or a supporting point, every paragraph must contain three things: a **topic sentence** (usually the first sentence in the paragraph), several sentences that develop the topic, and a conclusion or a transition to the next paragraph.

A clear statement of your main idea—usually a single sentence—is a good way to start a paragraph. The sentences that follow should support or expand on the main idea. The key to making the paragraph *unified* (an important quality of paragraphs) is to make sure that each of your supporting sentences relates directly to the main idea introduced in the topic sentence.

EXERCISE **25.1**

Go to our website (NELSONbrain.com) and read Brian Green's "The Case against Quickspeak." Study the fourth, fifth, and sixth paragraphs, and find in each the three basic components of a paragraph: the topic sentence, the supporting sentences, and the conclusion. Then compare your answer with ours. Answers for exercises in this chapter begin on page 451.

DEVELOPING YOUR PARAGRAPHS

How do you put a paragraph together? First, write your topic sentence, telling your reader what topic (main point or key idea) you're going to discuss in the paragraph. Next, develop your topic. An adequately developed paragraph gives enough supporting information to make the topic completely clear to the reader. An average paragraph runs between 75 and 200 words (except for introductions and conclusions, which are shorter), so you will need lots of supporting information for each point.

Unless you are writing from a detailed outline and have all the supporting ideas you need listed in front of you, you need to do some more thinking at this point. Put yourself in your reader's place. What does your reader need to know in order to understand your point clearly? Ask yourself the six questions listed as of page 309 to determine what *kind(s) of development* to use to support a particular topic sentence. The kind of development you choose is up to you. Let your topic and your reader be your guides.

1. Is a **definition** necessary?

If you're using a term that may be unfamiliar to your reader, you should define it. Use your own words in the definition. The reader needs to know what *you* mean by the term—and, besides, quoting from the dictionary is a boring way to develop a paragraph. In the following paragraph, Sarah Norton defines *biomimicry*, a term that many readers are unlikely to recognize.

> What is the relationship between air conditioning and termites? Mussels and superglue? Velcro and plant burrs? Self-cleaning glass and lotus leaves? The answer is that these and hundreds of other products and processes are innovations whose designs were based on plant, animal, or insect life. The term for this relationship is *biomimicry*, which is the science of applying natural models, systems, and elements to human dilemmas. The word comes from *bios*, meaning "life" and *mimesis*, meaning "imitate." Biomimicry is a discipline that uses nature's designs and processes to solve human problems in an efficient and sustainable way.*

You should include a definition, too, if you're using a familiar term in a specific or unusual way. In the following paragraph, Brian Green defines what he means by "slow food."

> The term "slow food" is often misunderstood. When I first heard of the Slow Food Movement, I assumed it was devoted to taking a long time to cook savoury meals. Instead, the term was coined in reaction to everything "fast food" represents, from poor-quality ingredients of unknown origin to hastily gobbled meals served in a plastic environment. "Slow food" can actually be cooked quite quickly, so long as the ingredients are of high quality and locally produced, and the meal is consumed in a relaxed and convivial environment.†

---

* Sarah Norton, "A Convenient Truth." Reprinted by permission of the author.

† Green, Brian. "Cooking under Pressure: Slow Food . . . Fast." *The Green Snail*. Voice of Pelham Newspaper, 2 Jan. 2010. Web. 9 Sept. 2012. Reprinted by permission of the author.

Paragraphs and Essays

EXERCISE **25.2**

Write a paragraph in which you define one of the following terms:

a bully	the ideal man (or woman)
leadership	sustainability
horror	diversity

> 2. Would **examples** help to clarify the point?

Providing examples is probably the most common method of developing a topic. Readers who encounter unsupported generalizations or statements of opinion are not convinced. They know they've been left dangling, and they will be confused. They may even become suspicious, thinking that the writer is trying to put one over on them. One of the most effective ways of getting your idea across to your readers is to provide clear, relevant examples. In the following paragraph, excerpted from a reading posted on our website (NELSONbrain.com), Sun-Kyung Yi uses examples to explain why her job with a Korean company proved to be a "painful and frustrating experience."

When the president of the company boasted that he "operated little Korea," he meant it literally. A Canadianized Korean was not tolerated. I looked like a Korean; therefore, I had to talk, act, and think like one, too. Being accepted meant a total surrender to ancient codes of behaviour rooted in Confucian thought, while leaving the "Canadian" part of me out in the parking lot with my '86 Buick. In the first few days at work, I was bombarded with inquiries about my marital status. When I told them I was single, they spent the following days trying to match me up with available bachelors in the company and the community. I was expected to accept my inferior position as a woman and had to behave accordingly. It was not a place to practise my feminist views, or be an individual without being condemned. Little Korea is a place for men (who filled all the senior positions) and women don't dare speak up or disagree with their male counterparts. The president (all employees bow to him and call him Mr. President) asked me to act more like a lady and smile. I was openly scorned by a senior employee because I spoke more fluent English than Korean. The cook in the kitchen shook her head in disbelief upon discovering that my cooking skills were limited to boiling a package of instant noodles. "You want a good husband, learn to cook," she advised me. (para. 8)*

* Sun-Kyung Yi, "An Immigrant's Split Personality," www.NELSONbrain.com.

Sometimes one or two examples developed in detail are enough to enable the reader to understand what you mean. In the following paragraph, Brian Green first defines what he means by "a rewarding career," and then he provides two examples to illustrate his definition.

If your career is stimulating, then chances are good that it can also be rewarding. A good career offers two kinds of rewards: financial and emotional. Rewarding work doesn't just happen; it's something you need to plan for. The first and most important step is to know yourself. Only if you know who you are and what you need to be happy can you consciously seek out career experiences that will bring you satisfaction and steer clear of those that will annoy or stress you. Are you genuinely ambitious, or is power something you seek because you think it is expected of you? The pursuit of status and a high salary brings some people pure pleasure. Many people, however, find leadership positions excruciatingly stressful. Career enjoyment depends to some extent on whether or not you are successful, and success is a state of mind. Consider two graduates from the same college program. One is a technician in a small-town television station who loves his work, takes pride in keeping the station on the air, and delights in raising his family in a community where he is involved in volunteer activities ranging from sports to firefighting. The other is a news director at one of Canada's major television networks; her work is highly stressful, full of risks, and continually scrutinized by viewers, competitors, and her supervisors. She thrives on the adrenaline rush of nightly production and loves the big-city life, the financial rewards of her position, and the national recognition she receives. Which graduate is "successful"? Certainly, both feel their careers are rewarding, according to their individual definitions of the term. (344–45)*

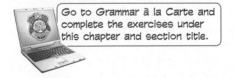

Go to Grammar à la Carte and complete the exercises under this chapter and section title.

EXERCISE **25.3**

Write a six- to ten-sentence paragraph based on one of the topic sentences that follow, using examples to develop it.

The teenage years are the hardest.

---

* Brian Green, "Career Consciousness," pp. 344–45.

Paragraphs and Essays

Fast food is killing us.
Social media are a harmful addiction.
Social media are a force for good.
Our school needs to upgrade its classrooms and labs.

---

3. Is a series of **steps** or **stages** involved?

Sometimes the most effective way to develop the main idea of your paragraph is by explaining how to do it—that is, by relating the process or series of steps involved. Make sure you break down the process into its component parts and explain the steps logically and precisely. The following paragraph explains the process of writing an effective email message. As you read it, number the steps the author identifies as the parts of the process. Has he left anything out?

> Email is no different from any other business correspondence: it must be clear and concise. Achieving clarity and conciseness is not difficult, but it does require planning. Begin with an introduction that briefly explains the purpose of your message. Next, outline how you are going to develop that message. Use numbered or bulleted points to guide the reader from your position statement through your reasoning to your conclusion. Reinforce your message with a conclusion that states any follow-up actions you require and that confirms the time, place, and responsibilities of those who are contributing to the project. Next, reread your message as if you were reading it for the first time. Revise to be sure that you have included all the necessary details: dates, reference numbers, times and places of meetings, and whatever other information is needed to get the right people together in the right places, on the right days, at the right times, with the right information in their briefcases. Use a spell checker, but don't rely on it to catch all your errors and typos. Remember: A clear message, clearly delivered, is the essence of effective communication. (para. 5)*

EXERCISE **25.4**

Write a paragraph developed as a series of steps telling your reader how to make or do something you are good at. (Choose a significant topic, not a trivial one.)

---

* Brian Green, "The Case against Quickspeak," www.NELSONbrain.com.

4. Would **specific details** be useful?

Providing your reader with concrete, specific, descriptive details can be an effective way of developing your main point. In the following paragraph, highlight the specific details the author uses to heighten the effect of her catalogue of torture instruments.

> Even in the Middle Ages, before electricity, there were many things you could do to torment a person. You could tie him up in an iron belt that held the arms and legs up to the chest and left no point of rest, so that all his muscles went into spasm within minutes and he was driven mad within hours. This was the twisting stork, a benign-looking object. You could stretch him out backward over a thin piece of wood so that his whole body weight rested on his spine, which pressed against the sharp wood. Then you could stop up his nostrils and force water into his stomach through his mouth. Then, if you wanted to finish him off, you and your helper could jump on his stomach, causing internal hemorrhage. This torture was called the rack. If you wanted to burn someone to death without hearing him scream, you could use a tongue lock, a metal rod between the jaw and collarbone that prevented him from opening his mouth. You could put a person on a chair with spikes on the seat and arms, tie him down against the spikes, and beat him, so that every time he flinched from the beating he drove his own flesh deeper onto the spikes. This was the Inquisitor's chair. If you wanted to make it worse, you could heat the spikes. You could suspend a person over a pointed wooden pyramid and whenever he started to fall asleep, you could drop him onto the point. If you were Ippolito Marsili, the inventor of this torture, known as the Judas cradle, you could tell yourself you had invented something humane, a torture that worked without burning flesh or breaking bones. For the torture here [was sup]posed to be sleep deprivation.*

In some paragraphs, numerical facts or statistics can be used to support your point effectively. However, ever since Benjamin Disraeli's immortal remark that the media publish "lies, damned lies, and statistics," critical readers tend to be suspicious of statistics. Be very sure that your facts are correct and that your statistics are current.

> Canadians are great travellers. We not only travel around our own country, exploring every nook and cranny from Beaver Creek in the Yukon

---

* "Tools of Torture: An Essay on Beauty and Pain," by Phyllis Rose. Copyright © 1991 by Phyllis Rose, used by permission of The Wylie Agency Incorporated.

Paragraphs and Essays

Territory to Bay Bulls in Newfoundland, but we also can be found touring around every other country on earth. Statistics Canada reports that we take more than 214 million overnight trips a year within our own borders. Abroad, we favour our next-door neighbour by a wide margin above other destinations, averaging around 18 million overnight trips a year to the United States. Mexico is our second-favourite destination, with over 1.1 million visits, followed by the United Kingdom (1 million) and Cuba (932,000). France (809,000) and the Dominican Republic (763,000) round out the top six. China ranks tenth in popularity with 250,000 visits, but Hong Kong, now part of China, attracts an additional 186,000 Canadian visitors, making their combined total ahead of Germany for seventh spot, followed by Italy, the Netherlands, and Spain. The top 15 Canadian destinations are rounded out by three more European nations: Switzerland, the Republic of Ireland, and Greece. We can make a rough estimate from these figures that, on average, a Canadian travels within Canada six times a year and takes a trip abroad twice in three years.*

EXERCISE **25.5**

Write an eight- to ten-sentence paragraph describing one of the following topics. Include details that involve several of the physical senses: sight, hearing, touch, smell, and taste. Be sure to begin with a clearly identifiable topic sentence.

Your favourite family meal
A great (or disastrous) camping trip
The best birthday party ever
Your favourite club, bar, or coffee shop
A horrible workplace

5. Would a **comparison** or **contrast** help to clarify your point?

A **comparison** points out similarities between objects, people, or ideas; it shows how two different things are alike. A **contrast** points out dissimilarities between things; it shows how two objects, people, or ideas are different. In the paragraph that follows, Sun-Kyung Yi contrasts the two sides of her "split personality."

---

* Brian Green, "Canadian, Eh?" Reprinted by permission of the author.

When I was younger, toying with the idea of entertaining two separate identities was a real treat, like a secret game for which no one knew the rules but me. I was known as Angela to the outside world, and as Sun-Kyung at home. I ate bologna sandwiches in the school lunch room and rice and kimchee for dinner. I chatted about teen idols and giggled with my girlfriends during my classes, and ambitiously practised piano and studied in the evenings, planning to become a doctor when I grew up. I waved hellos and goodbyes to my teachers, but bowed to my parents' friends visiting our home. I could also look straight in the eyes of my teachers and friends and talk frankly with them instead of staring at my feet with my mouth shut when Koreans talked to me. Going outside the home meant I was able to relax from the constraints of my cultural conditioning, until I walked back in the door and had to return to being an obedient and submissive daughter. (para. 2)*

In the following paragraph, the writer develops her topic—how lack of planning can kill a city—by comparing the anatomy of a city to that of the human body.

A poorly planned city dies from the centre out. When an unplanned urban area is growing rapidly, businesses and residential developments spring up wherever it is advantageous for them to locate. In time, they become plaque deposits on the very arteries that they chose to build on, gradually narrowing and choking the city's passageways. New routes cannot be constructed without major surgery, nor can the old ones be widened because of the poorly planned developments that line them. Without sufficient flow along its arteries, an organism begins to experience high pressure ... whether from traffic or blood. As the pressure builds, those who live and work in the city core seek to relocate to more convenient, less stressful surroundings, and the centre begins to die. Keeping arteries open and healthy requires advance planning and constant vigilance. In the human organism, a healthy diet and physical exercise will keep the blood flowing; in the urban organism, mass transit and well-planned traffic corridors will do the trick.†

_____

* Sun-Kyung Yi, "An Immigrant's Split Personality," www.NELSONbrain.com.

† Sarah Norton, "Our Cities, Ourselves." Reprinted by permission of the author.

Paragraphs and Essays

EXERCISE **25.6**

Write a paragraph comparing or contrasting two cities (or perhaps countries, generations, musicians, writers/books, sports teams, clothing brands, vacation destinations). Begin your paragraph with a clearly identifiable topic sentence and support it with fresh, original points. The differences in size, climate, and world status between London, England, and London, Ontario, will not grab a reader's attention; the differences in the two cities' ethnic mixes, employment possibilities, and cultural opportunities might interest a Canadian reader.

> 6. Would a **quotation** or **paraphrase** be appropriate?

Use a quotation when you find that someone else—an expert in a particular field, a well-known author, or a respected public figure—has said what you want to say better or more convincingly than you could ever hope to say it. In these cases, quotations—as long as they are kept short and not used too frequently—are useful in developing your topic.

In the following paragraph, Brian Green quotes humorist Robert Benchley and a Portuguese proverb to sum up what many of us have often thought but not been able to express so wittily and concisely.

> "Nothing is more responsible for the good old days than a bad memory." Robert Benchley got it right. Those who continually praise the past and decry the present are victims of selective memory. They are people who are dissatisfied with their lives and want to believe that conditions in the past were better. For these pessimists, today's glass is half empty, while yesterday's was half full. But under objective scrutiny, the pessimists' bias seldom stands up. Even when a few conditions from the past may be preferable to conditions in the present, innumerable other factors will have improved. We would do well to learn from the Portuguese about the pitfalls of the pessimists' selective nostalgia: "What was hard to bear is sweet to remember."*

A **paraphrase** is a summary of someone else's idea in your own words. It is fair to rewrite the idea, but you must still identify your source, the way the author of "The Myth of Canadian Diversity" does in the following paragraph.

---

* Brian Green. Reprinted by permission of the author.

[O]ur much-discussed ethnic differences are overstated. Although Canada is an immigrant nation and Canadians spring from a variety of backgrounds, a recent study from the C.D. Howe Institute says that the idea of a "Canadian mosaic"—as distinct from the American "melting pot"—is a fallacy. In *The Illusion of Difference*, University of Toronto sociologists Jeffrey Reitz and Raymond Breton show that immigrants to Canada assimilate as quickly into the mainstream society as immigrants to the United States do. In fact, Canadians are less likely than Americans to favour holding on to cultural differences based on ethnic background. If you don't believe Mr. Reitz and Mr. Breton, visit any big-city high school, where the speech and behaviour of immigrant students just a few years in Canada is indistinguishable from that of any fifth-generation classmate.*

College writing normally requires that you identify the source of any material you quote or paraphrase. The easiest way to do this is to include a parenthetical citation at the end of your quotation and full publication details in the Works Cited or References list at the end of your paper. If you give the author's name in the sentence leading up to the quotation, you need give only the page number(s) of the source in which you found it. If you do not give the author's name in your introduction to the quotation, you need to include it, together with the page number(s), in the parentheses at the end of the quotation. (If using APA style, provide the year of publication as well as the page number(s).)

If your quotation is short enough to be included in your sentence, put the period *after* the source information. For example,

> According to Brian Green, "A career can be defined as the employment you prepare for during the first quarter of your life, engage in during the best years of your life, and reap the rewards from when you are least able to enjoy them" (344).

> One writer takes a fairly cynical view of the typical career cycle: "A career can be defined as the employment you prepare for during the first quarter of your life, engage in during the best years of your life, and reap the rewards from when you are least able to enjoy them" (Green 344).

At the end of your paper, include a Works Cited or References list: a list in alphabetical order by authors' surnames of all of the books, articles, and other publications from which you have paraphrased, summarized, or quoted in your paper. Ask your instructor which documentation style is

---

* Published in the *Globe and Mail*, June 13, 1994, A12. Reprinted with permission of the *Globe and Mail*.

required: the Modern Language Association (MLA) style, the one approved by the American Psychological Association (APA), or some other style. For an example of a Works Cited list in MLA format, go to page 350 ("The Slender Trap"), and for an example of an APA References list, go to page 360 ("Eat, Drink, and Be Guilty"). For further information about both MLA and APA documentation styles, go to the Student Resources page of this book's website at **www.NELSONbrain.com**; click on "Format and Documentation."

When you plan the paragraphs of your essay, you will often need to use more than one method of development to explain each point. The six methods outlined in this chapter can be used in any combination. Choose whichever kinds of development will best help your reader understand what you want to say about your topic.

EXERCISE **25.7**

Working with a partner, identify the kinds of development used in the following paragraphs from essays in Unit 6 and the website (www.NELSONbrain.com). (More than one kind of development may be present in each.) Then turn to page 451 to check your answers.

1. "The Case against Quickspeak," paragraph 5
2. "Eat, Drink, and Be Guilty," paragraph 2
3. "Eat, Drink, and Be Guilty" paragraph 4
4. "Hockey, Fighting and What It Means to Be a Man," paragraph 4
5. "Career Consciousness," paragraph 3
6. "The Slender Trap," paragraph 4
7. "The Myth of Canadian Diversity," paragraph 1
8. "The Slender Trap," paragraph 3
9. "An Immigrant's Split Personality," paragraph 4
10. "An Immigrant's Split Personality," paragraph 10

EXERCISE **25.8**

Choose one of the following topics (or make up one of your own) and write a paragraph of approximately six to ten sentences using one or more of the methods of paragraph development discussed in this chapter. When you've completed your paragraph, exchange your work with another student, read his or her paragraph carefully, and identify the method(s) of development your partner has used. Were you given enough information to understand the topic? If not, what additional information did you need?

1. Life is like a game of _____.
2. Our school could do more to help students succeed.

3. Television is (not) a dying medium.

4. How to "get away from it all."

5. _____ is a profession with a future.

6. Yesterday's music is (not) better than today's.

7. How to assess a potential partner.

8. Canadians don't appreciate how lucky they are.

9. A near miss.

WRITING INTRODUCTIONS AND CONCLUSIONS

Two paragraphs in your paper are not developed in the way we've just outlined: the *introduction* and the *conclusion*. All too often, these paragraphs are dull or clumsy and detract from a paper's effectiveness. But they needn't. Here's how to write good ones.

The introduction is worth special attention because that's where your reader either sits up and takes notice of your paper or sighs and pitches it into the wastebasket. Occasionally, for a short paper, you can begin by simply stating your thesis. More usually, though, an **attention-getter** comes before the thesis statement. An attention-getter is a sentence or two designed to get the reader interested in what you have to say.

There are several kinds of attention-getter to choose from:

1. a little-known or striking fact (see "The Slender Trap," page 349)
2. a statement of opinion you intend to challenge (see "The Myth of Canadian Diversity," www.NELSONbrain.com)
3. an interesting incident or **anecdote** related to your subject (see "The Case against Quickspeak," www.NELSONbrain.com)
4. a definition (see "Career Consciousness," page 344)
5. a broad contextual statement for your thesis (see "Hockey, Fighting, and What It Means to Be a Man," page 352)

Add your thesis statement to the attention-getter, and your introduction is complete.

The closing paragraph, too, usually has two parts: a **summary** of the main points of your paper (phrased differently, please—not a word-for-word repetition of your thesis statement or your topic sentences) and a **memorable**

statement. Your memorable statement may take several forms. For example, it may do any of the following:

1. refer to the content of your opening paragraph (see "Career Consciousness," page 344)
2. include a relevant or thought-provoking quotation, statement, or question (see "The Myth of Canadian Diversity," www.NELSONbrain.com)
3. emphasize the value or significance of your subject (see "The Case against Quickspeak," www.NELSONbrain.com)
4. make a suggestion for change (see "An Immigrant's Split Personality," www.NELSONbrain.com)
5. offer a solution, make a prediction, or invite the reader to get involved (see "The Slender Trap," page 350; "Hockey, Fighting, and What It Means to Be a Man," page 353)

EXERCISE **25.9**

Using as many of the different kinds as you can, write an attention-getter and a memorable statement for each of the following topics.

1. College professors should (not) be required to take courses in how to teach.
2. Video game content should (not) be censored.
3. Honesty is (not) always the best policy.
4. What you wear tells who you are.
5. In our culture, men (women) have the easier role.
6. The notion of lifelong learning (i.e., continual retraining throughout a career) is (not) appealing to me.
7. On-demand video streaming providers (e.g., Netflix) will quickly destroy community movie theatres. Does it matter?
8. Canada's new preferred immigrant categories will (not) benefit the country over time.
9. Taxes on gasoline should (not) be earmarked for infrastructure repair and maintenance.
10. "The one who dies with the most toys wins." This popular saying says much about our culture.

KEEPING YOUR READER WITH YOU

As you write your paragraphs, keep in mind that you want to make it as easy as possible for your reader to follow your paper. Clear transitions and an appropriate tone can make the difference between a paper that confuses readers and one that enlightens them.

TRANSITIONS

Transitions are words and phrases that show the relationship between one point and the next, making a paragraph or a paper read smoothly. Like turn signals on a car, they tell the person following you where you're going. Here are some common transitions you can use to keep your reader on track:

1. **To show a time relationship:** first, second, third, next, before, during, after, now, then, finally, last
2. **To add an idea or example:** in addition, also, another, furthermore, similarly, for example, for instance
3. **To show contrast:** although, but, however, instead, nevertheless, on the other hand, in contrast, on the contrary
4. **To show a cause–effect relationship:** as a result, consequently, because, since, therefore, thus

The following paragraph has adequate development but no transitions:

> There are several good reasons you should not smoke. Smoking is harmful to your lungs and heart. It is annoying and dangerous to those around you who do not smoke. Smoking is an unattractive and dirty habit. It is difficult to quit. Most worthwhile things in life are hard to achieve.

Not very easy to read, is it? Readers are jerked from point to point until, battered and bruised, they reach the end. This kind of writing is unfair to readers. It makes them do too much of the work—more work than many readers are willing to do. The ideas may all be there, but the readers have to figure out for themselves how the points fit together. After a couple of paragraphs like this one, even a patient reader can become annoyed.

Now read the same paragraph with the transitions added:

> There are several good reasons you should not smoke. Among them, three stand out as the most persuasive. First, smoking is harmful to your

Paragraphs and Essays

lungs and heart. Second, it is both annoying and dangerous to those around you who do not smoke. In addition to these compelling facts, smoking is an unattractive and dirty habit. Furthermore, once you begin, it is difficult to quit; but then, most worthwhile things in life are hard to achieve.

In the revised paragraph, readers are gently guided from one point to the next. By the time they reach the conclusion, they know not only what ideas the writer had in mind but also how they fit together. Transitions make the reader's job easier and more rewarding.

TONE

One final point: as you write the paragraphs of your paper, be conscious of your **tone**. Your audience, purpose, and subject will all influence the tone you choose, which must be appropriate to all three. The words you use, the examples, quotations, and other supporting materials you choose to explain your main points all contribute to your tone.

When you are trying to explain something to someone, particularly if it's something you feel strongly about, you may be tempted to get highly emotional in your discussion. If you give in to this temptation, chances are you won't be convincing. What will be communicated is the strength of your feelings, not the depth of your understanding or the validity of your opinion. To be clear and credible, you need to restrain your enthusiasm or anger and present your points in a calm, reasonable way.

Here are a few suggestions to help you find and maintain the right tone.

- Be tactful. Avoid phrases such as "Any idiot can see," "No sane person could believe," and "It is obvious that ..." What is obvious to you isn't necessarily obvious to someone who has a limited understanding of your subject or who disagrees with your opinion.
- Don't address your readers as though they were children or ignorant. Never use sarcasm, profanity, or slang. (If you do, your readers will neither take you seriously nor respect you.)
- Don't apologize for your interpretation of your subject. Have confidence in yourself. You've thought long and hard about your subject, you've found good supporting material to help explain it, and you believe in its significance. State your thesis positively. If you hang back, using phrases such as "I may be wrong, but ..." or "I tend to feel that ...," your reader won't be inclined to give your points the consideration they deserve. If you present your argument with assurance and courtesy, your writing will be both clear and convincing.

The following paragraph is an example of inappropriate tone. The writer is enthusiastic about the topic, but the tone is arrogant and tactless, not persuasive.

> How dumb can people get? Here's this guy with a bumper sticker reading, "Out of work yet? Keep buying foreign!" on his "North American" car parked in a Walmart parking lot. What can you buy in a Walmart that's made in Canada? Zilch. And besides, the car this idiot is driving wasn't made in Canada or even the U.S. The engine was imported from Japan, and the transmission was made by Mexicans working for next to nothing. The plastic body moulding came from that model of capitalism and human rights, China, and the interior finishings were made in Taiwan. Not foreign? Give me a break. About the only part of this car that was made right here is the bumper that holds his stupid sticker. Meanwhile, parked right next to him was a "Japanese" car that was manufactured in Canada by Ontario workers. Sticker Guy is obviously too ignorant to get the irony.

Now read the paragraph below, which argues the same point but in a more tactful way.

> As the driver pulled into the parking spot beside me, I could hardly help noticing his bumper sticker: "Out of work yet? Keep buying foreign!" It was attached to a car produced by one of North America's "Big Three" automakers, but the message lost much of its force because of where we were: in a Walmart parking lot. There is precious little to buy in Walmart that has been produced in Canada. However, even that fact is beside the point, given the current internationalization of the auto industry. The car with the sticker on it, while nominally North American in origin, had an engine produced in Japan, a transmission built in Mexico, plastic body moulding made in China, and interior finishings imported from Taiwan. One of the few parts actually made in Canada, ironically, was the bumper to which the sticker was attached. Meanwhile, the car next to it, a "Japanese" mid-size, had been built in Ontario.

EXERCISE **25.10**

The following paragraph is a draft written for a general reader. The writer's purpose is to persuade his audience that fighting should be banned in professional hockey. Revise the paragraph to make it appropriate for its audience and purpose by deleting or rewording any lapses in tone. Then compare your answer with our suggestions on page 452.

Paragraphs and Essays

We've all heard the arguments: "It's part of the game," "It's what the fans want," "It prevents dangerous, dirty play." What nonsense! Fighting has no place in hockey or any team sport, and people who think differently are Neanderthals. Anyone with half a brain knows that fighting is banned in every other sport. What makes hockey any different? If the fans wanted fighting, they wouldn't watch the Olympics or World Championships. Ever seen the ratings for those events? Through the roof! Meanwhile, NHL ratings are in decline, and the game is treated as a third-rate sport in most of the world. Hockey can be a beautiful, fast, skilful, creative game, but when goons who have no purpose other than to fight are sent out onto the ice, it is a joke.

EXERCISE **25.11**

Do either A or B.

A. Using one of the thesis statements you prepared in Chapter 23, Exercise 23.7, write an essay of 400–500 words.
B. Using the outline you prepared in Chapter 24, Exercise 24.3, write a paper of approximately 500 words.

Jim Lopes/Shutterstock

Revising Your Paper 26

No one can write in a single draft an essay that is perfectly organized and developed, let alone one that is free of grammar, spelling, and punctuation errors. The purpose of the first draft is to get down on paper something you can work with until it meets your reader's needs and expectations. Planning and drafting should take about half the time you devote to writing a paper. The rest should be devoted to revision.

Revision is the process of refining your message until

- it says what you want it to say
- your reader(s) will understand it
- your reader(s) will receive it favourably

These three goals are the essentials of good communication. You can achieve them only if you keep your readers in mind as you revise. Because a first draft reflects the contents of the writer's mind, it usually seems fine to the writer. But in order to transfer an idea as clearly as possible from the mind of the writer to the mind of the reader, revision is necessary. The idea needs to be honed and refined until it is as clear to your reader as it is to you. By revising from your reader's point of view, you can avoid misunderstandings before they happen.

WHAT IS REVISION?

Revision means "re-seeing." It does *not* mean "re-copying." The aim of revision is to improve your writing's organization, accuracy, and style. Revising is a three-stage process. Each step requires that you read through your entire essay, painful though this may be. The goal of your first reading is to ensure that you've organized and developed your ideas in a way that your reader can follow. In your second reading, you focus on paragraphs and sentences—the building blocks of prose. Your third reading concentrates on correctness. Here are the steps to follow in revising a paper.

1. Improve the whole paper by revising its content and organization.
2. Refine paragraph and sentence structure, and correct any errors in grammar.
3. Edit and proofread to catch errors in word choice, spelling, and punctuation.

Inexperienced writers often skip the first two stages and concentrate on the third, thinking they will save time. They are making a mistake. They are wasting time—both theirs and their readers'—because the result is writing that doesn't communicate clearly and won't make a positive impression.

The best way to begin revising is to do nothing to the first version of your paper for several days. Let as much time as possible pass between completing your first draft and rereading it. Ten minutes, or even half a day, is not enough. The danger in rereading too soon is that you're likely to "read" what you *think* you've written—what exists in your head, not on the page.

If you haven't allowed enough time for this cooling-off period, don't despair. There are two other things you can do to help you get some distance from your draft. If your first draft is handwritten, type it out. Reading your essay in a different format helps you to "re-see" its content. Alternatively, read your paper aloud and listen to it from the point of view of your reader. Hear how your explanation unfolds, and mark every place your reader may find something unclear, irrelevant, inadequately developed, or out of order. To succeed as a writer—even if your message consists of a brief clinical record or an outline of a simple task—you must be able to get into the head of your reader and compose your message to complement the knowledge (and the lack of knowledge) that resides there.

STEP 1:
REVISE CONTENT AND ORGANIZATION

As you read your paper aloud, keep in mind the three possible kinds of changes you can make at this stage:

1. You can REARRANGE information. This is the kind of revision that is most often needed but least often done. Consider the order in which you've arranged your paragraphs. From your reader's point of view, is this the most effective order in which to present your ideas? If you are not already using a word-processing program, now is the time to begin. With a good word processor, moving blocks of text around is as easy as dealing a deck of cards.

2. You can ADD information. Adding new main ideas or further development of the ideas already there is often necessary to make your message interesting, clear, and convincing. It's a good idea to ask a friend to read your draft and identify what you should expand or clarify. (Be sure to return the favour. You can learn a great deal by critiquing other people's writing.)

3. You can DELETE information. Now is the time to cut out anything that is repetitious, insignificant, or irrelevant to your subject and reader.

Use the checklist that follows to guide you as you review your paper's form and content.

CONTENT AND ORGANIZATION CHECKLIST

ACCURACY

Is everything you have said accurate?
- Is your information consistent with your own experience and observations or with what you have discovered through research?
- Are all your facts and evidence up to date?

COMPLETENESS

Have you included enough main ideas and development to explain your subject and convince your reader? (Remember that "enough" means from the reader's point of view, not the writer's.)

- If your paper involves research, have you provided an appropriate source citation for every quotation and/or paraphrase?
- Have you attached a Works Cited or References list, if one is required?

SUBJECT
Is your subject
- significant? Does it avoid the trivial or the obvious?
- single? Does it avoid double or combined subjects?
- specific? Is it focused and precise?
- supportable? Have you provided enough evidence to make your meaning clear and convincing?

MAIN POINTS
Are your main points
- significant? Have you deleted any unimportant ones?
- distinct? Are they all different from one another, or is there an overlap in content?
- relevant? Do all points relate directly to your subject?
- arranged in the most appropriate order? Again, "appropriate" means from the reader's perspective. Choose chronological, climactic, logical, or random order, depending on which is most likely to help the reader make sense of your information.

INTRODUCTION
Does your introduction
- catch attention and make the reader want to read on?
- contain a clearly identifiable thesis statement?
- identify the main points that your paper will explain?

CONCLUSION
Does your conclusion
- contain a summary or reinforcement of your main points, rephrased to avoid word-for-word repetition?
- contain a statement that effectively clinches your argument and leaves the reader with something to think about?

TONE
Is your tone consistent, reasonable, courteous, and confident throughout your essay?

When you have carefully considered these questions, it's time to move on to the second stage of the revision process.

Go back to the essay you wrote for Exercise 25.11. That paper is a first draft. Use the Content and Organization Checklist on pages 327 to 328 to find and correct any errors or omissions in form and content.

STEP 2:
REVISE PARAGRAPHS AND SENTENCES

For this step, too, you should allow time—at least a couple of days—between your first revision and your second. Enough time must elapse to allow you to tackle your paper as if you were seeing it for the first time. Once again, read your draft aloud, and use this list of questions to help you improve it.

PARAGRAPH AND SENTENCE CHECKLIST

PARAGRAPHS

Does each paragraph

- begin with a clear, identifiable topic sentence?
- develop one—and only one—main idea?
- present one or more kinds of development appropriate to the main idea?
- contain clear and effective transitions to signal the relationship between sentences? between paragraphs?

SENTENCES

Sentence Structure

1. Is each sentence clear and complete?
   - Are there any fragments or run-ons?
   - Are there any misplaced or dangling modifiers?
   - Are all lists (whether words, phrases, or clauses) expressed in parallel form?
2. Are your sentences varied in length? Could some be combined to improve the clarity and impact of your message?

Grammar

1. Have you used verbs correctly?
   - Are all verbs in the correct form?
   - Do all verbs agree with their subjects?
   - Are all verbs in the correct tense?
   - Are there any confusing shifts in verb tense within a paragraph?

Paragraphs and Essays

2. Have you used pronouns correctly?
- Are all pronouns in the correct form?
- Do all pronouns agree with their antecedents?
- Have any vague pronoun references been eliminated?

When you're sure you've answered these questions satisfactorily, go to the third and last stage of the revision process.

EXERCISE **26.2**

Now apply the Paragraph and Sentence Checklist to the version of the essay you created in Exercise 26.1, and revise any errors in paragraph structure, sentence structure, and grammar.

STEP 3:
EDIT AND PROOFREAD

By now you're probably so tired of refining your paper that you may be tempted to skip **editing**—correcting errors in word choice, spelling, punctuation, and formatting—and **proofreading**—correcting errors in typing or writing that appear in the final draft. But these final tasks are essential if you want your paper to make a positive impression.

Misspellings, faulty punctuation, and messiness don't always create misunderstandings, but they do cause the reader to form a lower opinion of you and your work. Not convinced? Go to **www.youtube.com/watch?v= p_rwB5_3PQc** and see for yourself.

Most word-processing programs include a grammar checker and a spell checker. It is worthwhile running your writing through these programs at the editing stage. The newer programs have some useful features. For example, they will question (but not correct) your use of apostrophes, they will sometimes catch errors in subject–verb agreement, and they will catch obvious misspellings and typos.

But don't make the mistake of assuming these programs will do all of your editing for you. Many errors slip past a computer's database, no matter how comprehensive the salesperson told you it is. Only you or a knowledgeable and patient friend can find and correct all errors.

If spelling is a particular problem for you, you should first run your paper through a spell checker. After that, you're on your own. Read your paper backward, word by word, from the end to the beginning. Reading backward forces you to look at each word by itself and helps you to spot those that look suspicious. Whenever you're in doubt about the spelling of a word, look it up! If you find this task too tedious to bear, ask a good speller to read through your paper for you and identify any errors. (Then take this person out for dinner. If you get an A, add a show.)

Here are the questions to ask yourself when you are editing:

EDITING CHECKLIST

WORDS

Usage

Have you used words to *mean* rather than to *impress*?

- Have you eliminated any slang, pretentious language, or offensive language?
- Have you cut out any unnecessary words?
- Have you corrected any "abusages"?
- Have you checked the meanings of any words you're not absolutely certain about?

Spelling

Are all words spelled correctly?

- Have you double-checked any homonyms? (See Chapter 2, and double-check any words listed there that you've highlighted.)
- Have you used capital letters where they are needed?
- Have you used apostrophes correctly for possessives and omitted them from plurals?

PUNCTUATION

Within Sentences

- Have you eliminated any unnecessary commas and included commas where needed? (Refer to the four comma rules in Chapter 17 as you consider this question.)
- Have you used colons and semicolons where appropriate?
- Are all short and long quotations appropriately indicated? (See Chapter 20.)

Beginnings and Endings

- Does each sentence begin with a capital letter?
- Do all questions—and only questions—end with a question mark?
- Are all quotation marks correctly placed?

FORMATTING AND DOCUMENTATION (IF REQUIRED)

- Does your paper satisfy all formatting details specified by your instructor?
- Have you provided a reference for the source of every quotation and paraphrase?
- Have you attached a properly formatted Works Cited or References list?

Paragraphs and Essays

EXERCISE **26.3**

Now scan or key into your word processor the revised draft of the essay you produced for Exercise 26.2.[1] This is your last chance to make this essay error-free. There are two parts to this exercise.

1. Using the Editing Checklist above, revise errors in word usage, spelling, and punctuation. Save your file as "Draft 3" and print it.
2. Follow the "Tips for Effective Proofreading" below to find and correct any errors or typos you may have misscd. Save your file under a new name ("Draft 4" or "Final Draft") and print it.

TIPS FOR EFFECTIVE PROOFREADING

By the time you have finished editing, you will have gone over your paper so many times you may have practically memorized it. When you are very familiar with a piece of writing, it's hard to spot the small mistakes that may have crept in as you produced your final copy. Here are some tips to help you find those tiny, elusive errors.

1. Read through your essay line by line, using a ruler to guide you.
2. If you've been keeping a list of your most frequent errors in this course, scan your essay for the mistakes you are most likely to make.
3. Use the Quick Revision Guide on the inside front cover of this book to make a final check of all aspects of your paper.
4. Use the Correction Abbreviations and Symbols list on the inside back cover to check for errors your instructor has identified in your writing.

Your "last" draft may need further revision after your proofreading review. If so, take the time to revise the paper one last time so that the version you hand in is clean and easy to read. If a word processor is available to you, use it. Computers make editing and proofreading almost painless since errors are so easy to correct.

---

[1] If you do not have access to a word processor, complete this exercise using a different colour of pen for each draft. In order to learn your strengths and weaknesses, you must be able to identify the changes you made at each stage of the revision process.

EXERCISE **26.4**

Exchange with a partner the essay you each produced in Exercise 26.3. (This exercise works best if you choose a partner whose writing skills are better than your own.) Apply the three checklists to your partner's paper. Use a coloured pen, and note in the margins any problems you find in content and organization (Step 1), and correct on the paper errors you find in Steps 2 and 3. Be prepared to spend at least an hour on this exercise. Wise people know that the best way to learn a skill is to teach it. That's what this exercise requires you to do: teach your partner.

At long last, you're ready to submit your paper. If you've conscientiously followed the three steps to revision, you can hand in your paper confidently, knowing that it says what you want it to say, both about your subject and about you. One last word of advice:

DON'T FORGET TO KEEP A COPY FOR YOUR FILES!

EXERCISE **26.5**

Revise the following passage in three stages: first, apply all of the questions in the Step 2 "Paragraph and Sentence Checklist" on pages 329 to 330, and then apply all of the questions in the Step 3 "Editing Checklist" on page 331. Finally, review "Tips for Effective Proofreading" above. Then compare your final draft with ours on page 452.

Do you find it a struggle to pay the bills every month. When living beyond your means, even a small shortfall at the end of each month can quickly add up to a humongous debt. To beat this problem you can basically choose to spend less or earning more. At first, the former may seem the more difficulty choice, cutting back on what you spend may mean giving up some of the things you "need" such as eating out, movies, or the latest fashions. Doing

Paragraphs and Essays

without such expensive pleasures, however, often produce significant savings, you may even save enough to balance the monthly books.

Earning more money than what you now bring in and continuing to spend at your present pace may seem like a more attractive way to go, but is it realistic. There is the challenge of finding another job that pays better. Or adding part-time work to the job you already have, either way your going to loose even more of your already scarce study and leisure time. There is the fact that most people continue to spend at the same rate, regardless of how much money we make so its likely that, even with additional income, you'll still be in the hole at the end of the month. The best solution to the end-of-month budget blues is likely a combination of cutting costs where practical and adding to income where possible.

©iStockphoto.com/khr128

Using Research Resources Responsibly 27

PARAPHRASE OR PLAGIARISM?

In our culture, using someone else's words or ideas in your own writing without acknowledging their source is considered to be **plagiarism**, and it is a serious offence. Plagiarism is an attempt by the writer to deceive the reader into thinking he or she wrote the material. In the academic world, even when plagiarism is unintentional, it can lead to consequences ranging from a grade of zero on a paper to a failing grade in the course or even expulsion from the college or university. In the business world and in the media, a writer who plagiarizes can expect to be fired.

Many students think that it is all right to use information they've found if they change the wording of the material they want to "borrow." This is not so. *Any information or ideas that cannot be considered common knowledge must be acknowledged or credited. Even if you put someone else's original idea into your own words, you must tell your reader the source of the information.* Any material that is taken word for word from another writer must be put in quotation marks and its source given. (See "Crediting Your Sources," below.)

PARAPHRASING VERSUS PLAGIARISM

Paraphrasing is including another writer's idea in your essay but expressing it in your own words. The ability to paraphrase well is an immensely useful skill, but it is not easy to learn. You will need much experience before you can produce effective paraphrases. One of the reasons you are assigned research papers in college or university is to give you practice in paraphrasing. Here are the guidelines to follow:

1. A paraphrase must be a clear and accurate rewording of the author's idea.
2. A paraphrase must express the author's idea in your own words and sentences.
3. The source of your paraphrase must be included, using the documentation format that has been specified by your instructor or chosen by you.

To see the differences between paraphrase and plagiarism, study the paragraphs that follow. We have taken as our example a paragraph from "Career Consciousness," which you will find on page 345.

Original

It is not easy to find a career that provides stimulating, enjoyable, and meaningful work. Understanding yourself—your interests, needs, values, and goals—is an essential first step. Making long-term decisions consistent with your values and goals is the difficult second step. Too many people spend their lives in careers that make them miserable because they allow themselves to be governed by parents, friends, or simple inertia. Finally, once you have launched your career, never rest. Actively seek challenges and opportunities that stimulate you. Relish the rewards of meeting those challenges, being productive, and doing your job well. Continually strive to improve, not for the sake of your employer, but for your own sake. Your career will occupy three-quarters of your life, so make the most of it!

Unacceptable paraphrase

In "Career Consciousness," Brian Green points out that it is not easy to find a career that is stimulating, enjoyable, and meaningful. The first step is to understand yourself, your interests, needs, values, and goals. The second step is making long-term decisions consistent with your values and goals. Too often, people devote their lives to careers that make them unhappy because they permit themselves to be influenced by family, friends, or plain laziness. Once you have decided on a career, look for challenges and opportunities that are stimulating, and keep striving to improve, not for the sake of the employer, but for your own sake. Make the most of your career because it will occupy three-quarters of your life.

Neither a quotation nor a true paraphrase, this paragraph is an example of plagiarism. Its phrasing is too close to that of the original. Even though the paragraph acknowledges the source of the ideas, it presents those ideas in the same order and often in the same words as the original. And when the words are not identical, the sentence structure is. For example, compare these two sentences and note the correspondence between the two sets of italicized words:

Original

Too many people *spend* their lives in careers that make them *miserable* because they *allow* themselves to be *governed* by *parents*, friends, or *simple inertia.*

and

Unacceptable paraphrase

Too often, people *devote* their lives to careers that make them *unhappy* because they *permit* themselves to be influenced by *family*, friends, or *plain laziness.*

The second sentence is an example of what happens when an inexperienced writer tries to create a paraphrase by relying on a thesaurus to "translate" the original. The identical sentence structure is a dead giveaway—not only of what the writer was trying to do, but also of how he or she was trying to do it.

Better paraphrase

Two factors are essential to long-term career satisfaction. In "Career Consciousness," Brian Green says that the first is to know yourself and make a career choice that is consistent with your personal values and goals, rather than allow the decision to be made for you by others. The second, according to Green, is to continue to look for opportunities once you have begun your career. By continually seeking ways to improve your performance and meet new challenges, you will not only please your employer, but you will also make your job stimulating and satisfying.

USING ONLINE SOURCES

When using Internet sources for research, remember that the Internet is largely unregulated. Even seasoned researchers are sometimes fooled into thinking that a particular posting is factual when it is only someone's—and not necessarily an expert's—opinion. One of your responsibilities as a student researcher is to evaluate the sources of information you use to ensure that they are authoritative and creditable. Many websites try to give the appearance of being official and objective when, in fact, they have a distinct point of view that they are trying to promote. Unfortunately, there is no standard test or measure you can apply to distinguish between fact and propaganda.

One of the most popular sites for research material is *Wikipedia*, which is a gold mine of information. However, researchers must be aware that the entries in *Wikipedia* are written by subscribers. Can this information be trusted? Since entries are closely monitored by professional scholars and expert amateurs, as well as by *Wikipedia* employees, in many cases it can. But there is no guarantee that a *Wikipedia* entry is accurate, up to date, or unbiased. If you cannot rely on *Wikipedia* without question, imagine how careful you must be in using information from blogs and discussion forums!

Always check the trustworthiness of an Internet source. One way to confirm the accuracy of information you want to use is by consulting several different sources to see if they agree. If you are unsure about a source, check with your instructor to confirm whether information from that source is reliable for the research project you are doing.

CREDITING YOUR SOURCES:
MLA AND APA DOCUMENTATION

When you use material that you have found in your reading, you must tell the reader where that material came from. This process is called *documentation*, and it consists of two parts: parenthetical citations, which you insert into the text of your paper immediately after the quotations or paraphrases that you've used to support a main point, and a list at the end of the paper of all of the sources you refer to in your paper.

There are two reasons you must use source citations: first, they enable your readers to locate your sources if they want to read more about your subject; and, second, they protect you from the charge of plagiarism. Unfortunately, you cannot just name the author and title of the work(s) you have borrowed from. The standard style for papers in the humanities (English, history, art, philosophy, etc.) differs from the standard style required for papers in the social sciences (economics, psychology, sociology, political science, etc.). Your instructors may have specific requirements for acknowledging sources; if so, follow them to the letter. And don't be surprised if different teachers have different requirements.

As a student researcher, you need to be familiar with at least two documentation systems: MLA and APA. The initials stand for the organizations (Modern Language Association and American Psychological Association) that developed these formats for writers submitting papers for publication by these organizations in their respective journals.

In MLA and APA styles, in-text citations (basic information about sources) are given in parentheses immediately following the quoted or referenced material in the main body of your paper. In MLA style, in-text citations provide the author's last name and the page number in the document where the material was found. APA style requires the publication year, as well, in the in-text citation. At the end of the essay, a Works Cited (MLA) or References (APA) page gives detailed information about each source, including the author's name, title of the work, publisher, place of publication, and year of publication—not always in that order. The format of each reference depends on where you found the information: on the Internet; in a book, journal, or magazine; through an interview; and so on. In Unit 6, you will find an essay in MLA format (pages 347 to 350) and one in APA format (pages 355 to 361). For specific instructions on how to credit various kinds of sources in both MLA and APA styles, go to the Student Resources page on this book's website at **www.NELSONbrain.com** and click on "Format and Documentation."

EXERCISE **27.1**

Below we have provided three paragraphs (taken from readings in Unit 6 and on the book's website), each of which is followed by a paragraph that is intended to be a paraphrase of the original. Compare each paraphrase to the original and determine if it is an acceptable paraphrase or if it is plagiarism. Check your answers with ours on page 452 and then revise the plagiarized paragraphs to make them true paraphrases.

1. From "An Immigrant's Split Personality," www.NELSONbrain.com:

Original:

When I was younger, toying with the idea of entertaining two separate identities was a real treat, like a secret game for which no one knew the rules but me. I was known as Angela to the outside world, and as Sun-Kyung at home. I ate bologna sandwiches in the school lunch room and rice and kimchee for dinner. I chatted about teen idols and giggled with my girlfriends during my classes, and ambitiously practised piano and studied in the evenings, planning to become a doctor when I grew up. I waved hellos and goodbyes to my teachers, but bowed to my parents' friends visiting our home. I could also look straight into the eyes of my teachers and friends and talk frankly with them instead of staring at my feet with my mouth shut when Koreans talked to me. Going outside the home meant I was able to relax from the constraints of my cultural conditioning, until I walked back in the door and had to return to being an obedient and submissive daughter.

Paraphrase?

First-generation immigrants sometimes adopt two personalities: one outside the home and a different one inside. In her essay "An Immigrant's Split Personality," Sun-Kyung Yi says that she thought of her two identities as a secret game for which no one knew the rules but her. She was Angela in the outside world and Sun-Kyung at home. She ate bologna sandwiches, gossiped about teen idols with girlfriends, and waved hello and goodbye when outside her home. But in her home, she ate rice and kimchee, practised the piano and studied in the evenings, and bowed to her parents' friends. She could look directly at her teachers and friends and talk openly with them, but when she was with Koreans, she stared at her feet with her mouth closed. Outside, she was free of cultural constraints, but at home she was expected to behave like an obedient and submissive daughter.

2. From "The Case against Quickspeak," www.NELSONbrain.com:

Original:

People who write in quickspeak ignore the reason that rules for correct writing evolved in the first place. Writing that communicates accurately depends upon precise thinking. A message with a statement of purpose, logically arranged points, and a confirming summary is the work of a writer whose message has been thought through and can be trusted. In contrast, quickspeak, which can be bashed out in no time, reflects no planning, little coherent thought, and no sense of order or priority. The message, the reader, and ultimately, the writer all suffer as a result.

Paraphrase?

In "The Case against Quickspeak," a criticism of thoughtless writing in emails, Brian Green points out that writers who plan each message to include a topic sentence, carefully organized points, and a summation gain the trust of the reader; their messages are clear and credible. Those who write sloppily, with little thought or preparation, risk being misunderstood and often leave the reader confused and suspicious.

3. From "The Slender Trap," page 350:

Original:

If the media do not begin to provide young women with a positive and healthy image of femininity, we will see no lessening in the numbers of anorexia victims. If our cultural ideal of female beauty does not change to reflect a range of healthy body types, the pressures to realize idealized and unhealthy physical standards will continue, and young women's feelings of helplessness and inadequacy will persist. In order for anorexia to become less prominent among young women, healthier associations must replace the existing connections among beauty, success, and thinness. Young women must realize that self-inflicted starvation is not a means to empowerment, but a process of self-destruction.

Paraphrase?

In summing up her essay on anorexia nervosa, "The Slender Trap," Trina Piscitelli blames the media for not providing young women with a positive and healthy image of femininity; our culture for its unrealistic standards of beauty; and societal pressures that equate beauty, success, and thinness. Young women, Piscitelli concludes, must realize that starving themselves does not empower them but leads to their own destruction.

UNIT 6
Readings

Brian Green, "Career Consciousness"

Trina Piscitelli, "The Slender Trap"

Michael Adams, "Hockey, Fighting, and What It Means to Be a Man"

Aliki Tryphonopoulos, "Eat, Drink, and Be Guilty"

Online Readings (NELSONbrain.com)

Brian Green, "The Case against Quickspeak"

Sun-Kyung Yi, "An Immigrant's Split Personality"

"The Myth of Canadian Diversity" (Editorial)

Readings

CAREER CONSCIOUSNESS
Brian Green

1   A career can be defined as the employment you prepare for during the first quarter of your life, engage in during the best years of your life, and reap the rewards from when you are least able to enjoy them. Behind the cynicism of this observation lies an important truth: choosing a life's vocation is not a decision to be taken lightly. To justify the time and effort you will invest in your career, it should be stimulating, rewarding, and productive. The better you know yourself, the more likely you are to choose a career you can live with happily.

2   What would a stimulating career be like? Picture yourself getting up in the morning and looking forward to your day with eager anticipation. This may not be the popular image of most jobs, but it is one that can be achieved. Most people participate in leisure activities that they find interesting, even energizing. There's no rule that says you can't be as enthusiastic about your work as you are about your play. Many successful people have turned their interests into careers by getting paid for what they like to do. Many career professionals in the arts, for example, make their living by doing what they feel they were born to do: write, act, paint, dance, play or compose music, sing, design, or sculpt. Clive Beddoe loved to fly, and from that passion grew his career as a bush pilot and, later, his founding of one of Canada's most successful airlines, WestJet. Of course, it is not always possible to turn a passion into a career, but to deny what excites you, to relegate it to after-hours activities without trying to incorporate it into your working life, means you will spend most of your life wishing you were doing something else.

3   If your career is stimulating, then chances are good that it can also be rewarding. A good career offers two kinds of rewards: financial and emotional. Rewarding work doesn't just happen; it's something you need to plan for. The first and most important step is to know yourself. Only if you know who you are and what you need to be happy can you consciously seek out career experiences that will bring you satisfaction and steer clear of those that will irritate or stress you. Are you genuinely ambitious, or is power something you seek because you think it is expected of you? The pursuit of status and a high salary brings some people pure pleasure. Many people, however, find leadership positions excruciatingly stressful. Career enjoyment depends to some extent on whether or not you are successful, and success is a state of mind. Consider two graduates from the same college program. One is a technician in a small-town television station who loves his work, takes pride in keeping the station on the air, and delights in raising his family in a community where he is involved in volunteer activities ranging from sports to firefighting. The other is a news director at one of Canada's major television networks; her

work is highly stressful, full of risks, and continually scrutinized by viewers, competitors, and her supervisors. She thrives on the adrenaline rush of nightly production and loves the big-city life, the financial rewards of her position, and the national recognition she receives. Which graduate is "successful"? Certainly, both feel their careers are rewarding, according to their individual definitions of the term.

4   A job at which you do not feel useful cannot be either rewarding or stimulating for very long. It is human nature to want to contribute, to feel that your efforts make a difference. Camaraderie with co-workers, a pleasant daily routine, and even a good salary cannot compensate in the long run for a sense that your work is meaningless or unappreciated. Sadly, some people spend their entire working lives at jobs in which their contribution is so insignificant that their absence would scarcely be noticed. Everyone knows people who boast about reading magazines or surfing the Net on the job, and others who sleep through their night shift so they can spend their days fishing or golfing. Is this the way you want to spend 45 years of your life? All the junk literature and the rounds of golf don't add up to much without a sense that you are doing something worthwhile. It may take a few years, but when it comes, the realization that your work lacks meaning is soul-destroying.

5   It is not easy to find a career that provides stimulating, enjoyable, and meaningful work. Understanding yourself—your interests, needs, values, and goals—is an essential first step. Making long-term decisions consistent with your values and goals is the difficult second step. Too many people spend their lives in careers that make them miserable because they allow themselves to be governed by parents, friends, or simple inertia. Finally, once you have launched your career, never rest. Actively seek challenges and opportunities that stimulate you. Relish the rewards of meeting those challenges, being productive, and doing your job well. Continually strive to improve, not for the sake of your employer, but for your own sake. Your career will occupy three-quarters of your life, so make the most of it!

QUESTIONS FOR DISCUSSION

1. What kind of attention-getter does the writer use to open his essay?
2. In paragraph 5, identify the two main parts of the author's conclusion: the summary of the essay's main points and the memorable statement. What kind of memorable statement has he used? Is it appropriate for this essay? Why?
3. In what order has Green arranged his points: chronological, logically linked, climactic, or random? Can you rearrange the points without diminishing the effectiveness of the piece?
4. What kinds of development has the author used to develop paragraph 2? Paragraph 3? Paragraph 4?

Readings

5. How do the topic sentences of paragraphs 2, 3, 4, and 5 contribute to the coherence of this essay? Identify three or four transitional words or phrases the author has used within his paragraphs to make them read smoothly.

SUGGESTIONS FOR WRITING

1. How would you define a satisfying career?
2. Who is the most satisfied worker you know? What makes him or her happy with the job? How can you tell that this person is highly contented with his or her employment?
3. Who is the most dissatisfied worker you know? What makes him or her unhappy with the job? How does this person compensate for the lack of interest in his or her job?
4. If you had enough money invested so that you could live comfortably without paid employment, would you be happy? Why or why not?

THE SLENDER TRAP*

Trina Piscitelli

The following is a short documented essay prepared in the Modern Language Association (MLA) style. The annotations point out some features of MLA format and documentation. If your instructor requires a separate title page, ask for guidelines.

---

* Trina Rys, "The Slender Trap." Reprinted with permission from the author.

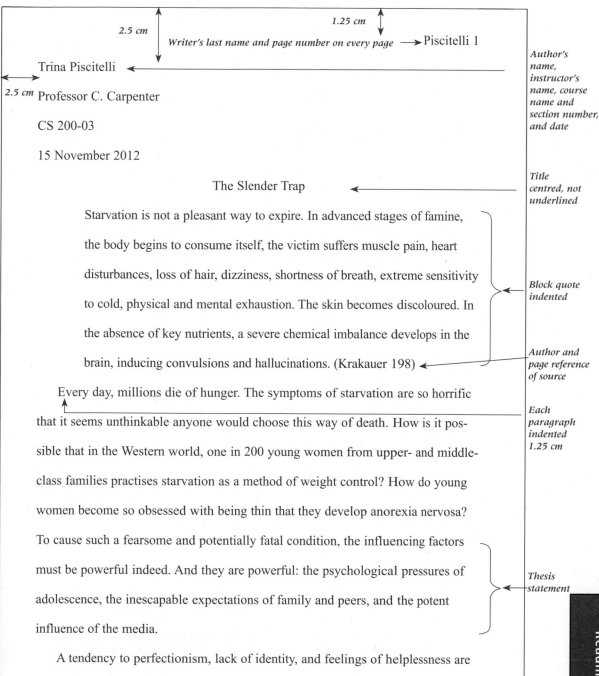

2.5 cm

1.25 cm

Writer's last name and page number on every page → Piscitelli 1

Author's name, instructor's name, course name and section number, and date

Trina Piscitelli

2.5 cm Professor C. Carpenter

CS 200-03

15 November 2012

The Slender Trap

Title centred, not underlined

> Starvation is not a pleasant way to expire. In advanced stages of famine, the body begins to consume itself, the victim suffers muscle pain, heart disturbances, loss of hair, dizziness, shortness of breath, extreme sensitivity to cold, physical and mental exhaustion. The skin becomes discoloured. In the absence of key nutrients, a severe chemical imbalance develops in the brain, inducing convulsions and hallucinations. (Krakauer 198)

Block quote indented

Author and page reference of source

Every day, millions die of hunger. The symptoms of starvation are so horrific that it seems unthinkable anyone would choose this way of death. How is it possible that in the Western world, one in 200 young women from upper- and middle-class families practises starvation as a method of weight control? How do young women become so obsessed with being thin that they develop anorexia nervosa? To cause such a fearsome and potentially fatal condition, the influencing factors must be powerful indeed. And they are powerful: the psychological pressures of adolescence, the inescapable expectations of family and peers, and the potent influence of the media.

Each paragraph indented 1.25 cm

Thesis statement

A tendency to perfectionism, lack of identity, and feelings of helplessness are three aspects of a young woman's psychology that can contribute to the development of anorexia nervosa. Young women who exhibit perfectionism are

Readings

Piscitelli 2

particularly susceptible to the disease because they often have unrealistic expecta-tions about their physical appearance. These expectations can lead to feelings of helplessness and powerlessness, and some young women with these feelings see starving themselves as a means to empowerment. Their diet is often the only thing they can control, and they control it with a single-mindedness that astonishes and horrifies their families and friends. As well as the need for control, anorexia in young women can be caused by a weak or unformed identity. Confused about who they are, many young women define themselves by how closely they approx-imate our society's notion of the ideal woman. Unfortunately, for the past half-century, Western society's ideal female image has been that of an unrealistically thin young woman. When women focus on this impossible image as the ideal and strive to starve their bodies into submission, they suffer emotional and physical damage.

In addition to an unstable psychological state, family and peer pressure can con-tribute to a fragile young woman's development of anorexia nervosa. By empha-sizing physical appearance, by criticizing physical features, and even by restricting junk food, family members can push a young woman over the cliff edge that sepa-rates health from illness. A home environment in which physical attractiveness is overvalued can be destructive for young women. Surrounded by family members and friends who seem to be concerned primarily about appearance, a young woman can begin to feel insecure about how she looks. This uncertainty can produce the desire—and then the need—to look better. And better means thinner. This flawed

Piscitelli 3

logic underlies the disease in many young women. A family or peer group that over-values physical appearance is often also critical of physical flaws. Critical comments about weight and general appearance, even when spoken jokingly, can be instrumental in a young woman's desire to be thin. Ironically, food restrictions imposed by parents can also contribute to anorexia in young women. Restricting the consumption of junk food, for example, has been known to cause bingeing and purging, a condition associated with anorexia.

While a young woman's developing psyche and the pressures of those close to her can exert tremendous influence, the root cause of the "thin is beautiful" trap is a media-inspired body image. Television, fashion magazines, and stereotypical Hollywood images of popular stars provide young women with an unrealistic image of the ideal female body. While only 5 percent of North American females are actually underweight, 32 percent of female television and movie personalities are unhealthily thin ("What causes ...?" para 6). The media's unrealistic portrayal of a woman's ideal body can cause a young woman to develop a sense of inadequacy. To be considered attractive, she feels she must be ultra-thin. Television's unrealistic portrayal of the way young women should look is reinforced on the pages of fashion magazines. Magazine ads feature tall, beautiful, *thin* women. Media images also perpetuate the stereotype that a woman must be thin in order to be successful. Thanks to television and movies, when we think of a successful woman, the image that comes to mind is that of a tall, well-dressed, *thin* woman. This stereotypical image leads impressionable young women to associate success

Paraphrase followed by source reference

Readings

Piscitelli 4

with body weight and image. When internalized by young women, these artificial standards can result in the development of anorexia nervosa.

If the media do not begin to provide young women with a positive and healthy image of femininity, we will see no lessening in the numbers of anorexia victims. If our cultural ideal of female beauty does not change to reflect a range of healthy body types, the pressures to realize idealized and unhealthy physical standards will continue, and young women's feelings of helplessness and inadequacy will persist. In order for anorexia to become less prominent among young women, healthier associations must replace the existing connections among beauty, success, and thinness. Young women must realize that self-inflicted starvation is not a means to empowerment but a process of self-destruction.

Works Cited list begins on a new page.

Piscitelli 5

Works Cited

Heading centred, not underlined

Krakauer, Jon. *Into the Wild.* New York: Villard, 1996. Print.

"What Causes Eating Disorders?" *Section 1: General Information.* Anorexia and

First line, flush left; subsequent lines indented 1.25 cm

Related Eating Disorders Inc. (ANRED), 2012. Web. 12 September 2012.

Entries in alphabetical order; double-spaced throughout

QUESTIONS FOR DISCUSSION

1. We've identified for you the author's thesis statement and plan of development. Compose a single sentence combining both the thesis statement and the main points Piscitelli uses to develop her thesis.
2. What two supporting points does the author use to develop the main point of paragraph 2? (See the fifth sentence ["As well as ..."], which serves as a transition between the two supporting ideas.)
3. What kind of development does Piscitelli use in paragraph 3?
4. Study the concluding paragraph carefully. The author's treatment of her summary and memorable statement is unusual and interesting. The second sentence of the conclusion summarizes the three main points that have been developed in the essay, but in an original, unpredictable way. Underline the clauses of this sentence, and write above each clause the number of the main point it reinforces.
5. What audience did Piscitelli have in mind when she wrote this essay? How do you know?

SUGGESTIONS FOR WRITING

1. Do you know something about eating disorders? If you have a friend or family member who suffers from bulimia, gorging, anorexia, or another related disorder, write an essay describing the causes, effects, and symptoms (features) of the problem or how it developed.
2. Men also suffer from eating disorders. How are their eating disorders different from those of women? Why do you think we seldom read about male anorexia, bulimia, etc.?
3. In April 2008, the French Parliament's National Assembly adopted a bill that would make it illegal for anyone (including fashion magazines, advertisers, and websites) to publicly encourage extreme thinness. What do you think about this approach to combating anorexia?

HOCKEY, FIGHTING, AND WHAT IT MEANS TO BE A MAN*

Michael Adams

1   The first rule of fight club was don't talk about fight club. The first rule of Canadian hockey seems to be never stop talking about it. The past few years

---

* "Hockey, Fighting, and What It Means to Be a Man," by Michael Adams. Published in *The Globe and Mail,* May 28, 2012.

have produced a huge amount of debate about the nature and value of our national sport. Rule changes, fighting, head shots, concussions, "big hits"— fans, journalists and concerned health professionals have hashed it all out again and again.

2   Why so much talk? Because there is a tension between the broad trends of social change and the take-no-prisoners machismo we see on the ice. A large proportion of Canadians feel they have a stake in the game of hockey. Eighty-four per cent of us say that hockey is "a key part of what it means to be Canadian."

3   That said, the millions of Canadians who feel some ownership over the game of hockey represent a range of constituencies. There are lovers of the sport who want a technically demanding, fast-paced game to watch. There are parents who want their kids to enjoy the camaraderie of a team sport while staying active during our long winters. There are Canadians who perk up around playoff time, feeling a sentimental, vaguely patriotic attachment to the game.

4   But the group that is understandably most important to the league and its advertisers is a set of hard-core fans, on average anglophone men aged 30 to 49 who feel quite at ease with the violence that makes some of hockey's other constituencies cringe. Just 18 per cent of serious hockey fans describe themselves as uncomfortable with the violence in hockey, as compared to 32 per cent of occasional fans and half (49 per cent) of those who say they dislike the game.

5   Old-fashioned masculinity does not have many places to prove its mettle these days. Our information economy prizes creativity and networking over physical strength. Our social mores less often call on men to defend women from rogues in the street, and more often ask them to meet women as equals at work and in social life. Even the military seldom affords opportunities to fight bad guys and scumbags: Historical and cultural understanding in complex places like Afghanistan may now be more important than target practice. For those who long for a venue in which to express their raw testosterone, a rock 'em, sock 'em game—complete with all the traditional etiquette, such as punishing aggressors, defending teammates and upholding manly honour—is a welcome release.

6   But even as some will wish for hockey to serve as a fight club–like refuge from a culture in which machismo seems outmoded and violence grows ever less acceptable, others will insist that sport does not exist in a vacuum. On a basic level, hockey must conform to society's ideas about acceptable behaviour. Off the ice, sneaking up behind someone and hitting them so hard they lose consciousness can get you jail time. On the ice, you risk a modest fine and a few games on the bench.

7   I suspect that hockey will eventually trend toward a compromise between the desire of hard-core fans for a tough, physical game and the belief of more

casual fans that whatever happens on the ice should not be so brutal as to debilitate players long after the final buzzer. In short, hockey will have to find a way to remain an arena that stands a little apart from ordinary social norms while at the same time remaining basically aligned with the contemporary Canadian expectation that no job (however rich the pay) should cost you your health or your life.

8   Some of the off-ice discussions that have emerged around hockey recently (the breaking of the code of silence about sexual abuse by coaches, and Brian Burke's continuation of his late son's campaign against homophobia) have revealed that a growing number of hockey stalwarts believe manly heroism in sport does not mean stoic silence in the face of any and all abuse. Might doesn't automatically make right. Changing the rules—and especially the unwritten codes—of professional hockey means changing our expectations about what it means to be a real man, even a heroic man, in the 21st century. And contrary to some tough guys' intuitions, it's men themselves who stand to gain the most from those changes.

QUESTIONS FOR DISCUSSION

1. What four categories of hockey fan does the author identify? In which category do you belong, or do you identify with more than one category?
2. The attention-getter of this essay takes up one paragraph. Which sentence in paragraph 2 is the thesis statement?
3. Hockey is really two different games: the one practised in Canada and much of the U.S., and the one seen in the Olympics and the World Championships, where there is virtually no fighting. Which game do you prefer? Why? When you watch Olympic and World Championship hockey, do you miss the fighting? Would fighting in those tournaments improve the game? Why?
4. In paragraph 5, the author identifies three different roles in which men have lost the opportunity to display traditional masculine traits and be rewarded with public recognition for their efforts. What are the roles in which "old-fashioned masculinity" has been displaced? What are some of the skills and abilities that men are now expected to display in place of brute strength?
5. In your own words, explain what the author means by "it's men themselves who stand to gain the most from [the changing expectations of what it means to be a real man]."

SUGGESTIONS FOR WRITING

1. Using Adams's four categories of hockey fans as a starting point, define what kind of fan you are, explain what you love about the game, what you hate about it, and why.

2. Write a comparison/contrast essay that explores your preference for one of the two different games of hockey identified in Question 3 above.

3. "Changing the rules—and especially the unwritten codes—of professional hockey means changing our expectations about what it means to be a real man, even a heroic man, in the 21st century." Has the concept of manliness changed? Find evidence to support your argument that what it means to be a man has or has not changed in the past 50 years.

EAT, DRINK, AND BE GUILTY
Aliki Tryphonopoulos

The following is a short research paper prepared in the American Psychological Association (APA) style. The annotations in the margins point out some basic features of APA format and documentation.

1.25 cm

Eat, Drink, and Be Guilty

2.5 cm

First two or three words of the title + page number on every page

Eat, Drink, and Be Guilty

Aliki Tryphonopoulos

COM 102-14

Professor B. Green

January 10, 2013

Title, author's name, course name and section number, instructor's name, date; centred on page, double-spaced

Readings

Title centred, not underlined or bold-faced → Eat, Drink, and Be Guilty

Paragraphs indented 1.25 cm

In consumer societies, individuals are often held responsible for problems such as debt or obesity, problems that are caused by overconsumption—buying more goods and services than we need. Overconsumption, however, may be normal

2.5 cm

behaviour in an abnormal environment (Egger & Swinburn, 1997), and we consumers may bear less responsibility for our problems than the environment that produces our behaviour.

Citation of secondary source

For example, researchers think unhealthy weight gain in the populations of developed nations may be the product of what scientists call obesogenic environments—environments that encourage us to become overweight. In Canada, 59% of the population is overweight or obese (Statistics Canada, 2005). While Canadians disagree about the causes of this health issue, we can no longer deny that our eating habits, exercise patterns, and consumer attitudes are shaped by the environment in which we live.

Paper is double-spaced throughout

Who has the time to make home-cooked meals anymore? We now work more hours than we have since the Industrial Revolution, when workers sometimes slept under their machines. Long workdays and long commutes consume much of our energy and time. Coupled with changing family economics (e.g., fewer stay-at-home parents), our busy schedules cause us to eat on the run, a habit that makes it difficult to control what and when we eat. The average Canadian family spends a third of its food budget on meals eaten outside the home (Samra, 2006). Profiting from our frantic lifestyles is the fast-food industry, which offers food that is convenient and tasty. Unfortunately, it is also high in fat, salt, and sugar, and low in

Eat, Drink, and Be Guilty 3

nutrients. More often than not, food portions are too large: a single meal can deliver more than our recommended calorie intake for the entire day.

Advertisers constantly remind us of the convenience of fast food through television spots (often during sporting events and children's programs), billboards, radio ads, even posters on the backs of washroom doors. After a study proved that the more fast-food ads children watched, the more calories they consumed, some countries banned fast-food commercials during children's television programming (Wilson, 2003), but no country has taken steps to protect adults from the ubiquitous advertising of calorie-laden, nutrition-deficient fast foods. A Burger King Whopper with a small side of fries, for example, provides 93% of an adult's daily recommended intake of fat (most of it saturated—or bad—fats), 38% of the cholesterol, 77% of the sodium, and 50% (or more, depending on your age, size, and level of physical activity) of the calories. On the nutritional side of the scale, the numbers are much lower: 27% of calcium, 35% of iron, and just 9% of the daily recommended intake of vitamins A and C. The amounts of other essential vitamins and minerals are negligible ("Foods from Burger King," 2012).

Paraphrase

Electronic source citation (author not known)

Unfortunately, the easy availability and targeted advertising of high-calorie, low-nutrition fast foods are not the only ways in which our environment adversely influences our health. Even those of us who do not live in the suburbs use our cars rather than our feet to get to the local convenience store. Why? Because we live in a culture that glorifies car ownership. Advertisers tell us the car is a safe, happy, family-friendly space, not to mention a symbol of social prestige. Also, we need a car so that we can hurry up and enjoy ourselves after working so hard to maintain

Readings

Eat, Drink, and Be Guilty 4

Source citation of the study referred to

and improve our standard of living: the goal of consumer culture.

Our collective laziness extends beyond getting behind the wheel rather than lacing up our runners. When we learn that less than 20% of young Canadians meet the national standard for daily physical activity (Blatchford, 2005), we worry about our children. Meanwhile, we adults choose passive leisure activities over active ones. We watch an average of 21 to 26 hours of television each week (Statistics Canada, 2006), immersing ourselves in a cultural environment of movies, television, celebrity tabloids, and video games, while exercising only our fingers. Ironically, these same media sources consistently present us with images of super-slim, super-fit bodies as if they were the norm. The world of electronic media is a world of buff beauty, wealthy consumerism, and happy endings (however short-lived), and it makes us passive viewers feel bad and even guilty by comparison.

Reinforcing our feelings of inadequacy, commercial advertising motivates us to buy—weight-loss pills, diet programs, even surgical procedures—but rarely to exercise. We consumers seldom perceive obesity as a problem that stems from the long work hours, poor nutrition, and inactive leisure activities that advertisers lure us into. We are more likely to identify our overweight and out-of-shape bodies as personal failings.

In Canada, as in many other wealthy nations, our cultural philosophy encourages overconsumption: we must keep up with the Joneses, the Smiths . . . and the Chans and the Singhs and the Garcias. The media promote and reinforce this philosophy. But not only do the media sell consumers on the pleasures of self-indulgence, they also feed the billion-dollar business of weight loss products.

Eat, Drink, and Be Guilty 5

And so we spend even more money—on the symptoms, rather than on the cause, of our obesity problem.

The negative connotations of being overweight are pervasive and cruel: children as young as six see overweight people as "lazy and [dishonest]" (Cassell, 1995, p. 424)—an attitude that carries over into adulthood. The weight-loss industry thrives on our prejudice and guilt: 25% of North American males and 50% of females are currently paying into one or more diet programs in an effort to free themselves from the cultural evil of "fat" (Cassell, 1995).

The daily pressures we encounter to indulge ourselves have led to poor eating practices, poor fitness habits, and negative feelings about the inevitable consequences. We are wrong to blame only ourselves. Eating too much and exercising too little are environmental problems. The solution, therefore, must involve societal as well as individual efforts. To maintain a healthy weight through good nutrition and sufficient exercise, we need a supportive environment. We need the participation of government, community, and family organizations; the cooperation of the agricultural and food industries; and the commitment and support of the health care system (Coles, 2005). It sounds difficult, but it is not impossible. Fortunately, a growing number of health care workers are beginning to see the importance of environmental factors—such as the consumer attitudes that underlie both overeating and indolence—as a major cause of the global obesity problem. South Korea, Singapore, and Sweden have already achieved success in nationwide campaigns that use multilevel action to address their obesity problems (Coles, 2005). Former U.S. president Bill Clinton is working nationwide with school boards and

Readings

Eat, Drink, and Be Guilty 6

food manufacturers to provide tasty, low-fat lunches in school cafeterias. We

Canadians must begin now to change our consumer culture, which encourages

poor nutrition and inadequate exercise and then condemns us for the inevitable

consequence: obesity.

Eat, Drink, and Be Guilty 7

Heading centred, not underlined

References

First line, flush left; subsequent lines indented 1.25 cm

Blatchford, A. (2005, April 21). Inactivity chief reason for youth obesity levels:

Fifth flabbiest in study of 34 countries. *Edmonton Journal*, p. A9.

Cassell, J. A. (1995). Social anthropology and nutrition: A different look at obe-

sity in America. *Journal of the American Dietetic Association, 95*, 424–27.

doi:10.1016/S0002-8223(95)00114-X

Entries in alphabetical order; double-spaced throughout

Coles, C. (2005). Obesity as a major malnutrition issue: Poor nutrition from

overeating may become a primary killer. *The Futurist, 39*(3), 15.

Egger, G., & Swinburn, B. (1997). An "ecological" approach to the obesity

Pandemic. *British Medical Journal, 315*, 477–80.

doi:10.1136/bmj.315.7106.477

Include the digital object identifier (DOI) if one is assigned

Foods from Burger King. (2012). *Self Nutrition Data.* Retrieved from

http://nutritiondata.self.com/foods-031000000000000000000.html

Samra, R. (2006, June 13). "Fast food doesn't have to be fat food." *Hamilton*

Spectator, p. 6.

Eat, Drink, and Be Guilty 8

Statistics Canada. (2005). *Measured adult body mass index (BMI), by age group and sex, household population aged 18 and over excluding pregnant females, Canadian Community Health Survey cycle 2.2, Canada and provinces* (CANSIM Table 105-2001). Retrieved from http://www5.statcan.gc.ca/cansim/pick-choisir?lang=eng&p2=33&id=1052001

Statistics Canada. (2006). *Average hours of television viewing, by province, and age/sex groups: Fall 2004* (Cat. No. 87F0006XIE). Retrieved from http://www5.statcan.gc.ca/access_acces/alternative_alternatif.action?l=eng&loc=87F0006XIE2006001.xls

Wilson, C. (2003, November 29). Food kills. *New Scientist, 180*(2423), 19.

Readings

QUESTIONS FOR DISCUSSION

1. What is the thesis of this essay? Summarize the main arguments the author uses to support her thesis.
2. In the first paragraph, the author suggests we live in "an abnormal environment." What does she mean by this? What examples does she present in the essay to support this statement?
3. Do you think that the author's proposal in the final paragraph is a realistic solution to the problems caused by our consumer culture? If not, what would you suggest as a more effective solution?
4. This essay uses the APA reference style. Compare the References list against the Works Cited list for "The Slender Trap," on page 350. Look at each part of each reference carefully. List some of the differences between the two styles.
5. APA style now requires researchers to provide digital object identifiers (DOI) when available. Although website addresses may change or disappear from the Web, DOIs remain searchable.
   a. Using a search engine, find and list the articles identifiable by the following DOIs: (1) 10.1503/cmaj.050445 and (2) 10.1139/h04-008.
   b. Using a search engine, find the following online articles and identify their DOIs: (1) "Who Pays for Obesity?" by Jay Bhattacharya and Neeraj Sood (American Economic Association) and (2) "The Formerly Fat Physician" by Ben Williams (*Canadian Medical Association Journal*).

SUGGESTIONS FOR WRITING

1. Write an essay discussing the root causes of another problem or illness that for many years was thought to be the individual's responsibility but that we now realize is a sociocultural problem.
2. Tobacco companies are no longer permitted to advertise or sponsor sports events, and their products are heavily taxed because they have been found to be harmful. Would you agree or disagree that the government should take the same approach with companies selling unhealthy food products? Explain.
3. The media are often criticized for promoting an unrealistic body image of women: tall, slim, buff. Does the same criticism hold true of the media's depiction of the male body image? Why or why not?
4. Do you think print advertisements and TV commercials should portray a broader, more realistic range of body types rather than representing only ideal images? If so, how would you respond to their argument "We'd lose money"?

Appendixes

APPENDIX A
A Review of the Basics

This appendix contains a brief overview of the basic building blocks of the English language. At the very least, you should know the kinds and parts of a sentence and the parts of speech before you tackle the complex tasks involved in correcting and refining your writing.

SENTENCES: KINDS AND PARTS

A sentence is a group of words expressing a complete thought. Sentences can be classified in two different ways: by function and by structure.

FUNCTION: FOUR KINDS OF SENTENCES

1. The **declarative** sentence makes a statement or conveys information.

George Clooney starred in *O Brother, Where Art Thou?*, a Coen brothers' film.

He played a character named Ulysses Everett McGill.

2. The **interrogative** sentence asks a question.

Did George Clooney do his own singing in *O Brother, Where Art Thou?*

Was Pete really turned into a frog, or was he turned in to the police?

3. The **imperative** (command) sentence gives an order or a directive.

Stop talking! I'm trying to listen.

The *request* is a modified form of imperative sentence. Its tone is softer:

Let's rent a DVD of *O Brother* and watch it tonight.

> 4. The **exclamatory** sentence is a strong statement of opinion or warning.

The scene in which Clooney insists on wearing a hair net to bed is hilarious!

Don't answer the phone! This is my favourite part of the movie!

STRUCTURE: BASIC SENTENCE PATTERNS

Every sentence can be classified into one of four patterns, depending on the number and kinds of clauses the sentence contains. (In the examples below, subjects are underlined with one line, verbs with two.)

> 1. A **simple sentence** consists of one independent clause. It has one subject and one verb, either or both of which may be compound (multiple).

a. Matt plays hockey for McGill. (single subject, single verb)

b. Matt and Caro play hockey with their friends on weekends. (compound subject, one plural verb)

c. Matt and Caro play hockey and drink beer with their friends on weekends. (compound subject, compound verb)

> 2. A **compound sentence** is made up of two or more independent clauses. The clauses may be joined by a **coordinating conjunction** or by a semicolon. (See Chapters 10 and 18.)

Minh paid for the flight to Cuba, *and* Kendra paid for their accommodation.

Either or both clauses in a compound sentence may contain a compound subject and/or a compound verb:

Minh and Kendra flew to Cuba, *but* Matt and Caro stayed home and sulked.

3. A **complex sentence** has one independent clause and one or more dependent clauses introduced by **subordinating conjunctions** (see page 374) or relative clauses introduced by relative pronouns (see page 372).

We <u>flew</u> to Cuba for our vacation *while* my <u>brother</u> <u>stayed</u> home to take care of our dogs.

<u>Matt</u> and <u>Caro</u> <u>stayed</u> home *because* <u>they</u> <u>couldn't</u> <u>afford</u> the trip.

4. The **compound-complex sentence** combines the features of sentence patterns 2 and 3 above. That is, it contains two (or more) independent clauses, together with one or more dependent clauses.

<u>Minh</u> and <u>Kendra</u> <u>flew</u> to Cuba, *but* <u>Matt</u> and <u>Caro</u> <u>stayed</u> home *because* <u>they</u> <u>couldn't</u> <u>afford</u> the trip and *because* <u>someone</u> <u>needed</u> to care for the dogs.

THE PARTS OF A SENTENCE

Every sentence or independent clause can be divided into two parts: subject and predicate. The subject half contains the subject (simple or compound), together with its modifiers. The predicate half contains the verb (simple or compound), with its modifiers and any other words or phrases that complete the sentence's meaning. These predicate completers may be direct objects, indirect objects, or complements.

1. The **subject** of a sentence is a noun/pronoun (or phrase or clause used as a noun).

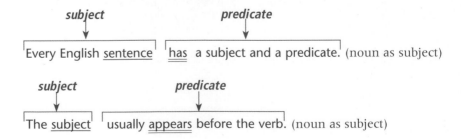

| *subject* | *predicate* |
| Every English <u>sentence</u> | <u>has</u> a subject and a predicate. (noun as subject) |

| *subject* | *predicate* |
| The <u>subject</u> | usually <u>appears</u> before the verb. (noun as subject) |

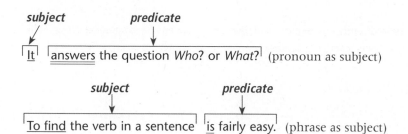

subject   *predicate*

It | answers the question *Who?* or *What?* | (pronoun as subject)

subject   *predicate*

To find the verb in a sentence | is fairly easy. | (phrase as subject)

2. The **verb** is the word or phrase that tells the reader what the subject is or does.

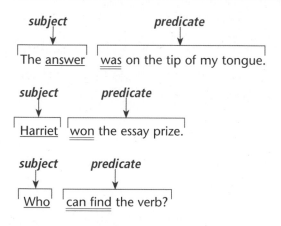

subject   *predicate*

The answer | was on the tip of my tongue.

subject   *predicate*

Harriet | won the essay prize.

subject   *predicate*

Who | can find the verb?

In the examples below, direct objects are indicated by a triple underline; indirect objects by a dotted underline; and complements by a broken underline.)

3. The **direct object** is the noun or pronoun that names the receiver of the action of the verb.

subject   *predicate*

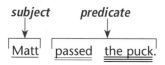

Matt | passed   the puck.

4. The **indirect object** is a noun or pronoun that tells to whom something is (was/will be) done. The indirect object comes before the direct object.

subject   *predicate*

Matt   passed Caro the puck.

5. An **object of a preposition** is a noun or pronoun that follows the preposition in a prepositional phrase.

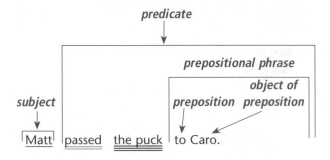

predicate

prepositional phrase

subject   *object of*
                  preposition preposition

Matt   passed   the puck   to Caro.

6. A **complement** is a noun, pronoun, or modifier that explains, renames, or describes the subject of a linking verb (e.g., *is*, *seems*, *appears*, *smells*, *tastes*).

Caro is the captain of the team. (noun complement)
The goal and the game are ours! (pronoun complement)
The crowd went wild. (adjective complement)

PARTS OF SPEECH

The words that make up sentences can be classified into nine grammatical categories or word classes. The function of a word in a sentence determines what part of speech it is. The word *rock*, for example, can belong to any one of three categories, depending on its context.

We stopped to rest in the shadow of an enormous *rock*. (noun)

The baby will usually stop fussing if you *rock* her. (verb)

I used to listen only to *rock* music, but now I prefer jazz. (adjective)

Here's another example, illustrating three functions of the word *since*.

We haven't seen Salima *since* Saturday. (preposition)

We haven't seen Salima *since* she left. (subordinating conjunction)

We haven't seen Salima *since*. (adverb)

1. NOUNS

A **noun** is a word that names a person, place, object, quality, or concept.

A. **Common nouns** are general names for persons, places, and objects: for example, *artist, politician; city, suburb; train, computer.*
 - **Concrete** nouns name things that can be seen and touched: *telephone, sister, puppy.*
 - **Abstract** nouns name thoughts, emotions, qualities, or values—things that cannot be seen or touched: for example, *ambition, success, honesty.*

B. **Proper nouns** name specific persons, places, and things and are capitalized: for example, *Queen Elizabeth, Homer Simpson, Bugs Bunny, CN Tower, Calgary, General Motors.*

C. **Collective nouns** name groups of people or things that act as a single unit: for example, *jury, class, committee, herd.*

2. VERBS

A. A verb is a word or phrase that tells what the subject of the clause is or does.

 - **Action verbs** tell what the subject does: The driver braked suddenly.
 - **Linking** (or *copula*) **verbs** connect the subject to a word or phrase identifying or describing the subject of a sentence: The driver was my older brother. He felt sleepy.

B. All verbs have different forms (called **tenses**) to indicate past, present, or future time.

Our team <u>played</u> badly last night. (action verb in past tense)

Mario <u>thinks</u> that we <u>will win</u> tonight. (present tense, future tense)

I <u>am</u> not so confident. (linking verb in present tense)

C. **Auxiliary** (or **helping**) **verbs** are used with a main verb to show tense or voice.

The auxiliary verbs are *be, have, do, may, can, ought, must, shall, will,* and their various forms.

By November, <u>we</u> <u>will have been</u> in Canada for six months. (future perfect tense)

D. The way verbs interact with their subjects is shown through a quality called **voice**. Active-voice and passive-voice verbs give different messages to the reader.

- **Active-voice** verbs show the subject doing or acting or being in a certain state:

  A <u>woman</u> in a BMW <u>took</u> my parking place. (doing)

  The <u>tornado</u> <u>destroyed</u> everything in its path. (acting)

  The <u>girl</u> <u>felt</u> ill. (being)

- **Passive-voice** verbs show the subject being acted upon:

  My parking <u>place</u> <u>was taken</u> by a woman in a BMW.

  Our <u>home</u> <u>was destroyed</u> by the tornado.

  (See Chapter 11, pages 159 to 160, for instructions on when to use passive-voice verbs.)

3. PRONOUNS

> Pronouns are words that substitute for nouns. They can act as subjects or objects.

There are seven classes of pronouns:

1. Personal Pronouns

	Singular (Subject/Object)	*Plural* (Subject/Object)
1st person	I/me	we/us
2nd person	you/you	you/you
3rd person	he, she, it/him, her, it	they/them

We would like *you* to come with *us* since *they* can fit only four people into the car.

2. Possessive Pronouns

	Singular	*Plural*
1st person	mine	ours
2nd person	yours	yours
3rd person	his, hers, its	theirs

The wonton soup is *yours*; the chicken wings are *hers*; the spareribs are *mine*; and the spring rolls are *ours* to share.

3. Indefinite Pronouns

Singular	*Plural*
any, anyone, anybody, anything	some, all, many
everyone, everybody, everything	some, all, many
someone, somebody, something	some people, some things
no one, nobody, nothing, none (sing.)	none (pl.)
one	several
each	both
either, neither	few, several, many

Is *no one* curious about *anything someone* is doing for the good of us *all*?

4. Demonstrative Pronouns

Singular	*Plural*
this	these
that	those

This paper is mine; *these* papers are yours.

That is my magazine; I've read *those*, so you can have them.

5. Relative Pronouns   *Singular and Plural*
                            (Subject/Object)

                            who/whom; whoever/whomever;
                            which/whichever; what/whatever;
                            that; whose

The Order of Canada, *which* was created in 1967, is awarded each year to Canadians *who* have distinguished themselves in the arts and sciences, politics, or community service, and *whose* contributions in *whatever* field are deemed worthy of national honour.

6. Interrogative Pronouns   *Singular and Plural*
                                 (Subject/Object)

                                 who?/whom?; whose?
                                 which?; what?

Jan is the leader on *whom* the team depended. *Who* could take her place? *What* can the team do now?

7. Reflexive/Emphatic Pronouns   *Singular*   *Plural*

1st person   myself   ourselves
2nd person   yourself   yourselves
3rd person   himself, herself, itself   themselves

We had planned to go by *ourselves*, but since Sharon invited *herself* along, Leo and Jon should have included *themselves* on the outing, too.

4. ADJECTIVES

> An **adjective** is a word that modifies or describes a noun or pronoun.

- Adjectives usually answer one of these questions: *What kind? Which? How many?*

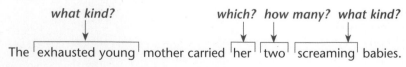

The exhausted young mother carried her two screaming babies.

- Pay special attention to the possessive pronoun adjectives: *my, our; your; his, her, its, their*. These words follow the same rules for agreement that govern the possessive pronouns listed above.

- Most adjectives have three forms:

  Positive (Base) Form: e.g., short, brief, concise

  Comparative Form:

  - Add -er to one-syllable words: e.g., shorter, briefer
  - Use *more* + base form for adjectives of two or more syllables: e.g., more concise

  Superlative Form:

  - Add -est to one-syllable words: e.g., shortest, briefest
  - Use *most* + base form for adjectives of two or more syllables: e.g., most concise

A few adjectives such as *bad* have irregular comparatives (*worse*) and superlatives (*worst*). Your dictionary will list these irregular forms.

5. ADVERBS

> An **adverb** is a word that modifies or describes a verb, an adjective, or another adverb.

- Adverbs commonly answer the questions *When? Where? How?*
- Adverbs often—but not always—end in -*ly*.

Rocco *foolishly* challenged the police officer. (adverb modifies verb)

The baby is an *extremely* fussy eater. (adverb modifies adjective)

My elderly father drives ⌐*very slowly.*⌐ (adverb modifies another adverb; adverb phrase modifies verb)

6. PREPOSITIONS

> A **preposition** is a word (or words) such as *in, on, among, to, for,* and *according to* that introduces a prepositional phrase. A **prepositional phrase** = a preposition + an object of the preposition (a noun or pronoun).

Prepositional phrases can function as adjectives, adverbs, or nouns.

Celeste is an old friend *of mine* *from Paris.* (prepositional phrases as adjectives modifying noun *friend*)

I'll wait *until seven o'clock.* (prepositional phrase as adverb modifying verb *wait*)

We all hope *for a better world.* (prepositional phrase as noun object of verb *hope*)

7. CONJUNCTIONS

Conjunctions are connecting words used to join two words, two phrases, or two clauses.

- **Coordinating conjunctions** (*and, but, or, for, so, nor, yet*) join grammatically equal elements in a sentence (e.g., the two parts of a compound subject; two independent clauses).

  Maureen *and* Gila are coming, *but* Tessa is not.

- **Subordinating conjunctions** (e.g., *because, although, when, since*) are dependent clause cues. They link dependent (or subordinate) clauses to independent clauses.

  Tom must go home early *because* he promised to cook dinner.

- **Conjunctive adverbs** are transitional expressions (e.g., *however, therefore, nevertheless, in fact*) usually used after a semicolon to join two independent clauses.

  I would like to go to the club tonight; *however*, I have no money.

- **Correlative conjunctions** are conjunctions used in pairs: for example, *both … and, not only … but (also), either … or, neither … nor*. These constructions are intensifiers. They make the meaning of a statement more emphatic by focusing the reader's attention on each element separately.

  Eva is beautiful *and* intelligent. (coordinating conjunction = statement)

Eva is *both* beautiful *and* intelligent. (correlative conjunctions = emphatic statement)

Luca invited all his friends to the party *and* gave everyone a gift. (coordinating conjunction = statement)

Not only did Luca invite all his friends to the party, *but* (*also*) he gave everyone a gift. (correlative conjunctions = emphatic statement)

8. ARTICLES

An **article** precedes the noun it modifies. The **definite article**, *the*, may be used with a singular or a plural noun; it denotes a particular person or thing. The **indefinite article**, *a/an*, is generally used with a singular **count noun** and signals an unspecified one of others. (Use *an* before vowel sounds, not just vowels: for example, *an* apple, *an* honest person.)

The student sitting next to you is asleep. (a particular student)

A student in the back row is snoring. (one of a number of students)

A number of factors determine the use or non-use of articles. For a summary of rules governing articles, go to "ESL Tips" on the Student Resources page of our website, NELSONbrain.com.

9. EXPLETIVES

Here and *there* are expletives, which are words used at the beginning of a sentence to postpone the subject until after the verb and thus emphasize it.

Here is your mail. (= Your mail is here.)

There are hundreds of copies still available. (= Hundreds of copies are still available.)

See Chapter 5, page 74.

APPENDIX B

List of Useful Terms

abstract noun (p. 369)

See **noun**.

action verb (p. 72)

A verb that tells what the subject is doing. See **verb**.

active voice (p. 157)

See **voice**.

adjective (p. 372)

A word that modifies (describes, restricts, makes more precise) a noun or pronoun. Adjectives answer the questions *What kind? How many?* and *Which?* For example, the com*petent* student, *five* home runs, my *last* class. When two or more adjectives modify a noun, they may require commas between them. **Coordinate adjectives** can be arranged in any order and can have *and* inserted between them. When there is no *and*, a comma is required (e.g., a spoiled, selfish child). **Cumulative adjectives** build upon one another and are not separated by a comma (e.g., an unopened cardboard box). See also "Parts of Speech" in Appendix A.

adverb (p. 373)

A word that modifies a verb, adjective, or other adverb. Adverbs answer the questions *When? How? Where? Why?* and *How much?* For example, Matt talks loudly (*loudly* modifies the verb *talks*); he is a *very* loud talker (*very* modifies the adjective *loud*); he talks *really* loudly (*really* modifies the adverb *loudly*). Adverbs often—but not always—end in *-ly*.

See also "Parts of Speech" in Appendix A.

agreement (p. 185)

Grammatical correspondence in person and number between a verb and its subject, or in person, number, and gender between a pronoun and its antecedent. See Chapters 12 and 14.

anecdote (p. 319)

A short account of an event or incident, often humorous, that is used to catch the reader's interest and illustrate a point. See Chapter 25.

antecedent (p. 194)   The word that a pronoun refers to or stands for. Literally, it means "coming before, preceding." The antecedent usually comes before the pronoun that refers to it: My sister thinks she is always right (*sister* is the antecedent of the pronoun *she*). See Chapter 15.

article (p. 375)   A determiner that precedes a noun. *A/an* is the **indefinite article** that signals an unspecified one of others: *a* stockbroker, *an* accountant, *a* village, *an* animal, *an* opportunity. Use *a/an* with a singular count noun when making a generalization: *A* stockbroker's job is stressful.

The is the **definite article** that signals a particular person, place, or thing that has been singled out from others: *the* stockbroker next door, *the* accountant who audits our books, *the* village where I was born. *The* is used when the speaker or writer and the audience are thinking about the same specific person(s) or thing(s). *The* is also used when an unspecified noun is mentioned a second time: I bought a box of chocolates, and my roommate ate half *the* box.

attention-getter (p. 319)   A sentence or more that comes before the **thesis statement** and that is designed to get the reader interested in what you have to say. See Chapter 25.

audience (p. 5)   The writer's intended reader or readers. Knowledge of your audience's level of understanding, interests, attitude toward the subject, and expectations of you as a writer is essential to successful communication. Your level of vocabulary, sentence structure, organization of material, the amount of specific detail you include, and tone should all reflect the needs of your audience. See Chapter 1.

auxiliary verb (p. 76)   A verb form that adds further meaning to the main verb. Some auxiliary verbs, also called **helping verbs**, show when an action took place (e.g., be, do/did, have/had, will), and some suggest possibility or probability (e.g., can, could, may, might, must, should, would). See Chapter 5.

chronological order (p. 283)   Events or ideas that are arranged in order of time sequence. See Chapter 22.

clause (p. 94)   A group of words containing a subject and a verb. If the group of words can stand by itself as a complete sentence, it is called an **independent** (or *main*) **clause**. If the group of words does not make complete sense on its own but depends on another clause, it is called a **dependent** (or **subordinate**) **clause**. Here's an example: The porch collapsed. This group of words can stand by itself, so it is called an independent clause. Now consider this clause: When Kalim removed the railing with his tractor. This group of words has a subject, *Kalim*, and a verb, *removed*, but it does not make complete sense on its own. For its meaning, it depends on *the porch collapsed*; therefore, it is a dependent clause. See Chapter 6.

cliché (p. 19)

A phrase that has been used so often it no longer communicates a meaningful idea. See Chapter 1.

climactic order (p. 284)

The arrangement of key ideas in order of importance. The most important or strongest idea comes last. Thus, the paper builds to a climax. See Chapter 22.

coherence (p. 141)

The logical consistency and stylistic connections between ideas, sentences, and paragraphs in a piece of writing. See Chapter 10 and "Keeping Your Reader with You" in Chapter 25.

collective noun (p. 171)

See **noun**.

colloquialism (p. 11)

A word or phrase that we use in casual conversation or in informal writing, but not in formal writing. Examples:

> Steve *flunked* his accounting exam.
>
> *Did* you *get* what the teacher said about job placement?
>
> I can't believe that *guy* is serious about learning.

command (p. 71)

A sentence that tells the listener or reader to do something. In this type of sentence, no subject appears, but "you" is understood. See Chapter 5. Examples:

> Look up unfamiliar words in the dictionary.
>
> Be all that you can be.
>
> Sit!

comma splice (p. 102)

The error that results when the writer joins two independent clauses with a comma. Example:

> The comma splice is an error, it is a kind of **run-on** sentence.

common noun (p. 369)

See **noun**.

comparison (p. 314)

Writing that points out similarities, showing how two different objects, people, or ideas are alike. See Chapter 25.

comparison and contrast	Writing that identifies both similarities and differences.
complement (p. 368)	A word or phrase that completes the meaning of a verb. Also called a *subjective completion*, a complement can be a noun, pronoun, or adjective that follows a linking verb. Examples:

> Ramani is the *manager*. (noun complement)
>
> The winner was *she*. (pronoun complement)
>
> The president's speech was *encouraging*. (adjective complement).

compound (p. 82)	A compound construction is made up of two or more equal parts. Examples:

> Walter and Pieter are brothers. (compound subject)
>
> Walter came late and left early. (compound verb)
>
> Pieter is quiet and studious. (compound complement)

compound complement	See **compound**.
compound sentence (p. 365)	A sentence consisting of two or more independent clauses:

> We had no time to warm up, but we won the game anyway.

See "Sentences: Kinds and Parts" in Appendix A.

compound subject (p. 82)	See **compound** and Chapter 5.
compound verb (p. 82)	See **compound** and Chapter 5.
concrete noun (p. 369)	See **noun**.
conjunction (p. 133)	A word that links two or more words, phrases, or clauses. Conjunctions come in three types: coordinating, correlative, and subordinating. There are seven **coordinating conjunctions**: *and, but, so, or, nor, for,* and *yet*. The **correlative conjunctions** include *either ... or, neither ... nor, not only ... but also,* and *both ... and*. Use a coordinating or correlative conjunction when the items being linked are of equal importance in the sentence. When you want to show that one idea is secondary to another, you should use a **subordinating conjunction**, such as *although, because, since, so*

	that, *though*, or *while*. See page 94 for a more comprehensive list of subordinating conjunctions.
conjunctive adverb (p. 374)	A transitional expression usually used after a semicolon to join two independent clauses (e.g., however, therefore, nevertheless, in fact).
consistency (p. 185)	In pronoun use, the maintenance of number, person, and gender. For example, a sentence that begins in the first person but shifts to the second person is incorrect: *We* chose not to drive to Calgary because, these days, *you* just can't afford the gas. See Chapter 14.
contraction (p. 42)	The combining of two words into one, as in *they're* or *can't*. Contractions are common in conversation and in informal written English. See Chapter 2.
contrast (p. 314)	Writing that points out dissimilarities between things, showing how two objects, people, or ideas differ. See Chapter 25.
coordinate adjectives	Adjectives that can be arranged in any order and can be separated by the word *and* without changing the meaning of the sentence. Commas come between coordinate adjectives not joined by *and*. Example: The lecture was *long, superficial,* and *boring.*
coordinating conjunction (p. 102)	A linking word used to join two or more words, phrases, or clauses of equal importance: *and, but, so, or, nor, for,* and *yet.* See Chapter 10.
correlative conjunctions (p. 133)	Linking words that appear in pairs and that join two or more words, phrases, or clauses of equal importance: *either ... or, neither ... nor, not only ... but also,* and *both ... and.* See Chapter 10.
count noun (p. 375)	A common noun that has a plural form and can be preceded by an indefinite article (*a/an*) or a quantity expression such as *one, many, several, a few of, hundreds of.* Examples: car, letter, dollar. See Appendix A.
cumulative adjectives	A series of adjectives in which each adjective modifies the word that follows it. No commas are placed between cumulative adjectives. Example: The bride wore a *creamy white lace* gown.
dangling modifier (p. 115)	A modifier that cannot sensibly refer to any specific word or phrase in the sentence. See Chapter 8.

definite article (p. 375)	See **article**.
dependent clause (p. 94)	A group of words containing a subject and a verb but not expressing a complete idea. It *depends* on an independent clause for its meaning. Also called *subordinate clause*. See Chapter 6.
dependent clause cue (p. 94)	A word or phrase that introduces a dependent clause: for example, when, because, in order that, as soon as. Also called a **subordinating conjunction**. See Chapter 6.
direct object	See **object**.
editing (p. 330)	The correction of errors in grammar, word choice, spelling, punctuation, and formatting. See Chapter 26.
formal level (p. 10)	The level of language often used (and expected) in university and college papers. Formal English avoids the use of contractions and of the first and second person. It uses no colloquial expressions or slang. See Chapter 1.
4-S test (p. 272)	A satisfactory subject is SIGNIFICANT, SINGLE, SPECIFIC, and SUPPORTABLE. See Chapter 22.
fused sentence (p. 102)	The error that results when the writer joins two independent clauses without any punctuation between them. See Chapter 7. Example: The fused sentence is an error it is a kind of run-on sentence.
general level (p. 10)	The level of language of educated persons. General-level English is used in college and professional writing. It is nontechnical and readily understood by most readers. It uses few if any colloquial expressions, no slang, and few contractions. See Chapter 1.
helping verb (p. 76)	See **auxiliary verb**.
homonyms (p. 26)	Two or more words that are identical in sound (e.g., bear, bare) or spelling (e.g., bank—a place for money; bank—a slope) but different in meaning. See Chapter 2.
indefinite article (p. 375)	See **article**.
indefinite pronoun (p. 195)	A pronoun representative of a person or thing (or people or things) that is unknown: for example, all, anyone, everything, somebody, no one, and both.

independent clause (p. 94)
A group of words containing a subject and a verb and expressing a complete idea. Also called *main clause*. See Chapter 6.

indirect object (p. 368)
See **object**.

infinitive (p. 151)
The form of the verb used with *to* (e.g., to visit, to be). See Chapter 11.

informal level (p. 10)
The level of language most of us use in conversation and in personal writing. It is casual, includes some slang and colloquial expressions, commonly uses contractions, and is written in first and second person. See Chapter 1.

irregular verb (p. 151)
A verb whose simple past and past participle forms are not formed by adding *-ed*: for example, eat (ate, eaten), lay (laid), ride (rode, ridden). See list on pages 152 to 155.

linking verb (p. 72)
See **verb**.

logically linked order (p. 284)
A pattern of organization that depends on causal connections among the main points. One point must be explained before the next can be understood. See Chapter 22.

main verb (p. 76)
The verb that follows the auxiliary or helping verb and tells the action in the sentence. See Chapter 5.

memorable statement (p. 319)
A sentence in the conclusion that will stick with the reader; it usually follows the summary and is usually the last sentence of the essay. See Chapter 25 for some of the many forms a memorable statement can take.

misplaced modifier (p. 111)
A modifier that is next to a word or phrase that it is not meant to modify. A misplaced modifier can change the meaning of your sentence. See Chapter 8.

modal auxiliary
A type of **auxiliary verb** that does not change form regardless of person or number. The modal auxiliaries are *may, might, must, can, could, will, would, shall, should,* and *ought to*.

modifier (p. 111)
A word or group of words that adds information about another word (or phrase or clause) in a sentence. See **adjective**, **adverb**, **dependent clause**, and Chapter 8.

non-count noun
A common noun that cannot be preceded by an indefinite article (*a/an*) or by a quantity expression (e.g., one, several, many, a couple of) and that has no plural form. Examples: traffic, mail, money.

noun (p. 72)   A word that names a person, place, thing, or concept and that has the grammatical capability of being possessive. Nouns are most often used as subjects and objects. There are two classes of nouns: concrete and abstract.

Concrete nouns name things we perceive through our senses; we can see, hear, touch, taste, or smell what they stand for. Some concrete nouns are **proper**: they name people, places, or things and are capitalized—for example, Justin Trudeau, Beijing, Canada's Wonderland. Other concrete nouns are **common** (woman, city, car, coffee); still others are **collective** (group, audience, crowd, committee).

Abstract nouns name concepts, ideas, characteristics—things we know or experience through our intellect rather than through our senses—for example, truth, pride, prejudice, self-esteem. See Chapter 5.

object (p. 367)   The "receiving" part of a sentence. The **direct object** is a noun or noun substitute (pronoun, phrase, or clause) that is the target or receiver of the action expressed by the verb. It answers the question *What?* or *Whom?* Examples:

Jai threw the ball. (Jai threw *what?*)

He wondered where the money went. (He wondered *what?*)

Munira loves Abdul. (Munira loves *whom?*)

The **indirect object** is a noun or pronoun that is the indirect target or receiver of the action expressed by the verb in a sentence. It is always placed in front of the direct object. It answers the question *To whom?* or *To what?*

Dani threw me the ball. (Dani threw *to whom?*)

Ian forgot to give his essay a title. (Give *to what?*)

The **object of a preposition** is a noun or noun substitute (pronoun, phrase, or clause) that follows a preposition—for example, after the *storm* (*storm* is a noun, object of the preposition *after*); before *signing the lease* (*signing the lease* is a phrase, object of the preposition *before*); he thought about *what he wanted to do* (*what he wanted to do* is a clause, object of the preposition *about*). Notice that what follows a preposition is always its object; that is why the subject of a sentence or clause is never in a prepositional phrase.

parallelism
(p. 121)

Consistent grammatical structure. In a sentence, for example, all items in a series should be written in the same grammatical form: words, phrases, or clauses. Julius Caesar's famous pronouncement, "I came, I saw, I conquered," is a classic example of parallel structure. The symmetry of parallelism appeals to readers and makes a sentence read smoothly and rhythmically. Lack of parallelism, on the other hand, is jarring: "My favourite sports are water-skiing, swimming, and I particularly love to sail." See Chapter 9.

paraphrase
(p. 316)

The rephrasing of another writer's idea in your own words. A good paraphrase reflects both the meaning and the tone of the original; it is usually about the same length as or shorter than the original. Whenever you borrow another writer's ideas, you must acknowledge your source. If you don't, you are plagiarizing. See Chapters 25 and 27.

parenthetical citation
(p. 254)

Brief information presented in parentheses at the end of a quotation or paraphrase to identify the source of the original information. See Chapter 25.

participle
(p. 151)

The form of a verb that can be used as an adjective (e.g., the *starving* artist, the *completed* work) or as part of a verb phrase (e.g., am *working*, have *purchased*).

The **present participle** of a verb ends in *-ing*.

The **past participle** of a **regular verb** ends in *-d* or in *-ed*.

For a list of past participles of **irregular verbs**, see pages 152 to 155.

passive voice
(p. 157)

See **voice**.

past participle
(p. 151)

See **participle** and Chapter 11.

person (p. 165)

A category of pronouns and verbs. *First person* refers to the person who is speaking (**I**, **we**). *Second person* refers to the person being spoken to (**you**). *Third person* is the person or thing being spoken about (**he, she, it, they**). Regular verb forms remain constant except in the present tense third-person singular, which ends in *-s*: *I* run; *you* run; *he/she/it* runs; *we* run; *they* run. See Chapter 12.

person agreement
(p. 207)

The consistent use of the first-, second-, or third-person pronoun throughout a sentence or a paragraph. See Chapter 16.

phrase

A group of meaning-related words that acts as a noun, a verb, an adjective, or an adverb within a sentence. Phrases do not make complete sense on their own because they do not contain both a subject and a verb. Examples:

> Please order *legal-size manila file folders.* (phrase acting as noun)
>
> I *must have been sleeping* when you called. (verb phrase)
>
> *Sightseeing in Ottawa*, we photographed the monuments *on Parliament Hill.* (phrases acting as adjectives)
>
> Portaging a canoe *in this weather* is no fun. (phrase acting as adverb)

plagiarism (p. 335)

Using someone else's words or ideas in your writing without acknowledging their source. See Chapter 27.

plural (p. 164)

More than one person or thing. See Chapters 12 and 16.

possession (p. 45)

Ownership, as denoted in writing by the addition of *'s* to a singular noun or just an apostrophe (') to a plural noun ending in *s.* See Chapter 2.

> The writer's goal was to tell as many fallen soldiers' stories as she could in one book.

possessive pronoun (p. 371)

A group of words that are already in the possessive form and do not require *'s.* The possessive pronouns are *my, mine, your, yours, his, her, hers, its, our, ours, their, theirs,* and *whose.* See Chapter 3.

prefix

A meaningful letter or group of letters added to the beginning of a word to change either (1) its meaning or (2) its word class.

1. *a* + moral = amoral

   bi + sexual = bisexual

   contra + diction = contradiction

   dys + functional = dysfunctional

2. *a* + board (verb) = aboard (adverb, preposition)

   con + temporary (adjective) = contemporary (noun, adjective)

   dis + robe (noun) = disrobe (verb)

   in + put (verb) = input (noun)

Some prefixes require a hyphen, as here:

all-Canadian

de-emphasize

mid-morning

preposition
(p. 373)

A word that connects a noun, pronoun, or phrase to some other word(s) in a sentence. The noun, pronoun, or phrase is the **object** of the preposition. See Appendix A.

> I prepared the minutes *of the meeting.* (*of* relates *meeting* to *minutes*)
>
> One *of the parents* checks the children every half hour. (*of* relates *parents* to *One*)

prepositional phrase (p. 79)

A group of grammatically related words beginning with a **preposition** and having the function of a noun, adjective, or adverb. A list appears on page 79. See Chapter 5.

present participle (p. 151)

See **participle** and Chapter 11.

pretentious language (p. 18)

Sometimes called *gobbledygook* or *bafflegab*, pretentious language is characterized by vague, abstract, multi-syllable words and long, complicated sentences. Intended to impress the reader, pretentious language is sound without meaning; readers find it irritating, even exasperating. See Chapter 1.

principal parts (p. 151)

The verb elements we use to construct the various tenses. The principal parts are the **infinitive** form (*to* + the base verb), the **simple past**, the **present participle** (*-ing*), and the **past participle**. See Chapter 11.

pronoun (pp. 72, 135)

A word that functions like a noun in a sentence (e.g., as a subject or as an object of a verb or a preposition). Pronouns usually substitute for nouns, but sometimes they substitute for other pronouns. See Chapters 5 and 15.

> *Everyone* must earn *her* bonus.
>
> *He* will promote *anything that* brings in money.

There are several kinds of pronouns:

personal: *I, we; you; he, she, it, they; me, us; him, her, them*
possessive: *mine, ours; yours; his, her, its, theirs*
demonstrative: *this, these; that, those*
relative: *who, whom, whose; which, that*

interrogative: *who? whose? whom? which? what?*
indefinite: all *-one, -thing, -body* pronouns, such as *everyone, something,* and *anybody;* and *each; neither; either; few; none; several*

Note: Possessive pronouns also have adjective forms: *my, our; your; his, her, their.* Possessive adjectives follow the same rules for agreement that govern pronouns. They must agree with their antecedents in person, number, and gender—for example,

Every young *boy* wants to be the goalie on *his* team.
(not *their* team)

pronoun form
(p. 185)

Pronoun form is determined by the pronoun's function in a sentence: **subject** or **object**. See Chapter 14.

Subject Pronouns		**Object Pronouns**	
Singular	*Plural*	*Singular*	*Plural*
I	we	me	us
you	you	you	you
he, she, it, one	they	him, her, it, one	them

proofreading
(p. 330)

The correction of errors in typing or writing that appear in the final draft. See Chapter 26.

proper noun
(p. 369)

See **noun**.

random order
(p. 284)

A shopping-list kind of arrangement of main points in a paper. The points could be explained in any order. Random order is appropriate only when all points are equal in significance and are not chronologically or causally connected to one another. See Chapter 22.

regular verb
(p. 151)

A verb whose simple past and past participle form are formed by adding *-ed*, or just *-d* when the verb ends in *-e*. See Chapter 11.

run-on (p. 101)

A sentence with inadequate punctuation between clauses. The two kinds of run-on sentences are **comma splices** and **fused sentences**. See Chapter 7.

sentence combining (p. 131)	A technique that enables you to produce correct and pleasing sentences. Sentence combining accomplishes three things: it reinforces your meaning; it refines and polishes your writing; and it results in a style that will keep your reader alert and interested in what you have to say. See Chapter 10.
sentence fragment (p. 88)	A group of words that is punctuated like a sentence but either does not have both a subject and a verb or does not express a complete thought. See Chapter 6.
simple past (p. 151)	See **tense** and Chapter 11.
single/singular (p. 164)	One person or thing. See Chapters 12 and 16.
slang (p. 17)	Non-standard language used in conversation among people who belong to the same social group. See Chapter 1.
subject (pp. 72, 272)	In a sentence, the person, thing, or concept that the sentence is about (see Chapter 5). In an essay, the person, thing, or concept that the paper is about (see Chapter 22).
subject–verb agreement (p. 165)	The agreement in number of subject to verb: both must be singular or both must be plural. See Chapter 12.
subordinate clause (p. 94)	See **dependent clause**.
subordinating conjunction (p. 135)	A word or phrase that introduces a dependent clause: for example, when, because, in order that, as soon as. See page 94 in Chapter 6 and page 374 in Appendix A for more comprehensive lists of subordinating conjunctions.
suffix	A letter or group of letters that is added to the end of a word to change (1) its meaning, (2) its grammatical function, or (3) its word class.

1. king + *dom* = kingdom
   few + *er* = fewer
   tooth + *less* = toothless
2. buy (infinitive) + *s* = buys (third-person singular, present tense)
   eat (infinitive) + *en* = eaten (past participle)
   instructor + *s* = instructors (plural)
   instructor + *'s* = instructor's (possessive singular)

3. your (adjective) + *s* = yours (pronoun)

    act (verb) + *ive* = active (adjective)

    active (adjective) + *ly* = actively (adverb)

    ventilate (verb) + *tion* = ventilation (noun)

Some words add two or more prefixes and/or suffixes to the base form. Look at *antidisestablishmentarianism,* for example. How many prefixes and suffixes can you identify?

summary (p. 319)	Part of the conclusion; a brief review of the main points of an essay. See Chapter 25.
tense (p. 151)	The form of the verb that indicates past, present, or future time. The verb ending (e.g., play*s,* play*ed*) and any helping verbs associated with the main verb (*is* playing, *will* play, *has* played, *had* played, *will have* played) indicate the tense of the verb.

There are simple tenses: **present:** *ask, asks*

past: *asked*

future: *will ask*

and perfect tenses: **present:** *has (have) asked*

past: *had asked*

future: *will (shall) have asked*

The simple and perfect tenses can also be **progressive**: *am asking, have been asking,* etc.

thesis (p. 275)	A thesis is the idea or point about a subject that the writer wants to explain or prove to the reader. A summary of the writer's thesis is often expressed in a **thesis statement**. See Chapters 22 and 23.
thesis statement (p. 288)	A statement near the beginning of a paper that announces the paper's subject and scope. See Chapter 23.
tone (p. 322)	A reflection of the writer's attitude toward his or her topic. For instance, a writer who is looking back with longing to the past might use a nostalgic tone. An angry writer might use an indignant tone or an understated, ironic tone, depending on the subject and purpose of the paper. See Chapter 25.
topic sentence (p. 308)	A sentence that identifies the main point or key idea developed in a paragraph. The topic sentence is usually found at or near the beginning of the paragraph. See Chapter 25.

transition (p. 321)	A word or phrase that helps readers to follow the writer's thinking from one sentence to the next or from one paragraph to another. See Chapter 25.
vague reference (p. 198)	A pronoun without a clearly identifiable antecedent. See Chapter 15.
verb (p. 150)	A word or phrase that says something about a person, place, or thing and whose form may be changed to indicate tense (or time). Verbs may express action (physical or mental), occurrence, or condition (state of being). See Chapters 5 and 11.

> Jessa *hit* an inside curve for a home run. (physical action)
>
> Laurence *believed* the Blue Jays would win. (mental action)
>
> Father's Day *falls* on the third Sunday of June. (occurrence)
>
> Reva eventually *became interested* in English. (condition)

Some verbs are called **linking verbs**: they help to make a statement by linking the subject to a word or phrase that describes it or renames it.

> William Hubbard *was* Toronto's first Black mayor. (*was* links *William Hubbard* to *mayor*)
>
> Mohammed *looks* tired. (*looks* links *Mohammed* and *tired*)

In addition to *am, is, are, was, were,* and *been,* some common linking verbs are *appear, become, feel, grow, look, taste, remain, seem, smell, sound.*

Another class of verbs is called **auxiliary** or **helping verbs**. They show the time of a verb as future or past (*will* go, *has* gone) or as a continuing action (*is* reading). They also show the passive voice (*is* completed, *have been* submitted).

voice (p. 157)	Verbs may be **active** or **passive**, depending on whether the subject of the verb is *acting* (active voice) or *being acted upon* (passive voice). See Chapter 11.

> In 2013, the <u>government</u> <u>introduced</u> a new set of tax reforms. (active)
>
> A new <u>set</u> of tax reforms <u>was introduced</u> in 2013. (passive)

wordiness
(p. 14)

The use of more words than necessary to communicate a thought. Wordiness results when information is repeated or when a phrase is used when a single word will suffice. See Chapter 1.

APPENDIX C
Answers to Exercises

Answers for Unit 1 Quick Quiz (page 2)

Note: Triple asterisks (***) indicate that a word or words have been deleted and not replaced. Each set of triple asterisks counts as one error.

[1]Having decided to buy a new stereo system for my car, I went to Awesome Auto Audio, a store **whose** advertisements in the paper said **their** quality and prices are unbeatable. [2]The salesperson could see that I was a more serious customer **than** the average car radio buyer and recommended that I consider V3A. [3]Of **course**, I didn't want to let him know that I didn't know what V3A was, so he **led** me to a special showroom, where I spotted a sign that read "Voice-Activated Auto Audio (V3A)."

[4]The salesperson switched on the system and demonstrated by saying, "**Louder**," which increased the radio's volume. [5]Then he said, "Techno," and the radio immediately switched to a techno station. [6]I thought this was **excellent**, so, **regardless** of the price, I told him to install it in my car. [7]In *** fact, I had convinced myself that **it's** safer to have a radio that doesn't need to be adjusted manually *** while I was driving. [8]Once I had presented my **credit card** and a **piece** of identification, I went to the parking lot to wait for the installation.

[9]Soon I was driving home and calling out, "Louder" and "**Oldies**" and "Classic rock," and the radio was obeying every command. [10]Suddenly, as I was turning a corner, another driver cut right in front of me. [11]Annoyed, I yelled, "Stupid!" and the radio *** abruptly switched to a call-in talk show.

Answer Key
If you missed the error(s)
in sentence ...   **See Chapter ...**

1	*who's, they're*	2 Hazardous Homonyms; 3 The Apostrophe
2	*then*	2 Hazardous Homonyms
3	*coarse, lead*	2 Hazardous Homonyms
4	*"louder"*	2 Hazardous Homonyms
6	*way cool*	1 "Slang" section
6	*irregardless*	1 "Language Abusages" section
7	*In actual fact*	1 "Wordiness" section
7	*its*	2 Hazardous Homonyms; 3 The Apostrophe
7	*manually, by hand*	1 "Wordiness" section
8	*Credit Card*	4 Capital Letters
8	*peace*	2 Hazardous Homonyms
9	*"Oldie's"*	3 The Apostrophe
10	*suddenly and abruptly*	1 "Wordiness" section

Answers for Chapter 1: Choosing the Right Words (pages 4 to 25)

Exercise 1.1

1. *humor.* You must use the root *humor* when adding an ending: e.g., *humorous.*
2. The word is spelled *harassment.* The stress is on the second syllable: har-<u>ASS</u>-ment.
3. The word is spelled *tattoo* and can be used both as a noun and as a verb.
4. People in Saskatchewan are more likely to experience a *tornado*; a *tsunami* is a gigantic sea wave, and a *typhoon* is a tropical storm.
5. *program, centre, skilful, traveller, judgment,* which are the preferred Canadian spellings.

Exercise 1.2

1. bases
2. criteria
3. data (the *singular* is datum)
4. ratios
5. nuclei (*or* nucleuses)
6. appendixes (*or* appendices)
7. formulas (*or* formulae)
8. phenomena
9. mothers-in-law
10. syllabuses (*or* syllabi)

Exercise 1.3

1. delayed
2. journeys
3. player
4. destroying
5. repayment
6. loneliness
7. policies
8. easier
9. laziness
10. necessarily

The root words in 1 to 5 end in a **vowel** plus *y*; these words do not change spelling when you add an ending. The root words in 6 to 10 end in a **consonant** plus *y*; change *y* to *i* when you add an ending to such words.

Exercise 1.4

1. cof-fee
2. man-age-ment
3. pre-cise
4. through (words of one syllable cannot be divided)
5. dis-trib-ute
6. mon-itor
7. grad-ual-ly
8. tech-ni-cian
9. dic-tion-ary (not dic-tion-ar-y. Use a hyphen to break a word only if three or more letters are left to begin the next line.)
10. busi-ness

Exercise 1.6

Informal paragraph: The vocabulary is casual and includes contractions and colloquialisms (e.g., "paying through the nose," "a lot of," "the best bets"). Written in the second person, the paragraph addresses the reader informally as "you." Most of the sentences are short and simple; two are exclamatory—common in speech, but not in formal writing.

General paragraph: Sentences here are longer and more complex than in the informal paragraph, but they are still easily understood. The vocabulary is less casual and more abstract (e.g., contrast the informal expression "We will have to change everything" with the general-level "We will have to transform our entire oil-based infrastructure"; and the informal "That's a big job!" with the general "That's an enormous undertaking!"). Written in the first person, the paragraph is still friendly in tone but less conversational than the previous paragraph.

Formal paragraph: The vocabulary is more abstract than concrete; there are no contractions or colloquialisms. The sentences are complex and relatively long; the parallel structure of phrases and clauses contributes to the formality of the passage, as does the third-person point of view. The tone is serious. The reader cannot imagine anyone speaking this paragraph; clearly, it was written for educated readers.

Exercise 1.7

1. formal	2. informal	3. general

Exercise 1.8 (suggested answers)

1. I prefer modern furniture to antiques.
2. I do not think there is any basis for believing in UFOs.
3. Getting up at 5 a.m. and repeating the same routine daily for three weeks wore me out.
4. I doubt that this innovation will succeed.
5. Because he is being transferred, Ravi plans to buy a new car.
6. I think Holly is pretending to be sick so she won't have to go to work.
7. Close friends usually share tastes and opinions.
8. My essay is as good as Kim's and deserves an equivalent mark, but our professor hates me.
9. Nothing suggests that this unusual situation will occur again, so we can proceed with confidence.
10. Our competitor's products are selling better than ours, even though they are not as good.

Exercise 1.10

On our recent trip to Montreal, just outside Dorval, we saw storm clouds ahead and realized that rain was likely. Within minutes, it began to rain so heavily that we couldn't see. When the rain turned to snow, we pulled into a nearby motel to wait for the storm to pass.

Exercise 1.11

For each item in this exercise, we have italicized the clichés and then provided a suggested revision.

1. The financial adviser told us there was a *window of opportunity* open to investors who could *think outside the box*. Then she gave us an *eye-popping ballpark figure* of what our *bottom line* would look like in five years if we put our money *in her capable hands*.

   The financial adviser told us there was a good opportunity for creative investors. Then she gave us an impressive estimate of the gains we could expect over five years if we entrusted our money to her.

2. While you may want *cutting-edge* stereo and television equipment and a *state-of-the-art* computer and car, you need to understand that your *lifestyle choices* must depend

on your income, not your desires. *At the end of the day*, your *take-home pay doesn't make the grade*.

> While you may want the very best stereo and television equipment and the latest model of computer and car, you need to understand that your choices must depend on your income, not your desires. Your salary is not sufficient to pay for your dreams.

3. Kayla knew that she *was in over her head* when the meeting *ground to a halt* because she had not *done her homework*. When she became office manager, she thought it would be *child's play* to get everyone *on the same page*, but she soon learned that careful preparation is *a must*.

> Kayla knew that she had underestimated the demands of the job when the meeting ended because she had not prepared for it. When she became office manager, she thought it would be easy to get everyone to agree, but she soon learned that careful preparation is vital.

4. *Experts agree* that *meaningful relationships* are important to mental health, even as divorce rates have *reached epidemic proportions* and loneliness has become *a fact of life*.

> Psychologists agree that close relationships are important to mental health, even as divorce rates have greatly increased and loneliness has become commonplace.

5. *Last but not least*, I want to thank George and Navika, my *tried-and-true friends* who have *stood by me through thick and thin*, even when there was *no light at the end of the tunnel*. The list of times when they have *lent me a hand* is endless.

> Finally, I want to thank George and Navika, my faithful friends who have been supportive in all circumstances, even when there seemed to be no hope. The list of their many kindnesses to me is endless.

Exercise 1.12 (suggested answers)
1. I would be happy to meet **you** any time, **anywhere**.
2. Don't be discouraged that Jessa's father **can hardly stand** you; he's **prejudiced** against **many** of her friends.
3. Television is probably the best example of a **medium** that remains popular **regardless** of the quality of the programming.
4. This course was **supposed** to be *** easy, but I could not **have** passed it without *** help.
5. Between you and **me**, the reason our group got a C+ on our project is **that** Jamie **did nothing** to contribute to it. (*Or:* **contributed nothing to it**)

Answers for Chapter 2: Hazardous Homonyms (pages 26 to 40)
Exercise 2.1
1. conscience, your
2. fourth, passed
3. principle, principals
4. Whether, lose, we're
5. woman, its

Exercise 2.2
1. you're, minor
2. course, cite
3. complement, dining
4. whose, advice
5. you're, past, too

Exercise 2.3
1. lose, then, your
2. conscious, dessert
3. two, it's
4. our, illusions
5. it's, whose

Exercise 2.4
1. Does, here
2. coarse, new
3. your, then
4. dinner, led
5. woman, choose, choose

Exercise 2.5
1. accepts, many
2. stationery, your
3. Where, desert
4. were, dose, lead
5. effective, choose

Exercise 2.6
1. The hiring committee will not **hear** from any candidate **whose** application is late.
2. Other **than** hope that the voters will **choose** our candidate, there isn't much more we can do.
3. I bruise easily, and **besides**, I faint at the **sight** of blood.
4. **Who's** the idiot who said that our **principal** purpose in life was to serve as a warning to others?
5. Driving **through** the **deserted** streets, we **passed** only a police officer and a stray dog.
6. You would do well to **choose** a **moral** rather than an **unprincipled course** of action.

Exercise 2.7

Nothing causes more arguments between men and **women than** money. Recently, my husband and I were driving **through** the countryside and became involved in a **minor** disagreement about **whether** to treat ourselves to a vacation or buy a new refrigerator. I argued that if we bought the appliance, this would be the **fourth** year in which we had not had a holiday. He countered that our fridge had **passed its** useful life, and a functioning refrigerator took **precedence*** over having fun. What began as a spat quickly **led** to a battle. Before we **knew** it, our good sense **deserted** us, and we were having a serious fight. At this point, we **passed** a farmyard containing several goats and pigs. Pointing to them, my husband asked if they were relatives of mine. "Of **course**," I replied. "**They're** my in-laws."

Did you find this error? If so, good for you! If not, be aware that our list of hazardous homonyms includes only the most commonly confused word pairs. There are dozens more that can trip you up—another reason you need to own and use a good dictionary.

Exercise 2.8

Many people today are **choosing** a quieter way of life, hoping to live longer and more happily by following the "slower is better" **principle**. Some, on the **advice** of **their** doctors, have been forced to slow down. One heart surgeon, for example, tells his patients to drive only in the slow lane rather **than** use the passing lane. They may arrive a few minutes later, but their blood pressure will not be **affected**. Others don't need to be prompted by their doctors. They **accept** that living at a slower pace doesn't mean **losing** out in any way. In fact, the opposite is true: choosing a healthy lifestyle benefits everyone. The **effect** of increased **peace** and **quiet** in your **personal** life leads to increased productivity, higher **morale**, and greater job satisfaction. Sometimes the improvements are **minor**, but as anyone who has **consciously** tried to slow the pace of life can tell you, the slow lane is the fast lane to longevity.

Exercise 2.10

These are examples only.
1. The wind [noun] was so strong that we couldn't wind [verb] the sail into position.
2. The supermarket will buy all of the produce [noun] your farm can produce [verb].
3. The hawk dove [verb] from high above, targeting a dove [noun].
4. Carefully, he wound [verb] a bandage around the wound [noun] on her arm.
5. They will present [verb] her with her birthday present [noun] at the end of the party.
6. Our local dump will refuse [verb] to take refuse [noun] from another municipality.
7. How can we object [verb] when the object [noun] that hit our house is from outer space?
8. Lead [adjective] poisoning can lead [verb] to severe illness.
9. There was a row [noun] when two people were caught smoking in row [adjective] seven.
10. Does [verb] this study prove that in our province's deer population, bucks are declining relative to does [noun]?

Answers for Chapter 3: The Apostrophe (pages 41 to 54)

Exercise 3.1

1. can't	5. let's	8. won't
2. she'd	6. hasn't	9. she'll
3. he'll	7. you're	10. we'll
4. we'd		

Exercise 3.2

1. they're	5. everyone's	8. you're
2. I'll	6. couldn't	9. we'd
3. it's	7. who's	10. won't
4. wouldn't		

Exercise 3.3

1. **There's** no way **we'd** go without you.
2. There **won't** be any problem if **you've** got an invitation.
3. **I'm** sure that contractions **shouldn't** be used in formal writing.
4. **They're** acceptable only in conversation and in informal writing.

5. **Let's** see if **she'll** do what she said **she'd** do.
6. **Don't** worry about your heart; **it's** going to last as long as you do.
7. When **everything's** coming your way, **you're** probably in the wrong lane.
8. **Wouldn't** it be great if everyone **who's** celebrating a birthday today could get together for a big party?
9. **I'd** support the idea only if the party **wasn't** held anywhere near my apartment.
10. "A **man's** got to do what a **man's** got to do. A **woman's** got to do what he **can't**."

Exercise 3.4

   I am writing to apply for the position of webmaster for BrilloVision.com that **you have** advertised in the *Daily News*. I have the talent and background **you are** looking for. Currently, I work as a web designer for an online publication, Vexed.com, where **they are** very pleased with my work. If you click on their website, I think **you will** like what you see. **There is** little in the way of web design and application that I **have not** been involved in during the past two years. But **it is** time for me to move on to a new challenge, and BrilloVision.com promises the kind of opportunity **I am** looking for. I guarantee you **will not** be disappointed if I join your team!

Exercise 3.5

1. Cass's voice
2. heaven's gate
3. families' budgets
4. crew's mutiny
5. soldiers' uniforms
6. everyone's choice
7. the all-candidates' debate
8. witness's testimony
9. teacher's attitude
10. Lady Gaga's style

Exercise 3.6

1. book's, its
2. Bikers', Larry's
3. whose, their
4. Dennis's, men's
5. month's, son's
6. Texas's, United States'
7. month's , men's, women's
8. whose, company's
9. consumers', WD-40's
10. its, your

Exercise 3.7

1. A **country's** health care system is one of **its** greatest assets.
2. Who says **nobody's** perfect? In my **mother's** opinion, I am.
3. Most **mothers'** beliefs about their **children's** characters are unrealistically positive.
4. Most **fathers'** opinions are negative when they first meet their **daughters'** boyfriends.
5. Did you ever notice that when you blow in a **dog's** face, he gets mad at you, but when you take him on a car ride, he **sticks** his head out the window?

Exercise 3.8

1. This **year's** hockey schedule puts the Stanley Cup **finals** halfway through baseball season.
2. The **candidates'** debate was deadly boring until the **hecklers** in the audience started a fistfight.
3. **Today's** styles and **tomorrow's** trends are featured in every issue of our magazine.
4. My **in-laws'** home is about a **half-hour's** drive north of Green Lake.

5. Have you noticed that since **everyone's** got a cellphone camera, **there's** been a dramatic drop in the number of UFO sightings?

Exercise 3.9

1. **Jacques'** brilliance is outshone only by his **wife's**.
2. Forming plural nouns by using **apostrophes** is one way to ensure that your writing **attracts** attention.
3. My **iPod's** playlists need editing; they're full of **songs** I no longer want to listen to.
4. Good writing **skills** may not guarantee success in **your** career, but their lack will certainly contribute to failure.
5. Golf requires different **clubs** for different shots: woods for long shots, irons for short **ones**, and a putter for character development.

Exercise 3.10

1. "Candy is dandy, but **liquor's** quicker."
2. **I've** posted a sign on my front lawn: "**Salespeople's** visits are always welcome. Dog **food's** expensive."
3. I haven't started the essay **that's** due tomorrow. It was supposed to take three **weeks'** work, so **it's** going to be a long night.
4. In Canada, as soon as **it's** warm enough to take off **your** shirt, you know **it's** mosquito season.

Exercise 3.11

1. Brittany's Twitter report on her trip to Europe read like an Ogden Nash poem: "**Britain's** a bore, **Spain's** a pain, but Greece's grand."
2. **Hedonists** are people who pursue pleasure for **its** own sake.
3. We will need **everybody's** maximum effort if we are to meet **tomorrow's** deadline.
4. Geoff devoted his two **years** at **Queen's** University to hard partying.
5. In **today's** competitive market, success depends on strategic **thinkers** who are familiar with a variety of cultures.

Exercise 3.12

1. Brain **cells** come and brain **cells** go, but fat **cells** live forever.
2. One of our **college's** objectives is to meet our **students'** social needs as well as their academic goals.
3. The Three **Tenors'** most spectacular concert was held in **Rome's** ancient Colosseum.
4. The health of **Canada's** economy depends on two things: its abundant natural **resources** and its pool of skilled **labourers** and well-educated **professionals.**
5. Research tells us that people from different backgrounds encourage creativity in one another: one **person's** problem is **another's** challenge.
6. "What do I think of computer dating? **It's** terrific if **you're** a computer."

Answers for Chapter 4: Capital Letters (pages 55 to 65)

Exercise 4.1

1. The **p**en is mightier than the **s**word.
2. **T**aped to the door was a sign that read, "**D**o not use as entrance or exit."
3. Richard Harkness summed up my feeling about committees when he wrote, "**A** committee is a group of the unwilling, picked from the unfit, to do the unnecessary."

4. On the first day of class, our teacher told us, "**F**or most of us, learning **s**tandard **w**ritten English is like learning another **l**anguage."
5. Finally, I want you to remember the words of Wendell Johnson: "*Always* and *never* are two words you should always remember never to use."

Exercise 4.2

1. At **L**oblaws, we argued over the cornflakes. Should we buy **K**ellogg's or **P**resident's **C**hoice?
2. After a brief stay in the **M**aritimes, **C**aptain Tallman and his crew sailed west up the St. Lawrence **R**iver.
3. Do you find that **V**isa is more popular than American **E**xpress when you travel to faraway places like **S**antiago, **R**ome, or **T**ofino?
4. Our stay at the **S**eaview **H**otel, overlooking the **P**acific **O**cean, certainly beat our vacation at the **B**ates **M**otel, where we faced **w**est, overlooking the city dump.
5. As a member of the Waterloo **A**lumni **A**ssociation, I am working to raise funds from companies such as **G**eneral **M**otors, **B**ell Canada, and the **CBC**, where our graduates have been hired.

Exercise 4.3

1. Many of the celebrations we think of as originating in the last 2000 years have much older roots; **H**alloween and **E**aster are two such festivals.
2. The celebration of **C**hristmas has its origins in ancient **B**abylon, where the birth of the son of **I**sis was marked by feasting and gift-giving.
3. The **R**omans, too, had a traditional celebration called **S**aturnalia, held at the end of December. The tradition of seasonal songs, known to us as *carols*, began in **R**oman times.
4. The Christmas tree and mistletoe date from pagan celebrations called **Y**ule, which were held in northern **E**urope on the shortest day of the year.
5. The observance of **R**amadan is one of the five pillars of the **I**slamic faith and is a month when **M**uslims show obedience and submission by fasting.
6. At the end of **R**amadan, a huge feast called **E**id lasts the entire night.
7. In the **J**ewish faith, the festival of **H**anukkah often occurs at the same time that **C**hristians are observing **C**hristmas.
8. The celebration of **H**anukkah involves the lighting of one candle each day on a nine-branched candelabrum.

Exercise 4.4

1. My favourite months are **J**anuary and **F**ebruary because I love all **w**inter sports.
2. This **M**onday is **V**alentine's **D**ay, when messages of love are traditionally exchanged.
3. In **s**ummer, big meals seem to be too much trouble; however, after **T**hanksgiving, we need lots of food to survive the winter cold.
4. In **C**uraçao, people celebrate **N**ew **Y**ear's **D**ay with elaborate fireworks displays.
5. By **T**hursday, I'll have finished my St. **P**atrick's **D**ay costume.

Exercise 4.5

1. While I enjoyed the movie *The Avengers*, I preferred the comic version and the old TV show of the same name.

2. Desperate for plot ideas, today's moviemakers often turn to comic books or even fairy tales, as 2012's *Jack the Giant Killer*, *Mirror Mirror*, and *Snow White and the Huntsman* demonstrate.

3. Did you know that a small painting called *The Scream* by Norwegian painter Edvard Munch recently sold for $120 million?

4. The album *Blonde* by **C**oeur de **P**irate is what I play most on my iPod; "**A**va" is my favourite single.

5. Most reviewers found Conrad Black's memoir, *A Life in Progress*, to be well written but wordy.

6. Although panned by reviewers and banned by libraries in several U.S. states, E. L. James's book *Fifty Shades of Grey* is a bestseller on the *New York Times* book list.

Exercise 4.6

1. Gore Vidal, author of *The Best Man*, once said, "**I**t is not enough to succeed; others must fail."

2. You must take some **s**cience courses, or you'll never get into the program you want at **C**amosun **C**ollege in the **f**all.

3. Our youth group meets in the **O**ttawa mosque every **T**hursday evening.

4. We went to Ho **L**ee **C**how for a bite to eat after the **g**ame and then went home to watch *This Hour Has 22 Minutes* on television.

5. In our **E**nglish course at **C**aribou **C**ollege, we studied *The Englishman's Boy*, a novel about life among the settlers of the **C**anadian **W**est.

Exercise 4.7

1. My most difficult course is **G**raphic **D**esign 201. We're required to submit both an essay and a **m**ajor **d**esign project in which we demonstrate everything we have learned in all our **a**rt courses.

2. I wonder how our **c**ollege gets away with requiring students to take **E**nglish and mathematics courses in addition to our **m**ajor subjects.

3. Leonard Cohen first became famous as a novelist when he published *Beautiful Losers*, but now he is better known as a singer-songwriter for albums such as *Old Ideas* and songs like "**H**allelujah."

4. The **a**phorisms of Steven Wright, a scientist and **h**umorist, appeal to my sense of **i**rony. Here's an example: "I'd kill for a Nobel **P**eace **P**rize."

5. I was raised a **B**aptist, but since taking **P**rofessor Chan's course, **I**ntroduction to **W**orld **R**eligions, I've been interested in **H**induism and **B**uddhism.

Exercise 4.8

Sherlock Holmes and his friend **D**r. **W**atson were on a camping trip in **B**ritish **C**olumbia's **R**ocky **M**ountains. During the night, Holmes awakened his friend and said, "Watson, look up. **W**hat do you see?"

Watson replied, "I see millions and millions of stars."

"And what does that tell you?" enquired Holmes.

"If I recall correctly, my **A**stronomy 200 course taught me that there are countless stars, **g**alaxies, and planets. From my knowledge of **a**strology, I observe that **T**aurus is in **S**corpio. From the position of the planets, I deduce it is about 3:30 in the morning, and according to my understanding of **m**eteorology, tomorrow will be a lovely **s**ummer day."

Holmes was silent for a moment and then said, "**Y**ou idiot, Watson! Someone has stolen our tent!"

Answers for Unit 1 Rapid Review

Note: Triple asterisks (***) indicate that a redundant word or words have been deleted. Each set of asterisks counts as one error.

[1]In 1908, **travellers** in the Nova Scotia wilderness reported being **thrilled** by the **sight** of a beaver dam because beavers were almost extinct at that time. [2]What a change 100 years has brought! [3]Now, the beaver is so common and so prolific that **it's** being hunted and trapped as a nuisance across Canada. [4]In fact, Canadian trappers are issued a quota for the number of **beavers** they are **allowed** to trap in their territory, and they must reach that quota or **lose** their trapping licence.

[5]**We're** not alone in our struggle to control these **large**, pesky rodents. [6]A *Canadian Geographic* film called *The Super Beaver* documents the **creature's** introduction to Tierra del Fuego, at the tip of South America, which has led to the *** devastation of the ecosystem. [7]The film tells us that only coral and humans have had a greater impact on **Earth's** environment than beavers! [8]They have migrated to the mainland of South America, where without rigorous and expensive government intervention, they threaten to destroy millions of hectares of **Argentina's** land as they expand their territory northward. [9]It's difficult to **accept** the fact that only 100 years ago, travellers in **Canada's** wilderness longed for a glimpse of what was then a rare and exotic animal.

Answers for Unit 2 Quick Quiz (pages 68 to 69)

Note: The superscript numbers refer to the original sentence numbers in the Unit 2 Quick Quiz on pages 68 to 69. Also, triple asterisks [***] indicate that punctuation has been deleted.

[1]After enduring one of those awful days in which nothing seems to go right, we can **sometimes** be cheered up by a story about someone even less competent than ourselves. [2]I began the day by spilling my coffee, losing my car keys, and **forgetting** my debit card PIN. [3]Things got worse. I was late for an important meeting and then discovered I had left **in my car** the documents I needed for the meeting.

[4]Slinking back to my office after this disaster, **I found** a newspaper open on my desk. [5]A Collingwood man had submitted a story about his neighbour, a woman who had recently moved from the city to enjoy the charms of country living. [6]The newcomer had written to the local town council *** [7]**to** complain about a "deer crossing" sign on a post across the road from her house. [8]When the official in charge of road signs called her to ask why she objected to the sign, [9]**she** replied that too many deer were being hit on her road, and the town should give them a safer place to cross. [10]**I felt** better after reading this story, and the next story made me feel even better.

[11]A woman from Guelph had bought a new car, **arranged** a loan with her bank, and arrived at the dealership to pick up her purchase. [12]There she was told that a worker had accidentally locked the keys in her car *** [13]**and** a mechanic **was** working on the driver's door trying to unlock the vehicle. [14]While waiting for the mechanic to finish, **she thought** the car looked so beautiful that she strolled around it, admiring her new purchase. [15]When she reached the passenger's side, she tried the door. [16]It opened! [17]When she told the mechanic that the car was open, he replied, "I know. I've already done that side."

[18]I don't know who put the newspaper on my desk, [19]**but it** must have been someone who knew the kind of day I was having. [20]After reading these examples about the stupidity of others, I realized my day hadn't been so bad. [21]In fact, by the time I got home from work, I felt quite cheerful, [22]**at** least in comparison to how I had felt eight hours before.

If you missed the error(s)
in sentence ...   **See Chapter ...**

1	*someone less competent than ourselves sometimes*	8	"Misplaced Modifiers" section
2	*my debit card PIN slipped my mind*	9	The Parallelism Principle
3	Comma splice	7	Solving Run-On Sentence Problems
3	*the documents I needed for the meeting in my car*	8	"Misplaced Modifiers" section
4	*Slinking back to my office, a newspaper*	8	"Dangling Modifiers" section
7	"Missing piece" fragment	6	Solving Sentence-Fragment Problems
8	Dependent clause fragment	6	Solving Sentence-Fragment Problems
9	Fused sentence	7	Solving Run-On Sentence Problems
10	*Feeling better after reading this story*	8	"Dangling Modifiers" section
11	*a loan with her bank was arranged*	9	The Parallelism Principle
13	"Missing piece" fragment	6	Solving Sentence-Fragment Problems
14	*While waiting for the mechanic to finish, the car looked*	8	Dangling Modifiers
17	Fused sentence	7	Solving Run-On Sentence Problems
19	"Missing piece" fragment	6	Solving Sentence-Fragment Problems
22	"Missing piece" fragment	6	Solving Sentence-Fragment Problems

Answers for Chapter 5: Cracking the Sentence Code (pages 70 to 87)

Exercise 5.1

1. I hate cellphones.
2. Today, however, cellphones are practically a necessity.
3. Public phone booths are very hard to find.
4. [You] Turn your cellphone off, please.
5. Our rehearsal was a disaster.
6. Two of the players were half an hour late.
7. [You] Take your time.
8. Few Canadians enjoy February.
9. Family Day makes no difference to the miserable weather.
10. The dance at Destiny's club was a rave riot.

Exercise 5.2

1. Canadians love doughnuts.
2. They eat more doughnuts than any other nation.
3. The Dutch invented doughnuts.
4. The Dutch word for doughnuts translates as "oily cakes."
5. An American sea captain created the doughnut hole.

6. <u>Captain Hansen Gregory</u> <u>impaled</u> his little cake on the ship's wheel.
7. Thus <u>Capt. Gregory</u> <u>created</u> the hole—and the doughnut.
8. The most popular <u>doughnuts</u> in Canada <u>are</u> Tim Hortons'.
9. <u>Tim Horton</u> <u>played</u> hockey for the Toronto Maple Leafs from 1951 to 1970.
10. In 1964, <u>Horton</u> <u>opened</u> his first doughnut store in Hamilton, Ontario.

Exercise 5.3

1. <u>Who</u> <u>wants</u> the last piece?
2. [<u>You</u>] <u>Drive</u> carefully.
3. Slowly down the spiral staircase <u>came</u> the <u>bride</u>.
4. <u>Have</u> <u>you</u> no heart?
5. [<u>You</u>] Then <u>give</u> me a kilogram of liver and a couple of kidneys instead.
6. Into the pool <u>leaped</u> the terrified <u>cat</u>.
7. There <u>are</u> two <u>electives</u> to choose from.
8. Which <u>one</u> <u>is</u> more interesting?
9. Here <u>is</u> just the <u>person</u> to answer your question.
10. <u>Were</u> <u>you</u> happy with the answer?

Exercise 5.4

1. <u>We</u> <u>are finding</u> most of the verbs.
2. Someday my <u>prince</u> <u>will come</u>.
3. <u>Have</u> <u>you</u> <u>planned</u> a party to celebrate his arrival?
4. This <u>book</u> <u>must have been written</u> by a genius.
5. The <u>verbs</u> <u>must be underlined</u> twice.
6. <u>Cam</u> <u>will have</u> another coffee and a doughnut.
7. <u>Do</u> <u>you</u> <u>know</u> anything about grammar?
8. <u>We</u> <u>have knocked</u> on the door several times.
9. <u>I</u> <u>will be looking</u> for verbs in my sleep.
10. <u>We</u> <u>must have practised</u> enough by now.

Exercise 5.5

1. <u>I</u> <u>am making</u> a nutritious breakfast.
2. <u>It</u> <u>does</u> not <u>include</u> pop.
3. <u>You</u> <u>can add</u> fresh fruit to the cereal.
4. The <u>toast</u> <u>should be</u> ready now.
5. My <u>doctor</u> <u>has</u> often <u>recommended</u> yogurt for breakfast.
6. <u>I</u> <u>could</u> never <u>eat</u> yogurt without fruit.
7. With breakfast, <u>I</u> <u>will drink</u> at least two cups of coffee.
8. <u>I</u> <u>don't</u> <u>like</u> tea.
9. <u>I</u> simply <u>cannot</u> <u>begin</u> my day without coffee.
10. <u>I</u> <u>should</u> probably <u>switch</u> to decaf.

Exercise 5.6

1. The security <u>guard</u> <u>is sleeping</u> again.
2. The security <u>guard</u> <u>is</u> often <u>found</u> asleep.
3. <u>Have</u> <u>you</u> ever <u>been</u> lonely?
4. There <u>has</u> never <u>been</u> a better <u>time</u> to invest.
5. <u>Marie</u> <u>is</u> carefully <u>considering</u> her options.

6. Where and when <u>are</u> <u>we</u> <u>meeting</u>?

7. <u>Teenagers</u> <u>are</u> sometimes <u>embarrassed</u> by their parents' behaviour.

8. <u>Could</u> <u>you</u> please <u>explain</u> one more time.

9. "<u>Ladies</u> <u>are requested</u> not to have children in the bar."

10. "The <u>manager</u> <u>has</u> personally <u>passed</u> all our water."

Exercise 5.7

1. <u>Any</u> of your friends <u>is</u> welcome at any time.

2. <u>Henry</u> <u>asked</u> for an extension on the grounds of mental incompetence.

3. <u>This</u> <u>is</u> the last of my money for the month.

4. <u>Exaggeration</u> in your writing <u>is</u> a million times worse than understatement.

5. Your <u>flu</u>, despite your precautions, <u>has infected</u> everyone in the office.

6. In their secret dreams, many grown <u>men</u> <u>would</u> still <u>like</u> to own a train set.

7. <u>Nothing</u> in the known universe <u>travels</u> faster than a bad cheque.

8. During the trial, before the decision, <u>you</u> <u>must have been</u> nervous.

9. Ninety-eight <u>percent</u> of all statistics <u>are made up</u>.

10. A <u>day</u> without sunshine <u>is</u>, in most respects, just like night.

Exercise 5.8

1. ~~According to my financial adviser~~, my earliest possible retirement <u>date</u> <u>is</u> 2052.

2. ~~By waiting on tables~~, ~~[by] babysitting~~, and ~~[by] borrowing from friends~~, <u>I</u> <u>manage</u> to make ends meet.

3. ~~Except for me~~, <u>everyone</u> <u>understands</u> prepositions.

4. ~~With the permission of the professor~~, <u>I</u> <u>will demonstrate</u> my mastery ~~of verb identi-fication~~.

5. No <u>book</u> ~~of Canadian humour~~ <u>would be</u> complete ~~without some shots at American tourists~~.

6. ~~Despite its strong taste~~, <u>espresso</u> <u>contains</u> no more caffeine ~~than regular coffee~~.

7. A daily <u>intake</u> ~~of more than 600 mg of caffeine~~ <u>can result</u> ~~in headaches, [in] insomnia, and [in] heart palpitations~~.

8. Six to ten <u>cups</u> ~~of coffee~~ <u>will</u> usually <u>contain</u> ~~about 600 mg of caffeine~~.

9. <u>One</u> ~~of the network's foreign correspondents~~ <u>will speak</u> ~~at noon~~ ~~in the auditorium about her experiences in Afghanistan~~.

10. Our teacher's <u>uncertainty</u> ~~about the date of the War of 1812~~ <u>made</u> us curious ~~about his knowledge of Canadian history~~.

Exercise 5.9

1. ~~In my opinion~~, <u>fear</u> ~~of flying~~ <u>is</u> entirely justifiable.

2. ~~In our basement~~ <u>are</u> <u>stacks</u> ~~of magazines~~ dating ~~from the 1950s~~.

3. The <u>rats</u> ~~in our building~~ <u>have written</u> letters ~~of complaint to the Board of Health~~.

4. <u>Some</u> ~~of us~~ <u>are staying</u> ~~for a planning session after the meeting~~.

5. ~~For reasons of privacy~~, <u>I</u> <u>am listed</u> ~~in the telephone book under my dog's name~~.

6. ~~After eight hours of classes~~, the <u>thought</u> ~~of collapsing in front of the TV~~ <u>is</u> very appealing.

7. ~~In future~~, [you] <u>be</u> sure to read ~~through your notes before the exam~~.

8. <u>Deciding</u> ~~between right and wrong, for most people~~, <u>is</u> not difficult.

9. <u>Acting</u> ~~on that decision~~, however, ~~for many people~~, often <u>is</u>.

10. ~~Of all the great Italian innovations,~~ ~~from Fellini films to opera,~~ ~~from spaghetti to~~ ~~Chianti,~~ the <u>best</u>, ~~in my opinion,~~ <u>is</u> cappuccino.

Exercise 5.10

1. <u>Maple sugar</u> and <u>wild rice</u> <u>are</u> native Canadian products.
2. <u>Professor Dasgupta</u> <u>handed out</u> the tests and <u>wished</u> us luck.
3. The <u>screen</u> <u>blinked</u> twice and then <u>went</u> blank.
4. <u>Elgar</u> and <u>Grieg</u> <u>are</u> the names ~~of my two unfortunate nephews~~.
5. My weird <u>brother</u> and his equally weird <u>wife</u> <u>chose</u> the names ~~in honour of their~~ ~~favourite composers~~.
6. <u>They</u> <u>could have done</u> worse and <u>chosen</u> Humperdinck and Shostakovich.
7. "A good sermon <u>writer</u> <u>creates</u> a brilliant opening, <u>develops</u> a stirring conclusion, and <u>puts</u> the two as close together as possible."
8. Today my <u>neighbour</u> and <u>I</u> <u>raked</u> the leaves, <u>dug up</u> our gardens, and <u>put away</u> the lawn furniture.
9. <u>Students</u> ~~with good time management skills~~ <u>can research</u>, <u>organize</u>, <u>draft</u>, and <u>revise</u> a first-class paper ~~by the deadline~~.
10. <u>Those</u> ~~with excellent time-management skills~~ <u>can keep</u> ~~on top of their schoolwork~~, <u>hold</u> a part-time job, <u>volunteer</u> ~~at a local charity~~, and still <u>find</u> time ~~for a social life~~.

Exercise 5.11

1. Video <u>games</u> and <u>Facebook</u> <u>take up</u> about three-quarters of my waking hours.
2. With the rest of my time, <u>I</u> <u>watch</u>, <u>read</u>, and <u>talk</u> about sports.
3. The <u>West Indies</u>, <u>British Isles</u>, <u>Australia</u>, and <u>India</u> <u>claim</u> to have the greatest cricket teams.
4. In Canada, <u>cricket</u>, <u>rugby</u>, and <u>jai alai</u> <u>are</u> not <u>played</u> or <u>followed</u> as much as elsewhere.
5. For Canadians, the <u>Habs</u>, <u>Sens</u>, <u>Leafs</u>, <u>Jets</u>, <u>Flames</u>, <u>Oilers</u>, and <u>Canucks</u> <u>are</u> household words.
6. <u>Referees</u> <u>control</u> the game, <u>call</u> penalties, <u>enforce</u> the rules, and <u>stay</u> out of the way.
7. <u>Soccer</u> or <u>football</u>, despite its many faults, <u>delights</u> and <u>infuriates</u> the greatest number of fans around the world.
8. A good <u>golfer</u> <u>drives</u>, <u>chips</u>, <u>putts</u>, and <u>lies</u> with skill and confidence.
9. <u>Winston Churchill</u>, <u>Gerald Ford</u>, and <u>Bill Clinton</u> <u>have</u> all <u>made</u> witty remarks about the game of golf.
10. A hot <u>bath</u>, a good <u>meal</u>, and a *Seinfeld* <u>rerun</u> <u>will help</u> me recover from my stressful day.

Exercise 5.12

~~During the holiday season,~~ <u>shopping</u> ~~for gifts~~ and <u>entertaining</u> relatives <u>are</u>, ~~for me~~, trials equivalent ~~to medieval tortures~~. <u>Stretching</u> limited funds to buy presents ~~for an~~ ~~ever-growing number of relatives~~ and <u>fighting</u> ~~through throngs of maddened consumers~~ ~~at the mall~~ <u>make</u> me think fondly ~~of the thumbscrew and the rack~~. <u>I</u> <u>stagger</u> ~~from store to~~ ~~store~~, overwhelmed ~~by the variety of goods for sale~~ and <u>pray</u> ~~for inspiration~~. How <u>could</u> <u>I</u> possibly <u>know</u> what to buy for Aunt Mildred, Uncle Morty, and cousin Millie and the rest?

~~After my shopping ordeal,~~ <u>I</u> desperately <u>need</u> a nap. But <u>it's</u> entertainment time! <u>Relatives</u>, <u>friends</u>, <u>neighbours</u>, more <u>relatives</u>, and total <u>strangers</u> <u>arrive</u> ~~in hordes~~. <u>We</u>

eat. We drink. We pretend to enjoy the traditional holiday meal. We eat some more. We exchange gifts and pretend to like our presents. We eat again. We reminisce and pretend to enjoy one another's company. And then, once more, we eat.

That's Christmas. [You] Give me the rack any time. I'd be a lot richer—and a lot thinner.

Answers for Chapter 6: Solving Sentence-Fragment Problems (pages 88 to 100)

Exercise 6.1

1. F   According to the government, our water is safe to drink.
2. S   Exhausted, I slept.
3. F   We are happy to help.
4. F   I am hoping to hear from you soon.
5. S   [You] Take another.
6. F   In case you were wondering, it is a wig.
7. S   [You] Close the door quietly on your way out.
8. F   The mayor is pausing to think of an appropriate reply.
9. S   Working as a server in a cheap restaurant is not rewarding.
10. F   Sentence fragments such as these make a poor impression on the reader.

Exercise 6.2

1. F	5. F	8. S
2. F	6. S	9. F
3. F	7. F	10. F
4. F		

Exercise 6.3 (suggested answers)

1. I wanted to stay home, but my girlfriend wanted to go to the movies **t**o see the new Coen brothers' film.
2. In volleyball, our college is well respected. Our team won the provincial championship last year**, p**lacing three players on the all-star team.
3. Whenever I go fishing, the fish aren't biting, but the mosquitoes are. Maybe I should give up fishing **a**nd start collecting insects instead.
4. My son is a genius. On his last birthday, he was given a toy that was guaranteed to be unbreakable. Guess what? **H**e used it to break all his other toys. (*Note:* "Guess what?" is a complete sentence because it is a command: *guess* is the verb and [*You*] is the subject.)
5. We weren't lost, but we certainly were confused. I realized this when we drove past City Hall **f**or the third time.
6. Correct.
7. My friends and I often go to the hockey arena during the winter**, n**ot to watch sports, but to hear concerts by some of the best local bands. These concerts give new meaning to the word *cool*.
8. Correct.
9. I enjoy reading travel blogs **a**bout faraway places that I have never visited and will probably never get to see. The fun is in the dreaming, not the doing.
10. Spending my days skiing and my nights dining and dancing **is** how I picture my retirement.

Exercise 6.4

1. S	5. F	8. S	
2. F	6. S	9. F	
3. F	7. F	10. S	
4. S			

Exercise 6.5

Ed forgot his wife's birthday. **He knew** he was in trouble from the moment he got home from work and saw her angry face. **He apologized** and **asked** how he could make it up to her. She replied that she wanted to find something in the driveway that would go from zero to 100 in less than five seconds, **n**o later than tomorrow morning. The next day, Ed left for work early, **l**eaving a colourful package tied with a large bow in the middle of the driveway. Ed's wife eagerly tore the paper and ribbon off the package **and discovered** a new bathroom scale. Ed is still missing.

Exercise 6.6

1. F   **After** my first attempt failed.
2. F   **If** there is life on other planets.
3. F   **Although** many people think sentence fragments are fine.
4. S   **Unless** there is a change in the weather, <u>I will go</u>.
5. F   Soon, **when** our oil reserves are depleted.
6. F   **Even though** the chef insists she does not overuse salt.
7. S   **If** he were any dumber, <u>he'd have</u> to be watered twice a week.
8. F   All of the salespeople **who** have not reached their quotas.
9. F   **Although** there is plenty of evidence that fish stocks are declining and water quality is deteriorating in the headwaters of our biggest rivers.
10. F   **When** you choose a hybrid car, **whether** it is gas-electric or diesel-electric, as your next vehicle.

Exercise 6.7 (suggested answers)

1. After my first attempt failed, I gave up trying to make pastry.
2. I won't be surprised if there is life on other planets.
3. Although many people think sentence fragments are fine, English teachers find them irritating.
5. Soon, when our oil reserves are depleted, we will finally learn to conserve energy.
6. Even though the chef insists she does not overuse salt, we found her *coq au vin* inedible.
8. All of the salespeople who have not reached their quotas this month will be put back on probation.
9. Although there is plenty of evidence that fish stocks are declining and water quality is deteriorating in the headwaters of our biggest rivers, the federal government refuses to take action.
10. When you choose a hybrid car, whether it is gas-electric or diesel-electric, as your next vehicle, you will be delighted with your cost savings.

Exercise 6.8

1. Walking is probably the best form of exercise there is. **Unless you're in the water.** Then, swimming is preferable.

2. The modern world is confusing for all of us. **If you can keep your head when all about you are losing theirs.** Perhaps you just don't understand the situation.

3. "The world is divided into good and bad people. The good ones sleep better. **While the bad ones enjoy their waking hours much more."**

4. Doing the job right the first time gets the job done. **While doing the job wrong again and again gives you job security.** This principle explains how my brother stays employed.

5. You know you have been teaching too long. **When capital punishment seems a reasonable response to sentence fragments.** Now is the time to think about early retirement.

Exercise 6.9

1. Internship programs provide experience and skill development for senior students. For small and mid-size companies, they are an important recruitment tool. Companies get to audition prospective hires at little cost. **While training the students on their systems and practices. Since both the students and the businesses gain.** Internships are a win-win.

2. Superglue is a remarkable product. **That can bond anything to almost anything else.** Nevertheless, all parents of toddlers know there is another substance. **That is much harder and stronger than Superglue.** The glue that outperforms all others is mashed banana. **Especially after it has dried in an infant's hair.**

3. The names of many Canadian landmarks have been changed over the years. One example is Kitchener. **Which was called Berlin until the First World War.** A second example is the Oldman River. **Until the residents of Lethbridge petitioned for a change to a more dignified name.** It was called the Belly River.

4. Most historians agree that Canada was named by Jacques Cartier. **Who thought natives were referring to the entire land mass when they told him their word for** *village*. Another legend says that Cartier overheard a Portuguese crewman who muttered, "Aca nada." **When he looked at the vast land.** In fact, the sailor was saying, "Nothing here."

5. Where the word *golf* comes from is a mystery. **Though we do know it does not stand for "Gentlemen only, ladies forbidden," as one legend suggests.** Early references to the word are interesting. **According to Katherine Barber, who is known as Canada's "Word Lady."** One of the earliest comes from the 1400s. **When the sport was banned because it was interfering with archery practice.**

Exercise 6.10
Corrections to fragments in Exercise 6.8

1. Walking is probably the best form of exercise there is **u**nless you're in the water. Then, swimming is preferable.

2. The modern world is confusing for all of us. If you can keep your head when all about you are losing theirs**, p**erhaps you just don't understand the situation.

3. "The world is divided into good and bad people. The good ones sleep better **w**hile the bad ones enjoy their waking hours much more."

4. Doing the job right the first time gets the job done **w**hile doing the job wrong again and again gives you job security. This principle explains how my uncle stays employed.

5. You know you have been teaching too long **w**hen capital punishment seems a reasonable response to sentence fragments. Now is the time to think about early retirement.

Corrections to fragments in Exercise 6.9

1. Internship programs provide experience and skill development for senior students. For small and mid-size companies, they are an important recruitment tool. Companies get to audition prospective hires at little **cost while** training the students in their systems and practices. Since both the students and the businesses **gain, internships** are a win-win.
2. Superglue is a remarkable **product that** can bond anything to almost anything else. Nevertheless, all parents of toddlers know there is another **substance that** is much harder and stronger than Superglue. The glue that outperforms all others is mashed banana**, especially** after it has dried in an infant's hair.
3. The names of many Canadian landmarks have been changed over the years. One example is **Kitchener, which** was called Berlin until the First World War. A second example is the Oldman River. Until the residents of Lethbridge petitioned for a change to a more dignified **name, it** was called the Belly River.
4. Most historians agree that Canada was named by Jacques **Cartier, who** thought natives were referring to the entire land mass when they told him their word for *village*. Another legend says that Cartier overheard a Portuguese crewman who muttered, "Aca **nada" when** he looked at the vast land. In fact, the sailor was saying, "Nothing here."
5. Where the word *golf* comes from is a **mystery though** we do know it does not stand for "Gentlemen only, ladies forbidden," as one legend suggests. Early references to the word are **interesting, according** to Katherine Barber, who is known as Canada's "Word Lady." One of the earliest comes from the **1400s, when** the sport was banned because it was interfering with archery practice.

Exercise 6.11

Because the chances of winning are so small**, l**otteries have been called a tax on people with poor math skills. Buying a lottery ticket will gain you about as much as betting that the next U.S. president will come from Moose Jaw **o**r that the parrot in the pet store speaks Inuktitut. While winning a lottery is not impossible**, i**t is so unlikely that you'd do better to use your money to light a nice warm fire. Although the winners are highly publicized**, n**o one hears about the huge numbers of losers **w**hose money has gone to pay the winners. In order for the lottery corporation to make its enormous profits**, m**illions of dollars must be lost whenever a lucky winner is declared.

Answers for Chapter 7: Solving Run-On Sentence Problems (pages 101 to 109)
Exercise 7.1 (suggested answers)
1. "Don't let your worries kill you. **L**et the church help."
2. I am busy right now**, so** you'll have to wait.
3. Remove your ear buds. **Y**ou can't hear the speaker.
4. Correct.
5. Consider hiring an event planner **if** you cannot arrange this function by yourself.
6. "We do not tear your clothing with machinery. **We** do it carefully by hand."

7. **After** you perfect your computer skills, reapply for this position. (*Or:* Perfect your computer skills; then reapply for this position.)

8. There are many factors to consider when hiring a new employee, **but** attitude is key.

9. "I don't want to achieve immortality through my work. I want to achieve it through not dying."

10. Many good films are made in Canada. I just wish I could tell which ones they were before buying a ticket.

Exercise 7.2

1. Computers do not prevent mistakes; they just make them faster.

2. Our company wants to hire a telepath to predict market trends. **T**he right person for the job will know where to apply.

3. All senior managers are required to attend the upcoming board meeting, **which** is in Bermuda.

4. Time is the best teacher; unfortunately, it kills all its students.

5. Allow enough time to complete the project. **A** rush job is not acceptable.

6. Place your hands on the table**, and** do not open your eyes.

7. I'm following the Toronto Maple Leafs this season **because** my doctor says I should avoid all excitement.

8. Correct.

9. "The English language makes no sense; **p**eople recite at a play and play at a recital."

10. We have not inherited the earth from our ancestors; **w**e are borrowing it from our children. (*Or:* Use a period.)

Exercise 7.3 (suggested answers)

1. In Canada, winter is more than a season. **It**'s a bad joke.

2. Twice a week, my wife and I go to a nice restaurant for some good food, a little wine, and pleasant conversation. **S**he goes Tuesdays, and I go Fridays.

3. **When** Emma backed her car out of the driveway, she forgot to check her rear-view mirror. **A**s a result, she managed to produce a significant alteration to the front end of a passing Honda.

4. We understand his feelings of rejection **after** he discovered that his family had moved to another city while he was out getting a pizza.

5. Home-cooked meals are generally more nutritious than fast-food meals**, but** this is not true of my mother's cooking. **H**ers rates below cardboard in nutritional value as well as taste.

6. Correct.

7. There are two students in this class named Xan. **O**ne is from China; the other is from Russia. **T**he latter's name is a nickname, a short form of Alexandra.

8. The first sign of adulthood is the discovery that the volume knob also turns to the left. **T**his realization does not happen overnight; for some people, the process takes years.

9. Football is always a great spectator sport, **and** hockey is usually fun to watch in the last period. **B**asketball is sometimes exciting for the last two minutes of a game**, but** baseball is consistently boring.

10. Evaluating Frank's progress is difficult when you realize that he has submitted none of the assignments, written none of the tests, and attended less than a third of the

classes. **Y**ou can see why I despair. (*Alternative revision:* Evaluating Frank's progress is difficult. **When** you realize that he has submitted none of the assignments, written none of the tests, and attended less than a third of the classes, you can see why I despair.)

Exercise 7.4 (suggested revision)

"I'm about to graduate, **but** I don't have any experience, **and** all the jobs I'm interested in demand experience. What should I do?" This is a common question. **Many** people are frustrated by the problem of how to get experience when no one will hire a person without it. According to employment experts and recruiters, there are several ways to overcome this problem. First, don't bother replying to job postings that clearly state experience is required **as** this wastes time and guarantees frustration. Second, look for part-time work in your field. **This** is a productive route to full-time employment **since** it gives you a chance to prove your worth to the company. Third, consider an internship or a co-op placement. **Like** part-time work, job placements allow you and the company to learn about each other and discover what both parties have to offer. Fourth, in your application, highlight how the skills and experience you gained in previous positions, even if they were unpaid, apply to the job you are seeking. Fifth, show initiative. **Research** the company you want to work for**, and** find out what skills they require. Join professional organizations and establish contacts through LinkedIn and other professional networks. Finally, be patient. **It** takes time to find the job of your dreams!

Exercise 7.5 (suggested answers)

1. "In answer to your letter, I have given birth to a boy weighing five kilos. I hope this is satisfactory."
2. "That isn't food**;** that's what food eats."
3. A <u>cup</u> of coffee in the middle of the afternoon <u>helps</u> to keep me alert. **T**he caffeine chases away my after-lunch slump.
4. CRNC is the home of the million-dollar guarantee. **I**f you give us a million dollars, we guarantee to play any song you want.
5. It's far too hot**;** no one feels like working**, n**ot even people who claim to like summer temperatures.
6. A fine <u>wine</u> during a special meal <u>is</u> my only vice**;** otherwise**,** I'm perfect.
7. Eat sensibly. **E**xercise regularly. **D**ie anyway.
8. People who do not turn off their cellphones in movie theatres are inconsiderate**, and** they should be ejected without a refund.
9. When a football or hockey game is on TV**, m**y husband becomes deaf. **H**e doesn't hear a word I say.
10. Our dog loves children**, e**specially when they are eating French fries or hot dogs. In her excitement, she has sometimes frightened a child**, but** she has never bitten anyone.

Answers for Chapter 8: Solving Modifier Problems (pages 110 to 120)
Exercise 8.1

1. I applied for (almost) | every job | that was posted.

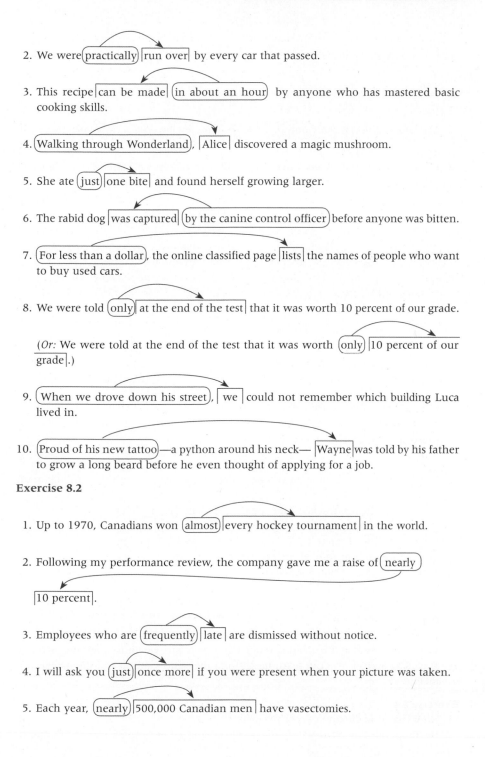

2. We were (practically) |run over| by every car that passed.

3. This recipe |can be made| (in about an hour) by anyone who has mastered basic cooking skills.

4. (Walking through Wonderland), |Alice| discovered a magic mushroom.

5. She ate (just) |one bite| and found herself growing larger.

6. The rabid dog |was captured| (by the canine control officer) before anyone was bitten.

7. (For less than a dollar), the online classified page |lists| the names of people who want to buy used cars.

8. We were told (only) |at the end of the test| that it was worth 10 percent of our grade.

   (*Or:* We were told at the end of the test that it was worth (only) |10 percent of our grade|.)

9. (When we drove down his street), | we | could not remember which building Luca lived in.

10. (Proud of his new tattoo)—a python around his neck— |Wayne| was told by his father to grow a long beard before he even thought of applying for a job.

Exercise 8.2

1. Up to 1970, Canadians won (almost) |every hockey tournament| in the world.

2. Following my performance review, the company gave me a raise of (nearly)

   |10 percent|.

3. Employees who are (frequently) |late| are dismissed without notice.

4. I will ask you (just) |once more| if you were present when your picture was taken.

5. Each year, (nearly) |500,000 Canadian men| have vasectomies.

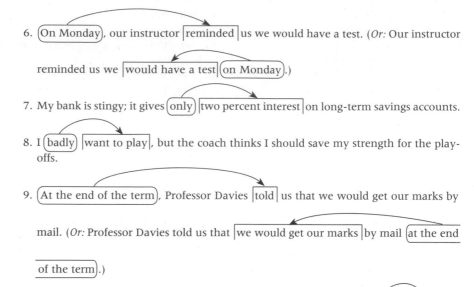

6. (On Monday), our instructor |reminded| us we would have a test. (*Or:* Our instructor

reminded us we |would have a test| (on Monday).)

7. My bank is stingy; it gives (only) |two percent interest| on long-term savings accounts.

8. I (badly) |want to play|, but the coach thinks I should save my strength for the play-
offs.

9. (At the end of the term), Professor Davies |told| us that we would get our marks by

mail. (*Or:* Professor Davies told us that |we would get our marks| by mail (at the end

of the term).)

10. Increasing numbers of Canadians are finding that they cannot (properly) |feed,

clothe, and shelter| their children in today's economy. (*Or:* Increasing numbers of

Canadians are finding that they cannot |feed, clothe, and shelter| their children

(properly) in today's economy.

Exercise 8.3 (suggested answers)
1. When applying for a job, you will find that experience is often the most important factor.
2. As a college English teacher, I am annoyed by dangling modifiers.
3. When you are writing, a dictionary is your best friend.
4. Opening the hood carefully, I found the engine was still smoking.
5. The surface must be sanded smooth before you apply the varnish.
6. The police had no trouble arresting the suspect, who was attempting to hot-wire a '99 Jeep Cherokee.
7. As an advocate of healthy eating, I believe fast-food restaurants are purveyors of poison.
8. Because Kara was driving recklessly, the police stopped her at a roadblock.
9. When we arrived at the meeting room 20 minutes late, we found everyone had left.
10. Travelling abroad, you can learn much from the sights you see and the people you meet.

Exercise 8.4
1. After changing the tire, release the jack.
2. Having decided on pizza, we should decide next whether to order beer or soft drinks.

3. After I waited for you for an hour, the evening was ruined.
4. Jogging through Stanley Park, I saw a cluster of totem poles.
5. After four days on the trail, we agreed that a hot shower and a cold drink were necessities rather than luxuries.
6. After I set the microwave on "Automatic," the turkey was cooked to perfection.
7. After you have completed the beginning, the ending is the second most important part of an essay.
8. Convicted of aggravated assault, she was sentenced to two years in the penitentiary.
9. After scoring the goal in overtime, the team led a huge victory parade through the city.
10. After I had lived with the same roommate for two years, my parents suggested that I try living alone.

Exercise 8.5
1. In our program, the women outnumber the men by almost a two-to-one ratio.
2. My guests were amazed by the tenderness of my *boeuf bourguignon*, which had been slow-cooked in red wine for two hours.
3. Only police officers are allowed to cross the line into the hotel where the heads of state are meeting.
4. Gnawing his stolen steak and growling, Henry's dog could not be coaxed to come out from under the table.
5. Swimming in the bay is forbidden if the water is polluted.
6. Because Cornish Rex cats do not shed hair, our neighbours bought one.
7. With your textbook closed, please summarize what you have read.
8. Having been to Monte Carlo and visited its magnificent casino, we think Las Vegas seems trashy and cheap by comparison.
9. On page 23 of *The New York Times*, a Guatemalan bishop was reported murdered.
10. After being convicted on drug charges, a 53-year-old truck driver who has lived in Canada since he was a baby has been deported to England, where he was born.

Answers for Chapter 9: The Parallelism Principle (pages 121 to 130)
Exercise 9.1 (suggested answers)
1. I am overworked and underpaid.
2. Our new office is ergonomic, functional, and attractive.
3. The three main kinds of speech are demonstrative, informative, and persuasive.
4. Wielding his knife swiftly and skilfully, the chef turned a tomato into a centrepiece that looked just like a rose.
5. My doctor advised me to take two aspirins and call her in the morning.
6. Most people would prefer to work rather than live on welfare.
7. You need to develop skill, strategy, and agility to be a competitive skateboarder.
8. Will and Kate are a perfect couple: attractive, intelligent, and energetic.
9. My name is hard to pronounce and to spell.
10. I had a hard time deciding whether to continue my education or to try to find a job.

Exercise 9.2
1. To me, Kahlil Gibran's poetry is sentimental and uninteresting.
2. Garlic and light are the two things Dracula detests.
3. We're seeking a roommate who is responsible, self-supporting, reliable, and quiet.

4. I'm looking for a car that is cheap to run, easy to park, and fun to drive.

5. The apostrophe is used for two purposes: contraction and possession.

6. The Internet provides us with limitless possibilities for research, convenient shopping, and endless ways to waste time.

7. Olympic athletes in the modern era can be categorized as able bodied, physically challenged, and chemically enhanced.

8. Travel provides an education in independence, patience, resourcefulness, and humility.

9. Our cafeteria now offers a number of healthy choices: there are plenty of gluten-free, lactose-free, and trans-fat-free items on the menu. (*Or:* ... there are plenty of items without glucose, lactose, or trans-fats on the menu.)

10. We are offering this once-in-a-lifetime opportunity for the discriminating buyer to purchase a unique home that is superbly constructed, thoughtfully designed, beautifully landscaped, and competitively priced.

Exercise 9.3 (suggested answers)

1. mechanically	manually	electronically
2. security	value	safety
3. achieve her goals	find true happiness	enjoy her family
4. humorous	wealthy	intelligent
5. daily exercise	wholesome food	regular checkups
6. creative	skilful	intelligent
7. generous	kind	considerate
8. look for bargains	choose quality	shop for value
9. lavish	expensive	well-attended
10. waiting patiently	reading quietly	humming softly

Exercise 9.5 (suggested answers)

1. • Install nameplates on all office doors.
   • Upgrade computers in all offices.
   • Replace damaged furniture.
   • Institute weekly office meetings.
   • Provide flexible hours where practical.

2. • Improve food at stadium concession stands.
   • Lower prices for general admission.
   • Increase the advertising budget by 20 percent.
   • Acquire high-profile players.
   • Update team logo and uniforms.

3. • Be in bed by 10:00 p.m. on weekdays.
   • Attend all classes and labs.
   • Reduce entertainment spending by 50 percent.
   • Submit assignments on time.
   • Restrict hours for Internet surfing and computer gaming.
   • Replace current crowd of friends.

4. • a conference room for 150 people
   • a nearby 18-hole golf course
   • full exercise facilities, including pool

- a separate dining room
- wireless Internet access in each room
5. • ability to work independently
- college diploma in business administration, hotel and restaurant management, or related program
- experience in the travel/tourism industry
- high-level computer skills
- fluency in at least one of French, German, Spanish, or Italian

Exercise 9.6

There can no longer be any question about the fact that our planet is getting warmer. The melting glaciers, **shorter winters**, record-breaking temperatures, and expanding deserts all point to a rapid warming trend. Many of us shrug our shoulders and leave solutions to this complex problem in the hands of governments, business leaders, **scientists**, and activists. We think, "How can one person do anything to make a difference?" We forget that if we all acted together, we could bring about a significant change for the better.

Buying more fuel-efficient cars, using our automobiles less, and even **doing** without them altogether would be a start, and imagine the impact if a million city dwellers decided to switch to public transit! We can turn our thermostats down in the winter and up in the summer—even a couple of degrees means a huge energy saving—and **change** to energy-efficient light bulbs. Would it be such a hardship to wear an extra sweater in the winter, **turn off** the air conditioning in the summer when we're out, or **switch** off the lights when we leave a room? Individual actions like these, if undertaken by enough of us, will not only save energy and reduce pollution but also demonstrate to business and government that we're serious, and **motivate** them to do more.

On a larger scale, we need to put more resources into research that will enable us to exploit wind power, capture solar energy, and **harness tidal forces**. We must insist on intelligently designed, energy-efficient buildings. Every project, whether large or small, will require the support and encouragement of individuals who buy thoughtfully, consume wisely, and **vote strategically**. All of us—individuals, corporations, and governments—need to dedicate ourselves to reducing, reusing, and recycling. Our comfort, our children's health, and our **grandchildren's lives** depend on it.

Answers for Chapter 10: Refining by Combining (pages 131 to 145)

Exercise 10.1 (suggested answers)
1. Our town may be small, **but** (*or* **yet**) it is not backward.
2. The final exam will be held on **either** Friday afternoon **or** Monday morning.
3. This book promises to help me manage my money, **so** I will buy it.
4. I have completed all the exercises, **and** my sentence skills are gradually improving.
5. This man is **neither** my father **nor** my husband.

Exercise 10.2
1. The office will close early today **if** this storm keeps up.
2. My favourite team is the Vancouver Canucks**, but** my father prefers the Montreal Canadiens.
3. Politicians often complain **that** newspapers distort the facts.
4. The protestors left the scene **when** the police arrived.
5. Art is long, **but** life is short.

Exercise 10.3

1. I sometimes have nightmares, **but** they don't usually bother me unless I eat pepperoni pizza as a bedtime snack.
2. **Because** the tortoise is slow but steady, it will win the race.
3. Declan procrastinates by playing video games **while** his homework lies unfinished.
4. **Although** I don't mind doing this exercise, I'll be glad when it's finished.
5. Olivia, **who** blogs incessantly, thinks all her thoughts are interesting. (*Or:* Olivia, **who** thinks all her thoughts are interesting, blogs incessantly.)

Exercise 10.4

1. **If** you want the rainbow, you've got to put up with the rain.
2. Borrow money from pessimists **because** they won't expect it back.
3. The early bird may get the worm, **but** the second mouse gets the cheese.
4. **When** everything is coming your way, you're in the wrong lane.
5. Hard work pays off in the future, **but** laziness pays off now.

Exercise 10.5 (suggested answers)

1. Don't worry about your heart, **for** it will last as long as you do.
2. The bank has added new service charges **that** I think are unjustified.
3. Office morale improved **when** she changed jobs.
4. Many people are not aware of the fact **that** "reality" television shows are, in fact, scripted.
5. **While** ancient scientists looked to the stars for guidance, **and** modern scientists look forward to travelling to the stars, Amanda looks for stars in dance clubs.

Exercise 10.6 (suggested answers)

1. I have a new tablet computer that came with e-reader and GPS apps.
2. Some people enjoy hockey, and others prefer soccer, [which is] the world's most popular spectator sport.
3. I want to leave class now and go home to lie down because my brain is full.
4. I was born in Sydney Mines, Nova Scotia, but I have not lived there since I was 10.
5. The Slow Food Movement, which began in Italy in 1986 as a reaction against fast food, has now spread to 150 countries.

Exercise 10.7 (suggested answers)

1. Whereas most of my friends hate to cook, I create special dishes whenever I can. I am taking a college chef program that will enable me to do what I love as a career.
2. I have no ambition, so I never move quickly except to avoid work. I believe that all deadlines are unreasonable and that it is always possible that no one will notice I am late or that my work is unfinished. I begin a task when I get around to it, and I never put off until tomorrow what I can avoid altogether.
3. China is a country with a population of more than a billion people. It is not easy to be an individual in China, for even if you think of yourself as "one in a million," there are a thousand other people just like you!
4. Lawyers, doctors, and businesspeople are professionals who, although they make up less than 10 percent of the Canadian workforce, occupy almost three-quarters of the seats in the House of Commons.

5. Blue-collar workers make up nearly 50 percent of the population, but they hold less than 10 percent of the positions in Parliament. Moreover, women, First Nations people, and minorities are also underrepresented in government, a fact that calls into question Canada's commitment to democracy.

Answers for Unit 2 Rapid Review (pages 143 to 144)

Note 1: The superscript numbers in the following indicate the original sentence numbers in the Unit 2 Rapid Review on pages 143 to 144.

Note 2: Triple asterisks (***) indicate that a word or words or punctuation has been deleted and not replaced. Each set of asterisks counts as one error.

[1]What simple activity can improve a child's grades, lessen the likelihood of drug use, and reduce the incidence of teen obesity and depression? [2]Research shows that eating together as a family produces these amazing results. **Here's** the proof.

[3]A recent study from the University of Minnesota concluded that shared mealtimes were the primary cause of significant improvements in children's health and well-being**,** [4]**especially** among girls. [5]Not surprisingly, the research shows that adolescents who eat meals with their family consume more fruit and vegetables, more calcium ***, and fewer soft drinks. [6]However, the benefits of sitting down to a family meal extend beyond better nutrition. [7]Studies show a correlation between family meals and improved academic performance, better mental health, and **reduced incidence** of substance abuse. [8]These benefits **increase** with each additional family meal per week.

[9]Television is the biggest obstacle to family mealtimes**. According** to the Canadian Paediatric Society, by the age of 15, children have spent more time in front of television than in front of teachers. [10]Rather than fight with their children to turn off the television and come to the table, **parents serve** meals to suit the children's TV schedule instead of the family's convenience. [11]Television-friendly frozen pizzas, TV dinners, and other fast foods are high in fat, carbohydrates, and sodium**,** [12]**while** their nutritional value is generally low.

[13]Accepting the benefits of eating together as a family is one thing**;** **doing** something about it is another. [14]Most teenagers are not convinced that family activities are beneficial (let alone "cool"), and there are many more interesting pursuits for adolescents**,** [15]**from** part-time jobs to sports to video games to computers to cellphones to television, and even homework.

[16]Experts in child and adolescent psychology offer some helpful guidelines. [17]First, turn off the television and agree **as a family** to turn off cellphones and let the household phone take messages during mealtimes. [18]Second, keep the conversation light, upbeat, supportive, and comfortable. [19]Family meals are not the time for serious, sensitive, or **controversial** subjects. [20]Third, set a goal. [21]You might begin with a commitment to sit down together twice a week and gradually increase the frequency *** [22]**as** everyone gets used to the idea.

[23]The experts' suggestions may not work for everyone. **Each** family will have to work out its own set of principles if family mealtimes are to succeed. [24]Negotiating your own "family rules" takes time**,** but the rewards are worth it!

Answer Key

If you missed the error(s) in sentence ...

	See Chapter ...
2 Comma splice	7 Solving Run-On Sentence Problems
4 Sentence fragment	6 "'Missing Piece' Fragments" section
5 *more calcium is consumed*	9 The Parallelism Principle
7 *the incidence of substance abuse is reduced*	9 The Parallelism Principle
8 Sentence fragment	6 "'Missing Piece' Fragments" section
9 Comma splice	7 Solving Run-On Sentence Problems
10 *Rather than fight ..., meals*	8 "Dangling Modifiers" section
12 Sentence fragment	6 "Dependent Clause Fragments" section
13 Fused sentence	7 Solving Run-On Sentence Problems
15 Sentence fragment	6 "'Missing Piece' Fragments" section
17 *take phone messages as a family*	8 "Misplaced Modifiers" section
19 *subjects that involve controversy*	9 The Parallelism Principle
22 Sentence fragment	6 "Dependent Clause Fragments" section
23 Comma splice	7 Solving Run-On Sentence Problems
24 Fused Sentence	7 Solving Run-On Sentence Problems

Answers for Unit 3 Quick Quiz (page 148)

[1]A Scottish newspaper reported recently that Scottish scientists had **dug** an excavation to a depth of 10 metres and discovered traces of copper wire that dated back more than 100 years. [2]Each of the artifacts **was** examined in a lab, and scientists **concluded** that Scotland had had a primitive telephone network more than 100 years ago.

[3]In the following weeks, English archeologists **began** their own excavations in the hope of finding something that would outdo the Scots. [4](Anyone **who** is familiar with relations between Scotland and England **knows** about the rivalry between the two long-time enemies.) [5]At the 20-metre mark in their excavation, the English made a discovery that **they** and their experts believed to be significant. [6]Laboratory analysis revealed what they had suspected: remnants of copper wire in the hole **were** evidence that the English had had an advanced communications network long before the Scots. [7]Everyone who **was** following the controversial discoveries now waited for the next revelation, the one **that** would settle the dispute once and for all.

[8]They did not have to wait long. [9]Within a week of the English announcement, amateur archeologist Wilf Johnson of Fenwick, Ontario, **reported** a startling discovery. [10]Wilf **had hired** his two cousins to help him dig down nearly 30 metres in an old apple orchard near his home, and, incredibly, **they** and Wilf found absolutely nothing. [11]The crack team of analysts from the Fenwick Lions Club **was** unanimous about the significance of this result: while the Scots and the English had been using copper wire for communication longer than anyone had thought possible, **we** in Canada had already been wireless for years.

Answer Key

If you missed the error(s) in sentence ...

See Chapter ...

1 *had digged*	11 "Principal Parts of Irregular Verbs" section
2 *Each ... were examined*	12 Mastering Subject–Verb Agreement
scientists conclude	13 Keeping Your Tenses Consistent
3 *archeologists begun*	11 "Principal Parts of Irregular Verbs" section
4 *Anyone that*	15 "Relative Pronouns" section
Anyone ... know	12 Mastering Subject–Verb Agreement
5 *them and their experts*	14 "Subject and Object Pronouns" section
6 *remnants ... was*	12 Mastering Subject–Verb Agreement
7 *Everyone who were*	12 Mastering Subject–Verb Agreement
the one which	15 "Relative Pronouns" section
9 *a startling discovery was reported*	11 "Choosing between Active and Passive Voice" section
10 *His two cousins had been hired by Wilf*	11 "Choosing between Active and Passive Voice" section
them and Wilf	14 "Subject and Object Pronouns" section
11 *The crack team ... were*	12 Mastering Subject–Verb Agreement
us in Canada	14 "Subject and Object Pronouns" section

Answers for Chapter 11: Choosing the Correct Verb Form (pages 150 to 163)

Exercise 11.1

1. ridden, rode
2. tore, torn
3. lay, lain
4. shaken, shook
5. grew, grown
6. knew, known
7. laid, laid
8. lent, lent
9. took, taken
10. went, gone

Exercise 11.2

1. I would have **called** more often if I had **known** you cared.
2. The phone **rang** and **rang**, but no one answered because they had all **gone** out for pizza.
3. After **lying** around all day watching TV, Emma **swore** she would do her chores before bedtime.
4. "Strike three!" called the umpire as I **swung** the bat, but I **ran** around the bases anyway.
5. While some have **swum** in the fountain of knowledge and others have **drunk** from it, Gary just gargles.
6. Claudio should have **known** better than to challenge me at chess because I have seldom been **beaten**.

7. Yasmin has **stolen** his car and **broken** his heart, or maybe it was the other way around.
8. Too late, we figured out that if we had **gone** to class and had **done** the homework, we would have **passed** the course.[1]
9. We should have **gone** out and **done** something interesting this evening instead of **sitting** around watching TV.
10. The lake had **frozen** solid, so after we had **eaten** supper, we **brought** our skates out and **spent** a couple of hours on the ice.

Exercise 11.3
1. A [You] Do not number your pages.
2. P Our cable line was gnawed through by a squirrel.
3. P Each year, Mount Washington is visited by thousands of tourists.
4. A "Some weasel took the cork out of my lunch!"
5. P Your essay was not formatted properly.
6. P The test questions were read to us by our instructor in a mumbling monotone.
7. P *Whale Music* was written by Canadian author Paul Quarrington.
8. A A small Canadian company made Quarrington's novel into a successful movie.
9. P Mandarin is spoken by most of China's 1.3 billion people.
10. P "Children should neither be seen nor heard—ever again."

Exercise 11.4
1. Your pages should not be numbered by you.
2. A squirrel gnawed through our cable line.
3. Each year, thousands of tourists visit Mount Washington.
4. The cork has been taken out of my lunch by some weasel!
5. You have not formatted your essay properly.
6. Our instructor read us the test questions in a mumbling monotone.
7. Canadian author Paul Quarrington wrote *Whale Music*.
8. *Quarrington's novel was made into a successful movie by a small Canadian company.
9. Most of China's 1.3 billion people speak Mandarin.
10. *One should neither see nor hear children—ever again.

* Passive voice is preferable in items 8 and 10. (Item 7 is debatable. If you want to focus on the novel, then passive voice [in the exercise] is preferable. If you want to focus on the author, then active voice [in the answer] is the better choice.)

Exercise 11.5 (suggested answers)
1. Two days after the test, the department posted the students' results.
2. We packed the car the night before we left on our vacation.
3. My sister is tutoring her new boyfriend.
4. After a slow start, the Mounties scored three runs in the fourth inning.
5. My activist brother downloaded my screen saver, a picture of a clear-cut forest.
6. In English, one can pronounce the sound "ough" eight different ways.

---

[1] While *pass* is not an irregular verb, its past tense, *passed*, is often confused with the adjective *past*.

7. Someone must do something about persistent telephone solicitors.

8. We require guests to wear shoes in the dining room.

9. Historians think Mozart wrote this piece of music.

10. After the class achieved disappointing results in the first semester, our professor tried a different approach.

Exercise 11.6

1. One calls the white part at the base of the fingernail the "lunula." ("Lunula" is a scientific term; we don't know who named it, so passive voice is preferable.)

2. We paid the bill as soon as we received the invoice. (Active voice is direct, clear, and effective.)

3. The human resources department will send a memo to your bank to confirm that you are a full-time employee. (Active)

4. I ate more food than I needed when I came off my diet. (Active)

5. When she couldn't watch her favourite show, Miranda broke the remote in a fit of rage. (Active)

6. The neighbour's dog barked at the letter carrier until she was too terrified to deliver our mail. (Active)

7. The investigators have not yet determined the cause of the accident. (Active is preferable unless you want to emphasize "the cause of the accident," in which case you'd use it as the subject and choose the passive verb.)

8. Next term, a senior professor will teach the honours seminar. (Passive-voice verb places emphasis on the course rather than on the unnamed professor; active voice emphasizes the teacher.)

9. We call the little indentation that connects your upper lip to the bottom of your nose the "philtrum." (Passive voice is more effective to express a scientific or technical fact; we don't know who gave the philtrum its name.)

10. Shakespeare created the word *assassination*. (Choose active voice if you wish to emphasize the creator of the word; choose passive voice if you wish to place the emphasis on the word itself.)

Answers for Chapter 12: Mastering Subject–Verb Agreement (pages 164 to 178)

Exercise 12.1

1. The <u>key</u> to power is knowledge.

2. Here are the <u>invoices</u> for this shipment of software.

3. In the future, instead of live animals, <u>people</u> may choose intelligent machines as pets.

4. At the front of the line stood <u>Professor Temkin</u>, waiting to see Santa.

5. <u>Jupiter and Saturn</u>, the solar system's largest planets, appear close together in the western sky.

Exercise 12.2

1. has	3. shows	5. is
2. succeeds	4. talks	

Exercise 12.3

1. This policy <u>change</u> <u>affects</u> all divisions of our company.

2. An <u>article</u> on the Internet <u>does</u> not always <u>contain</u> reliable information.

3. <u>Has</u> the lucky <u>winner</u> <u>collected</u> the lottery money?
4. Above all, a good <u>teacher</u> <u>demonstrates</u> respect for students.
5. The <u>pressure</u> of homework, part-time work, and nagging parents <u>has caused</u> many students to drop out of college.

Exercise 12.4
1. A primary source of Earth's oxygen <u>is</u> trees.
2. She <u>insists</u> on doing whatever <u>she</u> <u>pleases</u>.
3. A good manager <u>consults</u> with subordinates before making decisions.
4. We <u>do</u> our best work when <u>we</u> <u>are</u> unsupervised.
5. Civil servants with indexed pensions <u>stand</u> to gain from future inflation.

Exercise 12.5

1. is	3. are	5. causes
2. sleeps	4. are	

Exercise 12.6

1. contains	3. is	5. is
2. has	4. want	

Exercise 12.7

1. is	3. scores	5. works
2. appears	4. has	

Exercise 12.8

1. is	3. Has	5. find
2. are	4. was	

Exercise 12.9

1. is	3. makes	5. means
2. sounds	4. does	

Exercise 12.10
1. A group of unbiased students and faculty **has** been asked ...
2. Anybody who really **wants** to succeed ...
3. Correct.
4. The lack of these four nutrients **is** thought ...
5. You'll find that not only ragweed but also cat hairs **make** ...
6. Each of the contestants **thinks** ...
7. Neither the children nor their mother **was** willing ...
8. The lack of things to write about **causes** ...
9. Sophia, along with her agent, stylist, two bodyguards, and three Chihuahuas, **was** seen ...
10. The amount of money generated by rock bands on concert tours **is** ...

Exercise 12.11
There **are** many young people in Canada today carrying a large amount of debt. According to American Express, spending on fashion, travel, and fine dining **has** jumped dramatically in recent years. At the same time, wages among the group called Generation Y **have** stagnated, rising at a fraction of the increase in spending. Amex, for

example, together with other financial institutions, **reports** that spending on fine dining rose a staggering 102 percent over the past two years. At the same time, each of these institutions **notes** that fewer than 40 percent of credit card holders between the ages of 18 and 34 **make** the minimum payment on their card balance each month. This suggests that young people in the early stages of a career or even pre-career **are** sinking into debt while continuing to spend lavishly. It's the classic case of dousing a fire with gasoline! Parents, financial institutions, or the government **is** going to have to act to reverse this trend. But instead, bank representatives regularly visit campuses offering credit cards to undergraduates, and fewer than half of parents from the Baby Boomer generation **believe** it is important to save money for their children's inheritance. Generation Y, along with the Millennials and more recent generations, **is** going to have to get a grip on personal finances, or financial prosperity and even retirement will be an impossible dream.

Exercise 12.12

In a recent interview, hockey coach Randy Carlisle noted that the Stanley Cup playoffs, in which his team was not involved, **were** hard fought, but didn't feature very much excitement. "It was a grinding type of puck movement," he noted, adding that this is the type of hockey he wants his team to play. "There **weren't** a lot of goals scored off the rush," he said, since most of the scoring took place during penalties. "I think the games were played tight to the vest, but the pace of the games **was** up there," Coach Carlisle added.

So it is that fans of Randy Carlisle's team in the coming season **are** in for slow-moving, defensive hockey that will lull even the most enthusiastic fan to sleep. However, if the team along with Carlisle and his managers **is** successful, neither the fans nor the team owner **is** going to complain. Each fan, when assessing the success or failure of the players at the end of the season, **has** reason to applaud Carlisle's approach if the team wins. On the other hand, if the millionaire players and the organization itself **are** not successful, then this boring style of hockey will ensure that Carlisle's tenure behind the bench is short. Anyone in Carlisle's position, whether coach or players, **feels** the enormous pressure of fan expectations, and neither Coach Carlisle nor his general manager nor his highly paid players **want** to fail to meet those expectations.

Exercise 12.13

1. plural	5. singular	8. singular
2. singular	6. singular	9. singular
3. plural	7. plural	10. singular/plural*
4. singular		

* singular, if you are speaking of the department acting as a unit; plural, if you are speaking of the department members acting individually

Answers for Chapter 13: Keeping Your Tenses Consistent (pages 179 to 184)
Exercise 13.1

1. I enjoy my work, but I **am** not going to let it take over my life.
2. The umpire stands there, unable to believe what he **is** seeing.
3. Even though he was tired from a long day at work, Jay **made** it to the band rehearsal on time.
4. "The abdominal cavity contains the bowels, of which there **are** five: a, e, i, o, and u."

5. There will be a parade on Canada Day and the mayor **will be** the grand marshal.
6. Correct.
7. When the server goes down, no one in the office **is** able to work.
8. We told Dana that the exam was scheduled for 2:00 p.m., but she **didn't** believe us and **went** to the gym.
9. Mario goes to the fridge, gets a cold can of pop, and **proceeds** to drink it without offering me anything.
10. "I keep liquor on hand just in case I **see** a snake, which I also **keep** on hand."

Exercise 13.2
1. The class had just ended when in **walked** Wesley.
2. The game was exciting to watch, but the wrong team **won** on the last play.
3. First, he backcombed his hair into spikes, and then he **coated** it with glue.
4. The lights dimmed and the crowd held its breath; the Biebs **kept** them waiting for another minute or so before he **exploded** onto the stage.
5. The Peter Principle states that every employee **rises** to his or her level of incompetence.
6. Just as time ran out, Perry **launched** a three-point attempt from mid-court, but it **missed** the basket and the Chiefs lost their final home game.
7. The party was just getting started when she **decided** it **was** time to leave.
8. We'll do our best to be polite, but it **will** be difficult.
9. You will live a happy, healthy life until your forties, when you **will meet** a beautiful, dark-haired woman who **will make** you miserable, **[will] break** your heart, **[will] ruin** your health, and **[will] leave** you for another man.
10. I used to smoke, drink, and eat poutine whenever I could until I had a bout of indigestion that I **thought was** a heart attack and **scared** me into eating a healthier diet.

Exercise 13.3
   A woman *walked* into a veterinary office and **placed** a very limp duck on the examination table. The vet **checked** the duck for vital signs and then **shook** his head sadly and **told** the woman that her pet **was** dead. Terribly upset, the woman **insisted** the vet perform more tests to confirm that indeed her pet **was** deceased. The vet **left** the room and **came** back with a Labrador retriever, which **proceeded** to sniff the duck all over its body. After a moment, the dog **sighed** and **shook** her head. Then a sleek Persian cat **entered** the room and **examined** the duck from head to toe or, rather, webbed foot. The cat, too, sadly **shook** its head and **sighed** heavily. The vet **told** the woman that the animals **confirmed** his diagnosis: her pet **was** dead. Then he **presented** the woman with a bill for $350. She **was** outraged, given that the vet **had** spent less than 10 minutes examining her duck. The vet **explained** that his bill **was** $50. The Lab report and the cat scan **were** $150 each.

Answers for Chapter 14: Choosing the Correct Pronoun Form (pages 185 to 192)
Exercise 14.1
1. Liam and **I** stayed up all night trying to complete our assignment.
2. There wasn't much **we** could do to rescue it, however.
3. Ava and Katy were supposed to be in our group, but neither of **them** showed up.
4. When **we** poor, sleep-deprived students submitted the assignment, our professor glared at **us**.

5. Between **us**, **we** had managed to produce barely four pages.
6. After all, what do Liam and **I** know about the topic assigned to **us**?
7. Both of **us** thought "relative deprivation" had something to do with families.
8. **He** and I spent hours writing about being grounded by our fathers, forgetting our mothers' birthdays, and suffering our older siblings' bullying.
9. It never occurred to **him** or **me** that "relative deprivation" was a definition of poverty.
10. Liam and **I** have been frequently late and often absent from class this term, so when the prof adds our "class participation" mark to the grade we get on our major paper, whose topic we misinterpreted, it's unlikely that Liam and **I** can count on an A in sociology.

Exercise 14.2
1. **She** and her family are strict vegans; they don't eat dairy products, honey, or eggs.
2. **He** and his brothers started a yard maintenance company last summer.
3. The full moon affects humans and animals in strange ways, according to Lisbeth and **her**.
4. Mila returned the books to the library before **my boyfriend and I** had a chance to look at them. (Remember: courtesy requires that you put others before yourself.)
5. It is not up to you or **me** to discipline your brother's children; that responsibility belongs to **him** and his partner.
6. Luigi seems to be quite comfortable living with his mother; do you think **he** and Sofia will ever get married?
7. The contract was not signed by the deadline, so **my boss and I** will be up all night renegotiating it.
8. Except for **him** and his brother, no one was affected by the poison ivy.

Exercise 14.3
1. No one enjoys old movies more than **I** [do].
2. Only a few pasta fanatics can eat spaghetti as fast as **he** [can].
3. At last, I have met someone who enjoys grilled liver as much as **I** [do]!
4. You seem to have even less money than **I** [do].
5. Few people in our company flatter the CEO as much as **she** [does].
6. Correct, if you mean that Hans is more interested in history and archeology than he is his friend (him). Otherwise, write: Hans is more interested in history and archeology than **he** [is].
7. Although they have more talent than **we** [do], our team is in better condition.
8. No one in the world eats more doughnuts per capita than **we** Canadians [do].
9. Everyone wanted to watch the game except Max and **me**.
10. He doesn't write as well as **I** [do], but he does write faster.

Answers for Chapter 15: Mastering Pronoun–Antecedent Agreement (pages 193 to 206)

Exercise 15.1
1. Everyone is a product of ******* environment as well as heredity.
2. Nobody as smart as you are needs help with ******* homework.
3. The accident could not have been avoided, and fortunately no one was hurt, so no one should have to **apologize**.

4. Everyone who pays **the** membership fee in advance will receive a free session with a personal trainer.
5. It seemed that everybody in the mall was talking on **a** cellphone.
6. We will do our best to return everything found in the locker room to **its** owner.
7. Everyone from the provincial premiers to front-line health care providers agrees that electronic health records could provide huge gains in ******* efficiency.
8. Would someone kindly lend **a** copy of the text to Basil?
9. A bore is someone who sticks to **his** own opinion even after we have enlightened **him** with ours.
10. Anyone who wants an A for **this** essay should see me after class and give me **a** cheque.

Exercise 15.2
1. If anyone wants to change **his or her** mind, now is the time.
2. Each of the candidates has **her** appeal, but I choose bachelorette number 3.
3. Anyone who faithfully watches *The Bachelorette* needs to get out of **the** house more often.
4. Every movie-, theatre-, and concert-goer knows how annoying it is to have **an** evening's enjoyment spoiled by a ringing cellphone.
5. Everyone from the Bank of Canada to academics, marketers, and urban planners uses Statistics Canada surveys as the basis for ******* research.
6. When you turn off the highway, **you** must be very careful because the roads leading to the lake are not well marked.
7. Ultimate Frisbee is a game that every player enjoys, whether **the** team finishes first or last.
8. Put the sign at the curb so anyone looking for our yard sale won't have to waste ******* time driving around the neighbourhood.
9. A bandleader is someone who is not afraid to face **the** music.
10. Bridging the gap between the young upstarts who develop smartphone apps and the highly structured, rule-bound world of health care **they are** creating them for is not easy.

Exercise 15.3 (suggested answers)
1. Whenever Connor and Carlos play poker, **Connor** stacks the deck.
2. Fishing is fun even when I don't catch **anything** (*or* **a fish**).
3. Every time Cameron looked at the dog, **the dog** barked.
4. If your pet mouse won't eat its food, **give the mouse food** to the cat.
5. When the baby has finished drinking, **the bottle** should be sterilized in boiling water.
6. The lifeguard didn't hear my cry for help ******* because he was wearing earplugs.
7. The payroll manager met with the chief steward to tell her it was not **the manager's** responsibility to collect union dues.
8. My roommate and I, together with a couple of the girls from upstairs, play poker and blackjack once a week. **These evenings** are a lot of fun.
9. **Three minutes into overtime, her son scored the winning goal,** which Bella missed because she was arguing with another parent.
10. Our college strictly enforces the "no smoking" policy, so you can't have **a cigarette** even outside on campus.

Exercise 15.4

1. We were pretty sure Miss Grundy knew who was responsible for the cartoon **that** she found on her board this morning.
2. A grouch is a person **who** knows himself and isn't happy about it.
3. The sales clerk **who** sold me my DVD player didn't know what he was talking about.
4. Everyone **who** was at the party had a good time, although a few had more punch than was good for them.
5. The open-office concept sounds good to anyone **who** has worked in a stuffy little cubicle all day.
6. I wonder why we are so often attracted to people **who** are totally unsuitable for us.
7. Is this the dog **that** attacked the mail carrier **who** carries a squirt gun?
8. I think the ideal domestic companions would be a cat **that** cuddles and a husband **who** purrs.
9. Thanks to the Internet, I regularly order supplies from companies **that** are located in cities around the world.
10. Sales staff **who** want to earn promotions must have good interpersonal skills as well as thorough knowledge of the products [**that**] they are selling.

Exercise 15.5 (suggested answer)

Computing is not something I take to naturally, and although I have quite a good **computer**, I do not trust it. Anyone **who** is like me knows **her** communication with the outside world depends on **her** computer and the Internet, so when something goes wrong, we need help right away. Fortunately, I have a neighbour **who** is a computer genius. He is only 11 years old, but Raj is someone **who** seems to understand instinctively how **he** can solve computer issues.

Before calling Raj for help, I try everything I can think of to fix my frequent computer problems because Raj is a person with little patience for **his** less competent acquaintances. Raj is an intellectual **who** doesn't enjoy sports, but his parents make him go outside from time to time, and he and I kick **a ball** around in the yard. I waited until we had played for a few minutes before casually asking him if he would take a look at my current computing problem. He was delighted to quit kicking the soccer ball in favour of computing, and came right in.

Anyone **who** knows anything about computers knows when **she is** in the presence of genius. Raj's fingers flew over the keyboard and the computer responded with screens of information I had never seen before, almost purring with satisfaction as someone who knew what **he was** doing took the machine through its paces. After a couple of minutes, Raj sat back and told me the problem was fixed.

No one wants to appear ignorant, especially in front of **her** 11-year-old neighbour, so, not really expecting to understand, I asked him if he could tell me what the problem was. Raj got up and headed for the door while telling me it was a common error with **my computer**, an error called ID ten T. Seeing the puzzled look on my face, he told me to write it down and I would understand. As the door slammed behind him, I wrote out ID10T, and understood.

Answers for Chapter 16: Maintaining Person Agreement (pages 207 to 216)

Exercise 16.1

1. you have	5. we, our	8. you begin
2. you	6. he is	9. their
3. we've	7. you fill	10. our, our
4. our		

Exercise 16.2 (suggested answers)

1. A speed limit is the speed you go as soon as **you see** a police car.
2. People who don't learn from history are doomed to find **themselves** back in Grade 9 for a second try.
3. **Anyone who wants** to succeed in business must be well groomed and conservatively dressed. (*Or:* If you want to succeed in business, **you** must be ...)
4. If you are convicted on that charge, a fine is the least of **your** worries.
5. One cannot lead any farther than **one has** already gone.
6. "Middle age is that time of life when you've met so many people that everyone **you meet** reminds **you** of somebody else."
7. "Never try to impress a woman, because if **you do**, she'll expect you to keep up that standard for the rest of **your** life."
8. Many people are happy to ride with **you** in a limo, but what you want is someone who will take the bus with **you** when the limo breaks down.
9. Some women enjoy the pursuit of their ideal mate more than the capture and domestication of **their** prey.
10. When a company fails to maintain and upgrade **its** equipment, **it** often **pays** a high price for **its** neglect.

Exercise 16.3

1. It has taken Canadians far too long to acknowledge the seriousness of **their** environmental problems.
2. No one tests the depth of a river with both ***** feet**. (*Or:* No one tests the depth of a river with both of **his** feet.)
3. If you can't cope with the pressure, **you** must expect to be replaced by someone who can.
4. If any of you have signed up to attend the class party next Friday, **your** tickets are now available in the Student Association office.
5. Some people are like Slinkys: they have no useful purpose, but you can't help but smile when **you see** them tumble down the stairs. (*Or:* ... one can't help but smile when one sees them tumble down the stairs.)
6. When they feel frustrated or angry, it can sometimes be difficult for **teenagers** to control **their** temper.
7. "Good health" is nothing more than the slowest rate at which **one** can die. (*Or:* ... at which **you** can die.)
8. In the 1960s, some people took acid to make the world seem weird; now the world *is* weird, and **they** take Prozac to make it seem normal.
9. When taking multiple-choice tests, don't stop and think about questions you aren't sure of. Finish the test and then go back to the questions that stumped **you**.

10. When you're gardening, the best way to make sure **you are** removing a weed and not a plant is to grasp it firmly at the base of the stem and pull. If **it comes** out easily, **it is** a plant.

Exercise 16.4

(1) Second-person pronouns:

If **you are** a sports fan, you are already familiar with the astronomical salaries major players make. **You** sometimes lose sight of the fact that **your** favourite players live in the real world, and their salaries are sometimes out of touch with real life, at least as most people live it. You may be aware, for example, that all-time-favourite basketball player Michael Jordan made nearly $200,000 per day in the last year of his contract. If **you** compare Jordan's salary with the incomes of other famous people, however, **you find** some interesting numbers. For instance, you learn that, in his last year in professional basketball, Jordan earned 200 percent more than the total income of all the presidents of the United States, from George Washington to Barack Obama, *combined*. If **you** do a little more research, **you** also discover that, if Jordan were to save and invest all of his income for 250 years, he would accumulate less money than Bill Gates has now.

(2) Third-person pronouns:

If one is a sports fan, **one is** already familiar with the astronomical salaries major players make. **Fans** sometimes lose sight of the fact that **their** favourite players live in the real world, and their salaries are sometimes out of touch with real life, at least as most people live it. **One** may be aware, for example, that all-time-favourite basketball player Michael Jordan made nearly $200,000 per day in the last year of his contract. If **one compares** Jordan's salary with the incomes of other famous people, however, one finds some interesting numbers. For instance, **one learns** that, in his last year in professional basketball, Jordan earned 200 percent more than the total income of all the presidents of the United States, from George Washington to Barack Obama, *combined*. If **one does** a little more research, **one** also **discovers** that, if Jordan were to save and invest all of his income for 250 years, he would accumulate less money than Bill Gates has now.

Exercise 16.5

Second-person pronouns:

If **you are** searching for a less stressful, more satisfying life, **you** could investigate the "Slow Movement." **You** could start with the original Slow Food Movement, begun in Italy in 1986 as a protest against fast-food restaurants, specifically McDonald's, which was planning to build a restaurant in Rome near the historic Spanish Steps. The movement's objectives include eating healthy, buying local products, and making meals convivial occasions instead of wolfing down **your** food in a crowded, noisy, plastic environment.

You might also look into the Slow City Movement, an organization that certifies cities based on four criteria. To be declared a "Slow City," **your** city must respect strict environmental rules, encourage consumption of local products, discourage dependence on cars, and emphasize a sense of community. If the population of **your** city is more than 50,000, **you** need not apply, because cities over that size are automatically disqualified from Slow City status.

Third, why not check out the Slow Money Movement? This is an organization dedicated to changing the way **you invest**. Instead of putting **your** money in huge corporations with destructive environmental practices or health issues, like the oil or tobacco industries, the Slow Money Movement encourages **you** to invest in small food producers, sustainable enterprises, and local farms. Slow Money investors are not aiming to make less money but hoping to use their investments to encourage more responsible, ethical practices.

Another possibility **you** might find consistent with **your** principles is called simply the "Slow Movement," which promotes the idea of "connectivity." **You** might find this an appealing concept, as it seeks to make connections among **your** social network, environment, culture, food, and community. The Slow Movement promotes ideas such as Slow Travel, which encourages **you** to avoid packaged tours that zoom frenetically from place to place, in favour of slowing down, staying in one place for a few weeks, and getting to understand a little about the locale. The Slow Movement also promotes Slow Schooling, a type of education that seeks to replace one-size-fits-all learning and standardized testing with "connected learning": connecting students' learning to the community, culture, history, and geography of the place in which they live. The concept of the "edible schoolyard" might also appeal to **you**: students are responsible for producing, preparing, and serving the food they eat.

You can embrace several different aspects of the slower life, depending on **your** principles and preferences. **You do** not need to join a formal movement to change the way **you live**. The concepts behind these movements may give **you** ideas for revising **your** lifestyle, but maybe **you** should just consider living life more slowly, whatever that phrase means to **you.**

Exercise 16.6
Third-person plural pronouns: [Suggested answers]

People who are searching for a less stressful, more satisfying life *** could investigate the "Slow Movement." **They** could start with the original Slow Food Movement, begun in Italy in 1986 as a protest against fast-food restaurants, specifically McDonald's, which was planning to build a restaurant in Rome near the historic Spanish Steps. The movement's objectives include eating healthy, buying local products, and making meals convivial occasions instead of wolfing down **their** food in a crowded, noisy, plastic environment.

Researchers might also look into the Slow City Movement, an organization that certifies cities based on four criteria. To be declared a "Slow City," **a** city must respect strict environmental rules, encourage consumption of local products, discourage dependence on cars, and emphasize a sense of community. If the population of **the** city is more than 50,000, **its residents** need not apply, because cities over that size are automatically disqualified from Slow City status.

Third, **"Slow" investigators could** check out the Slow Money Movement. This is an organization dedicated to changing the way **people invest**. Instead of putting **their** money in huge corporations with destructive environmental practices or health issues, like the oil or tobacco industries, the Slow Money Movement encourages **investors** to invest in small food producers, sustainable enterprises, and local farms. Slow Money investors are not aiming to make less money but hoping to use their investments to encourage more responsible, ethical practices.

Another possibility **"Slow" researchers** might find consistent with **their** principles is called simply the "Slow Movement," which promotes the idea of "connectivity." **Many** might find this an appealing concept, as it seeks to make connections among **people's** social network, environment, culture, food, and **communities**. The Slow Movement promotes ideas such as Slow Travel, which encourages **tourists** to avoid packaged tours that zoom frenetically from place to place, in favour of slowing down, staying in one place for a few weeks, and getting to understand a little about the locale. The Slow Movement also promotes Slow Schooling, a type of education that seeks to replace one-size-fits-all learning and standardized testing with "connected learning": connecting students' learning to the community, culture, history, and geography of the place in which they live. The concept of the "edible schoolyard" might also appeal***: students are responsible for producing, preparing, and serving the food they eat.

People can embrace several different aspects of the slower life, depending on **their** principles and preferences. **They do** not need to join a formal movement to change the way **they live**. The concepts behind these movements may give **them** ideas for revising **their lifestyles**, but maybe **they** should just consider living a slower life, whatever that phrase means to **them**.

Answers for Unit 3 Rapid Review (pages 217 to 218)

[1]Having **begun** a new venture in our lives, we sometimes find that the experience does not meet **our** expectations. [2]Consider, for example, students **who** leave home to go to college. [3]They move to a new city, begin a new course of study, start making new friends, and begin to realize how stressful change can be. [4]Add to these challenges the inevitable shift in status that **accompanies** such a move, and we can see why many **students find** the transition from school to college to be far from smooth.

[5]**Students accustomed to being academic, athletic, or social stars** in high school may find that they have to prove themselves all over again. [6]This **challenge** is too much for some to cope with, so some former high achievers who fail to measure up in their new environment drop out. [7]These students often tend to quit in their first year, when **they** should still be experimenting and exploring their options.

[8]Students who were academically successful in high school may have a hard time when **they** and their less gifted peers move on to college. [9]**"Brains" have more to lose** in an academic environment where marks are awarded for performance, not effort, and deadlines are not negotiable. [10]These students **are** often shocked to receive a B or even a C on a mid-term paper. [11]On the other hand, students **who** made average grades in school are usually pleasantly surprised when they achieve a mark in the 60s or 70s in their first term at college.

[12]Those who were "late bloomers" in high school often treat the postsecondary environment as a fresh start and **begin** to blossom as they find new friends with interests similar to theirs. [13]In contrast, students who were social stars in high school may be frustrated by a new environment that dislodges **them** from the pinnacle of the popularity pyramid.

[14] When they reach their 30s or 40s, people who claim that high school was the best time of their lives often do so because their years in college **were** disappointing—in part because of their earlier success.

Answer Key

**If you missed the error(s)
in sentence ...**   **See Chapter ...**

1 *Having began*   11 "The Principal Parts of Irregular
                                               Verbs" section

  your expectations   16 Maintaining Person Agreement
2 *students that*   15 "Relative Pronouns" section
4 *shift ... that accompany*   12 Mastering Subject–Verb Agreement
  transition ... is found   11 "Choosing between Active and
                                               Passive Voice" section

5 *A student ... may find that they*   15 "Pronoun–Antecedent Agreement"
                                               section

6 *This is too much*   15 "Vague References" section
7 *these students ... when one*   15 "Pronoun–Antecedent Agreement"
                                               section

8 *them and their less gifted peers*   14 "Subject and Object Pronouns"
  move on   section
9 *There is more to be lost by ...*   11 "Choosing between Active and
                                               Passive Voice" section

10 *These students were*   13 Keeping Your Tenses Consistent
11 *students that*   15 "Relative Pronouns" section
12 *and began*   13 Keeping Your Tenses Consistent
13 *that dislodges him or her*   15 "Pronoun–Antecedent Agreement"
                                               section

14 *years in college was*   12 Mastering Subject–Verb Agreement

Answers for Unit 4 Quick Quiz (page 220)

[1]A hunter who had just shot a duck sent his dog to retrieve it, only to discover that the bird had fallen inside a fenced field. [2]The farmer who owned the field was standing nearby, so the hunter said, "Excuse me; that's my duck." [3]The farmer replied, "Why is it your duck? It's on my property!" [4]After some bickering, the farmer suggested a groin-kicking contest to decide ownership of the duck. [5]The hunter agreed and braced himself for the first blow. [6]The farmer's reaction suggested he'd had experience with this kind of contest before: he took a deep breath, drew back his leg, and kicked the hunter in the groin so hard that the hunter fell to the ground like a stone. [7]After five minutes, the hunter was able to haul himself to his feet. [8]After 10 minutes, he felt well enough to say, "OK. Now it's my turn." [9]At that, the farmer said, "Nah. You can keep the duck."

Answer Key

If you missed the error(s) in sentence ...	**See Chapter ...**
1 *it*	17 The Comma (Rule 4)
2 *nearby*	17 The Comma (Rule 2)
Excuse me (2 errors)	20 "Punctuating Dialogue" section
	18 The Semicolon
3 *Why ... duck* (2 errors)	20 "Punctuating Dialogue" section
	21 Question Marks
property	21 Exclamation Marks
4 *bickering*	17 The Comma (Rule 3)
6 *before*	18 The Colon
breath	17 The Comma (Rule 1)
leg	17 The Comma (Rule 1)
8 *minutes*	17 The Comma (Rule 3)
say	20 "Punctuating Dialogue" section
OK ... turn	20 "Punctuating Dialogue" section
9 *said*	20 "Punctuating Dialogue" section

Answers for Chapter 17: The Comma (pages 221 to 232)

Exercise 17.1

1. How many of you remember Sporty, Baby, Scary, Posh, and Ginger?
2. Correct.
3. In a typical Hollywood B Western, the villain rides into town and drinks, shoots, and leaves.
4. "Rachael Ray finds inspiration in cooking, her family, and her dogs."
5. Early investment of time and money can lead to a luxurious lifestyle, international fame, and a comfortable retirement.
6. Lee is an all-round athlete; he enjoys skiing, cycling, swimming, and showering.
7. Nicole has strong ambition, a cool head, good health, and an inquiring mind; most people hate her.
8. A good education, long-range planning, and pure luck led him to wealth, acclaim, and happiness.
9. Much of the world sees Canada as a land where French is spoken, ice and snow are year-round hazards, and violent hockey is a favourite pastime.
10. In fluent English and Italian, our tour guide described the construction of Notre Dame Cathedral, explained the causes of the French Revolution, and listed the ingredients in bouillabaisse.

Exercise 17.2

1. Rudi and I are good friends, yet we often disagree.
2. Correct.
3. Noah had the last two of every creature on his ark, yet he didn't swat those mosquitoes.
4. Money can't buy happiness, but it makes misery easier to live with.

5. *Con* is the opposite of *pro*, so Congress must be the opposite of progress.
6. Correct.
7. Flying may be the safest form of transportation, but why is the place where planes land called a "terminal"?
8. Pack an extra jacket or sweater, for evenings in September can be cold.
9. The phone hasn't worked for days, and the television has been broken for a month, but I haven't missed either of them.
10. Please pay close attention, for the instructions are a little complicated, and failure to follow the process precisely can result in disaster.

Exercise 17.3

1. First, you need to understand what an independent clause is.
2. In the end, we will be judged by how much happiness we have given others.
3. "Unless I get my husband's money pretty soon, I will be forced to live an immortal life."
4. According to company policy, you may not personally collect Air Miles points accumulated on business-related travel.
5. If you live by the calendar, your days are numbered.
6. According to my stomach, lunchtime came and went about an hour ago.
7. In most newspaper and magazine advertisements, the time shown on a watch is 10:10.
8. Even if a mixed metaphor sings, it should be stifled.
9. As her 40th birthday approached, Emily met the challenge by trading in her minivan for a sports car and one boyfriend for another who is 20 years her junior.
10. When the first robin heralds the return of spring, I begin to dream of lazy summer days beside the pool, with a cool drink in my hand and a ball game on the radio.

Exercise 17.4

1. Commas, like road signs, are signals that indicate how to proceed.
2. An optimist, of course, is someone who doesn't really understand the situation.
3. There is room in this world for all of God's creatures, right beside the mashed potatoes.
4. Our office manager, who recently received her MBA, has transformed our dysfunctional environment into a productive workplace.
5. Correct.
6. A compliment, like a good perfume, should be pleasing but not overpowering.
7. Correct.
8. One of our most experienced marketing people suggested, to our surprise, that we concentrate on making a better product instead of spending millions to persuade people to buy the inferior stuff in our current line.
9. Like some cheeses and fine wines, some people improve with age.
10. The new office manager, now in her second month in the job, has made many changes to our procedures, not all of them welcome.

Exercise 17.5

1. All power corrupts, but we need electricity.
2. If Barbie is so popular, why do you have to buy her friends?
3. No words in the English language rhyme with *month*, *orange*, *silver*, or *purple*.

4. My Facebook page, which now has more than 300 "likes," features pictures of me as an adorable baby.

5. "Our Superstore is unrivalled in size, unmatched in variety, and unparalleled in-convenience."

6. Why is it that one match can start a forest fire, but it takes a whole box of matches to start a campfire?

7. "The sooner you fall behind, the more time you will have to catch up."

8. Yield to temptation, for it may not pass your way again.

9. Sam packed a lunch, took a shower, changed into her hiking clothes, and, without a word to anyone, began her trek.

10. Noticing that he was being followed by two men in raincoats and hats, he slipped into a nearby café and exited by the back door.

Exercise 17.6

1. There is something wrong with this proposal, but I haven't yet figured out what it is. (Rule 2)

2. George Washington, the first president of the United States, was an officer in the British army before the American Revolution. (Rule 4)

3. While I respect your opinion and your right to express it, I disagree with everything you say. (Rule 3)

4. "Politics is the art of looking for trouble, finding it, misdiagnosing it, and then misapplying the wrong remedies." (Rule 1)

5. Did you know that, pound for pound, the amoeba is the most vicious animal on Earth? (Rule 4)

6. This department cannot support your proposal, nor can we recommend that any other department provide funding. (Rule 2)

7. The word *allegro*, thought by some to be a type of leg fertilizer, is actually a musical notation meaning "lively" or "quick." (Rule 4)

8. Further to your letter of last week, our personnel director will be pleased to meet with you on Thursday, but she can spare only 10 minutes for the meeting. (Rule 3, Rule 2)

9. The best feature of this book, a compact, concise, and clever guide to grammar, is its convenient spiral binding. (Rule 4, Rule 1)

10. Charlottetown, Quebec, and Kingston were the sites of the conferences that eventually led to Confederation, the birth of our nation, in 1867. (Rule 1, Rule 4)

Exercise 17.7

While a winter storm raged outside their Winnipeg home, a couple sat in their comfortable living room, reading magazines, watching television, and snacking on popcorn. When a newscaster announced that all cars should be parked on the side of the street with even numbers to facilitate snow removal, the husband sighed, got up, and put on his coat and boots to move the car. A week later, another storm hit the city, and this time the newscaster announced that cars must be parked on the side of the street with odd-numbered houses. Again, the husband dutifully went out to move the car. Two weeks passed before another storm brought heavy snow to Winnipeg, but this time, just as the newscaster was about to announce snow-removal arrangements, the power went out, as it often did during storms. The husband, distraught because he had not learned on which side of the street to park the car, appealed to his wife for advice. The wife looked up from her magazine, removed her glasses, and said in a quiet voice, "Dear, why don't you just leave the car in the garage this time?"

Exercise 17.8

As long as you are prepared and confident, you'll find that an employment interview need not be a terrifying experience. Some people, believe it or not, actually enjoy employment interviews and attend them with enthusiasm. Most of us, however, are intimidated by the prospect of being interrogated by an interviewer or, even worse, a team of interviewers. To prepare for an interview, you should first find out as much as you can about the company. Among the things you need to know are the title of the job you are applying for, approximately how much it pays, the name of the person or persons who will conduct the interview, the address of the company, and the location of the washrooms. Employment consultants usually recommend that you make an advance visit to the office of the firm to which you've applied in order to confirm how long it takes to get there and where the interview room is. While on your scouting mission, you can learn valuable information about the company's working conditions, employee attitudes, and even dress code. On the day of the interview, be sure to show up 10 or 15 minutes in advance of your scheduled appointment. When the interviewer greets you, you should do three things: memorize his or her name, identify yourself, and extend your hand. Your handshake should be brief and firm, not limply passive or bone-crushingly aggressive. Practise! Now all you have to do is relax and enjoy the interview.

Answers for Chapter 18: The Semicolon (pages 233 to 242)
Exercise 18.1
Sentences 2, 4, 6, and 9 are correct.

Exercise 18.2
1. Many are cold, but few are frozen.
3. This album is quiet and romantic, perfect for an intimate dinner.
5. I do not approve of political jokes because I've seen too many of them get elected.
7. Max, our most creative classmate, wrote the script; Sam, an organizational genius, produced the film; Gina, our best camera operator, was the director of photography; and I was made director because I'm not particularly good at anything.
8. The label on the bag of potato chips proclaimed, "You could be a winner! No purchase is necessary; look for details inside."
10. Here are the twins, looking adorable; their parents, who look in need of a good night's sleep; their babysitter, who appears to be on the verge of a nervous breakdown; and the family's four pet ferrets.

Exercise 18.3
Sentences 3, 8, and 10 are correct.

Exercise 18.4
1. If life deals you a handful of lemons, make lemonade.
2. Sadly, the swimming pool was closed; however, the hot tub was working just fine.
4. Our vacation in Europe was a huge success, except for Euro-Disney, which was a major disappointment.

5. Erin is always late; nevertheless, she is always worth waiting for.

6. She made herself feel better by shopping for new shoes, a guaranteed strategy for chasing the blues.

7. Cookie pieces have no calories because all the calories leak out when the cookie is broken.

9. The weather is terrible, as it has been all month; I have a head cold that is making me miserable; the power has been out for several hours, so I can't cook; and, to top it all off, my in-laws are arriving for dinner in about an hour.

Exercise 18.5

1. I didn't say it was your fault; I said I was blaming you.

2. The airline pilots were on strike, and the train tracks were blocked by a washout in northern Ontario; our only choice was to drive to Regina.

3. On my shopping list are carrots and onions for the stew; rhubarb and strawberries for the pie; Parmesan cheese, which Roshni likes to grate over the salad; and espresso coffee to have after the meal.

4. I'm reading a fascinating book on levitation; I just can't seem to put it down.

5. I already have a boyfriend; however, don't let that stop you from worshipping me from afar.

6. Correct.

7. Newfoundland and Labrador is Canada's newest province; actually, it was known as Newfoundland until 2004, when the full name was officially recognized.

8. Some people cause happiness wherever they go; some whenever they go.

9. Never argue with an idiot; he'll drag you down to his level and beat you with his experience.

10. "For the physics section of your exam, explain the nature of matter; include in your answer an evaluation of the impact of the development of mathematics on the study of science."

Exercise 18.6

1. Turn left when you come to the fork in the road; otherwise, you will end up at the nuclear waste-disposal site and come out all aglow.

2. Watch your pennies; the government will take care of your dollars.

3. As gasoline prices continue to rise, hybrid cars make more and more sense; the problem is their high purchase price.

4. If you can afford one, however, it will pay for itself in gas savings over the life of the vehicle; in fact, my calculations indicate that a hybrid will save me money after three years.

5. The Lord's Prayer is 66 words long; the Gettysburg address is 286 words; the Declaration of Independence is 1,322 words; but U.S. government regulations on the sale of cabbage total 26,911 words.

6. When I am tired, I listen to classic rock 'n' roll because it energizes me; however, when I am working at home, nothing stimulates my creativity like Mozart.

7. I am nobody, and nobody is perfect; therefore, I must be perfect.

8. "From the moment I picked up your book until I put it down, I was convulsed with laughter; someday I intend to read it."

9. Buying a house involves enormous responsibilities, not to mention enormous debt; consequently, I plan to live with my parents until I find a wealthy woman with her own home.

10. I'm sure you understand that I would like nothing better than for you to pass this course; however, there may be a small fee involved.

Exercise 18.7

1. I saw Michael Jackson; he sat right between the Sasquatch and me on the UFO.

2. Men never grow up, but some learn how to behave in public.

3. My new office chair was supposed to have been custom-fitted; however, when I sat down, I discovered that it had been custom-fitted for someone else.

4. When we skied silently through the north woods, we saw the tracks of a lynx that was stalking a snowshoe rabbit; we heard the cracking, groaning, and sighing of the river as ice solidified on its surface; and we felt the minus-40-degree temperatures nipping at our noses and fingers.

5. One movie reviewer loved this movie, another hated it, and a third thought it was so-so; however, audiences flocked to it and made the producers very rich. Apparently, critics do not have as much influence as they like to think.

6. In an advertisement for a product designed to help people quit smoking, Brooke Shields said, "Smoking kills; if you're killed, then you have lost an important part of your life."

7. Drive carefully and wear your seat belt; it's not only cars that can be recalled by their maker.

8. One of the products of the computer age was supposed to be increased leisure; however, most of us are now working through evenings, weekends, and vacations, thanks to mobile computing.

9. Some biblical figures are familiar to many different cultures; for example, the stories of Samson and Delilah and of David and Goliath are known throughout the world.

10. Every year at tax time, I am faced with the same problem: assembling my bills and receipts; figuring out my gas consumption; trying to recall which expenses were business-related and which were personal; finding my T-4s, T-5s, and other T-forms; and organizing this mess so my accountant can keep me out of jail for another year.

Exercise 18.8

A friend of mine had not been feeling very well for some time, so he finally went to the doctor for a complete physical examination. After many tests and two more visits, he was told to come back once more; he was also asked to bring his wife. When they arrived at the doctor's office, the doctor asked the wife to wait outside while he examined her husband. After several minutes, the husband emerged from the office and told his wife to go in; the doctor wanted to see her alone. The doctor asked the wife to sit down, and then he told her that her husband was seriously ill. While she listened attentively, the doctor outlined what she must do to save her husband. The doctor revealed that stress was the cause of the husband's illness; stress must be eliminated from his life. He must stop working immediately and stay at home. She would have to make sure he sat quietly in a comfortable chair while she brought him whatever he wanted. Even driving would be too stressful; she would have to take him wherever he wanted to go. She would have to cook his favourite meals, screen his telephone calls, bring him snacks while he watched

TV, keep the children away from him, and cater to his every wish. The wife listened to these instructions with concern; she left the office deep in thought. On the way home, the husband finally asked her, "What did the doctor say, dear?"

She replied, "My dear, I'm so sorry; unfortunately, nothing can be done."

Answers for Chapter 19: The Colon (pages 243 to 248)

Exercise 19.1

Sentences 1, 4, and 6 are technically correct.

Exercise 19.2

2. We cannot write the report until we are given accurate data.
3. Our weekly shopping list always includes pizza, pretzels, and pastries.
5. The essential characteristics of a good manager are decisive leadership, clear communication, and meaningful consultation.
7. A shin is a device for finding furniture in the dark.
8. We are looking for a computer firm that can supply three critical components: reliable hardware, adaptable software, and timely support.
9. Let me give you a perfect example of pride preceding a fall: Conrad Black.
10. In an effort to encourage me, my parents gave me a book for my birthday: *The Dog Ate My Resumé: Survival Tips for Life after College*.

Exercise 19.3

1. The only ways to get rich quickly are to win the lottery or marry money.
2. According to Leah, men are like Kleenex: soft, strong, and disposable.
3. The pioneers made their own candles, soap, butter, and beer.
4. Correct.
5. Correct.
6. My roommate, who loves horror movies, persuaded me to go with her to see *Nosferatu: The Vampyre* and *Evil Dead 2: Dead by Dawn*.
7. There are two sides to every divorce: yours and the idiot's.
8. My parents think I am lazy, selfish, ignorant, and inconsiderate, but what do they know?
9. Your paper lacks three essential features: a title page, a Works Cited list, and some original content in between.
10. Every time I walk into a singles bar, I can hear my mother's warning: "Don't pick that up! You don't know where it's been."

Exercise 19.4

After a long day at work, Gina couldn't wait to get home; however, she could not find *** her car keys. She looked in her purse, in her desk drawer, even in the filing cabinet. Knowing that she had a bad habit of leaving the keys in the ignition, she decided to check the car in the parking lot. When she saw that her car was missing, she panicked and called the police to tell them that her car had been stolen because *** she had stupidly left the keys in the ignition. Then she called the one person she didn't want to talk to at a time like this: her husband. When she explained what had happened, there was a long pause; eventually, he patiently reminded her that he had dropped her off at the office that morning. Embarrassed but relieved, Gina sheepishly asked her husband to come and pick her up. There was an even longer pause. "I will, just as soon as I convince this police officer that I have not stolen your car."

Answers for Chapter 20: Quotation Marks (pages 249 to 258)
Exercise 20.1
1. There are not many quotations that everyone who speaks English knows, but Shakespeare's "To be or not to be, that is the question" must be one of the most familiar.
2. Correct.
3. "It is good to obey the rules when you are young," wrote Mark Twain, "so that you'll have the strength to break them when you're old."
4. A dedicated non-athlete, Twain also observed, "I take my exercise acting as pall-bearer at the funerals of those who exercised regularly."
5. Will and Ian Ferguson describe Canadian cuisine in simple terms: "If you let a Canadian anywhere near a piece of food he (or she) is sure to fling it into a deep fryer. Or cover it with sugar. Or fling it into a deep fryer and *then* cover it with sugar."

Exercise 20.3
1. Although *Moneyball*, *The Iron Lady*, and *Lincoln* are all biopics, none of them is a fully accurate portrayal of its subject.
2. *The Huffington Post* is the most popular of all blogs, but *The Daily Beast* has a large following, and its "Children of War" entry was one of the year's best articles.
3. Canada's national anthem, "O Canada," was written by Calixa Lavallée in 1880, while the United States' "Star-Spangled Banner" was composed in 1814 by Francis Scott Key, using the melody of an old English drinking song, "The Anacreontic Song."
4. In her bestselling book, *Eats, Shoots and Leaves*, Lynne Truss devotes a chapter entitled "Airs and Graces" to colons and semicolons.
5. The year 1997 saw the release of two of the bestselling albums in Canadian history: Shania Twain's *Come on Over* and Celine Dion's *Let's Talk about Love*.
6. British newspapers are famous for clever headlines; among my favourites are *The Sun*'s "How Do You Solve a Problem Like Korea?" and, after Gordon Brown was elected prime minister, *The Daily Mail*'s "Gord Help Us Now!"
7. Pierre Elliott Trudeau made many memorable statements during his years in Parliament, but he is probably best known for two: "Just watch me!" and "Fuddle-duddle."
8. In her essay "Motherload," Dana DiCarlo writes, "My mother is the world's top travel agent for guilt trips."
9. The latest issue of *Consumer Universe* has an article about shopping aboard cruise ships entitled "Veni. Vidi. Visa," which can be loosely translated as "I came. I saw. I shopped."
10. The essay "Early Television Westerns" reveals that the musical theme for *The Lone Ranger* comes from "The William Tell Overture" by Gioachino Rossini, who also wrote the opera *The Barber of Seville*.

Answers for Chapter 21: Question Marks, Exclamation Marks, and Punctuation Review (pages 259 to 267)

Exercise 21.1

1. If we succeed, who will know**?**
2. I wonder who won the game last night.
3. Does the name Pavlov ring any bells**?**
4. Wouldn't it be great if, whenever we messed up our lives, we could simply press "Ctrl Alt Delete" and start all over**?**
5. The vice-president questioned our manager about the likelihood of completing this project on time and on budget.
6. I am curious about what the new minister of finance plans to do about our chronic deficit.
7. Please have a look at these tests and tell me if you agree that some of the students may have been cheating.
8. How can anyone just stand by while a child is being bullied**?**
9. If we continue to make a profit, I wonder if the new owners will close us down or move our operation offshore.
10. Why can't the sports fans who yell so loudly at players' mistakes put themselves in the position of those they criticize and be a little more forgiving**?**

Exercise 21.2 (suggested answers)

1. Row faster**!** It's gaining on us**!**
2. Never introduce a quotation with a semicolon.
3. Don't even think about it**!**
4. Just imagine**!** She actually got a job.
5. Turn the heat up. I'm freezing**!**
6. She's here at last. Let the celebrations begin**!**
7. Try it**!** You'll like it**!**
8. The fans were on their feet, screaming "Skate**!**"
9. "Lights, camera, action**!**"
10. Go for it**!** You'll never know unless you try.

Exercise 21.4

The symbol *** means a punctuation mark has been deleted.

1. Did you know that in English the word *karate* means empty hands**?**
2. If your goal is to be a millionaire before you are 35, you will have to *** make work the focus of your life and be uncommonly lucky.
3. The question of whether evolution is fact or myth doesn't worry most of the people in my biology class; they're more concerned about whether there's a dance on Friday night.
4. Do you think Deena has any idea how lucky she is that her supervisor didn't find out she took the day off to go to the casino**?**
5. The cure is readily at hand: drink plenty of liquids, take an aspirin with each meal, get lots of rest, and take three grams of vitamin C daily.
6. When her grandfather told her how large computers used to be, the wide-eyed child exclaimed, "Gosh**!** How big was the mouse**?**"

7. I think it was Mark Twain who once said, "Clothes make the man; naked people have little or no influence in society."

8. This is the first entry in my new book, *Words of Wisdom*: "If at first you don't succeed, skydiving is not the sport for you."

9. Your resumé is the second piece of writing that an employer will see; the first is the cover letter, which is one of the most important documents you will write in your career.

10. Today's passenger jets are so fast and the airlines so efficient that when you land in Amsterdam, it takes them only a couple of days to locate your luggage and fly it in from Brazil. (*Or:* !)

Exercise 21.5

No quality in business, government, or education is so widely discussed and studied as leadership; in fact, leadership studies have become a significant industry. Many documents have been written on the subject, from General Rick Hillier's *Leadership: 50 Points of Wisdom for Today's Leaders* to Patrick M. Lencioni's *The Five Dysfunctions of a Team: A Leadership Fable*. The best known is undoubtedly Dale Carnegie's *How to Win Friends and Influence People*, a bestseller since it was published in 1936. Organizations around the world offer courses, seminars, workshops, and conferences on leadership, and most of them sell out quickly. While these various forms of leadership training are undoubtedly useful, I cannot help thinking of great leaders like Winston Churchill, Mohandas Gandhi, and Nelson Mandela. They did not read books or take courses on leadership; how did they master the art? Former American president and WWII general Dwight D. Eisenhower may have answered this question when he said, "The leadership instinct you are born with is the backbone. You develop the funny bone and the wishbone that go with it."

Exercise 21.6

Canada's climate is not always friendly to the farming of tender fruit crops like cherries, peaches, grapes, pears, and apples. In fact, only in very special regions of the country can such crops be grown: the Okanagan Valley, the Niagara Peninsula, the Annapolis Valley, and a few other privileged spots in Quebec, the Maritimes, Ontario, and B.C. Even with the effects of global warming, growing tender fruit in Canada can be a risky business. Recently, an unseasonably warm March seemed to be a good omen for the crop, but when the fruit budded more than two weeks early, an April frost, which normally would not have affected the fruit, destroyed almost the entire crop. Technology has come to the rescue: wind machines have begun making an appearance in Canada's orchards and vineyards. These machines look like miniature wind turbines, but they are not driven by the wind; rather, they spin like a huge fan to drive warm air down onto the fruit trees and vines. At 20 metres, the air can be as much as 10 degrees warmer than at the level of the fruit, so pushing that warmer air down can prevent frost damage and save a valuable crop. There is a downside: the machines cost up to $50,000 each, cost about $40 an hour to run, and sound like a helicopter hovering over the orchard. Neighbouring residential areas may not be too sympathetic.

Answers for Unit 4 Rapid Review (page 268)

[1]A man bought a parrot at the pet store, only to find when he got it home that the bird's vocabulary was obscene. [2]He put up with the foul language for a while, hoping that the parrot would tone it down once he got used to his new surroundings. [3]Unfortunately,

it just got worse, and eventually the man had had enough. [4]"Quit it!" he yelled. [5]That really irritated the parrot, whose swearing became even more horrible. [6]Now really angry, the man grabbed the bird, threw him into the freezer, and slammed the door. [7]At first, there were sounds of a struggle; then there was a terrible silence. [8]The man began to fear he had injured his pet. [9]He opened the freezer door. [10]The parrot climbed onto his outstretched hand and said these words: "I'm awfully sorry about the trouble I gave you. I'll do my best to improve my vocabulary." [11]The man was astounded. [12]What could have brought about this miraculous change in the parrot's behaviour? [13]Then the parrot asked, "By the way, what did the chicken do?"

Answer Key

If you missed the error(s) in sentence ...

		See Chapter ...
1	*store only*	17 The Comma (Rule 4)
2	*while hoping*	17 The Comma (Rule 4)
3	*Unfortunately it*	17 The Comma (Rule 3)
	worse and	17 The Comma (Rule 2)
4	*"Quit it"*	21 "The Exclamation Mark" section
5	*parrot whose*	17 The Comma (Rule 4)
6	*angry the*	17 The Comma (Rule 3)
	bird threw	17 The Comma (Rule 1)
	freezer and	17 The Comma (Rule 1)
7	*first there*	17 The Comma (Rule 3)
	struggle then	18 The Semicolon
10	*words "I'm*	19 The Colon
12	*behaviour*	21 "The Question Mark" section
13	*asked*	20 Quotation Marks
	By the way, ... chicken do?	20 Quotation Marks

Answers for Chapter 22: Finding Something to Write About (pages 271 to 287)

Exercise 22.1

1. Not significant.
2. Not single.
3. Not supportable without a great deal of research.
4. Not single.
5. Not significant.
6. Not single or specific.
7. Not supportable. (How can we know?)
8. Not specific or supportable unless you're an expert in the field.
9. Not supportable.
10. Not significant or specific. What about Velcro?

Exercise 22.2

1. Not specific. If limited, the subject could yield several possibilities: for example, "Bottled water is an environmental catastrophe"; "Bottled water is a waste of

money"; "The water-bottling industry is depleting Canada's limited sources of pure water."

2. Not specific. You could limit it in several ways so that it passes the 4-S test: for example, "What makes a male/female attractive to Canadian teenagers" or "How the notion of physical attractiveness has changed since my parents' generation."

3. Not significant. This could be useful if revised to instruct dishwasher users how to conserve water or energy. If your dishwasher is a human being, the topic has humorous potential.

4. Not specific and not supportable without a great deal of research. Apply one or more limiting factors to it: for example, "Effects on the elderly of Russia's transition to a market economy."

5. Not specific. What about them? How do they work? What are their advantages and disadvantages?

6. Not significant.

7. Not specific or supportable. It needs limiting: for example, "Weather forecasting is becoming more precise" or "Basic palm-reading techniques."

8. Not single. Choose one hero from one war.

9. Not specific. What about them? How to use them? Why they are useful? What they are used for?

10. Not specific. Limit the discussion to one kind of Internet piracy: for example, "The impact of Internet piracy on the gaming software industry."

Exercise 22.6

1. "Seattle Seahawks" is not relevant. The team is not Canadian.

2. "Better looks" and "improved appearance" are the same point.

3. Shovelling snow is not significant when compared to the other problems, and it overlaps with "adjusting to the climate."

4. "Changing hairstyles" is not generally a cause of stress, and it certainly is never a major one.

5. The "great white" is a species of shark; it is not a characteristic of all sharks.

6. "Cause of eye strain" is not an advantage, so the point is not relevant to the subject.

7. "Sun" and "solar" are the same point.

8. "Government can launch infrastructure projects to boost employment" does not support the subject. With lower taxes, the government has less money to spend on infrastructure.

Exercise 22.8

Subject	Order	Main Points	
1. How to prepare for a job interview	chronological	_1_	Visit the company's website.
		_4_	Dress appropriately.
		_2_	Prepare answers to standard interview questions.
		_3_	Ask a friend to role-play the interview with you.

Subject	Order	Main Points
2. Differences between spoken and written language	climactic	__3__ Speech is transitory; writing is permanent.
		__1__ Speech is spontaneous; writing isn't.
		__2__ Speech can't be revised; writing can.
3. How to write a research paper	chronological	__3__ Read and take notes on selected research sources.
		__4__ Draft the paper.
		__2__ Compile a working bibliography of research sources.
		__1__ Define the subject.
		__7__ Type and proofread final draft.
		__5__ Insert source citations and reference list.
		__6__ Revise the paper.
4. How colleges benefit society	logical	__2__ They provide students with a higher level of general education.
		__3__ They contribute to increased national productivity.
		__1__ They provide students with job skills.
5. Effects of malnutrition	logical	__3__ Malnutrition affects the productivity and prosperity of nations as a whole.
		__1__ Malnutrition impedes the mental and physical development of children.
		__2__ Undernourished children become sickly adults unable to participate fully in their society.
6. Why pornography should be banned	chronological	__1__ It degrades those who make it.
		__3__ It brutalizes society as a whole.
		__2__ It desensitizes those who view it.

7. and 8. Decide on your own climactic arrangements for these questions. Be sure you can explain your reasoning.

Answers for Chapter 23: The Thesis Statement (pages 288 to 299)

Exercise 23.1

1. Three essential components of a strong and lasting relationship (are) good communication, sexual compatibility, and mutual respect.

2. Don Cherry simultaneously amuses and provokes viewers (with) his opinions about hockey violence, his taste in clothing, and his perspective on international hockey.

3. If I were you, I would avoid eating in the cafeteria (because) the food is expensive, tasteless, and unhealthy.

4. The responsibilities of a modern union (include) protecting jobs, increasing wages, improving working conditions, and enhancing pensions and benefits.

5. If we are to compete internationally, our company (needs) a strong board of directors, creative executives, and dynamic middle managers.

6. The original Volkswagen Beetle, the Citroen CV, and the Morris Minor (are) three cars that will be remembered for their endearing oddness.

7. Fad diets are not the quick and easy fixes to weight problems that they may seem to be; (in fact, they are) often costly, ineffective, and even dangerous.

8. Taking the time and trouble to buy locally grown foods is better (not only for) you, (but also for) the local economy and the environment.

9. Do you lack basic skills, study skills, or motivation? (If so,) you are at high risk of failing your first year of college.

10. What makes a great movie? Not top stars or a huge budget. Great movies—those that are destined to be viewed generations from now—(are based on) a fortuitous combination of memorable stories, unforgettable characters, and brilliant direction.

Exercise 23.2

Sentence 1 is grammatically parallel.

Exercise 23.3

1. Correct.
2. The campus pub that we are designing should be open and inviting, efficient for food preparation and service, acoustically superior for concerts, and centrally located on campus.
3. The company is seeking new employees who are well educated, honest, disciplined, and reliable.
4. Some of the negative effects of caffeine include nervousness, sleeplessness, heart palpitations, and potential mild addiction.
5. The new agreement includes a small pay increase, improved health benefits, more sick time, and slightly higher pensions.

Exercise 23.4

1. Four types of essay writing are description, narration, exposition, and persuasion. (parallelism)

2. In a competitive environment, this corporation needs to improve its products, increase its sales, and reduce its workforce. (A new logo is not significant when compared to the other items.)

3. Increasingly, scientists are finding links between the environment and health concerns such as diabetes, cancer, and aging. (Cold sores are not significant among the other ailments mentioned.)

4. Cloud formations, wind direction, temperature variation, and barometric pressure are all signs that even an amateur can use to predict the weather. (parallelism)

5. The Summer Olympic events that gain the largest television audience are track and field, volleyball, basketball, and gymnastics. (The 100-metre race is part of track and field.)

Exercise 23.5 (suggested answers)

1. violent video games? No, a different topic.

   There are three reasons that watching television is a valuable way to spend time: it teaches us many things, it provides relaxation, and it supplies us with topics to discuss with others.

2. A 30-hour workweek would increase our company's productivity.
   - Employees will be more productive: Good point, but note overlap between "less tired," "more focused," and "more productive."
   - It would allow employees to get part-time jobs: No, doesn't support the thesis.
   - More free time improves employee satisfaction: "Family time" and "leisure time" overlap. "Free time" covers both.
   - Work hours will not be in sync with those of suppliers and clients: No, doesn't support the thesis; the lack of compatible work schedules may well decrease productivity.
   - Reduction in work hours will be compensated for by reduction in absenteeism: This point should be provable, but you will need hard evidence to support it; note that sick leave is a form of absenteeism.

   A. Three reasons that our company should reduce the workweek to 30 hours are that workers would be more productive, absenteeism would be decreased, and employees would be more satisfied.

   B. Our company should reduce the workweek to 30 hours because workers would be more productive, absenteeism would be decreased, and employees would be more satisfied.

3. Immigration is a good policy for Canada.
   - Immigrants offer new skills: Yes, good point.
   - Immigrants may find adjusting to life in Canada difficult: No, doesn't support the thesis.
   - Immigrants may bring investment dollars: Yes.
   - Immigrants must often learn a new language: No, doesn't support the thesis.
   - Immigrants enrich Canadian culture: Yes, supports the thesis.

   A. Immigration is a good policy for Canada because immigrants offer new skills, often bring investment dollars, and enrich Canadian culture.

   B. Immigration is a good policy for Canada: immigrants offer new skills, investment, and cultural enrichment.

4. Most of us look forward to vacations, but the kind of vacation we enjoy depends on the kind of people we are.
   • beach resorts: Yes, a kind of vacation.
   • gambling trips: Yes, a kind of vacation.
   • Cancun, Mexico: No, it's an example of a beach resort.
   • adventure vacations: Yes, a kind of vacation.
   • Buckingham Palace: No, it's an example of a cultural attraction in London.
   • too much sun: No, doesn't support the thesis.
   • mountain climbing: No, it's an example of an adventure vacation.
   • touring cultural attractions: Yes, a kind of vacation.
   A. Different people like different kinds of vacation; (for example), some people like to relax at a beach resort, some people like to gamble, some people like to have adventures, and other people like to tour cultural attractions.
   B. Some of the kinds of vacations that different people like to take (are) relaxing at a beach resort, playing games of chance, enjoying adventure travel, and touring cultural attractions.
5. A satisfying career
   • interesting: Yes, but an overused word; "stimulating" expresses the idea more originally and more accurately, and is the word the author chose when he came to draft the paper.
   • well-paid: Yes.
   • respected: Yes, but could be combined with "well-paid" under "rewarding" (a more comprehensive main point).
   • provides opportunities for advancement: Yes, but overlaps with "rewarding" and "makes employee feel appreciated."
   • makes employee feel needed and appreciated: Yes, but rephrase as "productive" to maintain parallel phrasing and avoid overlap with "provides opportunities for advancement."
   A. To enjoy a satisfying career, an employee (must be) interested, rewarded, and productive.
   B. (If)one's career is interesting, rewarding, and productive, it will be truly satisfying.

Now compare these thesis statements to the one the author used in his final draft, on page 344.

Exercise 23.9

Thesis statement: ... choosing a life's vocation is not a decision to be taken lightly. To justify the time and effort you will invest in your career, (it should be) stimulating, rewarding, and productive.

Topic sentence: What would a stimulating career be like?

Topic sentence: A good career offers two kinds of rewards: financial and emotional.

Topic sentence: It is human nature to want to contribute, to feel that your efforts make a difference.

Conclusion: Your career will occupy three-quarters of your life, so make the most of it!

Answers for Chapter 25: Paragraphs (pages 307 to 324)

Exercise 25.1

Paragraph 4:

Topic sentence —

Supporting sentences

Conclusion —

Although I am usually able to decipher the gist of quickspeak, I'm seldom sure that I have translated the message accurately. In many cases, this failure stems from the fact that the writer didn't provide complete or accurate information. Take the example that introduces this essay. I know there will be a meeting (about what?) on Tuesday (which week?) at 9:00 (a.m. or p.m.?). Where is this meeting? Who will be present? What documents am I expected to bring? Without the answers to these questions, how can I prepare? Far from saving time, quickspeak actually wastes it. Now I have to respond to the email sender to find out the answers to these questions. At least three messages will be needed where one would have done. If only the writer had recognized this basic rule of writing: to be brief takes time!

Paragraph 5:

Topic sentence —

Supporting sentences

Conclusion —

Email is no different from any other business correspondence: it must be clear and concise. Achieving clarity and conciseness is not difficult, but it does require planning. Begin with an introduction that briefly explains the purpose of your message. Next, outline how you are going to develop that message. Use numbered or bulleted points to guide the reader from your position statement through your reasoning to your conclusion. Reinforce your message with a conclusion that states any follow-up actions you require and that confirms the time, place, and responsibilities of those who are contributing to the project. Next, reread your message as if you were reading it for the first time. Revise to be sure that you have included all the necessary details: dates, reference numbers, times and places of meetings, and whatever other information is needed to get the right people together in the right places, on the right days, at the right times, with the right information in their briefcases. Use a spell checker, but don't rely on it to catch all your errors and typos. Remember: A clear message, clearly delivered, is the essence of effective communication.

Paragraph 6:

Topic sentence —

Supporting sentences

Conclusion —

People who write in quickspeak ignore the reason that rules for correct writing evolved in the first place. Writing that communicates accurately depends upon precise thinking. A message with a statement of purpose, logically arranged points, and a confirming summary is the work of a writer whose message has been thought through and can be trusted. In contrast, quickspeak, which can be bashed out in no time, reflects no planning, little coherent thought, and no sense of order or priority. The message, the reader, and, ultimately, the writer all suffer as a result.

Exercise 25.7

1. process (series of steps)
2. definition + statistics
3. paraphrase + statistics

4. statistics
5. examples + contrast
6. examples
7. examples + numerical details
8. descriptive details + examples
9. quotations
10. quotation and contrast

Exercise 25.10

Those who support fighting in hockey argue that "It's part of the game" or "It's what fans want" or "It prevents dangerous, dirty play." Even a quick look at the facts shows that such arguments are baseless. Like hockey, sports such as football, soccer, and basketball are fast, aggressive, and violent, but fighting is banned in all of them. If fighting was what fans demanded, then there would be few viewers for the Olympics or for World Championship tournaments. The fact that these events draw unequalled ratings demonstrates that hockey fans do not need fights to draw them to the game. Meanwhile, NHL ratings are in decline in Canada, and the rest of the world views hockey as a third-rate sport. Hockey can be beautiful, fast, skilful, and creative, but when players whose only skill is fighting are sent into the game, it becomes nothing more than a brawl.

Answers for Chapter 26: Revising Your Paper (pages 325 to 334)
Exercise 26.5 (suggested answers)

Do you find it a struggle to pay the bills every month**?** When **you live** beyond your means, even a small shortfall at the end of each month can quickly add up to a **significant** debt. To **overcome** this problem**,** you can ******* choose to spend less or **earn** more. At first, the former may seem the more **difficult** choice**. Cutting** back on what you spend may mean giving up some of the things you "need," such as eating out, **going to** movies, or **buying** the latest fashions.   Doing without such expensive pleasures, however, often **produces** significant savings. **You** may even save enough to balance the monthly books.

Earning more money ***** and continuing** to spend at your present pace may seem like a more attractive **option**, but is it realistic**? First,** there is the challenge of finding another job that pays better **or** adding part-time work to the job you already have. **Either** way**, you're** going to **lose** even more of your already scarce study and leisure time. **Second, it is a** fact that most people continue to spend at the same rate, regardless of how much money **they** make. **So it's** likely that, even with additional income, you'll still be **overdrawn** at the end of the month. The best solution to the end-of-month budget blues is likely a combination of cutting costs where practical and adding to income where possible.

Answers for Chapter 27: Using Research Resources Responsibly (pages 335 to 341)
Exercise 27.1

1. This "paraphrase" is plagiarism. The writer has made little attempt to rethink or rewrite the author's original. Many of the phrases in this attempt at paraphrasing have been taken word for word from the original source.
2. This paragraph is an acceptable paraphrase. The writer has made the idea her own by expressing the gist of Green's paragraph in her own words.

3. Good try, but this paragraph is closer to plagiarism than it is to paraphrase. While the writer has made an effort to express the author's ideas in her own words, she hasn't been entirely successful. Her paragraph begins well, but after a strong start, she drifts into repeating the original author's words (e.g., *a positive and healthy image of femininity* and *beauty, success, and thinness*). The second sentence begins with Piscitelli's words (*Young women ... must realize*) and even uses the author's "not ... but" sentence construction.

INDEX

Note: A page reference followed by *n* (for example, 191n) refers to a footnote at the bottom of that page.